AF600699

MORAL COMBAT

Women, Gender, and War in Italian Renaissance Literature

GERRY MILLIGAN

Moral Combat

Women, Gender, and War in Italian Renaissance Literature

UNIVERSITY OF TORONTO PRESS
Toronto Buffalo London

Toronto Buffalo London
utorontopress.com

ISBN 978-1-4875-0314-7

Toronto Italian Studies

Library and Archives Canada Cataloguing in Publication

Milligan, Gerry, 1972–, author
Moral combat : women, gender, and war in Italian
Renaissance literature / Gerry Milligan.

(Toronto Italian studies)
Includes bibliographical references and index.
ISBN 978-1-4875-0314-7 (cloth)

1. Italian literature – 16th century – History and criticism. 2. Women in literature. 3. War in literature. I. Title. II. Series: Toronto Italian studies

PQ4055.W6M55 2018 850.9'9287 C2017-907832-1

This book has been published with the financial assistance of The College of Staten Island – City University of New York.

University of Toronto Press acknowledges the financial assistance to its publishing program of the Canada Council for the Arts and the Ontario Arts Council, an agency of the Government of Ontario.

Funded by the Government of Canada
Financé par le gouvernement du Canada

Contents

Illustrations

Acknowledgments

I offer my deepest gratitude to my parents and family, who instilled in me a commitment to education. In not so insignificant ways, this book is a result of the lessons they taught me – in particular to seek and respect knowledge. Indeed, it was my grandmother, an Italian-American navy-yard riveter in the Second World War, who first sparked my interest in women's experience of war. Without her stories as well as those of my veteran grandfathers, this book would likely never have been conceived. I also thank the Battle of Normandy Foundation who sent me and an entire class of twenty Tennessee undergraduates to France so that we could study warfare through direct contact with a land that still bears the scars of 1944. My encounters with war survivors, and their willingness to speak about a time so many decades before, continue to inform my thoughts about armed conflict. For having introduced me to the Italian Renaissance, I thank Sal Di Maria and Robert Rodini, both of whom inspired a passion for the Cinquecento and both of whom recommended that I pursue an academic career. I thank Rodini in particular, who encouraged me to complete my graduate studies when I had left them.

It is fitting that a book primarily concerned with strong women of the Renaissance has been so greatly influenced by modern women who study the period. My greatest debt is to Jane Tylus, my mentor and friend. She not only introduced me to gender theory, she taught me how to read texts as destabilizing forces that ask more questions than they answer. I am grateful for her support and advocacy, as well as her generosity in reading nearly every page I have written. I extend my thanks to Diana Robin for her continued interest in my success. For nearly fifteen years, she has kindly shared with me her thoughts (and publications) about early modern women and war and, most importantly, about how to write about peace. I give my warmest thanks to Deanna Shemek and Julia Hairston, whose company is always a delight, and who never fail to offer provocative conversations about Renaissance gender. Deanna and Julia graciously offered their feedback on early versions of chapters 2 and 5, respectively. Both provided insightful readings that deepened my analysis and saved me from historical errors. I am very thankful for the friendship and guidance of Virginia Cox, a true *guerriera* of Italian women's writing. I have benefited in unknowable ways from her scholarship, and I treasure our West Village dinners discussing obscure women poets. She read an early version of the first chapter; any improvements that resulted in the many rewrites are thanks to her.

The research for this book began during a fellowship at Harvard's Center for Renaissance Studies at Villa I Tatti in Florence, Italy. I am grateful to the selection committee who chose to support a project on gender and war as well as the vast community of people who guarantee the continuation of this special place. While at I Tatti, I was fortunate to encounter so many of the brilliant minds of Italian Renaissance studies. Some of the most important elements of this book, including its structure, title, and much of its content, resulted from conversations during that year. For both their intellectual contributions and their conviviality, I thank Holly Hurlburt, Cynthia Klestinec, Sharon Strocchia, Maddalena Spagnolo, Flora Dennis, Valeria Cafà, Gabriele Pedullà, Peter Howard, Guido Ruggiero, and Konrad Eisenbichler. To Holly I extend special thanks for her willingness to read parts of the manuscript and for her reminder of why history matters. Above all, I thank Michael Rocke, an insightful interlocutor about all things Renaissance as well as an incomparable host. Over the many years of visiting Italy, I have benefited from the generosity of Alexandra Lawrence, Cathy Ramsey Portolano, Sarah Beck, Elena Hogan, and Pier Giorgio Frand Genisot, all of whom have repeatedly welcomed me into their homes and provided warm hospitality, inspiring conversation, and lots of laughter.

I am grateful for the constant support of my academic institution, the College of Staten Island-CUNY. A dean's travel award as well as several PSC-CUNY summer travel grants made research in Italy possible. I thank my fellow Renaissance scholars at the CUNY Graduate Center, Monica Calabritto, Paolo Fasoli, Eugenia Paulicelli, and Clare Carroll, as well as my colleagues at the College of Staten Island. In particular, I thank Paola Ureni, Giancarlo Lombardi, Chiara Ferrari, Steven Monte,

Lucas Marchante, and Jane Marcus Delgado. They have made my time at CSI both enriching and playful. I also am thankful for the wonderful graduate and undergraduate students with whom I have worked at CUNY and NYU. In particular, I thank Fabio Battista, who assisted with the notes for this book, Valerie Hoagland, who created the index, and Daniela D'Eugenio, who kindly assisted with the Latin translations of Foresti. At NYU, Anna Wainwright, Shannon McHugh, Jessica Goethals, Melissa Swain, and Bryan Brazeau each contributed in his or her own way to this project.

I gratefully acknowledge the permission to reproduce in this book a portion of it published elsewhere. Part of chapter 3 originally appeared as "Proving Masculinity before Women: Laura Terracina and Chiara Matraini Writing on Warfare" in *The Poetics of Masculinity in Early Modern Italy and Spain* (Toronto: Centre for Reformation and Renaissance Studies, 2010). I am forever indebted to Suzanne Rancourt, the exemplary editor at the University of Toronto Press. Her steady guidance, along with the careful readings of the anonymous readers as well as the editorial staff, made this book possible. Each reader of this text offered keen suggestions for improvement, and any errors that remain in the book are entirely mine.

Finally, I thank my New York "family" for their support over these years. They graciously stopped asking why it was taking so long to complete my book or even why anyone would want to spend such a long time writing one. The true hero in this story is Ben Medley, my partner in life and a fellow student of masculinity studies. Not only his love but also his unwavering confidence in my abilities were crucial to the successful completion of the project. I read his presence in every page.

MORAL COMBAT

Women, Gender, and War in Italian Renaissance Literature

Introduction

On 20 October 1999, the Italian government passed legislation that allowed women to join the armed forces, making Italy the last NATO country to do so.[1] The law incited much debate regarding women's right and ability to fight. While some argued that the law was necessary to satisfy the requirement of equality of the sexes under the Italian constitution, another equally vocal group expressed concerns that women were timid, weak, and suited to procreation rather than killing.[2] Such initial hesitations notwithstanding, women in the Italian military were accepted relatively quickly within the ranks of enlistees. By 2004, the complaints that had been common about women's timid nature or physical weakness were less frequent.[3] The change in perception did not, however, result in a large number of female enlistees. In March of 2017, Roberta Pinotti – the first female Italian minister of defence – lamented that the female presence in the Italian armed forces was only 5 per cent.[4]

More than a decade after Italy allowed women to join the military, the United States took a different step towards gender equality in the armed forces. On 24 January 2013, U.S. Secretary of Defense Leon E. Panetta lifted the 1994 ban on women's serving in ground combat. The event made women's role in warfare the centre of national attention, reinvigorating a long-standing debate about women's militancy. In fact, both the "Combat Exclusion Policy" of 1994 and its repeal in 2013 provoked a flurry of commentary on topics such as women's physical abilities, their psychological "nature," and their vulnerability to sex crimes if captured.[5] What also came to the surface in these discussions was a widespread discomfort with the idea of women and killing both women killing others, and women being killed. The policy shift concerning women's right to participate in combat thus prompted existential questions regarding the value of human life. Most strikingly, it unveiled the tacit social compact to extinguish certain people (in this case based on gender) while protecting others.

The policy changes in the United States and Italy, along with the various studies and public reactions that accompanied them, might suggest that the controversy over women in war is a modern phenomenon. It is, however, an ancient question, famously debated by the Greeks and Romans. Although the question of women's militancy would occasionally resurface throughout the Middle Ages, the first sustained discourse about women's militancy across several literary genres and among numerous authors is likely in the Italian sixteenth century. In philosophical texts as well as in fictional epics and biographies, authors throughout the Italian Cinquecento debated the role of women in war as well as wrote texts that featured female characters who fought in combat, led armies, or suffered as victims of violence. It is fascinating that the themes of those works that specifically addressed women as combatants – despite extraordinary differences in technologies of warfare – resemble the debates of the modern era. Like our modern contemporaries, fifteenth- and sixteenth-century writers raised questions about the weakness of women, the decorum of women who kill, the novelty of female combatants, and women's vulnerability to sexual assault. What is perhaps the most striking aspect of our modern debate is how little the conversation has changed.

One contributing factor leading an increasing number of Renaissance writers to turn their attention to women and war may have been the large-scale violence that beset Italy in the first half of the sixteenth century. Although warfare was recurrent throughout medieval Italy, the Italian Wars (1494–1559) brought an unprecedented measure of violence to the peninsula. What began as a dispute between the French monarchy and the Habsburg Empire over control of Milan and Naples led to more than sixty years of bloodshed throughout Italy. The wars not only destroyed countless lives, they also changed the collective psyche; *Italianità* (Italianness) became associated with defeat and occupation.[6] This perception was rooted in a very real political shift, as most of the Italian peninsula was subject to foreign imperial rule after the signing of the Peace of Cateau-Cambrésis (1559).

It is thus no surprise that warfare is at the heart of so many texts in the period; but what might be striking is how often gender is implicated in these works. This book will show how women authors praised men for victories just as they also wrote scathing critiques of men who were defeated or did not protect them. If a battle was lost, authors described female war victims, rather than male, in order to signify war's injustices; women's sufferings (considered to be inherently more tragic) were symbolic of the greater ills of society. In texts that depicted women not as victims but as *combatants* in war, the critique of men's military failings remained pervasive. Narratives of women's militancy implicitly and explicitly suggested that when women became warriors, they did so to compensate for men's dereliction. Whether authors argued for or against women's ability to fight in combat, they affirmed the ideology that warfare was ultimately the moral responsibility of men. Indeed, the present book's title, *Moral Combat,* takes its name from the intersection of morality, masculinity, and militarism.

Precisely because warriors were overwhelmingly gendered as masculine, any woman warrior, even if only a fictional character in an epic poem, flagged the possibility that real women might take up arms and fight. Indeed, as we will see, some chivalric epics of the sixteenth century explicitly addressed the incongruity that viragos fought in the pages of poetry much more frequently than in real life. The legendary and exceptional aspect of women warriors was part of the fictional virago's poetic impact, but it was also her poetic baggage. Her "marvel" made her compelling to authors and readers, and yet this exceptionalism also coloured all narratives about women warriors with a hue of fiction, so that tales of even historical women seem shaped more by fantasy than by fact. There were, to be sure, women who fought in war, and we will consider texts that discuss historical as well as fictional viragos. It will also become quickly apparent that the lines between fiction and history were continually blurred. Authors of historical biographies cited fictional characters as proof of women's real-life virtues, just as poets of fictional viragos compared them to historical women. My study will not attempt to parse fiction and history but rather seek to understand how literary texts functioned as agents in the cultural discourse of war and representations of war.

Although warrior women occupy much of the space of this book, the project considers textual representations of women as warriors, non-combatants, commanders, pacifists, victims, and active observers of war. It is thus the first study in English to tackle gender and war in Italian Renaissance literature through such a broad lens. The most significant work on the topic up to this point has been done by the French scholar Frédérique Verrier, who has written three monographs that survey fifteenth- and sixteenth-century texts on women's militancy.[7] A trailblazer, Verrier has unequivocally proven just how vast the literary representation of women warriors is and just how central women are to the discourse of Renaissance militancy. My own work expands on Verrier's investigation to show that women's militancy was enmeshed in a larger question of gender that was as much about men as it was about women. When Renaissance men and women debated women's militancy (e.g., women as capable or incapable in war, pacifists by nature, lacking training, etc.), they were simultaneously confirming the unquestioned and ahistorical truism that men are the militant sex. Without exception, all of the texts that I will analyse cannot escape what Joshua Goldstein has aptly called the "universal gendering of war" – the process by which war was, is, and has always been gendered as masculine.[8]

This book will consider how texts fashion a discursive construct of gender in warfare (e.g., women as non-combatant innocents, men as warriors who protect women) as well as how these gender roles are rewritten, challenged, and reaffirmed. One text that both critiques and perpetuates the "gendering of war" is Francesco Filelfo's (1398–1481) epic poem, the *Sforziade*. The poem comes from the mid-fifteenth century, a period long before the great Italian Wars but one in which cities were often targets of local power struggles. In the work, we see how lived gender realities did not always align with scripted gender roles. Women lament that they are by nature non-combatants – indeed, unable to fight – but these same women are also depicted in battle, fighting to protect themselves and their city. One episode, describing a siege attack, serves to introduce the very questions that will be addressed more systematically in the following chapters.

The Renaissance Gendering of War and the *Sforziade*

The *Sforziade* is a Latin text written in praise of the Duke of Milan, Francesco Sforza (1401–1466), and tells, among other things, of his siege of Piacenza in 1447. Just before the siege, the author, Filelfo, depicts the women of Piacenza lamenting their fate:

> Ah woe, nature or God has dealt us a sad fate – our being the female race. No living creature is more submissive, nor more exposed to every evil. We are unwarlike, nor do we have the power to reason, more excellent than any other: Our minds are always weak with fear. We have no useful physical strength. (translation Robin, *Filelfo* 79)[9]

The female chorus, much like women in classical tragedy, complains of the precarious status of women in war.[10] Theirs is a problem of nature, for women have "no useful physical strength," "no power to reason," and are fundamentally "unwarlike." In Filelfo's account, women are damned to suffer this world as victims of men's violence.[11] The laments of Piacenza's women are, after all, in response to the abuse of the invading soldiers: "Over here a young girl is dragged off; and right over there a pure wife submits, with her husband watching her, to whatever lust and madness dictate" (translation Robin, *Filelfo* 77).[12]

On this occasion and throughout Filelfo's moving account of the siege of Piacenza, the author portrays women as non-combatant and passive embodiments of innocence who are defiled in war. They are "Beautiful Souls," a term of Hegel's borrowed and revised by Jean Bethke Elshtain in her groundbreaking book *Women and War* to describe the way that women are often represented in the context of warfare.[13] Like Elshtain's Beautiful Souls, the women of Piacenza are non-combatant nurturers, and they present themselves as the innocent victims in an inexorable force of men's wars. Such vulnerable women must be protected by men, and thus Elshtain suggests that the foil to the Beautiful Soul is the male "Just Warrior," construed as violent and answering the call to war, willingly or not. Elshtain is quick to state that this is not the relationship of real women and men to war; rather, it is the "sedimented lore" that has overshadowed the plurality of other stories, a lore that has secured "women's location as non-combatants and men's as warriors" (*Women* 4).

My study will scrape away this sediment and attempt to explain how war was gendered in the crucial moment of the Italian Renaissance, a moment when powerful women ruled principalities and kingdoms but also a period, particularly in the sixteenth century, when men's ability to carry out their military duty was often ridiculed as Italy witnessed capitulation to foreign occupying troops. This book will analyse the gendering of war in the Italian Renaissance on several fronts. The first two chapters will review the discourses that surrounded the ability of women to fight, confirming or resisting the notion of women as non-combatants. Chapter 1 specifically addresses how philosophical and didactic treatises tackled the question of women in the military, while chapter 2 instead focuses on chivalric epic poetry, a genre known for virago protagonists but also one that engages a potentiality of real women combatants. Chapter 3 looks at women armed with the pen rather than the sword; women authors wrote orations, poems, and letters to insist that men take up the sword in order to perform their masculine moral obligation as protectors of women. The remainder of the book then turns to representations of historical women in war. Each chapter considers literary and historical representations of women, particularly those biographies found in the so-called Illustrious Women genre. Chapter 4 considers women and war as they are presented from the ancients to Boccaccio, while chapters 5 and 6 are anchored by two sixteenth-century editions of Boccaccio's work. The study engages the intersection of fiction and history and takes into account the stakes of writing about powerful women at a time when women ruled from the thrones of France and England.

All discussions of women and war, be they abstract treatises or historical biographies of fighting viragos, necessarily turned around the axis of men's role in warfare. Implicit in any text was the understanding that men were obliged to fight. This obligation could be used to motivate men to action, as well as to condemn or justify violence. An example of the complexity of this mechanism is found in the *Sforziade,* where the text both challenges and reinforces the cultural ideology that casts men as the protectors of women. Both the men of the town of Piacenza and the men of the invading army are depicted as assuming the role of women's champions. The men of Piacenza fight to defend their families and homeland and notably their wives: "They scorn death because of the sweetness of glory, fear for their sons, sad duty toward their parents, and intense dread for their wives and the city of their birth" (translation Robin, *Filelfo* 74).[14] Likewise, Francesco Sforza, the invading general, offers the people of Piacenza the hand of *amicitia* and protection from the Venetians who were at the time occupying the city. Diana Robin analyses Sforza's speech (and the poem as a whole) to suggest that the poet slyly uses the guise of a celebration of Sforza's military might to critique warfare. Robin states that Sforza's speech "exemplifies the two contradictory faces of patronage: even as he holds out the benefits of safety, protection, and self-determination to the Piacenzans if only they surrender, he warns them of the vengeance his troops will take if they must penetrate the city's walls forcibly" (*Filelfo* 69). To this analysis, we add that such "patronage" is staunchly gendered as masculine. Sforza offers, in a most ironic way, a manly protection of the feminine *urbs* by threatening to sack it. When the Piacenzans refuse Sforza's brand of protection, Sforza motivates his men to attack with a new speech that vilifies the townspeople, calling them "ingrates." The Beautiful Souls of Piacenza do not accept his manly protection, and so Sforza unleashes his troops on the city.

Sforza claims that the people of Piacenza are defeated because of God's punishment for subjecting themselves to the Venetians, "like slaves."[15] He thus effectively transforms the feminine city and the women who live within her walls from vulnerable innocents to sinning criminals. It is a rhetorical move that also allows the author to show just how high the stakes are when women's gender role is nudged from Beautiful Soul to enemy combatant. The loss of innocence effectively makes women, children, and the elderly fair game.[16]

The poetic account of the siege of Piacenza in 1447 encompasses the principal themes in the gendering of war: women are deemed unfit for fighting; women are victims in war and need men's protection; men fight for just cause, including the protection of women; and, in the dark, circular logic created in the poem (and one that is repeated in wars today), men fight to protect their wives from invading troops who claim that they are protecting the very women they are attacking.[17] Despite these social attitudes, the reality is that during war the fundamental discourse is survival. And thus the urgency of siege warfare often means that everyone – whether male or female – fights.

Even the author Filelfo recounts that the women, along with the elderly and children, participated in the defence of Piacenza when it was besieged (Robin, *Filelfo* 74). It is an act that seems hard to negotiate with the same women's lament about the "unwarlike" nature of their sex and their inability to fight. However, once we move out of the context of the rhetoric of women in war – the *war story* – and into that of historical reality, we find militant women to be more visible.[18] As military historian John Lynn has shown, it is "ordinary, not extraordinary" for resident women in early modern Europe to be "participants in the defense of towns, either working alongside men to maintain walls and dig trenches or, in many cases, taking up arms themselves to repel the enemy."[19] How authors like Filelfo reconcile representations of combatant women (in siege warfare and otherwise) with the more pervasive discourses of women's inability to fight is the focus of the second half of the book.

Biographies and Combatant Women

The most common literary depictions of combatant woman that we see in the sixteenth century are of women in siege warfare. These stories are both fictional and historical, and they are found in histories, chronicles, and biographical *vitae*. A typical example of this narrative trajectory is the story of Marulla, a fifteenth-century Veneto woman who fought off attacking Turks and chased them to their ships. Her tale was recorded in Marco Antonio Sabellico's *History of Venice* (fol. 222v) (written 1480; published 1554) and was then retold by Matteo Bandello (c.1480–1562) in his *Novelle* as well as by Francesco Serdonati in his anthology of "Illustrious Women" *(Donne Illustri)* published in 1596.[20] In the present book, chapters 4, 5, and 6 focus on biographies of women like Marulla as well as women in war who were not combatants. The chapters are organized in a loose chronological way that will permit us to trace possible shifts across time. We will see that compendia of illustrious women became quite fashionable in the sixteenth century and that, by the end of the century, these collections of women's biographies were recounting tales of women's militancy with extraordinary frequency. For example, in the 1596 compendium of illustrious women by Francesco Serdonati, more than one-third of his 109 biographies tell about historical combatant women.[21] If we gather all of Serdonati's women who were praised for their heroic acts in war, including holding men at knife-point or causing explosions on enemy ships, we find that nearly two-thirds of the women in his text were *illustrious* for their involvement in warfare. Such figures tell us that in contrast to modern putative beliefs, women's fame – at least by the late sixteenth century – is linked in great part to war.

The fascination with compiling encyclopaedic texts of militant women's biographies did not end in the sixteenth century. Collections about militant women were published during the Risorgimento and in fascist Italy, and in our own times we have seen compendia of militant women's lives such as *Amazons to Fighter Pilots: A Biographical Dictionary of Military Women* as well as the extensive *Women and War: A Historical Encyclopedia from Antiquity to the Present*.[22] Such modern compendia, like their Renaissance antecedents, are celebratory texts of women's competencies, but they are also engaged in an archaeological enterprise that is dedicated to unearthing and asserting the existence of warrior women in history against an ideology that continues to erase them. These compendia (modern and otherwise) always take the stance that, despite contemporary assumptions, women warriors are not mythological. They are dedicated to revising and correcting history, demonstrating that women participated in warfare. If such scholarship is any indication, it seems that we have only scratched the surface of the extent of women's involvement in combat.[23]

In this book, I take a different approach to the topic of women's militancy. I will not reveal untold stories of historical women combatants. Rather, my intent is to reach a better understanding of how the narrative representations of women and war were crafted; why some women were chosen and others were not; how descriptions of women's militancy were influenced by the cultural realities surrounding historical women; and finally, why and how historical biographies were often painted with a brush of fiction. Moreover, I seek to understand the relationship between tales of exceptional women and the critique of men.

This is a book that shuttles between literature and the unknowable realities of life experience. We cannot ignore the fact that, despite all of the Renaissance and modern biographies of militant women, Joshua Goldstein can confidently state that women amount to less than 1 per cent of all warriors in history.[24] Goldstein's statistic is of course disputable, but there is no doubt that the percentage of women warriors is a small one. It is also likely that scholars will not change the overwhelming consensus that wars were fought by men, not women; and, even with the contributions of excellent archival research, it is also unlikely that this 1 per cent will ever grow to a number that is truly significant. I propose, thus, to shift the focus away from the empirical data of women warriors to the multifaceted debate that formed around women warriors and to turn Goldstein's number of 1 per cent on its head. Given the small number of women warriors, the extent of the discursive production that formed around their existence is remarkable, and it suggests something much more complex than we might have otherwise realized. Indeed, a profound cultural rupture was triggered by a remarkably small number of women. Thus, we begin not with the woman warrior but with the formidable discursive force she engendered.

1 The Philosophical History of the Armed Woman

The Renaissance debate about warrior women was the continuation of an ancient conversation among men about women's physical weakness, men's moral obligation to protect the vulnerable, and women's political and moral commitment to domestic concerns. It was also a conversation about power, one that both challenged and perpetuated women's status as inferior to men. At the core of the debate about women's militancy is the notion that women are *naturally* inferior in combat and are significantly different from men in their tendency to violence and/or their willingness to fight. The discussion is, however, not limited to scientific claims of women's physical (in)capacities. Writers on all sides of the debate also raise questions of morality and economic stability by focusing on societal, familial, and religious obligations.

The texts that are the focus of this chapter are philosophical, non-narrative, and generally didactic in nature.[1] For the most part, they are not discussed chronologically; nor are they placed within historical contexts. This will be the task of other chapters. In this chapter, instead, I have traced various themes of competing notions of women's militancy in order to underscore the complexity and the existence of a pervasive discourse that has largely been ignored.

Plato and the Reception of the *Republic*, Book V

The most influential sources for Renaissance discussions of women's militancy are Plato's and Aristotle's diverging opinions on the matter. The principal component of the argument is found in Book V of Plato's *Republic*, where the speaker, Socrates, will suggest that men and women should share responsibilities in society, including protection of the *polis* in warfare. When the notion of women's equality is raised, Socrates asks a question that pushes parity between the sexes to its perceived extreme: if women are to be equal, then, Socrates inquires, shouldn't they be educated in gymnasia, music, and war? A radical notion indeed, for after raising the idea of women's pursuing male activities, Socrates notes that women will be ridiculed, particularly for being naked in the *palestra* and above all for "bearing arms" and "riding astride horses" (Plato, *Republic* V). Yet, he assures us, this ridicule will diminish over time.

Socrates' explanation of women's role in his ideal society begins with the statement that women should not be confined to domestic spaces. He uses a suggestive example of male and female guard dogs, an example that points, if only implicitly, to his more direct discussion of women at arms:

> Do we separate off male and female dogs from one another, or do we expect both to share equally in standing guard and in going out to hunt? Should all activities be shared, or do we expect the females to remain indoors on the grounds that bearing and nursing the pups incapacitate them for anything else, leaving to the males the exclusive care and guarding of the flocks? (Plato, *Republic* V.142)

Such comparisons of animals and humans generate much attention in the debate on women's militancy. This passage in particular is incorporated by Thomas Aquinas in his dispute about women combatants, where Aquinas faults Plato for not recognizing that humans and animals differ because animals need not concern themselves with household management (Blythe 252–4). But it was Plato's intention here and indeed throughout Book V of the *Republic* to suggest solutions to civic as well as household management concerns. To Aquinas's dismay, Plato advocates that women should be trained, as are men, to best realize their potential, even a military one. This progressive outlook towards women's education does not mean that Plato saw women as physically and intellectually equal to men; he in fact states the opposite: "one sex [male] excels the other in every respect" (*Republic* V.146). Nonetheless, both sexes participate in all aspects of the republic, and for the class of citizens called "guardians" this includes warfare. As Plato states, "It is obvious that men and women will take the field together" (*Republic* V.158). Military defence is a shared duty. However, each sex performs different tasks:

> Then wearing virtue as a garment, the guardians' wives must go naked [in exercising, like men] and take part alongside their men in war and the other functions in government, and no other duties will be required of them. Owing to the weakness of their sex, however, they shall perform the less burdensome tasks. (Plato, *Republic* V.148)[2]

Plato's thoughts on women in general and more particularly on their ability at arms were a continual point of contention throughout the Renaissance.[3] According to James Hankins, Uberto Decembrio (13?? –1427), a collaborator on the first Latin translation of the *Republic*, is "baffled" by Plato's idea that women should fight (116).[4] However, Uberto's son and the translator of a heavily annotated second, corrected version of the *Republic*, Pier Candido Decembrio (1392–1477), accounts for women at arms as stemming from the idiosyncrasies of ancient Athens.[5] Hankins further explains that Cardinal Basilios Bessarion (c.1400–1472) is more amenable to Plato's philosophy of armed women.[6] The extensive Latin commentary on the *Republic* by Sebastian Fox Morcillo (1556) also favours Plato's opinion, specifically under the auspices of following one's natural strengths.[7]

The subtle variations among later sixteenth-century translations and commentaries give us further indications of the reception of Plato. In a 1554 Italian edition of the *Republic*, Panfilo Fiorimbeni translates the above-cited passage about guardians' wives by emphasizing not only the "lightness" but the "ease" of the tasks to be carried out by women owing to the weakness of their sex: "Ma di questi ufficii alle donne i piu leggieri & più facili dar si deono per l'imbecilità del sesso" (Plato, *Republica* 190r) (But of these [military] offices, women should do those that are lighter and easier because of the weakness of their sex).[8] The "ease" of tasks is of course an ambiguous term and does not follow the more famous Latin translation by Marsilio Ficino, which merely calls for women's work to be the lighter.[9] The Italian translator Fiorimbeni also characterizes women's effort in military duties as less "important" than men's in his brief descriptive commentary that precedes the book:

> Voleva Socrate che gli huomini, & parimente le donne fossero nella medesima disciplina ammaestrati, & che i studi delle cose di guerra, & di pace, tanto publici, quanto privati, fossero alle donne comuni con gli huomini, distribuendo però le cose di maggiore importanza a gli huomini, & alle donne le più lievi. (Plato, *Republica* 175r)

> (Socrates wished that men and women would be equally trained in the same discipline and that the studies of war and peace, public as well as private, would be shared by women and men, distributing, however, the tasks of greater importance to men and to the women the lighter ones.)

Fiorimbeni's commentary on the lesser "importance" ("importanza" is a term that is again more ambiguous than "heavy" ["pesante"]) of women's wartime work thus allows for an interpretation that debases the labour of women in a way that the dialogues themselves do not. These alterations, taken together with the fact that his index omits women in the military while it highlights less prominent discussions about women, point to the translator's general scepticism about women's abilities at arms.[10]

On the other hand, Plato's ambi-sex army finds great fortune in Renaissance Italy's best-known utopia, *La città del sole* (1602), written in Italian and later published in Latin by Tommaso Campanella (1568–1639). Campanella's *City of the Sun* argues for women's inclusion in the military.

> E le donne pure imparano queste arti [militari] sotto maestre e mastri loro, per quando fusse bisogno aiutar gli uomini nelle guerre vicine alla città; e se venisse assalto, difendono le mura. (68)

> (The women are also taught these skills [military arts] by their masters and mistresses in the event that they should be needed to help the fighting men in the vicinity of the city. In case of an assault, they can defend the walls.) (69)[11]

Women, like men, are both militarily trained and are trainers; but in regard to their sex, they engage primarily in defensive battle and are not sent on long-distance missions.

In an interesting passage that is added only to the later Latin edition, *Civitas soli* (1623, 1637), Campanella's speaker states that the women of the City of the Sun have convinced him that Plato not Aristotle was correct about women's abilities at war:

> Consuetudo quidem aptas bello mulieres facit et aliis usibus. Itaque Platoni consentio, ex quo istas vidi et rationes Caietac nostri non satis approbo, minime vero aristotelicas. (*La città del sole / Civitas soli* 60–3)[12]

> (Training, clearly, renders women adept at war and other duties. Thus after having met these women, I am in complete agreement with Plato. On the other hand, I disagree in all ways with our Gaeta and even more so with Aristotle.)

Like Plato, Campanella points to women's physical weakness as a factor in social organization. Women's physical weakness determines, for example, the sort of labour that is assigned to the sexes: to men work that requires "fatica grande e viaggio" (hard labour and travel) (48, 49) and to women professions that are particularly sedentary.

> Universalmente, le arti che si fanno sedendo e stando, per lo più son delle donne, come tessere, cucire, tagliar i capelli e le barbe, la speziaria, fare tutte le sorti di vestimenti; altro che l'arte del ferraro e delle armi. (Campanella, *Città* 48–9)[13]

> (Universally, the tasks that are performed seated and standing, are for the most part assigned to women, like weaving, sewing, barbering, pharmacy, every kind of clothes making, but exclude the work of the blacksmith or of the arms maker.)

Thus, weakness not only influences the tasks women perform in combat, it also bears on other professional choices. These occupational restrictions place unexpected limits on women in a utopia that otherwise heralds women's ability to perform at the level of men.

Campanella's dialogue ends with a discussion on astrology and a reflection on the contemporary world. In this break from his utopic vision, he comments that "si vede che in questo secolo regnano le donne" (122) (in this century, women reign [123]), and he goes on to list several women rulers, including Catherine de' Medici, Isabella of Spain, Elizabeth I of England, and Bianca Cappello in Tuscany. In a list of ten female princes, he includes a group of women who do not seem to fit with their noble sisters, "l'Amazzoni tra la Nubbia e 'l Monopotapa" (122) (the Amazons between Nubia and Monopotapa [123]). These are not European royalty but African women who had been described as warriors ("guerriere") in recent accounts.[14]

Proximity and the Woman Combatant

Campanella's list of European regents and Amazons exemplifies a typical conflation of two types of illustrious women: women rulers and women combatants. Although these categories may seem distinguishable in important ways, female rulers and combatants are often casually listed alongside one another. Such an association likely shows how both professions shared a prestige of power that was typically identified as masculine; but it also points to a more culturally specific notion of the concept of warrior, one that may not match our own modern distinctions between strategic commander and weapon-bearing soldier. In medieval and Renaissance accounts of warfare, a person might be called "warrior" even though he (or possibly she) did not wield weapons (McLaughlin 196). Despite this pre-modern categorization, I will argue in subsequent chapters that the matter of bearing weapons was an important distinction for female viragos. While men might have been called "warriors" when they were in fact commanders, there was an assumption that any man could, if needed, bear arms. The case for women is clearly more complex.

Perhaps more striking than the conflation of female commanders and combatants is the fact that women writers are also often listed alongside warriors and commanders in praises of exceptional women. This strange commingling of female ruler, combatant, and author is evident in texts such as Ariosto's *Orlando furioso* (canto 37, 1–23) and Bandello's *Novelle* (4.19), where readers are expected to accept that a virago and a woman poet should be praised in the same breath.[15] It is indeed a rather common Renaissance conceit of the pro-woman literature to discuss how women might succeed at arms and letters if they were to be trained, notably eliding over the great differences between these two professions. While most texts list women writers and warriors alongside one another with no explanation, Girolamo Camerata's *Trattato dell'honor vero* (1567) provides a rare accounting for this phenomenon. He suggests that while the gods of war and letters (Mars and Mercury) are separate for men, they are co-joined in Minerva for women. Men must choose to be either soldiers or intellectuals, but a woman can be both.[16]

I will show how the conflation of the woman of arms, letters, and politics was instead untenable (*pace* Camerata). Of these illustrious professions, the warrior woman is the most problematic, embodying as she does the irreconcilability of feminine social decorum and killing. The difference among these exemplary women is contained within the very language that writers such as Ariosto, Bandello, and Camerata use to suggest that they are similar. Most notably, the praise of female writers, rulers, and warriors betrays a problem of proximity. We will see that women writers and rulers are hailed as local members of the *polis* while warriors are always on the margins of society, often lurking in the unknown. The mode that Campanella (and other writers of his time) utilizes in order to praise women for their militancy while maintaining a putative feminine gender identity is to distance fighting women from the space and time of the reader. As scholars researching Amazons have shown, travel writing had exploited the exotic potential of distant lands by often depicting fantastic tales of tribes of warring women in Asia, the Americas, and northern Europe.[17] Campanella adopts a similar approach when he describes soldier women in the distant and fictional island of the City of the Sun. So too the African context of Nubia proved to be sufficiently removed from the realities of European social constraints that the author could name the Amazon-like warriors of Monopotapa in his list of illustrious women, women whose qualities were strikingly different from those of the more local Bianca Cappello and Catherine de' Medici.

And thus, the woman warrior remained distanced from reality through either time, or space, or utopistic fiction. Indeed, Plato's and Campanella's texts are similar in that they both describe fantastic worlds. Fiction permitted the shifting of entrenched cultural and social boundaries in order to create utopias that seem even today impossibly foreign to humanity. What is striking, however, is that the fictions of the *City of the Sun* or of the *Republic* were not fantastic enough to break the perceived natural truth of women's physical weakness. Despite their ability to imagine worlds entirely different from their own, both Plato and Campanella saw the bodies of women as immutably weaker than men's. Thus even utopian women, circumscribed by their bodies, saw their roles in combat restricted and constrained.

Aristotle and Women's Weakness

The classical tradition had rather broadly attributed feminine weakness as deriving from women's humidity and coldness. This argument was, according to the medical writer Scipione Mercurio (c. 1540–1615), written in "one thousand places" by Aristotle and Hippocrates.[18] The ancient scientific discourse, however, was not limited to physical weakness, for such notions as humidity and coldness were also coupled with emotive and psychological traits. Women, Aristotle tells us in the *History of Animals*, are less able to overcome fear, less spirited, and less willing to exact violence (Book IX, part 1).[19] These are characteristics that implicitly, if not ever explicitly stated by Aristotle, cast women as unfit for combat. And finally, as weakness and fear would have been seen as incompatible with the act of ruling a state, it is no surprise that Aristotle clarifies in the *Politics* that women are to be the subjects of men: "the relation of the male to the female is by nature that of better to worse and ruler to ruled" (*Politics* 16).[20]

Aristotle never directly poses the question of arming women (except when quoting Plato), but it seems clear that in his estimation, the female body – cold, humid, weak, timid, and non-violent – made women unsuitable for combat.[21] The exclusion of women from combat for reasons of an "inferior" body prevented women from being accorded the status that was awarded to warriors. Moreover, Aristotle's emphasis on the body acted as scientific proof of women's weakness and their consequent unsuitability for combat.

This scientific perspective was cited to overturn Plato's pronouncements on women's ability at war. For example, Giambattista Gelli (alternatively Giovan Battista Gelli, 1498–1563) invokes animals to argue that women are weak. In his dialogue *La Circe* (1549), he reverses Plato's corollary by stating that if female animals are as strong as the males, this only further emphasizes women's relative inferiority to men; the sexes in animals are not divided by weakness while in humans they are.[22] Giovanni Francesco Lottini (1512–1573) states that even though women can be trained to be warriors, their "delicate" bodies make it unwise. His *Avvedimenti civili* (1575, published posthumously) obliquely references Plato's discussion of the strength of female animals by arguing that, unlike female animals, people must live together, and that since women are weak, they can best serve the community by staying in the home. Women should watch over family and home, and they should greet their husbands, returning home from a day of work, with food prepared on the table.[23] Avoiding any comparison to animals at all, Ercole Filogenio merely states that weakness and timidity were what made women unsuited for war: "One finds in women a natural timidity, for which she does not desire to be among arms, nor put herself in any other risk" ("Si ritrova nella Donna una naturale timidità, per la quale non ardisce porsi tra l'armi, nè ad alcuno altro rischio").[24] And finally, even pro-woman authors such as Tomaso Garzoni (1549–1589) found women's weakness to be incontrovertible science. Citing Aristotle, Galen, and Isidorus, Garzoni accepted women's natural physical inferiority as it was received from medical science and particularly Aristotle. [25]

The weakness of women's bodies also justified their domesticity. A Renaissance commonplace, taken in part from Xenophon's *Oeconomicus*, is that a woman stays indoors "as her body is less capable of endurance," while men are occupied outside the house, either in business or on military campaigns.[26] This notion of women's "anatomy as destiny" is hardly unique, and it nicely circumscribes women's lives by virtue of their sexuality or reproductive roles. What is particular to the case of the woman warrior, however, is that when men discuss women's bodies in relation to warfare, they often focus discussion on the "weakness" of the female body rather than childrearing or sexuality. The debate about the woman warrior thus offers a rare case where men discuss women's bodies in terms that are not overtly eroticized – recognizing that implicit in this debate there is an erotic argument of vulnerability. The importance of this fact is that we, as scholars, need to consider warfare when we think of discursive modes of differentiating the sexes. That is, the (non-)combatant body, much like the procreative body, is one way that early moderns (and perhaps moderns) have divided the sexes.[27]

If writers since the ancients had cited women's weakness as a reason to exclude or limit women's participation in the military, there were a select few who were ambivalent towards or outright rejected this ideology. Tomaso Garzoni, for example, acknowledges women's "softness" in several ancient scientific sources, but he also argues for women's fortitude in historical military acts.[28] Others, such as Galeazzo Flavio Capra, redefine physical strength and claim that women are entirely capable of combat. In his 1525 defence of women, *Della eccellenza e dignità delle donne* (*On the Excellence and Dignity of Women*), Capra argues that physical strength should be measured using different parameters, because women exhibit what we might call a strong constitution (they live more moderately and are thus sick less frequently).[29] Moreover, Capra, like the medical writer Scipione Mercurio,[30] suggests that women used to have more strength but have undergone a general atrophy due to a cultural prohibition from engaging in military exercise. According to Capra,

> Li altri beni del corpo cioè la sanità e le forze non sono men ne le donne che negli uomini e posto ancora che fussero in esse minori, non sono tanto momento che possano torgline una minima parte ancora de la loro eccellenza. Perché la sanità consiste in gran parte nel regolato vivere, il che è ne la vostra voluntà, e perché più modestamente e con migliore regola viveno le donne, più rade volte infermano …

Quanto a le forze, noi leggiamo de le Amazone e de molte altre andare use in battaglia e che hanno già molti trionfi e innumerabili vittorie rapportate. La quale consuetudine se infin a questi tempi fusse perseverata, ne l'ora presente ancora veder si potrìa quante fossero le feminili forze. Ma perché tale usanza è interrotta, e le forze e li essercizi militari si conservano e aumentano essercitandoli, par che da nulla siano tenute le forze de le donne. (Capra, *Della eccellenza* 109–10)

(The other qualities of the body, that is health and strength, are no less in women than in men. And even if they were less in women, they are of so little importance that they would take away only the tiniest bit of their excellence. Because health consists in great part in regimented living, which is your will, and women live more modestly and with better routine, more rarely do they fall ill …

Regarding strength, we read of Amazons and of many other women who were accustomed to going to battle and who have reported many triumphs and innumerable victories. Which habit, if it were preserved up until the present day, one would be able to see how great is feminine strength even now. But because such a custom was interrupted, and because strength and military exercises are maintained and grown by exercising them, it seems that but nothing is left of women's strength.)

The treatise goes on to argue that women are cognitively superior to men and that ultimately large battles are won with intellect. Finally, Capra makes an intriguing argument that too much physical strength leads to temerity and thus causes men to be worse in battle.[31]

A Christian and Medieval Context

The ancient debate about women and war that sprang from Aristotle and Plato would continue in the Middle Ages, but the discussion of women in the military was shaped increasingly by a Christian context as well as by contemporary historical events. Particularly important were the accounts of Christian women, especially cloistered nuns in the midst of war. Jane Tibbetts Schulenburg provides many examples of medieval Christian women's creative strategies for protecting themselves in times of invasion, including self-mutilation and making their bodies repellent by placing rotting meat under their clothing (127–76). But there are also examples of more aggressive actions in war. As the now-classic study by Megan McLaughlin suggests, women warriors were more common in medieval Europe than in the classical world or early modern Europe (196). She further explains that the rise and fall of women's participation in medieval warfare depended in part on attitudes towards gender variance but more so on the shifts in the technologies of war; particularly the reduction of the domestic configuration of warfare, where family units fought together (200–2). McLaughlin and scholars after her have thus shown that female rulers fought in battles, women accompanied the crusades, and women of all sorts aided in the defence of cities. Although these tales are often recorded in distorted lore, the flashy tales of Sichelgaita riding armed alongside her husband or of Eleanor of Aquitaine dressed as an Amazon pledging herself to fight in the second crusade may give us some idea of women who fought or at least the legends that formed around them.[32] Furthermore, as Christian writers sought justification for female militancy, there were exceptional women from the scriptures, such as Judith and Deborah, who did not go unnoticed. They were women who achieved their ends through a mix of force and "astuzia" (cleverness), and thus they brought a new dimension into the discourse of women and war that could counterbalance the matter of women's physical weakness.[33] The popularity of the biblical heroine was undeniable: Deborah, the prophetess who helped guide the Israelite army to a victory over the Canaanites (Judges 4:4–16), was heralded by Peter the Venerable in a letter to his beloved Eloise (quoted in Blythe 245), and Judith would of course become iconic in fifteenth-century Italy when both Donatello and Botticelli crafted masterpieces depicting her beheading of the general Holofernes. Moreover, Judith as well as another Old Testament heroine, Esther, would continue to grow in fame as writers such as Lucrezia Tornabuoni and Lodovico Domenichi retold their stories in verse.[34]

Despite the legendary, biblical, and historical examples of women in the midst of wars, the Dominican theologian and preacher Giordano da Pisa (c.1255–1311) was still able to negate the existence of women warriors as well as preclude them from future combat by stating that women cannot fight because they have not done so in recent times. In a sermon of 1304 he states,

> Il quarto e ultimo deffetto delle femine è perch'elle sono divietate da battaglia: si è però che non ne sono use; non usano le femine de combattere, e però non ci sono menate. Ben si legge che un tempo femine combattero, ma questa fu cosa strana e disusata, che non fu mai più; e fu questo ben

vero, e fecer battaglie, e mantennero il reame gran tempo, e furono ne le battaglie de' Troiani, ciò si dice settemila; ma poi venner meno. E però ne le donne tutti i sopradetti difetti sono ragunati.[35]

(The fourth and last defect of women is why they are forbidden from battle: it is because they are not used to it. Women are not accustomed to battle and thus are not brought along. Certainly, we read that at one time women fought, but this was a strange and unusual thing. We know that this has never happened since, that it was very true, that they made war, that they maintained their realm for a great amount of time and that they were in the battles of the Trojans. Some say seven thousand of them fought, but then these women disappeared. And for this reason, in women all the above defects are assembled.)

Giordano's passage is fraught with ambiguities. In his explanation of women's exclusion from battle, he invokes an ancient Amazon history wherein women fought. His words could be taken to suggest – as Renaissance proto-feminists would do after him – that contemporary women should fight but cannot since they lack proper training. It is, however, an unlikely interpretation, as Giordano couches his theory in a context of women's "defects." Unlike later Renaissance proto-feminists, Giordano does not seem to advocate for the training of women warriors as much as explain their absence through a myth of Amazonian extinction. Living women are defective, and presumably Amazons were as well; they were, in his estimation, "strange" and "unusual." His text forecloses any space for contemporary women in the military and ultimately exemplifies how the Amazon myth could be used to damn as well as justify women's militancy.

Given that real women were fighting in a time when men such as Giordano continued to deny the existence of militant women, late-medieval Christian Europe makes for a fascinating time to explore cultural attitudes towards women in the military. It was a time of ambivalence: figures such as Matilda of Canossa (1046–1115) were gaining fame for their militancy, while tenth- and eleventh-century movements such as the *Pax Dei* were attempting to legislate that women, children, and the elderly were to be protected during war since they were non-combatant innocents.[36]

In the best study on the medieval philosophical tradition of armed women, James Blythe considers how writers in the Middle Ages struggled with the mixed legacies of Christianity and classical antiquity, with particular regard given to the reception of Plato as filtered through Aristotle (in a moment when Plato's *Republic* was as yet unavailable).[37] Blythe's study discusses the writings of two Italian philosophers, Ptolemy of Lucca (c. 1236–1327) and Giles of Rome (1243–1316). Both medieval thinkers give serious consideration to the Platonic argument that women should fight, and yet both will ultimately conclude that women are unsuited for combat. The more interesting discussion is put forth by Ptolemy of Lucca, who follows scholastic convention to argue for and against women in combat. In support of women warriors, he states that there were several past societies in which women fought successfully, and that women can alter their nature and virtue through exercise and thus should take part in war: "If therefore, feminine virtue is greatly strengthened in gymnasia and in warlike activities, it would seem to be appropriate for the practice of war to pertain to them."[38] At first Ptolemy might seem to be a direct precursor to Capra's thesis that contemporary women merely lack training, yet Ptolemy will also claim that women's bodies, which are not as strong as men's, predispose them to serve in a social role of childbearing and nurturing (Blythe 260–2). And finally, he will make a surprising example of the Amazons as proof of how women are not meant to fight. Referencing an aspect of the Amazon legend (one that was also visually depicted a century earlier in the outstanding pavement mosaic of Otranto's cathedral), Ptolemy notes that Amazons had to manipulate their bodies by removing their right breasts in order to be successful fighters, a sign of the physical limits of the female body.[39] For Ptolemy and other followers of Aristotle, we are again reminded, the female body and social gender politics are often indivisible.

The Sixteenth-Century *Querelle*

Despite the fact that Ptolemy and Giles ultimately exclude women from the military, their treatises stand as medieval forerunners to the later Renaissance *querelle des femmes*. In her survey of women and militancy in sixteenth-century treatises, Frédérique Verrier argues that, across the sixteenth century, defences of women demonstrate an "intellectualization" of war, where women could offer a new approach to warfare, one that focused more on cleverness than mere force (*Le miroir des Amazones* 114).[40] Beyond the use of astuteness, almost all of the *querelle* texts also confronted the questions of women's weakness, social decorum, and custom. Pompeo Colonna (1479–1532) advocated women's participation in war as a moral question of public engagement, and Giovanni Francesco Lottini (1512–1573), Stefano Guazzo (1530–1593), and Sperone Speroni (1500–1588) all suggest that the received opinion of women's inability to fight is merely an effect of custom.[41] Guazzo in particular suggests that, in time, people could become accustomed to such a "strange" sight, a situation that he makes analogous to the fable of the green donkey, a story which demonstrates how people can become accustomed to what at first might seem strange or outrageous:[42]

> et se bene a voi pare che si disdica loro il vestir l'arme come cosa poco conforme alla dignità donnesca, questo aviene perché non vi è l'uso, come si vuol parere di tutte l'altre cose inusitate ; ma quando si vedessero più d'una volta ridotte, sotto l'insegne militari, non vi parrebbe più cosa strana, ne disdicevole, il che ci vien dimostrato con la volgarissima favola dell'asino verde. (131)

> (and if you think it seems a good thing to denounce the wearing of arms as something that does not become ladylike dignity, this happens because you are not accustomed to it, as happens with all unusual things. But when women would be seen more than once bearing military insignia, it would no longer appear to be a strange thing, nor disreputable, which is demonstrated to us in the most popular fable of the green ass.)

Lodovico Domenichi's *La nobiltà delle donne* (1549)[43] argues that not simply custom but the malicious intentions of men have kept women from realizing their military potential. Domenichi begins by praising Lycurgus and Plato for knowing that women should be able to participate in all things that men do, "including all that pertains to the art of war: shooting with a bow, sling, or rocks; in combat with arms by foot, on horseback, in encampments, in ordering troops, in leading an army …" (26v–27r).[44] He then explains that women are not fighters because men have stifled them, and he notes that the suppression of women is against nature and divine justice:

> Ma contra la divina giustitia, & contra gli ordini della natura, essendo superiore la licentiosa tirannia de gli huomini; la liberta data alle donne è loro, dalle inique leggi interdetta, dalla consuetudine & dall'uso impedita, & dalla educatione totalmente estinta: percioche la femina subito che è nata da i primi anni è nell'otio tenuta in casa: & quasi che ella non sia atta a più

alto negotio; niente altro le è permesso comprendere ne imaginare se non l'ago e 'l filo, mentre poi sara giunta a gli anni al matrimonio; e data nelle forze della gelosia del marito; overo è rinchiusa nella perpetua prigione d'un monasterio di monache. Tutti gli uffici publichi le sono dalle leggi prohibiti. (27r)

(Going against divine justice and the order of nature, since the licentious tyranny of men is great, the freedom given to women is banned by unjust laws, impeded by custom and use, and by education totally snuffed out. Therefore, as soon as a girl is born, from her earliest years she is kept at home in idleness and hardly is she fit for any loftier affairs. She is not allowed to comprehend or imagine anything other than a needle and thread. Then once she has arrived at a marriageable age, she is given to the throes of a husband's jealousy, or she is confined in the life imprisonment of a convent of nuns. All public offices are by law prohibited to her.)

Domenichi and Speroni will both refer to Amazons as exemplars of women's military potential. Speroni in particular elaborates at length about the history of Amazons as well as "viragine" of his own day, including Maria and Margarita of Hapsburg (196). Indeed it was commonplace for writers to have recourse to the Amazons. They are, as Verrier has pointed out, a ubiquitous but problematic presence in nearly all sixteenth-century discussions of women's ability to fight.[45] As we have seen above, some authors will invoke Amazons as a negative example, while others seem to cite them as a matter of staying uncommitted to the debate about the armed woman.[46] Armed women were legendary and thus unthreatening if kept at a geographical or temporal distance.

Moderata Fonte and Lucrezia Marinella

Two Venetian women authors, Moderata Fonte and Lucrezia Marinella, address this gap between the conditions of living women and the viragos of utopistic fiction in their own philosophical works at the end of the sixteenth century. They are the first women to make a sustained contribution to the debate, with the exception of a prodigious forerunner, the Italo-Franco author Christine de Pisan (1363–1430). De Pisan's works included an outstanding treatise on the art of war, an encomium to the living Joan of Arc, and a proto-feminist manual for women. It was in her manual known as *The Treasure of the City of Ladies* that she advocated for women's militancy, stating that the wife of a nobleman should acquire training in warfare:

> We have also said that she ought to have the heart of a man, that is, she ought to know how to use weapons and be familiar with everything that pertains to them, so that she may be ready to command her men if the need arises. She should know how to launch an attack or to defend against one, if the situation calls for it. She should take care that her fortresses are well garrisoned. (129)

De Pisan's noble wife is not an Amazon or creation of utopistic fiction but rather a prudently prepared real woman, perhaps not unlike Margaret Paston of England, who famously watched over her manor in times of war while her husband was away. It is interesting that de Pisan's ideal wife is not only prepared in military matters but is also quite conventional; in the remainder of the manual she is circumscribed by obligations of childrearing and chastity. Such a broad range of skills and responsibilities (war-ready woman, mother, and chaste wife), although not always reconciling with modern notions of feminist thought, shows that de Pisan did not view the military arena as precluding more putative and traditional understandings of femininity. Moreover, McLaughlin, in her seminal essay on medieval women warriors, points out that de Pisan's advice was not pro-woman fantasy but was instead reflective of real-world practice. She states that de Pisan's emphasis on the wife's preparing for war is likely a result of medieval warfare structures, where family units fought together and/or men were frequently away on campaigns while women were responsible for defending the home (203).

As warfare technologies and structures changed, so too did the role of women in wars, and these changes may partly account for the fact that more than 150 years would have to pass after de Pisan's texts for Italian women writers to return to the topic of armed women in the real world. Possibly because of such changes, the armed woman who is discussed by the late-sixteenth-century female authors is no longer taken from the realities of contemporary society; rather, she inhabits a *possible* world, one of abstract philosophy or epic poetry.

The Venetian author Moderata Fonte (1555–1592) was to my knowledge the first Italian woman to write a philosophical text that directly addressed the matter of armed women. Fonte's first venture into the debate about women warriors was embedded in her chivalric-epic poem, *I tredici canti del Floridoro* (1581). In the *Floridoro* (studied in the following chapter, which is dedicated to the genre), Fonte makes an authorial intervention to say that if girls were given the same training as boys, they would succeed in fields that are exclusively held by men, such as the military. This same argument is then restated in her later philosophical dialogue on the virtue of women, *The Worth of Women* (*Il merito delle donne*) (1592, published 1600). Leonora, one of an all-women cast of speakers, states that if women do not bear arms, "non è lor mancamento ma di chi dà loro creanza, poiché si è visto chiaro di quelle che sono state già tempo allevate sotto tal disciplina" (*Merito delle donne* 62) (that isn't because of any deficiency on their part; rather, the fault lies with the way they were brought up) (*The Worth of Women* 100).[47] Fonte's dialogue, however, discusses the issues of women's nature in a way that raises the thorny matter of women's weakness regarding their potential at arms. One speaker claims that men are stronger than women "so they can be in service of women" (*The Worth* 59), while another, Corinna, virtually advocates Aristotle's entire philosophy on women's cold and phlegmatic nature: "ci rende per consequenzia più quiete, più deboli, più apprensive di natura, facili a credere ed a piegarsi" (*Merito* 47) (this makes us calmer than men, weaker and more apprehensive by nature; more credulous and easily swayed) (*The Worth* 83). There is no challenge to the notion of women's weakness. Instead, this weakness underscores the reason that women are deserving of better treatment by men. Fonte's speakers thus engage in a precarious strategy, claiming weakness as a component of women's strength, while at the same time arguing that women should be trained at arms (*The Worth* 100).

The dialogue effectively asserts that women, although weaker than men, can perform heroic acts of strength. The speaker Leonora lists ancient examples of courageous women from legend, the ancient past, and the Old Testament (e.g., Camilla, Hippolyta, Zenobia, Judith), but she also provides several examples of communities of brave women. These women are not warriors but rather women who aided men's fighting or women who ended men's wars: women of Aquileia, Carthage, and Rome who cut their hair to give to men to make bowstrings; women of Sparta who shamed husbands to fight; and the Sabine women who restored peace (*The Worth* 101–3).[48] Fonte's exemplary women encompass what is a conventional cast of characters: classical, legendary, and biblical. Yet in her case the exclusion of contemporary women is politicized by her belief that male suppression had stifled their existence.

The role of a living woman warrior is reserved for the character Leonora herself, who recounts a dream that she is fighting hand-to-hand combat with men and "hacking them to pieces," only to find when she awakes that it was her cat "battling" with a "troop of valiant mice" (*The Worth* 119).[49] In her typical playful way, Fonte seems to be urging her readers to imagine a possible world while remaining in the real one. Proximity again determines the potential of women warriors. The real world is governed by cultural codes that circumscribe women's behaviour, and Fonte's speakers are certainly not gender rebels. Leonora, in fact, states that she would ride horseback and go hunting, only "if she were a man"; presumably, as a woman, she would not (*The Worth* 140). And just as with hunting, Fonte's outfitting of women warriors seems to depend on a hypothetical situation. If men do not fulfil their duty to fight with honour, she states, "I'd like to see us women arming ourselves like Amazons of old and going into battle against these men" (*The Worth* 230).

Fonte's chivalric-epic poem and her treatise were an inspiration for another Venetian woman writer, Lucrezia Marinella (1571–1653), whose extensive writings include a chivalric epic with female warriors as well as a treatise that took up the matter of armed women. Marinella's treatise *La nobiltà et l'eccellenza delle donne, co' difetti et mancamenti de gli uomini* (*The Nobility and Excellence of Women and the Defects and Vices of Men*) (1600 and then expanded in 1601) was a direct response to the misogynist treatise *I donneschi difetti* (*Womanly Defects*) (1599) by Giuseppe Passi.[50] Like Fonte's dialogue, *The Nobility and Excellence of Women* also proposes that a lack of education and training has caused women's absence from military activity. When Marinella arrives at her discussion of the training of women at arms, she aptly cites Plato and her fellow Venetian feminist, Moderata Fonte, as allies to women. Marinella uses Fonte's chivalric-epic *Floridoro* as a challenge to men, to try the experiment of raising a boy and a girl equally in the liberal and military arts.[51] Marinella refashions the debate of arms and letters into a feminist problem, for they are the fields to which women were denied access, and, not incidentally, they are the words ("Et Lettere Et Arme") that surround Minerva on the frontispiece of the earlier 1600 edition (see figure 1.1).

In the treatise, Marinella explains that the exclusion of women from military studies is due to a deliberate and concerted effort on the part of men because of their fear of women's rule.

> Ma poco sono quelle, che dieno opera à gli studi, overo all'arte militare in questi nostri tempi; percioche gli huomini, temendo di non perdere la

LE NOBILTA,
ET ECCELLENZE
DELLE DONNE:
ET I DIFFETTI, E MANCAMENTI
DE GLI HVOMINI.

Diſcorſo di Lucretia Marinella.

In due parti diuiſo.

CON PRIVILEGIO.

IN VENETIA,

Appreſſo Giouan Battiſta Ciotti Seneſe. M. DC.

Con licentia de i Superiori.

Figure 1.1 Frontispiece from Lucrezia Marinella, *Le nobiltà et eccellenze delle donne, et i difetti e mancamenti de gli huomini.* Venice: Ciotti, 1600. Reproduced with permission of the Ministero dei beni e delle attività culturali e del turismo. Biblioteca Nazionale Centrale di Firenze

signoria, et di divenir servi delle donne, vietano à quelle ben spesso ancho il saper leggere, & scrivere. (*Nobiltà* 1601, 32)

(But in our times, there are few women who apply themselves to study or the military arts, since men, fearing to lose their authority and become women's servants, often forbid them even to learn to read or write.) (*The Nobility* 79)

Marinella is one of the few writers to suggest outright that women are actively excluded from fighting, not just that custom has kept women from doing so: "O Dio volesse, che à questi nostri tempi fosse lecito alle donne l'essercitarsi nelle armi, et nelle lettere, che si vedrebbono cose meravigliose, & non piu udite nel conservare i regni, & nell'ampliarli" (*Nobiltà* 1601, 33) (Would to God that in our times it were permitted for women to be skilled at arms and letters! What marvellous feats we should see, the like of which were never heard, in maintaining and expanding kingdoms) (*Nobility* 80). But, presumably because women have been denied such education, Marinella's treatise focuses its discussion of war not on women's past deeds but on a utopic vision of a world that *could* be: "Chi sarebbe piu pronto di fare scudo con l'intrepido petto in difesa della Patria delle donne? & con quanta prontezza, & ardore si vedrebbono versare il sangue, & la vita insieme in difesa de maschi" (*Nobiltà* 1601, 33) (And who but women, with their intrepid spirits, would be the first to take arms in defence of their country? And with what readiness and ardor they would shed their blood and their lives in defence of males) (*The Nobility* 80).

Marinella does provide some historical examples of women and war, despite admitting that she has "fuggita la fatica di voler leggere tutte l'Historie" (*Nobiltà* 1601, 34) (avoided the fatigue of reading every history book available) (*The Nobility* 81). In her chapter 7, "Delle donne nell'arte militare, & nel guerreggiare illustri, & famose" (On Illustrious and Famous Women in the Art of War and Fighting), she describes the valour of legendary Amazons, as well as of several of the women who will be discussed throughout the current volume.[52] She must have particularly revelled in the stories of contemporary Italian women, some of whom fought victoriously at the walls of Pisa or against the Turks. Such brave soldiers stood in stark contrast to the women described in Giuseppe Passi's chapter on fearful women in his misogynist tract *I donneschi diffetti*. From its inception, Marinella's text is an erudite response to Passi's misogynist book, and it tackles each of his chapters with a corresponding counter-argument. For example, to Passi's chapter 27, which was unambiguously called "Delle donne codarde, ville [*sic*], timide e paurose" (Of Cowardly, Fainthearted, Timid and Fearful Women), Marinella wrote her chapter 17, "De gli huomini vili, paurosi, & di poco animo" (Of Cowardly, Fearful and Small-Spirited Men). It is interesting that Passi's examples of fearful women are not about women in war but rather about their reactions to more domestic threats such as mice and flies (251). Marinella instead will claim that fearful men are much more dangerous than fearful women, particularly because of men's role in warfare. Fear of death, she says, is a dangerous trait: "colui, che teme la morte poco stima, & pregia la buona fama, o l'honore" (he who fears death will little value or esteem good fame or honour) and, citing Aristotle, she states that this fear "sforza l'huomo a commettere cose vergognose" (forces men to do shameful things) (*La nobiltà* 1601, 230; translations mine). Her examples will move from failed male warriors in *Orlando furioso* to historical war leaders who, once they feared death, became ineffective. Notably, this moment exposes how Marinella invokes the discourse of men's dominance and obligation in war just as she seeks to resist it.

Torquato Tasso and Francesco Serdonati

Marinella, like Fonte before her, authored a chivalric-epic that embodied women warriors, in effect creating a fiction that showed how a world might seem if such gender equality were indeed enacted. The remaining two authors of this chapter (both male) also wrote of women's militancy, in several genres, and they have been singled out in this chapter for their innovative approach to opening alternative discourses of women's militancy.

Torquato Tasso's *Discorso della virtù feminile e donnesca* (*Discourse of Women's and Ladies' Virtue*) (1580, published 1582) and Francesco Serdonati's *Della perfezione delle donne* (*On the Perfection of Women*) (1596) are treatises that attempt to challenge the putative notions of women's militancy at the close of the sixteenth century. In each text, the virtue of utility will be the determining factor of whether they ultimately advocate for or against the arming of women. Tasso's text presents a complex picture of contemporary women rulers, questioning their roles in government as well as combat. Serdonati, writing the century's longest discussion of women and the military, focuses on a "natural" equality of the sexes and then demonstrates the social imperative of women's militancy.

Torquato Tasso and the Question of Utility

The slim *Discorso della virtù feminile e donnesca* begins by rehearsing Aristotle's position that women are inferior to men in speculative reasoning as well as strength; and yet, according to Tasso, there are some women who transcend this inferiority by nature of their birthright. Tasso explains that although "feminine virtue" ("virtù feminile") may be characterized by modesty and household management, some women, such as his addressee, Eleanora d'Austria Gonzaga (1534–1594), Duchess of Mantua, may demonstrate a much different sort of virtue, one that is derivative of their "heroic" and "royal" blood. These are not merely women but "donne" (ladies), and accordingly they inherit a lady's virtue, "virtù donnesca," which, as Tasso tells us, derives from the term *domina,* suggesting their right to rule.

Tasso was not the only Italian male author to explain to a young noble girl how a woman ruler differs from other women. More than fifty years earlier, Antonio De Ferraris wrote a letter to the Italian-born future queen of Poland, Bona Sforza (1494–1557), in which he reminds the young Sforza of the difference between a princess and an ordinary girl:

> If princes are superior to others (not only on the basis of law and custom, as most people think), then very great must be the distance between you and other girls. You are born for commanding, they for obeying. They work the distaff and spindle; you concentrate on law and moral education. They devote themselves to developing their bodies, you to cultivating your mind. They obey their mistress, make wool, and sew with silk and delicate threads of gold. You, who have the task [...] of commanding even men, read books of the saints and of philosophers. Learn to follow the example of illustrious women to seem worthy of having the power of commanding even men because fortune has gathered in you all of her gifts.[53]

Similarly, the courtier Scipione Ammirato wrote to the new Grand Duchess of Tuscany, Christine of Lorraine, his own advice. In the essay "Alcuni ammaestramenti per le gran principesse" (Some Lessons for the Grand Princess), he explains that while common women must occupy themselves with sewing and weaving, a princess's duty is to govern and rule.[54]

Even within this micro-tradition of didactic literature addressed to princesses, the term "virtù donnesca" (lady's virtue) is the innovation of Tasso. Particular to Tasso, the notion of "lady's virtue" is troubled at best, for *donne* are not characterized by fortitude but by "la leggiadria e la delicatura" (gracefulness and delicateness) (*Discorso* 64).[55] Furthermore, he is ambivalent in his presentation of *ladies'* ability to rule or fight even though he states that the etymology of "donne" would suggest that they are meant to rule. Tasso's philosophy of women's virtue is not a straightforward praise of women but rather a contorted compromise of competing Greek thought, which, according to Tasso himself, negotiates between the camp of Plutarch's and Plato's pro-woman writings and the opposing one of Thucydides' and Aristotle's subjugation of women.[56]

Tasso's text hesitantly addresses the matter of armed women while advocating for men's military service. Twice Tasso refers to women's abilities in "military activities" ("uffici militari") to remind us that Plato believed women could rule and fight just as men did, and that any difference between the two sexes is one of culture not nature:

> Crede Platone che l'istessa virtù sia quella della donna e quella dell'uomo, e che s'alcuna differenza è in loro, sia introdotta dall'uso e non dalla natura; e ne' libri civili vuol che le donne sian partecipi della republica e degli uffici militari, non meno che gli uomini.
>
> ... così parimente [natura] produce l'uomo e la donna atti a tutti gli uffici civili e militari. (*Discorso* 54)

> (Plato believes that the virtue of woman is the same as that of man, and that if there is any difference in them, it is caused by use and not by nature; and in his political writings he thinks that women should participate in the republic and in military offices no less than men.
>
> ... so [nature] produces man and woman fit for all civil and military offices.)

And while Tasso's essay may at first seem to advocate for women at arms, Plato's position on women's innate abilities is one that Tasso refutes. He instead supports the Aristotelian claim of the differences (and inequalities) between the sexes, focusing on the matter that women are weaker. "Fortezza" (strength) is unequivocally the virtue of men.[57] The text thus offers contradictory positions that are resolved through silence. If Tasso begins his treatise by citing Plato's pronouncements on women in the military, he then otherwise ignores the debate about women and the military, allowing for the *physical* frailty of women to dominate the argument. This silence is however complicated by the main focus of the *Discorso*, on Tasso's third category of noble ladies.

Tasso's praise of "ladies" leads him to an acrobatic discussion of the virtues of "heroic women" ("donne eroiche") that in all but one case sidesteps mention of combat.[58] In short, the author seems uneasy with the term he has chosen. He explains how some women are born of a "heroic spirit" ("animo eroico") and others are not quite "heroic women" yet resemble them: "non si possono chiamar donne eroiche, molto nondimeno alle donne eroiche s'assomigliano" (one can't call them heroic women, even though they greatly resemble them).[59] On the other hand, when the discussion turns to what Plato claimed to be women's other competency, "uffici civili" (civil matters), Tasso demonstrates a more lucid defence of women. He heralds women's ability to rule, and he provides a list of notable female regents: Queen Catherine de' Medici, Queen Elizabeth I of England, and Maria of Austria.[60] As Maria Luisa Doglio has pointed out, that women often ruled was by Tasso's time an indisputable fact, and thus, for Doglio, Tasso's reconciliation of the reality of women rulers with Aristotelian writings on gender is a matter of contextual/historical necessity (16). However, I would argue that in Tasso's treatise the praise of women rulers is fraught with ambivalence. On closer examination of his text, we find that Tasso also suggests that queens and regents may be nothing more than elegant palace dwellers.

To pursue this argument, we can look at several ways in which Tasso addresses the usefulness of women. First, his unusual caveat on heroism and ladies suggests that a woman may choose *not* to rule and still be a "donna eroica": "Il regio governo nondimeno, quantunque grande e nobile, può e suole dalla donna eroica esser rifiutato" (*Discorso* 64) (Nevertheless, government rule, however grand and noble, can and usually is rejected by the heroic woman). Tasso's world of illustrious women is an intriguing one: "heroic women" possibly neither rule nor fight, but simply delight in their gracefulness and elegance. This is a duty that contrasts entirely with a letter of Scipione Ammirato to the Grand Duchess Christine of Lorraine, which explains how a princess should synchronize her spirit with her husband's by accompanying him on horseback, in running with lances, and in hunting, as well as in ensuring that courtiers are properly trained.[61] All this, Ammirato reminds his Grand Duchess, is because "ella più d'esser principessa che donna" (she is more princess than lady). The difference between a woman's and a lady's occupation is also stressed in Tasso, but, unlike

Ammirato, Tasso does not regard utility as the purview of the "donna eroica." Tasso states that *women* ("femine") must worry themselves with what is useful (i.e., the house, family) while *ladies* ("donne") occupy themselves with decorum: "l'una avrà per oggetto l'utile, e l'altra il decoro" (*Discorso* 64) (one will have utility as her objective, the other will have decorum).

The occupations of common women (the house) and ladies (decorum) allow the author to make an argument for male superiority that is unexpected in what is on the surface a proto-feminist treatise. In Tasso's elaboration of the "double standard," he tells us that both sexes are subject to social control. Women are shamed for their lack of chastity and men for their lack of courage.[62] He states that,

> Ma onde aviene che la donna impudica sia infame, e l'uomo impudico infame non sia riputato? Forse per la stessa ragione per la quale la timidità, che si biasima nell'uomo, non è vergognosa nelle donne, perciò che così l'uomo come la donna è onorato e disonorato per il proprio vizio e per la propria virtù, e non per gli altri. (*Discorso* 58)
>
> (But how does it happen that an indecent woman is called wicked while an indecent man is not? Maybe for the same reason that fear, which is shameful in men, is not shameful in women. Thus, men and women are honoured or dishonoured for their respective vices and virtues and not for other ones.)

Tasso explains that men are honoured for their courage, women for their modesty. When men and women fall short in these virtues, they are dishonoured. Tasso explains that this social control of behaviour is necessary for the public good. Specifically, it is men's courage that guarantees well-being and security. For Tasso, fear causes men to "gittar l'arme e a far altre cose contra il decoro" (*Discorso* 58) (to cast off arms and to do other things against decorum). Shame corrects fear and thus engenders military success. He explains that this philosophy of shame follows Aristotle's *Politics,* which explains that citizens must be compelled to do good through infamy: "l'infamia a' timidi s'attribuisce" (*Discorso* 58) (we attribute disrepute to the cowardly).[63]

There is one moment in the essay in which Tasso suggests that noble ladies are as capable as men in warfare, stating, "Ne alcuna distinzione d'opere e d'uffici fra loro e gli uomini eroici si ritrova" (*Discorso* 67) (there is not found any distinction of works and offices between them [heroic women] and heroic men). The claim is followed by the important example of Maria of Hungary, sister to Emporar Charles V and aunt of the dedicatee, who, Tasso states, was a valorous captain in wars and a prudent king in governing. Though this passage may seem to suggest that "donne eroiche" act heroically in war, it should be remembered that this was a choice for women. "Heroic ladies" did not need to fight; they were only compelled to perform delicateness and decorum.[64] If we situate Tasso's text in a discourse of utility, men offer the state a service of security that ladies (even his "donne eroiche") often did not. For Tasso, men are always bound to (re)demonstrate courage at arms or risk accusations of failed manhood and effeminacy.[65] When women demonstrated such acts, it was truly exceptional.

Serdonati (c.1540 Florence–c.1603 Rome?)[66]

The Florentine grammarian and *poligrafo* Francesco Serdonati wrote a lengthy essay that seems to be a response to and revision of Tasso's notions of women's labour and the military. Serdonati's essay *Della perfezione delle donne (On the Perfection of Women*) (479–90) is found in his edition of the translation of Boccaccio's *On Famous Women.* The book itself is a fascinating collection of a translation of Boccaccio's compendium of illustrious women followed by fifty biographies of women added by Giuseppe Betussi in 1547 that is then followed by a hefty addition of women's biographies by Serdonati. Betussi's and Serdonati's biographies of illustrious women are discussed in chapters 5 and 6, but here we turn to the philosophical essay that Serdonati places ahead of his catalogue of famous women.

Serdonati's text is dedicated to the Grand Duchess of Tuscany, Christine of Lorraine, the very same princess whom Scipione Ammirato reminded to accompany her husband on horseback and with lances. In his essay *On the Perfection of Women*, Serdonati never acknowledges Tasso outright, but he follows Tasso's lead by discussing the etymology of "donna" and its use in contemporary parlance (*Della perfezione* 483–4). He discusses the engendering power of the term "donnesca," and, in what I see as a sly defiance of Tasso's text, Serdonati states that when writers use the term, it is as if they are *asking* women to rule:

> veggiamo nelle antiche memorie di quei gran padri della lingua nostra, che quando voleano esprimere qualche gran forza, e mostrare che qualche cosa fusse stata comandata signorilmente ... dicevano donnescamente

imporre, è donnescamente parlare, volendo quasi mostrar, che alle donne s'aspettava comandare. (*Della perfezione* 483)[67]

(We see in the ancient stories of the great fathers of our language, that when they wanted to express some great force and show that something has been commanded as a lord [...] they would say one did it "donnescamente" or one speaks "donnescamente," wanting to almost show that, from women ["donne"] one expects rule.)

The treatise is an unequivocal defence of women, stating its purpose as challenging the "universal opinion" that women are not suited for great works and "heroic deeds" (*Della perfezione* 479–80). Citing Plato in the defence of women, Serdonati, in a more provocative move, draws on Aristotle for his central argument of women's perfection, and thus makes allies of the historic two camps around the *querelle des femmes*, typically represented by Plato (pro-woman) and Aristotle (anti-woman).[68] Avoiding the question of physical strength, Serdonati says that all "virtù" are within women's potential if they are given the time and training to practise them.[69] Serdonati asserts that women's recent lack of military activity is not a matter of natural disposition but of cultural construction. Furthermore, women are occupied in domestic affairs because they respectfully follow society's rule and dutifully obey their parents: "per ordini degli huomini, e per modestia loro si sono prese nella cura e nel governo delle case, e per obedire all'instituzione de padri e delle madri" (*Della perfezione* 481) (women are involved in the care and management of the house out of the laws of men, for their own modesty, and in order to obey the guidance of their fathers and mothers). Like certain modern feminists, Serdonati honours women by acknowledging the value of domestic chores, stating that "non sono al genere humano di minore utilità" ([such work] is of no minor utility to the human species); but he privileges a more public service. Indeed, he is most enthusiastic about women's roles in civic and military functions:

Ma qualunque volta le donne hanno atteso ad esercizi nobili, e virili sono riuscite, riescono, e sempre riusciranno eccellenti a par degli huomini. E ciò si pruova agevolmente, perché la più nobile e la più malgevole opera, che in questa nostra mortal vita si faccia è il governare e reggere tanto le Città e' regni, quanto i campi, e gli eserciti, e maneggiare le guerre; e questa non è opera di huomini soli, come molti falsamente

> si danno ad intendere, che le donne anche ci hanno la parte loro. (*Della perfezione* 482)
>
> (But whenever women have attempted noble and manly endeavours, they have succeeded; they succeed; and they will always succeed excellently and equal to men. And this easily shows why the most noble and the most demanding work that exists in this mortal life is governing and ruling, not only cities and realms, but also battlefields and armies, as well as managing warfare. And this is not the work of men alone, as many falsely understand, for women also have their part.)

Significantly, Serdonati shifts the discourse of utility, so important to Aristotle, Xenophon, and of course Tasso, away from domestic duties and on to the public concerns of governing the city and managing wars. And more importantly, this is true for both men and women.

The bulk of his essay is dedicated to women in combat; in his eleven pages he provides what is likely the lengthiest discussion on women and war in the sixteenth century. After his philosophical argumentation, he provides a standard list of examples of women warriors of ancient and distant lands (Amazons, Sauromati, Saci, Spartans, Athenians, Indians) as well as adding some less common examples such as the legendary founders of Milan (the Insubri). He quickly explains that if one does not see examples of women warriors in the present day, it is merely because women are not trained:

> E se oggidì non si veggiono sovente tali pruove, ciò nasce, perché oggidì le donne comunemente non esercitano tali mestieri, che se le donne de tempi nostri s'essercitassero nell'arme, come già fecero molte antiche, farebbono le medesime pruove, che fecero quelle. (*Della perfezione* 488)
>
> (And if today we don't frequently see such exemplary deeds, this is born of the fact that nowadays women do not commonly practise such professions. If women in our own time were to train at arms, as did the ancients, they would prove their valour, as did the ancients before them.)

Such language resembles that of his contemporaries Moderata Fonte and Lucrezia Marinella; but what makes Serdonati's work so compelling is that he promotes a genuine *need* for women to fight in the military. History, he claims, had shown that a fighting force of women and men was necessary to combat the very real Turkish threat. Even if Christian women warriors were not to be found fighting the Turks, Persian women were. Serdonati states that when Sultan Selim I (1465–1520) defeated the Persian shah, Ismail (1487–1524), at the 1514 battle of Chaldiran, the Turks were amazed to find women's bodies dressed in armour among the Persian dead – women who had died fighting for liberty and their homeland:

> si trovarono molte donne Persiane fra la cavalleria loro, le quali combatterono da franchi cavalieri, ne furono conosciute per donne se non poi nello spogliare morti, che ve ne furon trovate molte, che havean sostenuto onorata morte per la patria, e per la libertà con danno inestimabile, e stupore maravilioso de Turchi ... (*Della perfezione* 489)
>
> (Many Persian women were found among their cavalry. Women who fought as earnest knights were not recognized as women if not for when their dead bodies were stripped. There were many of them who had an honourable death with unbelievable wounds, all for their *patria* and for liberty, all to the stupor and wonder of the Turks ...)

Although the women were fighting on the losing side, they fought like "franchi cavalieri" (confident knights). Moreover, taken in the context of the longer work (we recall that following Serdonati's essay are more than a hundred biographies, many of which depict real women in war defeating men), the essay thus functions as the abstract hypothesis followed by empirical evidence.

Serdonati's ideology not only argues for the equitable military education of women, it also reverses Tasso's theory of women's utility. As we reflect on the argument for and against women in the military and the gendering of war in the early modern period, we may find that, at its core, this debate has much more to do with the distribution of labour than the question of women's physical weakness. One could argue that the debate about armed women was in some sense a multiplying of new Renaissance *oeconomici.* Women's courageous actions in war proved, in effect, their utility. The contribution of women to society was then underscored in praises of women in war, which frequently depicted their acts of heroism during the desperate moments of siege warfare.

Conclusion

All authors, including Serdonati, had to contend with Plato and Aristotle as the authoritative voices on women's militancy. Lodovico

Domenichi, Moderata Fonte, and Lucrezia Marinella all claimed that Plato's writings had had little effect on real women because women's militancy had been intentionally suppressed in order to maintain men's superiority. Francesco Serdonati and Tommaso Campanella instead deliberated on Plato's argument of social expediency and declared that women's exclusion from fighting was a waste of resources. Other authors merely cited Plato as authoritative proof for their own claims of women's potential. Aristotle, on the other hand, was the source authors used to state that science disproved all of these arguments.

Despite all of the treatises and dialogues that sought to argue otherwise, women in the sixteenth century did not participate in combat in notably larger numbers. This does not mean, however, that the discourse of women's militancy had no effect on the lives of men and women. What may not be at first apparent is that the mere question of women's potential militancy was a matter of life and death. As innocents, women were not to be targeted during war; laws such as the previously discussed *Pax Dei* as well as war practice customs were established to protect them. Although these laws and customs did not successfully protect all women at all times, they did perpetuate the ideology that women were not to be harmed in warfare. Women, however, were also imperilled by this characterization as "innocent non-combatants." Since they did not fight, women, along with children and the elderly, were labelled as "disutili" (useless) or "bocche inutili" (useless mouths) during siege warfare. Because of their status as useless to the war effort, they were often cast out of cities into the arms of the enemy so as to preserve food rations.[70] Those people who were expelled, unsurprisingly, did not always fare well in enemy camps. Thus, the utility of women – as defined by the discourse of women's militancy – was a high-stakes matter in the Renaissance.

It is my claim that the discourse of women's militancy – that is, not just the act of women fighting – had a great effect on the lived realities of men and women. Women were both imperilled and protected by their status as both "useful warriors" and "innocent non-combatants." But so too were men affected by this discourse. The deaths of men, as the warrior sex, were considered less tragic than women's. Moreover, men were morally obliged to fight and protect the vulnerable, and thus they could be controlled through shaming mechanisms if they were derelict in their duties. The positive aspect of men's warrior status, on the other hand, was that men could maintain their claims of superiority and gain access to fame, glory, and honour as well as the monetary benefits that were associated with these concepts.[71]

Finally, the discourse of the armed woman challenged not only women's position in the patriarchy but one of the fundamental ways that the gender binary was framed. As Torquato Tasso's essay explained, women are controlled through a shaming mechanism that condemns sexual promiscuity; men are defined by courage and are shamed for cowardliness. Despite the multitude of real lives that proved otherwise, war and masculinity remained synonymous. The woman warrior was thus not only a challenge to social practice, she was a challenge to the way that gender – as well as society more generally – was understood.

It is no surprise that a concept so fraught with social disruptions did not bring about any real change in the status of women in the military. What is surprising, however, is the proliferation of the discourse of the armed woman during the Italian sixteenth century. The following chapters will consider the cultural and historical contexts that might have contributed to this phenomenon.

2 The Poetic and the Real: The Chivalric-Epic Commentary of the Armed Woman

Sixteenth-century heroic poetry became increasingly verisimilar in its depiction of new combat technologies.[1] Contemporary military realities that were found in verse included amplified use of infantry, the pitching of fortified camps, the changing role of the commander, and, most famously, the gunpowder revolution. Given this literary trend of verisimilitude, the prominence of the female knight in sixteenth-century chivalric epic is all the more striking. The irony cannot be lost on us that in a context of increasing poetic war realism, armed ladies proliferated in heroic poetry while they still remained rare in real-world combat. It is a point that has escaped most scholarly discussions about historicity and verisimilitude in sixteenth-century epic. And it may be that this critical silence points to a symptom of the sixteenth-century epic itself. The chivalric epic was, as we will see, a genre that expanded the role of female warriors while muting almost any extra-diegetic commentary on their textual presence. So what can we know of these women warriors who battle across the pages of the most famous poems of the European Renaissance?

In the last few decades, we have witnessed an impressive scholarly interest in the viragos of Renaissance epic and romance, including monographic studies devoted to the development and origins of the woman warrior character.[2] Many scholars have considered the literary virago within a context of historical militant women, while still others have discussed her in the context of fifteenth- and sixteenth-century women rulers.[3] Some of these studies have proffered that the numerous viragos of sixteenth-century poetry are literary imaginings inspired by historical women such as Caterina Sforza and, more convincingly, have argued that these characters reflect both the celebration of and anxiety about women's increasing political power, particularly in courtly contexts. This chapter will approach the issue from a different perspective. The primary thrust of my inquiry is the question of how poetic women warriors are situated within the Renaissance debate of women's role in the military, a debate that, as I discussed in the previous chapter, permeated many genres during the sixteenth century.

Unlike previous studies, this chapter frames the literary woman warrior not as (only) a symbol or a metaphor but as a "woman" and a "warrior." This methodological shift thus takes a new approach, which raises new questions such as whether armed maidens are invoked to celebrate gender equality or to condemn a perverted emulation of male aggression. To be clear, the warrior women considered in this chapter are not real women but are literary inventions, primarily from the epic genre. Considerable attention is thus given to how literature and generic convention inflect the chivalric virago: the interplay between a fantastic and a material armed woman, the reception of the virago within and beyond the text, and the containment of the chivalric virago within a recursive construct. The trajectory of the chapter, loosely moving from chivalric epics written by men to those penned by women, is in part chronological, but it also serves to highlight that women authors (working in a genre that is steeped in a history of masculinity) both challenged and reinforced the putative notion that women were non-combatants.

Women's Militancy and Ancient Epic

The previous chapter focused on philosophical writings that openly discussed the question of women's military abilities. Heroic narrative, on the other hand, appeals to the issue of women's abilities at arms with a certain poetic evasiveness. Epic poems engage in a play between intertext and the mundane to create an armed woman who is at once symbolic and real. That is, the virago of epic poetry is likely both a metonym for the abstract virtues of women and a literary incarnation of women's military potential; the extent to which she is one or the other will have extra-textual implications. The degree to which the author successfully inserts her into a narrative of historic realism may be ultimately and ironically determined by the faithful adherence to the tradition of literary trope. And here the ancients provide the germinal examples.

Bernard Schweizer has controversially claimed that "epic and masculinity appear to be coterminous,"[4] and it would be reasonable to argue, regardless of one's opinion of Schweizer's statement, that within epic, war and masculinity are bound together in a semantic knot. Epic's foundational text, the *Iliad*, relegates women to the home just as it confirms men's obligation to the battlefield. When Andromache begs Hector to consider his family and not risk his life, the hero famously responds, "Go home, now, attend to tasks that are yours, your shuttle, your loom, and supervise your maids at work, but trust martial affairs to men" (6.490–2).[5] The sexes are indeed repeatedly identified by the dichotomy of "war and weaving, city and house."[6] Despite his gendering of war, Homer also provides two of the earliest citations of Amazons, where warring women ("Amazones antianerai") are praised as formidable opponents (3.189; 6.186).[7]

Homer's brief mention of the Amazons does not convince even the most hopeful reader that he believed that women could be warriors. Indeed the Renaissance writer Francesco Bracciolini (1566–1645) notes that Homer, like the later Aristotle, saw women as weak, while Virgil and the Renaissance epic poets who followed him would attribute fortitude to women warriors.[8] Such a reception of Homer is not surprising given that the Homeric Amazons are inconsequential in the story and are so brief an allusion that they likely confirm male dominance in warfare by creating the exception that proves the rule.[9] While the Homeric Amazons had little impact on the development of Renaissance warrior women, post-Homeric characters such as Amazon Queen Penthesilea resonated in Renaissance texts, most importantly via their adaptations by Virgil.[10]

Virgil was undoubtedly the most influential writer for Italian Renaissance iterations of female militancy.[11] This is not to say that Virgil genders war as feminine. As most readers of the *Aeneid* would quickly note, warfare in the epic is nearly exclusively masculine.[12] From the trajectory of Ascanius growing into his role of warrior patriot (*Aeneid* XII, 586–92), to the speech of Mercury that scorns Aeneas for his bejewelled (read feminized) sword when war was calling out for him (*Aeneid* IV, 219–78), warfare in the *Aeneid* is the ultimate destiny if not goal of manhood. And yet, even as the epic raises the warrior man to the sublime and relegates women to the loom, it also creates Camilla, the most important and lasting model of a female warrior.[13] The genre of classical epic thus arguably instals a cast of problematic exemplars in its temple of war.

The centrality of Virgil's Queen Camilla to the Renaissance discourse on warrior women cannot be overstated; already in the Middle Ages her story is cited by each of the *tre corone* of the Trecento.[14] She is made the subject of a fresco cycle by Nicolò dell'Abate (Poggi Palace, Bologna, 1550), and she is referenced by nearly all medieval and Renaissance writers who discuss women's strength. Moreover, the characteristics of Virgil's Camilla provided a model (at times a problematic one to be resisted) for all subsequent literary descriptions of female warring protagonists. Most obviously, she is chaste, athletic, and a queen. She is an accomplished horsewoman and a master of archery, hand-to-hand combat, and the hunt. And although she is compared to Penthesilea and Amazons in general, she is in fact not exactly an Amazon but rather a Volscian huntress who adapts her hunting skills for battle.[15] Finally, it is her family history – child of an exiled father and absent mother, raised on the milk of wild beasts – that destines her to become an anomaly: a woman unlike other women.

As Giampiera Arrigoni has suggested, Camilla's extraordinary childhood may intimate how it is possible for women to deviate from the trajectory of the weaving domestic woman in order to become a mistress of the hunt, the professional stepping-stone for many women warriors.[16] Camilla was promised by her father to the goddess Diana and nursed on the milk of a wild mare. She is thus both spiritually and biochemically altered, different from other women who are raised by human mothers. Such a wildling upbringing and, more particularly, unusual nursing might also be applicable to the women soldiers who fight alongside Camilla, though we ultimately learn little about them. This wildling origin will be taken up in the Renaissance, most famously with Ariosto's Marfisa and Tasso's Clorinda. Given its persistence, we may need to consider this sylvan childhood as fundamental not only for Camilla's militancy but for her Renaissance progeny as well. It is certainly an aspect of epic that will be problematized by texts at the end of the sixteenth century.

Such a biological argument, however, does not explain the case of a different example of militant women found in the *Aeneid*. These are the Latin mothers, who after the death of Camilla are inspired to fight from atop the city walls: "From the walls, even the mothers, with a peak of effort – real love of country shows the way – when they saw Camilla, excited they threw their weapons with force and with heart of oak ... and [they] burn to die in the front line in defence of their walls" (*Aeneid* XI, 891–5; prose translation Horsfall 47).[17] In his description of the Latin mothers, Virgil suggests that not only the sylvan huntress but also the Roman matron is capable of fighting in war if pushed by necessity. And, of course, it is notable that it was a woman warrior exemplar, Camilla herself, who inspired these women to arms.

Andreola Rossi notes that there are several ancient historical cases that parallel the Latin matrons' acts; and I would add that these women also resemble Renaissance women fighting at city walls during siege warfare. It is thus striking that the Latin matrons are *not* emulated more frequently in Renaissance heroic poetry. When they do appear, these groups of women are typically in minor roles. For example, Tasso imitates Virgil's episode of the Latin matrons in his *Gerusalemme liberata,* when a group of Saracen women who are watching Clorinda are inspired to fight from the walls (*Gerusalemme liberata* XI.58, 3–8). The brief moment seems to be an unlikely attempt to comment on the role of women in warfare.

Conversely, it is the ahistorical warrior Queen Camilla who found great fortune in later literature. Indeed, Renaissance authors repeatedly depict singular heroines or groups of misandrist Amazons – choices that likely point to both the generic tendency of epic to emphasize individual heroism (e.g., Bradamante, Marfisa, Clorinda) on the one hand, and the period's fascination with tales of exotic Amazons (e.g., the island of man-killing women of *Orlando furioso* XIX–XX) on the other. The fact that the most influential Renaissance poets did not imitate Virgil's Latin matrons is even more intriguing when we consider that groups of women similar to Virgil's matrons are found in other ancient epics as well.

There exists a close parallel to these women in the *Posthomerica* of Quintus, a poem written centuries after Virgil but likely based on texts that were also influential for Virgil.[18] In Quintus's tale of the Trojan War, Trojan women were said to be inspired both by Penthesilea's success against the Greeks and by a rousing speech by Hippodameia:

> Friends, let the hearts within your breasts be brave,
> No less than those of our husbands, who for the fatherland
> Are fighting the foe on behalf of our children and ourselves
> With no relief from suffering. Let us also fill
> Our hearts with courage and take an equal share of fighting.
> We are not far removed from the strength of men.
> The vigor that there is in them is also in us.
> Eyes and knees are the same, and everything is alike.
> The light and liquid air are common to us all.
> Our food is the same. So what advantage is given to men
> By heaven? Let us not shrink in battle. (*Posthomerica* 1.409–19)[19]

As the narrator reports, the speech was successful in rousing the women to leave their looms and reach for weapons:

> These words filled them all with a passion of hateful fighting.
> They were ready to rush out headlong from their walls
> Under arms, in their eagerness to defend
> Their city and their people; so roused in them was their spirit.
> ...
> ... They cast aside their wool
> And baskets, putting their hands to grim weapons
> (*Posthomerica* 1.436–46)[20]

Although they are inspired to go to arms (once again by a heroine woman), these Trojan mothers, unlike their Latin counterparts, do not ultimately fight. They are not, as Andreola Rossi states, "able to bridge the gap between weaving and warfare" (*Contexts* 119). Just as they turn to join the fight, the women are persuaded by one in their group to abandon their plan, since women's physical weakness precludes them from fighting. As "Prudent Theano" states, "You rush without a thought. Your strength won't equal / that of the Danaans who are trained in fighting / ... / Therefore stay away from the noisy battle / and busy yourselves with the looms inside your homes" (*Posthomerica* 1.454–69; Quintus 14). Although motivated by brave spirits and presumably morally engaged in the protection of their city, the Trojan women are ultimately returned to a discourse that qualifies them as the vulnerable sex.

To my eye, the Trojan mothers of Quintus and the Latin mothers of Virgil establish a cultural commentary on women's militancy (both pro and con) that is much more convincing than the heroic deeds of individual and exemplary viragos such as Camilla. And yet, neither classical group will be central to the poems of Boiardo, Ariosto, or Tasso. We do, however, find moments of militant verisimilar women in other early modern poems. Margherita Sarrocchi's *Scanderbeide* (1606 and 1623), for example, depicts a Christian captain who, in an attempt to defend the city of Croia, dresses the city's women in men's armour so that the invading Turks will be deceived (VI, 41).[21] The scene borrows loosely from ancient sources and directly reflects historical biographies nearly contemporary to Sarrocchi. Most striking is the resemblance of Sarrocchi's tale to that of the women of Corciola, who were dressed as soldiers standing atop the walls in order to frighten off the Turks in 1571, at least a hundred years after the setting of Sarrocchi's historical epic but only a few decades before she composed the poem.[22] Although it differs in important ways from that of Virgil's fighting mothers, the scene shows that the Renaissance epic did at times produce images of women in war that reflected contemporary war narratives and practices; moreover, it shows the sort of interplay that might happen between historical tales of illustrious women and the poetic epics depicting fictional armed women. Indeed, by the end of the sixteenth century, it is the genre of the pseudo-historical *illustrious woman* biography, not heroic poetry, that will depict communities of militant women more in line with Virgil's Latin matrons. Sixteenth-century chivalric epics, on the other hand, are invested in the exploitation of the heroic, virginal, and noble virago figure, and thus we now look to these projections of legendary female heroism and prowess.

Believe It or Not: The Armed Maiden of Chivalric Epic

In the opening canto of Ariosto's *Orlando furioso,* an anonymous errant knight unsaddles the Saracen king Sacripante just as the king is planning his sexual assault on the fair Angelica. Sacripante's humiliation is redoubled when a messenger proclaims that the victorious knight was a "valiant and courageous woman," none other than Bradamante, a woman "as beautiful as she is brave" (I, 70.1). The scene is the first of many where male opponents find themselves defeated at the hands of women, and unsurprisingly, this defeat causes extreme "pain" and "shame" for Sacripante as he considers what has transpired. Yet this humiliation stirs neither the narrator nor the characters to pause and reflect on the strangeness of a female warrior. The narration simply pushes forward. I will argue that this moment and others like it have a cumulative effect suggesting that, although it is humiliating to lose to a woman, it is not always unexpected; or, perhaps more precisely, that women opponents are understood to exist within a realm of possibility and not merely as fantasy.

As Eleonora Stoppino has shown, the woman warrior, and Bradamante in particular, would have been familiar characters to Ariosto's readers. The virago was part of the "constellations of literary memories," borrowed and recrafted by authors in the intertext of chivalric literature (19). Ariosto himself gives a sly nod to such familiarity in the virago's most famous episode at the Rocca di Tristano (Tristan's

Castle), which first appears in the 1532 edition.[23] In canto 32, Bradamante seeks lodging in Tristan's castle, which has a strict law that a knight seeking lodging must defeat the male guest who arrived before him. On the other hand, a woman who wishes to stay at the castle must be judged as more beautiful than any previously arrived female guest. Bradamante enters as a knight by challenging three male knights and defeating them handily. Upon entering the castle, her sex is revealed when she lifts her helmet and inadvertently loosens her bound hair so that it falls to her shoulders. The scene is told first as a simple description of events: "uscì con l'elmo; onde caderon sparsi / giù per le spalle, e la scopriro a un tratto / e la feron conoscer per donzella" (XXXII, 79) ([her hair net] came off with the helmet. / Whence her tresses fell loose upon her shoulders, / at once discovering her and revealing she was/ a damsel).[24] And it is then repeated in the subsequent stanza in a hyperbole of awkward similes:

> Quale al cader de le cortine suole
> parer fra mille lampade la scena,
> d'archi e di più d'una superba mole,
> d'oro e di statue e di pittura piena;
> o come suol fuor de la nube il sole
> scoprir la faccia limpida e serena:
> così, l'elmo levandosi dal viso
> mostrò la donna aprisse il paradiso. (XXXII, 80)
>
> (As when the stage appears at curtain drop
> amidst a thousand lanterns, full of
> archways, proud structures, gilding, statues,
> and paintings; or like the sun, which often
> reveals its limpid, serene face from out of
> a cloud: so the damsel seemed to open paradise
> by taking off her helmet.)[25]

What is even more fascinating than the unusual likening of Bradamante's fallen tresses to a stage or sun is that the lord of Tristan's castle seems quite unaffected by the gender of his guest. The baroque-styled similes provide an ironic spectacle of wonder staged between author and reader. I use the term "ironic simile" as this spectacle serves to highlight the difference between an exaggerated if tired trope of revealing the female underneath armour and the casual response it produces.

The only reaction the lord is said to have is one of respect, for he realizes that he must be gazing at the Bradamante he had seen on previous occasions.[26]

Previous occasions, indeed, for narrative poetry had been replete with female warriors named Bradiamante, Bradamante, and Braidamante.[27] This diverse group of Bradamantes demonstrates that sixteenth-century readers would have been quite familiar with her namesakes as well as any number of armed women.[28] In this context of decades of women warriors, the simile of stage curtains dropping to reveal the armed lady seems almost quaint. And it is this proliferation of literary viragos that incites a nagging question – in what ways did or didn't Ariosto's contemporaries respond to the woman warrior as literally what she was, a woman at arms?

The reception of the female warrior (both inside and outside the text) is complicated by the silence of nearly all authors of heroic poetry on the credibility of women at arms. Modern readers would likely concur that the lack of discussion about women's militancy does not suggest that women warriors were typical real-world sights for Ariosto's and Tasso's sixteenth-century contemporaries. But I also hesitate to suggest that women warriors were only symbolic figures of virtue or that they were so common a literary trope that they had become nothing more than representations of something, indeed *anything,* other than armed women.[29] To suggest that the fictional armed maiden is purely metonymical, a signpost for feminine fortitude or some other abstract virtue, ignores the repeated poetic choice of the author, precisely in a culture that was discussing the possibility of women at arms and the failures of armed men. It could be instead that the power of the literary armed woman, particularly in Ariosto, lay precisely in the interplay between imagination and the material world, an interplay that resists the categorical dismissing of the female militant body.

Tresses of Golden Hair

Throughout the genre, such negotiation between reality and fantasy is played out in the trope of the revelation moment like that of Bradamante at Tristan's castle. The scene, which is repeated throughout the corpus of heroic poetry, stages a woman who performs feats of martial prowess and then removes her helmet to expose (always beautiful) feminine aspects and long healthy tresses of hair.[30] I will refer to this moment as the "revelation moment," as it is an occasion that not only reveals the sex of the armed person but also highlights the troubling yet titillating transgression of putative gender roles. It is furthermore a moment that is grounded in identity politics. This section considers what was at stake in the revelation moment, first looking at what it means to be a knight as well as the particular significance of armour in communicating knightly identity. It then focuses on what sort of challenge the female knight poses to this masculine unity by considering several revelation moments.

The armoured body is imbued with a host of political signifiers (e.g., honour, knight, masculine) that are at best vague; in the extreme they are empty signs that posture as significant through recursive sequences.[31] As an example of this dizzying recursive dynamic, one need only think of the Medici reintroduction of chivalry into humanist Florence.[32] In a moment of particularly heightened neo-chivalric artifice, Pulci wrote *La giostra* (1469) and Poliziano wrote the *Stanze per la giostra* (published 1484) on the occasion of chivalric tournaments that the Medici staged with princes fashioned as knights. Of course, the victorious Medici princes (Lorenzo in 1469 and Giuliano in 1475), wearing full chivalric regalia, knew little of real combat. The specific recursive aspect of knighthood is apparent when we consider that the tournament, the artistic imagery, and even Poliziano's poem itself were all modelled on an idea of chivalry that was received from medieval tales of knights; and even this medieval literature was set in a still earlier period, often a fictive Arthurian one, that was meant to depict a practice of martial character that had likely never existed. Such circularity was aptly reflected in Lorenzo's heraldic device, *"Le temps revient,"* a motto that was interpreted by Pulci in his *La giostra* as "Tornare il tempo, e 'l secol rinnovarsi" (Time returns, and the century renews itself) (stanza 64). As one considers how the concept of a "knight" would be understood for Italians of the Renaissance, it becomes clear that any signifier one might consider pointed not to a reality of martial valour but rather to a previous literary incarnation that was itself always as much a textual as a historical construct.[33]

The female knight who repeatedly appears from beneath a suit of armour forces the question "What is a knight?" Is a knight male? noble? And is this knight even necessarily militant?[34] These are important questions, since the claim to a chivalric past as well as a performance of the symbols (armour, coats of arms, titles, etc.) that accompanied this chivalric past were used by the nobility (and upper-class bourgeoisie such as the Medici) in its claim to power. Thus, the staging of female knighthood would have been more than a literary exercise that placed women's bodies in men's metal suits.[35] If the chivalric knight could be a woman, did this open up the class of "knight" or even "nobility" to a wider cast of characters based on merit or martial valour rather than sex or inherited bloodlines? After all, these women were often better knights than their male counterparts. Could those who wore suits of armour and laid claim to power and titles be stripped of that power just as they could be stripped of armour? The revelation of the woman knight beneath a gleaming suit of armour was thus a moment that court poets such as Ariosto and Tasso knew could both tantalize their readers and challenge the very court system that funded their existence.

In the *Furioso*, the narrative force of the revelation moment is aided by the fact that armour is ascribed an intrinsic value of virtue. Like a magic lance, armour has the power to protect its wearer (or at least certain wearers) not just from external forces but from internal weakness. Armour notably protects from moral failings: the knight Ruggiero is hindered from raping Angelica by the difficulty he has in removing his armour (X); Orlando performs countless acts of violence against nature and innocent people only after removing armour (XXIII); and Bradamante attempts to fall on her sword only to be saved by her own armour (XXXII). Armour also performs a semantic role, obscuring the body beneath it as well as revealing aspects of the wearer's identity. If armour has a dual function – obscuring and revealing – we might consider armour not as a mask but as a problematic veil.[36] We know that the person beneath the metal surface is a knight because we have read this identity precisely on the surface; but what is problematized in Ariosto is that we have misread "knighthood." An armoured knight is (to use Butler's terms on identity) "founded and indeed, continually refounded" on what is "refused or repudiated."[37] Here the most obvious negative identity is woman. Commonly understood, a knight is, among other things, non-woman.[38] Thus the unveiling of the feminine face and hair from beneath a helmet and suit of armour works at two ends simultaneously: it is an audacious demand that women be included within the identity of knighthood, and it is simultaneously a cleaving apart of two identities: armour (at least as it was traditionally understood) and the body beneath the armour. A woman revealed beneath a suit of armour compels the viewer to question a woman's place at arms, but it also compels the viewer to question the discourses that had come to constitute knighthood and the idealized masculinity to which it corresponds.

The shuttling of identity between a metal suit and a feminine body, between the meaning that is suggested by the veil itself and that which shimmers beneath the veil, reveals a commentary not only on gender, chivalry, and war but also on subjectivity itself. The female knight, typically seen as master of her own destiny, is in some texts revealed to be living a closeted existence, dissimulating a true feminine identity beneath a construction of a more militant persona. Carmela Cristofaro has argued that armour represented a transitional identity that obscured an authentic non-combative feminine nature in both Torquato Tasso's and Bernardo Tasso's epics. She particularly points to Bernardo Tasso's *Amadigi* (1560), when the woman warrior Mirinda, after discovering her noble lineage, removes her armour to become her "beautiful" and arguably authentic self (Cristofaro 63). Although Mirinda remains courageous, the warrior role is presented as but an assumed character waiting to be replaced by a genuine identity:

> Spogliata che si fu la Damigella
> l'arme che nascondean tanta beltade,
> e di bel cavalier fatta donzella,
> degna di star fra l'altre alte e lodate,
> d'un manto fatto d'opra ricca e bella
> si coperse le ben proporzionate
> membra, che non potea far la natura
> con maggior simmetria, né più misura. (*Amadigi*, XI. 6)[39]
>
> (Once the maiden had undressed
> removing the armour that was hiding such beauty,
> and turned herself from a handsome knight into
> a damsel, worthy of inclusion among the highest and most praised women,
> she covered with a richly made and beautiful mantle
> her well-proportioned limbs, nature could not have made
> with greater symmetry or good measure.)

Bernardo Tasso's Mirinda provides an unexpected psychological dimension to the woman warrior and furthermore insinuates that the non-normative identity of "militant woman" was in fact the constrictive one, an image well aided by the metaphor of armour. This reading reminds us that the revelation moment is a complex one, and that identity is not always portrayed as a liberated maiden who wields a sword and wears armour. Nor is the unarmed maiden, at least in Bernardo Tasso's epic, the *natural* identity of Mirinda. She is just as much artifice as is the person of the male knight, signified by the suit of armour. This is communicated in the seventh and eighth verses of the above-cited octave, "membra, che non potea far la natura / con maggior simmetria, né più misura" (her well-proportioned limbs, nature could not have made / with greater symmetry or good measure). These lines use a negative assertion to argue a positive one, and such syntax opens interpretation to at least two possibilities: nature could not have done better in forming this woman or nature could not make a woman such as this. Perhaps more interesting is the poetic choice of using the enjambment in the seventh line, "her well-proportioned limbs, nature could not have made / with greater symmetry ...," thus ending the line with an assertion that flirts with the suggestion that the woman's body is indeed beyond the natural. In my reading, Bernardo Tasso raises the possibility that both the maiden *and* the virago are fictive constructs and that, beneath the signifying armour, there lies merely another signifier.

We will find a similar discomfort with fixed identities in the work of Bernardo's son, Torquato Tasso, later in this chapter, but first I will focus on the revelation moments in Ariosto's *Orlando furioso*. I have privileged the *Furioso* in this study because it enacts what I see as the most important shift in the discourse of the armed maiden: it makes a woman knight (Bradamante) the central Christian protagonist. Moreover, this virago is likely more "knight" (with all of that word's moral connotations) than her male beloved and fellow dynastic founder, Ruggiero.[40]

Ariosto's project of dismantling putative notions of knighthood runs throughout the poem and is most obvious in the episode at the Island of Man-Killing Women (cantos 19–20), an episode that features not the poem's protagonist Bradamante but yet another principal female warrior, Marfisa. The island of Amazon-like women is protected by a select group of male knights, among them Guidone. When Marfisa arrives at the island, she challenges the knights and defeats all of them except Guidone. The final battle between Guidone and Marfisa continues into the night hours, and thus the battle is called off until the following day. When both Marfisa and Guidone enter the castle to rest for the evening, both are equally amazed in a double revelation moment; one knight reveals herself to be a woman, the other a youth. The reactions of the knights as each removes his or her helmet may also expose what Ariosto never states outright, that contemporary armed women were indeed not implausible; or at least that they shouldn't be.

Let us compare the two reactions. Guidone is astounded: "ch'alle chiome / s'avede con chi avea fatto battaglia" (seeing, from Marfisa's tresses whom it was he had been fighting) (XIX, 108: 3–4). Marfisa, seeing Guidone's young face, is also stupefied: "Si maraviglia la donzella, come / in arme tanto un giovinetto vaglia" (The damsel was amazed that such a youth should be so powerful a fighter) (XIX, 108: 1–2). Though both are "amazed," Ariosto expressly states Marfisa's reasons. She marvels that a youth could be "so powerful a fighter." Guidone on the other hand is simply stunned to see "whom" he is fighting. Though Marfisa's gender has surely triggered Guidone's marvelling, the phrase is structured so that it avoids a clear statement on women's military potential. The omission, though admittedly subtle, is important, particularly given the repetition of such a scene throughout the poem and the genre as a whole.

Guidone's reaction to his opponent's gender varies, for instance, from that of Rodomonte, who in canto 35 appears to be completely stunned that a woman (this time Bradamante) could defeat him: "Di maraviglia il Pagan resta muto, / ch'una donna a cader l'abbia condotto" (The pagan was left mute with wonder / that a woman had brought him down) (XXXV, 50; translation, Shemek, *Ladies Errant* 108). The particular circumstances that characterize this encounter may give us some notion of just how different Rodomonte is from Guidone. The most obvious difference is that Rodomonte's battle is with Bradamante and not Marfisa. And though some critics claim that the opponents react differently to each of the two women, I argue that these reactions correspond more closely to the circumstances of the fight or the identity of the men than to that of the women.[41] Notably, there is also no revelation moment; Bradamante had announced her identity before the match. It is this fact – the knowledge before the battle that the opponent is a woman – that leads Rodomonte to exhibit the most important aspect of the scenario, an outmoded conception of gender construction. Rodomonte approaches his opponent Bradamante as though he is entering a battle of courtly love, not one of arms. Using the Petrarchan arsenal of praising her face, hair, and eyes, he then moves to more licentious imagery, saying he would use his "prowess" to put her beneath him: "Io son di tal valor, son di tal nerbo, / ch'aver non dei d'andar di sotto a sdegno" (I am of such valor, I am of such prowess, / that you needn't disdain to go under me) (XXX, 47; translation Shemek, *Ladies Errant* 107). Clearly, this sort of man is precisely the sort that Ariosto would show to be "stunned" that a woman could wield her own sword and topple him.[42]

Taken together, Sacripante, Guidone, Rodomonte, the lord of Tristan's castle, and the rest, are actually a selection of male *readers*, men who interpret and/or misinterpret the significance of a woman at arms. Rodomonte is the most misguided, for he fails to read armour in its knightly context. He sees not a virago but a vulnerable damsel, who happens to carry weapons and wear armour, and thus he casts Bradamante as a sexual object to be conquered on the field of erotics rather than the field of battle. The young Guidone, instead, is more open to recognizing female strength and military prowess, which is unsurprising as he has been living in a society of Amazonian women as their guest/prisoner. He may be *stupefatto* (stupefied), but the narrator is careful not to couch his marvel in terms of women's militancy. And finally, the lord of Tristan's castle, even after a narrated hyperbolic simile that equates Bradamante's sex to a stage at curtain drop, does not marvel at her sex; he merely affords her the respect her reputation deserves.

Finally, these revelation moments bring us back to the matter that the unveiling of the warrior woman was primarily meant to fill the reader with wonder and delight. This might be a simple expectation if – as Ariosto states in canto 20 – modern authors did not tell of such armed ladies. But as Ariosto was well aware, moderns had been writing about women at arms for some time. He had himself borrowed two of his viragos from his fellow modern Ferrarese poet Boiardo. He is correct, however, to suggest that armed ladies were repeatedly *represented* by these writers as never-before-seen marvels of delight, slipping off helmets to expose long locks and their gender at once. After two centuries of having tresses reveal the maiden beneath a steel suit, one wonders if the power of repetition might have enacted a development of reader response. Could armour ever become, for example, gender-neutral? Or did the repetition of the revelation moment, at least in its more common iterations, become yet another way of reinforcing, founding, and refounding the masculine gendering of war?

Virgins of the Forest

As the poets of epic and romance hinted at a world of redrawn gender lines, they also pressed the bounds of the erotic economy, and one aspect bears overwhelmingly on the virago's identity construction – chastity. Albert Russell Ascoli has argued that, in duels of domination, the armoured male knight is impenetrable, "like a virgin."[43] Yet, the female knight, as the genre progresses, is actually a virgin (though in other genres such as biography and the *novella* she is also a wife, widow, or prostitute),[44] and it is possible that the limited representation of all viragos as virgins is another poetic commentary on the ability of women to fight. For not only is chastity associated with the ancient goddesses of the hunt and war (Artemis and Athena) and the great Camilla herself, chastity is also a formal construct of exceptionality.[45] Virginity could mark these women as different from their female companions and thus provide a justification of the inversion of male and female roles.[46] It also denotes a potentially transitory moment in a woman's life. For many of the characters, virginity is a phase from which a woman can pass into marriage and motherhood, and thus achieve a womanhood that is typified as complete. Marriage could therefore indicate not only a woman's maturity but an end of militancy, and such a closure was emphasized in literature through various means: a male spouse is the dowry given to Marulla, a successful warring virgin; a mother comforts a virgin soldier at the walls of Pisa, stating that the war is her marriage and the walls her husband; and of course, the epic-romances themselves often involve a marriage of a virago to the man who can defeat her in a duel.[47]

If virginity is an identity that is gazing forward to a potential (if not always desired) change, the other trait inherited by the Renaissance daughters of Camilla, a wildling childhood, is instead a characteristic that looks back to a fixed and fixing origin. Being nursed on the milk of wild beasts is common to viragos in Ariosto, Tasso, Sarrocchi, and Gonzaga, among others, and this along with Amazon parentage may be the most common link among sixteenth-century warrior women.[48] Nurse milk, even if not in fictional wildling contexts, is a matter that was frequently discussed in the Renaissance prescriptive literature. Writers such as Francesco Barbaro credited the mother's milk with a particular importance in the building of the body and mind of the child: "The power of the mother's food most effectively lends itself to shaping the properties of body and mind to the character of the seed."[49] Thus, the role of animal nurse milk is one way that authors may have sought to explain the existence of armed women within the structure of a society that could not otherwise accommodate them. This is all the more reason why Ariosto's Bradamante, a noble Christian woman of conventional parentage (i.e., no wildling nurse milk), is critical to the study of the warrior virago.

The genealogy of Bradamante has received much recent attention. Chimène Bateman points to Bradamante's conventional origin in combination with her epic destiny as founder of the Este dynasty to show how she embodies both epic and romance, while Eleonora Stoppino exposes Ariosto's presentation of Bradamante as a revisionist veneer that is laid over an uncomfortable literary past (26–57). It was a past that would have been known to Ariosto's readers, in which she had appeared as a Muslim princess and a Christian illegitimate daughter (81–7). Ariosto not only legitimizes Bradamante, he also alters Marfisa, a character who was primarily the creation of Boiardo, by softening her impetuous nature and giving her an origin story.[50] Marfisa is fixed within a genealogy of warriors (daughter of Galiziella) and, even more importantly, may be the first virago in the Italian tradition since Camilla to be nursed on the milk of wild beasts (XXXVI).[51] Such origin stories inform how we view the agency of women – the choice they are shown to make between warrior identities or more conventional womanhood. If Marfisa seems both destined to be and unalterably a warrior, Bradamante becomes even more the master of her own life.

Though scholars have been tempted to emphasize the categorical differences between Marfisa and Bradamante, it would be reductive to suggest that there are distinct models of warrior women in heroic poetry.[52] The lines between the perpetually chaste virago and the destined bride are blurred through poetic nuance. I thus step lightly when I note that Ariosto leaves Marfisa in the realm of literary convention while he brings Bradamante closer to the courtly women readers of the poem, placing her in a Christian aristocratic genealogy. But it is undeniable that there is an affinity between Bradamante and the upper-class women readers of the *Orlando furioso* (particularly at the Este court) that could arguably have moved them to imitate the character's spirit if not her military acts. Even Bradamante's marriage draws her closer to courtly female readers, just as it makes a direct comment on women's militancy. As has been convincingly argued by Deanna Shemek and Julia Hairston, Bradamante's militancy does not end once she is wedded. Rather, she will return to battle and avenge the murder of her husband after the poem's conclusion.[53] The revival of Bradamante's militancy is prophesied to happen once she is both a mother and a widow, and thus female militancy is presented not as the profession of only the resolute virgin (e.g., Marfisa) but as an identity that is not necessarily contained or reversed by motherhood and marriage.

The Inspired and Marvelling Reader

Given the spectrum of warring women (loving ladies, chaste viragos, and entrapped ladies seeking freedom from their armour), contemporary readers must have also had a diverse range of reactions to the cadre of armed women that battled through the woods of *ottava rima.* First, we know that the chivalric romances were widely read by women readers, a fact that garnered the attention of moralists.[54] And we know that the general popularity of the romances caused them to permeate into daily life in interesting and even intimate ways: palace frescoes and wedding chests (*cassoni*) depicted scenes from the *Orlando furioso,* and enthusiastic parents named baby girls after Marfisa and Bradamante.[55]

Although it is difficult to trace the impact of women warriors on the early modern female readership, we do know that certain women writers found inspiration in the deeds of epic maidens. The convent dramatist Beatrice del Sera comments that it was the reading of "l'armate donne" (armed women) who "ebbon per vanto / di far battaglia contro ai grandi e regni" (del Sera 94) (could boast / of doing battle against the mighty and kings) that inspired her to write. Chivalric poetry also inspired another woman author, Maddalena Campigli, to state, "in qualunque disciplina le nobili e gentili Donne vengono essercitate, non rimangono a dietro punto a' più valorosi huomini che si ritrovino" (When noble and gentle women apply themselves in any discipline, they are in no way inferior to the most valorous men).[56] And there are more indirect instances where we can trace the impact of Ariosto's viragos on future female authors, such as when the author Moderata Fonte crafts a sonnet on women's independence in her *Worth of Women* by incorporating lines from Marfisa's speech (canto 26. 79, 7–8; *Worth* 49–50).

These moments are only select literary responses among what must have been those of countless women readers of chivalric romance, and yet most scholars, including myself, would be hesitant to suggest that tales of armed maidens inspired emulation of military exploits by contemporary women.[57] This stance, however, does place the hermeneutical process in question. Did literature influence male readers differently from female readers? We know from contemporary accounts that men's deeds in chivalric tales were thought to be imitated by the boys who read them.[58] We can point to the famous general Blaise de Monluc, who warned men and boys to avoid chivalric epics so that their military abilities would not be tainted by chivalric codes.[59] Could women not be similarly affected by tales of armed maidens? After all, in an albeit hyperbolic "Exhortatione" penned by Ortensio Lando, the author noted that women had adopted habits of wearing helmets and riding horseback and always carrying "Ariosto nelle mani" (Ariosto in their hands); and, according to Lando, they were especially reading the part that spoke of arms.[60] We also know that historical militant women had typically been compared to fictional viragos; the militant Countess Matilda was called Penthesilea, and Maria of Pozzuoli made Petrarch believe in the feats of Camilla. In a reverse dynamic, Lando claimed that literary viragos seemed plausible after considering the histories of real women such as Maria of Pozzuoli, Caterina Sforza, and Sienese women (46). And finally, the landscape of historical and poetic armed maidens became completely intertwined in the case of the book *Donne illustri del Furioso* (*Illustrious Women of the Furioso*) (1563), a title that suggests it is a historical anthology of biographies gleaned from the fiction of Ariosto.

This evidence compels the scholar, as it compelled Lando, to question the interdependence of myth, history, and legend. Was the poetic armed maiden so far from reality that no reader could take her seriously? Did her exceptionality make her "recuperable" and "less threatening" (Cox, *The Prodigious* 161)?[61] Is it not also possible that our notions of gender are so deeply imbedded in a binary that divides around warfare that we are unwilling to imagine that Bradamante inspired young girls to don a cuirass and sword?[62] Of course we know that even if girls were inspired by chivalric-epic to fight, they did not break social conventions in any numbers that would be considered significant. This, however, should not stop us from asking whether the warrior woman of epic and romance was received as an armed woman or merely as a delightful dalliance that was contained by stanzas of *ottava rima,* a fantastic amusement like a magical flying hippogriff. In effect, I have proposed two reader receptions: the first, where women knights are seen as fantasy, would reconfirm the masculine dynamics of war (particularly erotic ones),[63] while the second, where a woman knight might stand in for an armed woman, would offer a potential rupture of the recursive process of signification. In this second dynamic, "knighthood" could come to mean something new, and along with it, other terms like "women" and "vulnerability" would evolve.

This alteration of an ideology, where culture conceives of women as militant, would inherently mean that the pervasive notion of women as vulnerable might change. This is a feminine potential that is staged in *Furioso,* canto 26, when Marfisa, dressed in women's clothing, becomes the target of Mandricardo's schemes to win her and trade her. After Mandricardo defeats the male knights that surround Marfisa, he plans to take her as his reward. Mandricardo misreads Marfisa because she is, for the only time in the poem, dressed in women's clothing. The warrior maiden responds that she is both woman and knight, and in one of the most memorable lines of the poem, she tells him that she belongs to no one but herself:

Io ti concedo che diresti il vero
Ch'io sarei tua per la ragion di guerra,
Quando mio Signor fosse o cavalliero
Alcun di questi c'hai gittato in terra:
Io sua non son, né d'altri son che mia
Dunque me tolga a me chi mi desia. (XXVI. 79)

(I allow that you would be correct
that I would be yours by custom of war
if one of these men you have overthrown
were my lord or my champion.
I am none of theirs; nor do I belong to anyone but myself.
So, let whoever desires me, first reckon with me.) (translation mine)

In the brief episode, Ariosto dramatizes not only the delight of women warriors but the social change that female militancy could offer. Even if, as Cesare Segre has noted, Ariosto did not find chivalry a preferred way of life, he certainly exploited the moral codes of chivalry to expose the inequalities that existed in society, inequalities that could be erased, at least hypothetically, by arming women.[64] Whether such a reception actually seeped out of fantasy and into the realm of potential real change is only knowable in the hints we might read in the cracks of a monolithic culture that genders war as masculine. Although there has been no systematic arming of equal numbers of men and women even into the modern day, there is some evidence that the woman warrior of heroic poetry at least caused some discomfort among men off the page. Perhaps the strongest evidence we have that the armed maiden encroached on the realm of – if not reality – at least a potential reality was that the character type invoked anxiety in writers such as Ortensio Lando, who in the text mentioned above exhorts men to take notice of these warring women.

We can also gauge reception of the female knight by male readers by considering the debate over the poetic merits of the *Orlando furioso.* As is well known, the *Orlando furioso* was at the centre of a fervent debate that was fuelled by a Counter-Reformation climate and a poetic formalism that grew more rigid after the translation of Aristotle's *Poetics* into Latin in 1536 and into Italian in 1549.[65] Although the debate only infrequently considers warring women, it merits some attention.[66] One of the more important early contributions to the debate that addressed the issue of armed women was by Giovan Battista ("il Pigna") Nicolucci, who defended Ariosto's fictional viragos as verisimilar by suggesting that, even though the poet had created sword-wielding heroines, they were believable, since the women in the poem are, relatively speaking, less skilled than men, "Per *relatione;* come, che esse donne poco pratiche sieno à rispetto dell'huomo" (quoted in Shemek, *Ladies Errant* 84). Characters such as Bradamante and Marfisa were realistic as long as men were more valiant. Moreover, Pigna explains, these female warriors reflected a reality outside of Ariosto's poetry. He states that they refer to a specific historical context, one that is foreign and exotic:

> Da prima elle nelle battaglie traposte non erano: ma poi che nelle guerre di Spagna, che ottocento anni durarono, gli Arabi d'Africa le consorti & meretrici loro trassero, & lor diero il potere alla libera guerreggiare, molte molto honoratamente riuscendo mostraro, che le donne nelle cose ch'a far si pongono, non son niente da meno de gli huomini. & à poco à poco questo uso di far che le nobili signore tali fossero, chente hora nella Fiandra la Regina Maria d'Austria veggiamo, nelle spagnuole infanti s'introdusse, & indi in Francia trapassò ... (quoted in Shemek, *Ladies Errant* 85)

> (In the beginning, women were not placed amidst battles. But once the Arabs of Africa brought their consorts and their prostitutes into the Spanish wars, which lasted eight hundred years, and gave them the power to combat freely, many women succeeded in showing most honorably that women are not at all inferior to men in whatever things they set out to do. And little by little this custom of assuring that noble ladies were such as we see in Flanders in Queen Maria of Austria was introduced also to Spanish royal children, whence the custom passed into France ...)[67]

Pigna's tale reconciles armed women in two distinct literary genres, the historical narrative and the heroic poem. The generic representations of women warriors pivot around the question of social class; the epic woman knight is noble, while the *bellatrix* in the histories and biographies of the European fifteenth and sixteenth centuries is typically from the lower classes. Militant noblewomen, when they were depicted in histories and biographies, were instead typically commanders, not bearing weapons, and not depicted as killing.[68] Since epic viragos are noble and present on the battlefield, the apologist finds that the way to incorporate them into history is to create a genealogy that begins with women from the lower classes. Pigna thus creates a third, bridge narrative that is separate from the histories or the epics, where Arab wives and prostitutes brought a tradition to Europe and eventually into the royal house of Queen Maria of Austria.[69] It is a history of armed women that puts into question the decorum of the armed woman and surely could not have been seen as unequivocal praise for the Queen.

Pigna's explanation of the genealogy of women warriors is conventional in that it locates their origin as both foreign and non-Christian. It is a categorization that perpetuates the classical tradition of casting the female combatant on the "wrong" side, a dynamic best known in Virgil's Camilla, who fights for the losing side and "wears in vain" her armour (XI, 703).[70] Thus, Pigna's defence of Ariosto – one that hinges on historicizing the virago – accomplishes its task by returning all women warriors to an origin story as foreign and Muslim.

Torquato Tasso

This notion of Christian versus non-Christian virago lies at the centre of the famous chivalric-epic of Torquato Tasso, the *Gerusalemme liberata*. Clorinda, the principal warrior woman of the *Gerusalemme liberata,* self-identifies as a Muslim until she discovers that she is the daughter of the Christian king and queen of Ethiopia.[71] Like Camilla and Marfisa, Clorinda was raised without a mother and briefly nursed on the milk of a wild beast, but her nativity story is also descended from the Greek writer Heliodorus's *Aethiopica.* Clorinda, like the girl Charikleia in Heliodorus's story, was born a white baby to a black African queen; both women experienced supernatural births caused by their mothers, who gazed at the painted image of a white woman during conception (Quint; Stephens; Bearden). Where Charikleia's mother gazed upon an image of Andromeda, Clorinda's mother looked upon the image of St George's maiden.

Clorinda's exceptional childhood, one that even had visible biological effects on her body, might explain her prowess at arms.[72] She is different from other *unaltered* women such as her friend Erminia, who steals and awkwardly dons Clorinda's armour and in so doing underscores an implied incongruity of the *nature* of women and armour.[73] Of course, Clorinda too is caught in a bind between self-representation and a "natural" identity. She is white and Muslim but discovers that she is the child of black Christian parents; and, more relevant to this study, her origin story (mother gazing on the maiden of St George) shows that she is conceived from the image of a vulnerable woman, not a virago.[74] Strikingly, both Tasso's story of Clorinda's birth and Heliodorus's tale of Charikleia involve mothers who gaze on women who are paragons of female vulnerability (St George's maiden and Andromeda respectively), and both women were to be sacrificed to a monster until being miraculously saved by men. The linkage between Andromeda and the maiden recalls another more famous intertextual Andromeda, that of the *Orlando furioso*. In Ariosto's text, the Andromeda story is retold twice, where first Angelica and then Olimpia are chained to a rock in preparation for their sacrifice to a sea monster, metaphorically binding them to a discourse of feminine vulnerability and dependency on male prowess.

Tasso instead writes a different Andromeda tale to describe Clorinda's nativity. The significance of the moment is of course that Clorinda discovers she is not Muslim by birth nor, in a certain sense, does she have a female warrior protector. The discovery of her maternal figures, the vulnerable maiden of St George and – more distantly – Andromeda, differs significantly from that of Ariosto's Marfisa, who learns that her mother was the famous warrior Galiziella, a devotee of the goddess Diana. Thus, the origin story of Clorinda creates a dynamic of waiting, even if unknowingly, to have an authentic identity restored. If Clorinda is, as David Quint has it, a character waiting for baptism, she is also waiting for her knight to save her (*Epic and Empire* 242–3). She is also quintessentially hybrid: Muslim and Christian, black and white, and warrior (nursed on wild tiger's milk) and non-militant (descendant of Andromeda and St George's maiden). In Clorinda's last moments, she converts to Christianity, but the result of her militancy is left more ambiguous. While some critics claim that her conversion to Christianity also marks a turn to an "authentic" state of non-combatant, it seems more plausible that the moment of conversion provides Tasso a moment to underscore the conflict within Clorinda's pysche about militancy.[75] Although she is baptized into Christianity and thus resolves her conflicted religious identity, she is still the product of two irreconcilable origin stories (warrior and maiden). She is, like all women, unable to will away the inheritance of a gender script of vulnerability.

Tasso's ambivalence about Clorinda's militancy is reflected by the poet in his theoretical writings as well as in his personal correspondence. In his *Giudizio sovra la Gerusalemme conquistata* (1593/5), Tasso states that he has crafted a "marvel" by writing about the warrior woman. In his own estimation, he has even outdone Homer, who missed a poetic opportunity when he did not write of Penthesilea in the *Iliad*:

> S'alcuno desiderò mai nell'*Iliade* Pentesilea, non può desiderar nella mia *Gerusalemme* la persona finta d'una guerriera, ad imitazione delle Amazoni; né so conoscere la cagione per la quale Pentesilea si rimanesse tra le cose da Omero tralasciate; perché dovendo il poeta cercar la maraviglia, niuna cosa ci par più maravigliosa dell'ardire o della fortezza feminile. (521)[76]

> (If one were to ever desire Penthesilea in the *Iliad*, he would not wish to see in my *Gerusalemme* the imaginary person of a woman warrior, in imitation of the Amazons. Nor do I understand the reason for which Penthesilea remains among the things that Homer neglected. Given that poets must seek out marvels, nothing seems more marvellous than the ardour or fortitude of women.)

In the passage, Tasso clarifies that the warrior woman makes for a good story. Moreover, he stipulates that the virago is a fiction, a "finta persona," and that she is one of the many "marvels" that a poet must employ. Any poem, even the *Iliad*, would be lacking without her.

This judgment of a "marvel" does not align with Tasso's remarks about militant women that he wrote in previous texts on the subject. In his *Discorsi del poema eroico* (written 1580s, published 1594), Tasso quotes Aristotle's *Poetics* and states that poets should avoid writing about strength in women altogether.[77] In a separate work, a letter written by Tasso to his Florentine friend and poetic revisor Orazio Capponi, Tasso instead contradicts the emphasis placed on the "marvel" of the woman warrior. In this letter, Tasso claims that he has included women warriors in his poem because they were a historical element in the Crusades:

> perché, dice il conte di Prochese ne la sua *Istoria*, in questa guerra fu combattuto non solo fra gli uomini, ma fra le donne: peroché molte donne cristiane passarono in Asia e si mescolarono ne le battaglie; e le donne saracine difesero le città con virile ardimento, e oltr'a ciò con tutte le insidie femminili procurarono d'allettare i cristiani nel loro amore e di convertili a lor fede. (*Prose* 798–9)

> (because, as the Count of Prochese states in his *History*, this war was fought not only among men but also among women, since many Christian women went to Asia and mixed in the battles. And the Saracen women defended the city with manly ardour, and moreover, with all their feminine traps they managed to tempt Christian men in their love and to convert them to their faith.)

At the very least, Tasso's prose writings on women warriors display the same sort of ambivalence we see in his poetry. It is perhaps for this reason that he will cut the only Christian woman warrior, Gildippe, from his revised *Gerusalemme conquistata* (*Jerusalem Conquered*).

What is apparent from Tasso's letters to Capponi and from Pigna's defence of the female knight in Ariosto is that within the poetic texts and the contemporary reception of them, there was a cultural reaction afoot: readers were responding to the fictional viragos by attempting to situate their credibility in the physical and real world. Such a discourse makes it imperative that we as modern readers of Renaissance epic no longer appeal to the figure of the poetic armed woman as an immaterial symbol. Rather, we might think of her as a signifier of abstract feminine virtue as well as something much more corporeal. In moving on to look beyond Ariosto and Tasso, we find chivalric epics, often written by women, that openly commented on the "real" relationship of women and war. The debate about women's militancy was, for these authors, poetic inspiration.

Laura Terracina and Making War Modern Again

The most published woman author of the sixteenth century was Laura Terracina (c. 1519–1577), a daughter of a courtier at the Spanish-Neapolitan court.[78] The work for which she was best known was a poetic reworking of and commentary on Ariosto's *Orlando furioso* entitled the *Discorso sopra tutti i primi canti d'Orlando furioso* (Discourse on all the first cantos of the *Orlando furioso*) (1549). In her *Discorso* she does not so much address the question of women warriors as comment on Ariosto's own authorial intervention about exemplary militant women.

We recall that, in the *Orlando furioso,* Ariosto makes two authorial interventions that ostensibly praise women's military potential, in cantos 20 and 37. Canto 20, discussed above as it follows Guidone's and Marfisa's revelation moment, begins by praising women of the distant past and constructing a link between arms and writing.[79]

> Le donne antique hanno mirabil cose
> fatto ne l'arme e ne le sacre muse
> e di lor opre belle e gloriose
> gran lume in tutto il mondo si diffuse.
> Arpalice e Camilla son famose,
> perché in battaglia erano esperte et use;
> Safo e Corinna, perché furon dotte,
> splendono illustri, e mai non veggon notte. (*Orlando furioso* 20.1)

> (In feats of arms, as in the cultivation of the Muses, the women of old achieved distinction, and their splendid, glorious deeds irradiated the whole earth. Harpalice and Camilla achieved fame for their practised skill in battle; Sappho and Corinna shine, on account of their learning, with a radiance that night will never darken.) (translation Waldman 229)

The incipit links martial women and learned women in an analogical structure: Harpalyce and Camilla are to war as Sappho and Corinna are to poetry. This is not the traditional humanist discussion of arms and letters but rather a celebration of women's accomplishments in fields from which they have conventionally been excluded. The reason we have not heard of women's achievements, Ariosto tells us in both canto 20 and canto 37, is that men have not written about them. Thus, the problem does not lie with women but rather with the male writers who have suppressed them. On the other hand, Ariosto explains that he and a cadre of other male authors (Bembo, Strozzi, Alamanni, et al.) are champions of women, taking up the pen in women's defence. His role in this defence of women, he tells us, will be to praise women whose deeds far "surpass" those of even Marfisa (20. 3).

But Ariosto undermines his own praise of militant women. The narratives that follow the two encomia tell of women who destabilize society: Amazon man-killing women and a society where a male tyrant is overthrown by female rule.[80] More troubling is that, within the praises themselves, the only women who are mentioned as military heroines are a host of ancient and legendary Greeks and Romans. The contemporary examples of excellence in these encomia (including women writers) are slim, and in fact are primarily limited to Vittoria Colonna, notably a writer rather than a warrior.[81] Ariosto's analogy is thus incomplete; Sappho is to Vittoria Colonna as Camilla is to no contemporary woman. The absence of contemporary armed women is then further underscored when the only recent heroic acts mentioned are those of Colonna's deceased husband, Francesco, the Marquis of Pescara, the hero about whom Colonna assiduously writes. Thus, in one of the Renaissance's most famous defences of women, the warrior maidens of ancient glory are effectively stripped of their armour and turned into poets who praise brave men. The stories of women who surpass Marfisa are, as one expects with Ariosto, deferred.

Laura Terracina, on the other hand, reflects on the continual discussion of ancient women at arms and asks why authors continue to praise them when there is the modern example of Isabella Colonna (1513–1570) before our eyes.[82] Canto 20 of Terracina's *Discorso sopra tutti i primi canti d'Orlando furioso* (Discourse on all the first cantos of the *Orlando furioso)* begins with an introductory reflection on the common practice of praising women at arms: "Fra quanto io sento in questa parte, e in quella / Donne famose in arme & in costumi" (Canto 20, introduction) (Among the things I hear about both here and there, [are] women famous at arms and deeds).[83] The canto names some ancient illustrious women, but it is devoted to praising Isabella Colonna, a woman who was a fellow Neapolitan and whose troops engaged in armed conflict over property claims with Isabella's relative Ascanio Colonna. The canto's most interesting move is to request that authors stop praising ancients and instead speak of living women: "Lasciamo di parlar di queste antique / E di voi sol, dica la mia rima" (20. 8, vv 1–2) (Let's stop speaking of these ancients / And of you alone my rhyme will speak)).

Lasciamo di parlar di queste antique
E di voi sol, dica la rima mia,
Perche fra le moderne, e fra l'antique

Non trovo uguale a voi, fra qual si sia,
E se pur fama, e nome hebber l'antique
In quel tempo, hor per voi ciascun l'oblia,
Safo, e Corinna perche furno dotte:
Splendono illustri, e mai non veggon notte. (20. 8)

(Let's stop speaking of these ancients, and of you alone let my rhyme speak because among the moderns and the ancient women I cannot find an equal to you in any company. And if the ancients had fame and name in that time, now because of you each is forgotten. Sappho and Corinna, because they were learned, shine with a radiance that night will never darken.)

Like all of Terracina's *Discorso,* this canto reworks Ariosto's poem in thematic and structural means. She fragments the first stanza of each Ariostean canto and builds a stanza of her own around his poetry.[84] She also revises Ariosto in more substantive ways, for not only does she take her subject of Isabella Colonna from Ariosto (37. 9; 46. 8), she also uses the same examples of illustrious women that he used when he described Vittoria Colonna (Camilla, Harpalyce, Sappho, and Corinna), adding Ariosto's very own Bradamante.[85] And, unlike Ariosto's Vittoria Colonna, Terracina's Isabella Colonna is both a poet and a warrior, accomplishing "fatta ne l'armi, e ne le sacre muse" (deeds in arms and in the sacred muses) (20. 2, v 8); also, "Voi l'arme oprate ogn'hora, e la scrittura / Come le donne antique opravan spesso" (You engage at arms and in writing every hour / just as ancient women often did) (20. 4, vv 1–2). Although we know very little about the historical Isabella Colonna's sword-wielding exploits, it is still a momentous turn to contemporary women. It is hard not to compare Ariosto's and Terracina's encomia of Colonna women: one, a poet not a warrior, and the other battling hourly with both sword and pen, heir to Sappho, Camilla, and Bradamante herself.

Laura Terracina was only one of many women writers who engaged with epic poetry. This chapter concludes with a discussion of three female authors who brought their own innovations to the genre. Three post-Tridentine women penned chivalric-epics, all with fresh commentaries on women and militancy: Moderata Fonte (1555–1592), Margherita Sarrocchi (1560–1617), and Lucrezia Marinella (1571–1653).

Moderata Fonte, Margherita Sarrocchi, and Lucrezia Marinella

The first extended and provocative commentary about women and war that is written into the text of narrative epic is by Moderata Fonte.[86] Fonte does not miss the opportunity to remark on the incongruity between the epic representation of women warriors and the reality of the sixteenth century in which she writes. In her *Tredici canti del Floridoro* (*Thirteen cantos of Floridoro*) (1581), an incomplete poem that was meant to be a longer chivalric-epic, there is an entire secondary plot that focuses on identical twin princesses, separated at birth, where one is raised conventionally while the other is raised as a warrior. In canto 4, Fonte argues that the reason we do not find women warriors in real life is due entirely to cultural bias:

Sempre s'è visto e vede (pur ch'alcuna
Donna v'abbia voluto il pensier porre)
Nella milizia riuscir più d'una,
E 'l pregio e 'l grido a molti uomini torre;
E così nelle lettere e in ciascuna
Impresa che l'uom pratica e discorre
Le donne sì buon frutto han fatto e fanno,
Che gli uomini a invidia punto non hanno.

E benché di sì degno e sì famoso
Grado di lor non sia numero molto,
Gli è perché ad atto eroico e virtuoso
Non hanno il cor per più rispetti volto.
L'oro che sta nelle minere ascoso
Non manca d'esser or, benché sepolto,
E quando è tratto e se ne fa lavoro
E' così ricco e bel come l'altro oro.

Se quando nasce una figliola un padre
La ponesse col figlio a un'opra eguale,
Non saria nelle imprese alte e leggiadre
Al frate inferior né disuguale,
O la ponesse in fra l'armate squadre
Seco o a imparar qualche arte liberale,
Ma perché in altri affar viene allevata
Per l'educazion poco è stimata.[87] (canto 4, stanzas 2–4)

> (Numerous women throughout history have attained success in military life, outstripping the achievements of many of their male comrades, and the same still occurs whenever a woman turns her energies to this kind of activity. The same may be said of the profession of letters, and all other activities in which men engage: women's achievements have been and are such that they have no cause to envy men.
>
> And even if there are not many women who have attained this degree of excellence and fame, that is only because, for various reasons, they have tended not to turn their energies toward heroic and challenging deeds. The gold that lies buried in the mines is still gold, even though it is buried from sight, and when it is mined and worked it is as precious and exquisite as any other gold.
>
> If when a daughter was born to him, a father were to have her engage in the same pursuits as a son, the girl would not prove inferior to her brother in any lofty and glorious enterprise, whether she were placed alongside him in the ranks of an army, or set to learn some liberal art. But because girls are given a different kind of upbringing, their abilities are not rated highly.) (translation Cox, *Floridoro,* in *The Worth* 262–3)

Whereas Ariosto had complained that women's valour was unknown because of the suppression and jealousy of male writers, Fonte presents a darker and perhaps more realistic vision. She states that women of martial valour do not inhabit the real world because real women are suppressed by cultural forces. Like Plato, she sees the limitation of women's labour as wasted potential. In her metaphor, potential is the gold that lies buried, waiting to be mined by a culture willing to give women the chance to be soldiers.

After the publication of Fonte's *Floridoro,* another woman poet, Margherita Sarrocchi, penned the historical epic *Scanderbeide* (1606, 1623), a poem on the military travails of Albanian warrior-prince George Castrioti or Scanderbeg (1405–1468).[88] Sarrocchi avoids polemical disputations on women's military might and opts instead for a gender commentary embedded in a narrative of resistance. The warrior daughter of Sultan Murad II, Rosmonda, is described as extraordinary in beauty and intelligence, and, as Rosmonda tells us in her own words, she is unlike other women: I "disdain[ed] the delicate inclinations of women and decided to train for higher endeavors" (13.21; 245).[89] The lengthy descriptions of her beautiful face, her undulating and "alluring" hair as well as her regal and gem-studded vestments contrast with references to the other principal virago, Silveria. As her name suggests,

Silveria is a woman living in the wilderness. She was abandoned by her father as a baby and allegedly nursed by a wild bear (Sarrocchi 13.5–27; 241–6).

The disparity between the two women's descriptions is telling. On Rosmonda:

> Con l'elmo ella il bel viso or non asconde,
> scintillan gli occhi un più ch'uman splendore;
> parte annodate son le chiome bionde
> e parte in preda ad un lascivo errore.
> Malagevole è il calle a poggiar, onde
> l'irriga l'ostro un cristallin sudore,
> cui ondeggiando intorno i vaghi crini
> paion legati in or, perle, e rubini. (*Scanderbeide* 13.11; 411)

> (No helmet hid now her beautiful face, her eyes sparkled with extraordinary brilliance, part of her blond hair was tied up, other locks hung in alluring waves. The path was hard to climb and a crystalline sweat ran down her rosy cheeks, which, with her beautiful hair undulating at the sides, seemed to be bound in gold, pearls and rubies.) (translation Russell 242)

Silveria, on the other hand, is described not only as beautiful but also as virile: "Giusta e vaga natura in lei comparte, / ma robusta e virile ogni fatezza" (Nature had bestowed on her features good proportions and grace, but also a virile energy) (13.16; 243). She is dressed in animal skin, has unkempt hair, naked "breasts and knees" and "well-developed and well-shaped limbs" (13.14, 15; 243). The contrast between the two women, one whose physical portrait is limited to a Petrarchan conceit (albeit an athletic version of the more static Laura) and the other who is described in more bodily terms, is the same contrast that will indicate class difference in historical biographies of warring women, discussed in chapters 5 and 6 of this book. Where biographies traced a figure of the noble woman as regal ruler and the peasant woman as fighting warrior, the narrative of Sarrocchi, as we will see, might actually open a new discourse, one that brings social mobility to armed common women and the chance to exercise real combat to noble women. Moreover, Sarrocchi also resists the epic conventions that had gendered beauty, strength, and honour from its generic inception.

Rosmonda meets Silveria only because a townswoman has told Rosmonda that Silveria, "a fiercely savage woman," had killed the townswoman's two sons. The townswoman tells the lengthy story of Silveria's abandonment as a baby and subsequent nursing by a wild bear. In the townswoman's story, Silveria is the conflation of the man-killing witch, Amazon warrior, and beastly savage. The crying townswoman thus appeals to Rosmonda to vindicate the death of her sons. The townswoman explains that she seeks a woman as her champion not because of her feminine traits but because of Rosmonda's manliness: "not because of your feminine beauty, in comparison with which any woman's boast is empty, but thanks to your manly valor and strength" (13.3; 241).

In both her story of Silveria's life and her assessment of Rosmonda's "manly" qualities, the townswoman proves to be a bad judge of character. First, Silveria is not the ferocious and wild savage who typically kills men. We learn that she normally hides "bashfully" when strangers approach; and most importantly, we discover that she has killed the two sons only after an attempted rape. The townswoman has also misjudged Rosmonda. The queen's displays of courage and ability at arms may be "feminine" rather than "manly," as she is shown to posses a distinct feminine strength and valour that will influence the story's resolution. In response to Silveria's tale of the attempted rape, Rosmonda unambiguously claims, "Men have never died for better reason" (13.25; 245). The two women form an immediate bond, based on mutual respect and feminine solidarity. In addition, when Rosmonda states that she disdains "the delicate inclinations of women," she does not, as the townswoman had wrongly believed, assume a manly identity. For example, Rosmonda proudly refers to herself on several occasions as the *daughter* of the sultan. Sarrocchi's two warring maidens effectively break the binary of feminine beauty versus manly strength (the binary that the townswoman herself mentions) and allow for a different potential of women, a possible feminine valour or feminine strength.

The encounter of the two viragos inspires Rosmonda to persuade Silveria to leave her life of hunting wild beasts and to fight in combat. Rosmonda's speech echoes a literary trope, those scolding lectures made to male warriors who had been "snared" in the lures of women (e.g., Aeneas, Hercules, Ruggiero, Rinaldo). Indeed, Rosmonda uses the language of honour and recognition, commonplaces normally reserved for men, to motivate Silveria from the entrapment of her sylvan nest: "Your proud superior mind ought to disdain humble deeds destined to remain obscure, for that is a valueless reward indeed!" and

> Vincer tigre e leone e orso e cinghiale
> avventando lontan dardi e quadrella
> di paventoso rischio è gloria frale,
> sol dovuta di boschi a pastorella.
> Guerriera invitta tu, donna reale
> meco amata sarai più che sorella,
> Solo in guerra acquistar puote l'uom forte
> gloriosa vittoria o illustre morte. (13.40–1; 417)

> (To overpower tigers, lions, bears, and boars, and to be able to shoot darts and arrows a long way, is not a very impressive achievement, only one becoming a country shepherdess. As the invincible warrior that you are, if you come away, you will be loved even more than a sister by a royal woman such as myself: only in war can a strong human being attain celebrated victories or a glorious death.) (translation Russell 249–50)

War is the only means of achieving "celebrated victories or a glorious death." Without war, women, even exceptional country shepherdesses who kill lions and tigers, are left in obscurity. The episode taken as a whole seems to call women to assume a new feminine strength, leave their domestic spaces, and enter into the world of military glory.

The Venetian poet Lucrezia Marinella knew of both Fonte's and Sarrocchi's epics when she wrote her epic poem inspired by the fourth crusade (1202–4), *L'Enrico*.[90] The Venetian warrior Claudia is one of three viragos in the text, and in her introduction during a catalogue of warriors, the narrator pauses to reflect on the culture that has excluded women from the military.

> L'ultima è Claudia altera, che discese
> Dal gran sangue latin, progenie augusta
> Costei ne' suoi primi anni avid'apprese
> De' prischi eroi l'alta virtù vetusta,
> E'n cheta pace e'n militari offese
> Si mostrò ognor magnanima e venusta;
> Mostra che l'uso e non natura ha messo
> *Timor nell'un, valor nell'altro sesso.* (II, 29; emphasis mine)

(The last one is the proud Claudia, born of imperial Latin blood. As a young child she learned the great virtue of ancient heroes; she showed herself as magnanimous and generous both in peace and in war. *She shows that habit, and not nature, put fear in one sex and valor in the other.*) (*Enrico* 46; emphasis mine)

The last two verses indicate, much as Moderata Fonte had done, that custom, not anatomy, has determined women's social destiny, and Marinella's verse suggests that this constructed division of the sexes is identifiable in a binary of fear and valour. By categorizing the sexes with psychological characteristics rather than physical ones, Marinella shrewdly avoids the more common and damning categorical division of weakness versus strength.[91]

Marinella also characterizes the gendering of labour as a social construct. The world in which Marinella wrote perceived the division of the sexes as reflected in a corresponding *natural* division of the professions: war and weaving. Homer had long ago established this dichotomy when in the *Iliad*, as cited above, Hector tells his wife that weaving is for women, war for men. And in 1554, nearly two millennia later, Federico Luigini da Udine could still criticize Virgil's Camilla and Ariosto's Bradamante for giving up the distaff (*canocchia*).[92] But for pro-woman writers, the confrontation between the needle and the sword was also a point of contention. In his *Amadigi*, for example, Bernardo Tasso praises women as capable of every deed: "Che le donne, ad ogn'opra, ad ogni cosa / di man, d'ignegno, di valore e d'arte, sian'atte" (11, 2) (That women, in every labour and everything / with hands, intellect, valour and art are able), but he will also add that if only contemporary women would wield swords instead of needles, there would be more written about them.[93]

Lucrezia Marinella seems to answer Bernardo Tasso while silencing the misogynist detractors in one fell strike of a sword. In her *Enrico*, when the armed Claudia meets the famed Byzantine warrior Oronte in battle, he strikes her and haughtily tells her that, "it would have been better if [she] had stuck to womanly occupations rather than looking for praise and victory among warriors!" (24. 28, 5–6; *Enrico* 337).[94] She returns the blow and breaks through Oronte's shield, causing a small cut that leads him to "quiver" in fear. Marinella extracts women from a prescribed life of domestic labour and suggests that the reason that women have been kept from the military is actually men's fear of being defeated by them.

Conclusion

From its very beginnings, heroic poetry told the stories of courageous warrior women, but it was in the Italian Renaissance that armed women stepped into the poetic limelight. Authors of the late fifteenth and sixteenth centuries created scores of warrior women, most of whom imitated classical generic types such as Amazons or beautiful noble maidens. Of these types, the noble virago, in the image of Virgil's Camilla, enjoyed the greatest fortune in sixteenth-century epics, becoming a central figure in the two most celebrated poems of the age, Ariosto's *Orlando furioso* and Tasso's *Gerusalemme liberata*. The popularity of poetic women warriors was not matched in real-world combat. Even when historical records did discuss women in war, the descriptions were rarely like those of the female knights of Ariosto or Tasso. Historical biographies praised noble women as commanders who remained distant from the battlefields, while women who bloodied their hands were described as low-born, typically fighting in siege warfare alongside a community of women at the city walls. Thus, chivalric poems consistently pushed the question of verisimilitude and historicity by casting women in knightly roles where they mounted formidable competition to men's military prowess. The question of the historicity of women warriors inspired writers such as Torquato Tasso and Gian Battista Pigna to situate the poetic virago in a context of real women warriors. Later female poets, such as Moderata Fonte and Lucrezia Marinella, instead proposed their own theories of why real women did not fight like poetic viragos. These women authors suggested that while poets could imagine an armed virago, society prevented real women from realizing this potential.

As literary viragos proliferated in the texts, they were contained within certain literary tropes. Ariosto is likely the first major author to reintroduce Virgil's trope of a wildling childhood (i.e., Camilla nursed by a mare). This trope was to be adapted by nearly every author after him, creating a variation on a theme where baby girls are nursed by wolves, tigers, horses, and bears. The most significant trope for my study, however, is the revelation moment, where women's armour is partially removed to show a female body beneath it. I have argued that this moment is one that focuses the reader's attention not only on questions of gender and knighthood but also on the literary form itself. The lyrical revelation moment points to all of its precursors throughout the genre of chivalric literature and acts as both narrative marvel and parody of the marvel it is meant to incite.

The omnipresent virago notably loses her centrality in literature after the sixteenth century. She occasionally returns in theatre or operatic melodrama, but never with the same frequency until perhaps our modern day.[95] Her two hundred years of fame, however, did influence Italian culture. Writers sought to justify the presence of fictional armed women; moralists warned of the possibility that these women might gallop off the pages into the cities of Renaissance Italy; and some poets began to incorporate the same sincere commentary on women's militancy that had surfaced in political philosophy. Why these warrior women became such a poetic trend is always a matter of conjecture, but what is implied in these texts is that their appeal may have had much more to do with men at arms (and the particular historical and literary contexts of these men in sixteenth-century Italy) than with a concerted effort to bring women onto the battlefield.

3 Women Writers Demanding Warrior Masculinity: Catherine of Siena, Laura Terracina, Chiara Matraini, and Isabella Cervoni

> E per l'azione dobbiamo incitare i nostri uomini senza essergli delle palle di piombo ai piedi e dobbiamo essergli accanto nella dura battaglia, che è la battaglia per la nostra salvezza, per la nostra libertà e per quello di tutto il popolo italiano.
>
> – Noi donne: Organo dei gruppi di defesa della donna (10 July 1944)
>
> (And as for action, we must urge our men without being lead balls chained to their feet. We have to be beside them in the hard battle, which is the battle for our salvation, for our freedom, and for that of all of the Italian people.)

The preceding quotation from the newspaper *Noi donne* (*We Women*) of 1944 reminds us that women often appear in the rhetoric of war as inspiration for men to fight. This text, apparently written by women, indicates that the authors actively sought to cultivate a role for women in encouraging men's militancy, supporting war through companionship and, presumably, through love. Such a role is also frequently signalled in literary representations of the Middle Ages and Renaissance. Women were depicted as affectionately, if ambivalently, sending men into battle or tending to men's wounds so that they might return to combat. Men were responsive to such gender dynamics. One commonplace scenario involves men who redoubled their military efforts after gazing on the image of a beautiful woman or after being reminded of their obligations as protectors of the female sex. Men's militancy, however, was not portrayed as entirely altruistic; such masculine bravery had a payoff. Military victory was nearly always rewarded with wealth and status. In addition, there was at least the potential for the love of women. In her discussion of the masculinity of medieval knights, Ruth Mazo Karras explains that the love of women was ostensibly given as both gratitude for men's protection and an acknowledgment of men's admirable prowess, two motives that are discursively related. Moreover, Karras thoughtfully contrasts the experience of men and women in stating that "women no doubt experienced it differently, but from the masculine point of view love was a commodity that could be earned" (54). We might thus begin where Karras finished and seek to learn more about the experience of women when men took up arms, often purportedly in their name.

Some insight into women's perspective is provided by the corpus of Renaissance texts on war written by women. Several of these texts feature female authors who urged men to fight. This chapter will look specifically at the complex rhetorical strategies of persuasion employed by these authors. What is immediately apparent is that these women are not passive vulnerable maidens, saved by men from a world of violence. In contrast to the fictions of chivalry, the selections below show that male champions do not always rescue women, and women authors do not simply effuse gratitude and love. Instead, when we turn to texts written by women, we often find authors encouraging men into battle by employing a threatening tone, chiding men to change their behaviour and thus earn women's praise. In this strategy, a woman bestows or withholds praise in order to attain a desired response. The praise of women was thus imbued with a discourse of shame. Men could be shamed by a woman who accused them of unmanly behaviour, and a woman might experience shame if she was associated with a defeated or cowardly man.

The use of shame as a motivating force for battle is not limited to Renaissance women. It is perhaps one of the more pervasive tactics in war rhetoric, and it is deployed by both sexes. As a pithy example, I take a citation again from *Noi donne,* the women's newspaper of the Second World War, in which women admonished other women for trying to keep their husbands out of the line of fire. In bold font on the front page we find the epigram "Meglio essere la vedova di un eroe che la moglie di un codardo" (1) (Better to be the widow of a hero than the wife of a coward). As is evident from this striking statement, shame is not only used to perpetuate warfare but binds the two sexes in a militant cycle. Italian women of the Middle Ages and Renaissance also employed the rhetoric of gender shaming in order to incite combat.

This chapter seeks to analyse not only the frequency of this rhetoric but the complexity of it as well. In the discussion below, I have given a preference to texts in which women used shame to demand militancy. This is but one of the many ways that women wrote about war. I leave the exploration of other equally important perspectives to others.

I begin with a brief survey of lyric poets, and then turn to four female authors (Catherine of Siena, Laura Terracina, Chiara Matraini, and Isabella Cervoni) who employed lyric as well as other literary forms to demand that men take up arms.[1]

Scouting the Territory

Even the most cursory look at women's literature of the fourteenth through seventeenth centuries reveals a surprising number of women writing about warfare. Indeed, Olivia Sears identified at least fifty women poets of the Cinquecento writing about war in their verses. Sears focused on the important figures of Vittoria Colonna and Veronica Gambara, as well as a group of Sienese poets, to discuss the intersections of women's war poetry and love lyrics. In addition to this formidable list of poets, we might also consider the numerous female epistolary writers, diarists, and cloistered chroniclers who felt compelled to write about their own experiences of living in a war-torn land. Although women have often been cast as uniformly pacifist, these writers did not depict their thoughts on war with a singular pro-peace (or pro-war) message. The plurality of voices is, however, often identifiable within one or more of the competing female discourses addressed by Jean Bethke Elshtain, those of pacifist, civic bellicose mother, or mythic Penelope awaiting her soldier-husband's return.[2]

Within this pantheon of female authors, the most famous is certainly Vittoria Colonna (1490–1547), poet, religious reformer, and wife and daughter of two *condottieri*. In her long poetic career, she demonstrates extraordinary ambivalence towards war, an ambivalence that she herself will reference as a result of her own gender. Colonna's epistolary poem "Excelso mio signore, questa ti scrivo" (My august lord, I write this to tell you),[3] written on the occasion of the dual imprisonment of Vittoria's father and husband after a defeat in battle, is one of the best-known verses about war written by a woman in the Renaissance. The epistolary poem, written to her husband the Marquis of Pescara, Ferrante Francesco D'Avalos, puts the question of men's honour during war squarely at odds with the honour of performing the duties of a family man:

> la vostra gran virtù s'è dimostrata
> d'un Hettor, d'un Achille; ma che fia
> questo per me, dolente, abbandonata? (vv 28–30)

> (You showed yourself to have the greatness of a Hector, an Achilles; but what do I care for that, grieving and abandoned as I am!)

Colonna asks how a man's military *virtù* is of any benefit to her, a wife abandoned. She is clear that she did not wish for her husband to be at war: "Altri chiedevan guerra; io sempre pace" (Others preached war, but I was for peace) (v. 37), and she proceeds to escalate her criticism of war by engaging her husband in an admonishment of masculine pursuits. She states that he, inconsiderate of her needs, thinks of nothing but "honor":

> Non nuoce a voi seguir le dubbie imprese,
> m'a noi, dogliose, afflitte, ch'espettando
> semo da dubio e da timore offese;
> Voi, spinti dal furor, non ripensando
> ad altro ch'ad honor, contr'il periglio
> soleti con gran furia andar gridando.
> Noi timide nel cor, meste nel ciglio
> semo per voi; e la sorella il frate,
> la sposa il sposo, vol la madre il figlio;
> ma io, misera! cerco e 'l sposo e patre
> e frate e figlio; sono in questo loco
> sposa, figlia, sorella e vecchia matre. (vv 40–51)

> (You men are not harmed by attempting your bold enterprises, but what of us women, suffering, afflicted, torn apart by fear and doubt as we wait for you? You, fueled by fury, thinking of nothing but honor, delight to race furiously into the face of danger, while we wait, fearful at heart, sad-eyed on your account; the sister longs for her brother, the bride her husband, the mother her son. But I, alas! long for husband and father, brother and son; I feel myself at the same time bride, daughter, sister, and aged mother.)

The poem, written from her home in Ischia while her husband and father were in an enemy's prison, reveals a woman's desperation and anger as well as other themes that are often lost in the more typical war story.[4] Her verse, unlike most contemporary texts on war, tells of the impact of martial victories and losses on human relationships, and her poetics reflect and engage quite specifically her gender, centring as they do on the differing drives for masculine honour and feminine affect. Her frustration is a sentiment that is reflected in Paolo Giovio's writing about Colonna during his stay on the island of Ischia. In his *Dialogus de viris ac foeminis actata nostra florentibus* (*Notable Men and Women of Our Time*), Giovio tells of the plight of abandoned women deprived of their husbands and relatives during the Italian wars.[5] Giovio's dialogue, however, also offers a perspective on this dynamic from the viewpoint of male combatants, one that is lacking in Vittoria's poem to her husband. Men's departure for battle weighs on the minds of men as well as women. For example, we see the Marquis del Vasto, the adopted son of Colonna, struggling with the conundrum of masculine duty. He is torn between the duty to defend Naples against an impending attack by French galleys and the duty to protect the women on Ischia who will be left without a male defender if he were to leave (Zimmermann 90).

In both Colonna's epistolary poem and Giovio's dialogue, Vittoria Colonna and the other women of Ischia are the iconic abandoned women calling for peace and the return of the fighting men who have left them.[6] It is a scenario that echoes throughout classical and early modern literature, from Ovid's ventriloquized female voices in the *Heroides* to Gaspara Stampa's complaints of the distance of her *lord,* "the son of Mars," Collaltino.[7] Throughout her poetic corpus, Vittoria Colonna calls for peace within Italy, and such protests against war represent a position that has long been gendered as feminine, at least since Plato and into our own modern-day "peace movements" (Elshtain, "Reflections," 226–56; Goldstein 330–1).

But the gendering of war as masculine and peace as feminine is a facile binary, for even the peace-loving Vittoria Colonna will write poems praising wartime honour. In fact, the militant heroic legacies of Colonna's husband and adopted son figure much more prominently in her poetry than do her critiques of war. We might take for example the sonnet "Or che pien d'alto sdegno e pietà grande" (Now full of lofty disdain and great piety), a poem written to her adopted son del Vasto to encourage him to defeat the Turks and receive the honour that she regrets was denied to her husband (Colonna, *Rime* 204). The same woman who had critiqued fighting as mere posturing for honours that unnecessarily took men from their families now wishes those same honours for her son.

Colonna was not unconventional in this respect. The notion that a female writer could honour and even elevate her husband by writing of his military pursuits had been prefigured by the poet and tutor Antonio Tebaldeo (1463–1537), who stated that his pupil Isabella d'Este might learn to write poetry and exalt her husband Francesco Gonzaga's military prowess. In this short excerpt of Tebaldeo's *capitolo* about d'Este, feminine writing is in dialectic with masculine war:

> Che gaudio arà quando contexta e messa
> udrà da lei ogni sua palma in verso!
> Lui al far serà pronto, al scriver essa.
>
> (What pleasure it will give him when he hears from her all his victories woven into rhyme! He will be ready to act; she to write) (quoted in Cox, *Women's Writing* 52–3)

While Isabella d'Este's literary tutelage did not bear the fruits predicted by Tebaldeo, the dynamic of fighting husband and poetic wife was perfectly performed by Vittoria Colonna and her spouse. She also sought to guarantee the legacy of her late husband by asking the historian and physician Paolo Giovio to write a biography of him, where d'Avalos would figure as the ideal military general (Zimmermann 95). In fact, she thanks Giovio for his idealizing prose in her sonnet "Di quella cara tua serbata fronde" (With that prized, reserved branch, Apollo), where she states that his histories will secure glory and immortality for d'Avalos's wartime bravery.

> Di quella cara tua serbata fronde
> ch'a' rari antichi, Apollo, ampia corona
> donasti, alor ch'a l'alma tua Elicona
> gustar l'acque più chiare, e più profonde,
>   or che 'l gran Iovio ne l'estreme sponde
> del pario Oceano a l'Indico risona,
> con sì lucido onor che si ragiona
> le prime glorie altrui girli seconde.
>   orna di propria man la fronte altera,
> ché la sua dotta musa oggi è sol quella
> che rende il secol nostro adorno e chiaro.

Questo al Sol vivo mio sua luce intera
serberà sempre, e quel subietto raro
farà s'degna istoria eterna e bella.

(With that prized, reserved branch, Apollo,
Which you gave, an ample crown, to those
Rare ancients who tasted the clearest,
Deepest waters of your spring at Helicon;
Now that the great Giovio resounds
From the Parian to the Indian ocean,
With such blazing honor, that the glories he bestows
Reduce earlier ones to second place;
Deck by your own hand his lofty forehead,
Since his learned music is now the only one
Which renders our century adorned and famous.
He will preserve for my living Sun his entire light,
Forever, and that rare subject will make
So worthy a history eternal and splendid.) (quoted and translated in Zimmerman 101)

Colonna's writings perhaps offer the most literary expression of a Renaissance woman's predicament in warfare, fraught with competing discourses of masculine prestige and familial and affective needs. Such masculine prestige was transferable to women. That Colonna augmented the reputation of the deceased d'Avalos in order to bolster her own fame even after his death is not just a cynical argument but a reality of Renaissance life. The *Diary of Sister Bartolomea Riccoboni* suggests precisely this transference of fame, when the author tells of how one nun was pleased to think that if a relative died in religious combat it would elevate her status as well. Riccoboni records how Sister Paola, the mother of the Lord Cardinal Giovanni Dominici, was cheerful when her fellow sisters comforted her over the fact that her son was risking his life. As the diary states, "When the sisters comforted her, with a cheerful expression she replied, 'Dear daughters, you can be sure that I feel no anguish, considering that he is toiling for God's honor; and if I should hear that he was killed while defending the holy church, I would feel the highest joy, for he would make me out to the be the mother of a martyr'" (78).

Fame notwithstanding, many women did suffer the psychological and emotional predicament of a gendered war system that might end a man's life. The fact that men's status could run counter to the wishes of a mother, daughter, or wife is most poignantly stated by Veronica Gambara (1485–1550). Gambara had been intimately aware of the gruesome realities of war; she was present with her mother, Alda, in her castle when it was besieged in 1511, and her father was killed in battle in 1512.[8] Yet, in a letter of 1537 she expresses the difficult paradox of welcoming war while simultaneously loving peace. She worries that if there is a "truce," her son may not receive the military honour that war would bring him. The unusual text is written to Agostino Ercolani, apparently wishing for an attack by the French so that her son might fight and gain prestige:[9]

> Ippolito mio è in campagna, e dubito che fra poco converrà andare in Piemonte con le genti tutte, perchè si dice che il Re di Francia viene con grossissimo esercito. Il povero figliuolo ha spesa la vita; se si facesse una tregua, come si va dicendo, vedete dove egli si ritroverebbe. Fui sempre nemica della guerra, ed ora conviene ch'io la desideri; or vedete dove io sono ridotta. (*Rime e lettere* 247)
>
> (My Ippolito is in the countryside, and I suspect that soon it will be necessary to go to Piedmont with all the other people, because they say that the King of France is coming with an enormous army. The poor child has spent up his youth, and if there were a truce, as everyone is saying, you see where he would end up. I have always been an enemy of war, and now it is necessary to desire it. Now you see what I have been reduced to.)

One does not doubt Gambara's sincere wish for peace, and yet she is a product of a time that conferred status and wealth on fighting men.[10] She is strikingly frank in expressing her dilemma, complaining, "vedete dove io sono ridotta" (you see what I have been reduced to).

Gambara's letter also reflects the cultural pressures that saw war as the duty of men. This duty is evident in Gambara's sonnet "La bella Flora, che da voi sol spera" (Famous heroes, the bella Flora in you alone) in which she writes in the female voice of Florence to incite the citizens of the city to regain the ardour of their past glory and fight:[11]

> La bella Flora che da voi sol spera,
> famosi eroi, e libertate e pace,
> fra speranza e timor si strugge e sface,
> e spesso dice or mansueta, or fera:

"O de' miei figli saggia e prima schiera,
perché di non seguir l'orme vi piace
di chi col ferro e con la mano audace
vi fe' al mio scampo aperta strada e vera?
Perché sì tardi al mio soccorso andate?
già non produssi voi liberi e lieti,
perché lasciaste me serva e dolente.
Quanta sia in voi virtù dunque mostrate,
e col consiglio e con la man possente,
fate libera me, voi salvi e queti." (*Rime* 112–13)

(Famous heroes, the bella Flora in you alone
places her hope for liberty and peace.
She is torn and undone between hope and fear;
and she cries out repeatedly, at times gently and then wildly:
"Oh, most noble and wise rank of my sons,
why do you not wish to follow the steps of those
who with their swords and brave hands
made a true and liberal passage for my rescue?
Why do you come to my relief so late?
I did not bear you to be glad and free
so you could leave me grieving and enslaved.
Now demonstrate how great your virtue is,
and with counsel and with a powerful hand
make me free and render yourselves safe and peaceful.")

Gambara chooses to use the feminine voice of Flora to beg for aid from her "sons" ("figli") so that she no longer might be "enslaved" in pain. In a tradition dating to the origins of Italian literature and specifically in imitation of Petrarch's "Italia mia," Gambara makes of the homeland a woman's body, and to this body she gives a voice.[12]

A very different war will be cause for another poet, Girolama Corsi Ramos (fl. 1490–1509), to write about Florence under attack, again so that her citizens might take up arms. After the French invasion of 1494 that began the so-called Italian Wars, Corsi, a Tuscan woman living in the Veneto, wrote a caudate sonnet, not bemoaning the pitiful state of Florence but rather shaming the city for its pusillanimity for giving the French passage without resistance:[13]

Nel bel paese mio toscho gentile
vassene il gallo, ognhor bechando el grano
e le galine che li viene a mano
tutte l'alletta e chiama a suo chovile.
Oymè, marzocho, come fosti vile
a darli il passo e tuo governo in mano!
Tempo non ci verrà molto lontano
che habito mutarai, 'dioma e stile. (vv 1–8)

(Into my fine noble land of Tuscany goes the Gaulish rooster, pecking at his grain, and all the hens that come his way he lures and calls to his lair. Alas, Marzocco, how cowardly and base to give him free passage and deliver yourself into his hand! The time will not be long in coming when you change your clothes, language, and customs.) (quoted and translated in Cox, *Lyric Poetry* 305)

Corsi writes to Florence, not addressing her as the "bella Flora," servant to oppressors, but through one of Florence's other symbols, the lion. Florence, here gendered as the masculine Marzocco, has become "cowardly" ("vile") and given its government away to a mere rooster, a metonymic reference to France, and as such has failed his manly duties. Combining fears of sexual penetration and diabolical births, Corsi warns the lion that this rooster is making Florence its nest, and if the rooster is not expelled soon, a basilisk (the legendary serpent that killed with its gaze) would be hatched from the egg:

Vedi che in la tua paglia cova el gallo,
Perhò cerca cazarlo
Prima che 'l basilisco esca dell'uovo. (vv 17–19)

(See that the rooster is brooding in your straw. Chase him out before the basilisk hatches from the egg.) (quoted and translated in Cox, *Lyric Poetry* 305)

The same French invasion of Italy that inspired Corsi to castigate men, prompted Camilla Scarampa (1476–1520) to lament the state of "miserable Italy."

Misera Italia, il ciel pur te minaccia.
Una voce me intona nell'orecchia,
ché, se non svegli tua virtute vecchia,
convien ch'ogni tua pompa si disfaccia.

Sciolta non sei ancor dell'un de' braccia
de' barbari, che l'altro s'apparecchia.
Chi vuol veder miseria in te si specchia,
poi, lagrimando, per pietà s'agghiaccia;
ché, per le nostre tante adverse voglie,
de 'sti rabiosi can sei fatta preda,
che van stracciando le tue belle spoglie.
Or tal lo proverà, che par nol creda:
saran comune tante amare doglie.
Chiudemi gli occhi, Dio, che ciò non veda.

(Wretched Italy, heaven still threatens you. A voice thunders in my ear that if you do not revive your ancient prowess, all your splendors will be undone. You have barely escaped from one of the arms of the barbarians when the next awaits you. Whoever wants to see pity, for in punishment for our perverse desires, you have been made prey by these dogs who are now tearing away at your fair remains. Those will soon feel the truth of this who seem now not to believe it: all these bitter woes will be common to all. Close my eyes, God, that I shall not see that day.) (quoted and translated in Cox, *Lyric Poetry* 307)

She wonders if Italy will awake and prevent the destruction of another invasion. Scarampa's poem, emotive as it is, lacks the stinging condemnation of men found in Gambara and Corsi. Instead, the poet postulates that the cause of the recent destruction is the "adverse voglie" (perverse desires) of all Italians, and her call to action is addressed to a general, personified Italy.

The verses of Colonna, Gambara, Corsi, and Scarampa provide only a glimpse of the rich poetic landscape that is produced by women writing about war. For these women, war is as much a muse as is love. Moreover, some Cinquecento publishers elevated these poems, making war and politics emblematic of women's poetic voice. For the most obvious example we need only think of Lodovico Domenichi's important 1559 anthology of women poets, *Rime diverse d'alcune nobilissime et virtuosissime donne* (*Diverse Rhymes of Several Most Noble and Virtuous Women*), where the incipit poem is a sonnet by Aurelia Petrucci (1511–1542), "Dove sta il tuo valor, Patria mia cara" (Where is your valor, my dear homeland? [translation from Cox, *Lyric Poetry*]), a damning condemnation of Sienese warring factionalism.[14]

Women's voices in the rhetoric of war raise important questions about gender and writing. To what effect do these authors refer to their sex in writings on war? How might texts written by women about war have been received? And furthermore, in what ways did such texts that employ deliberative rhetoric (such as the above sonnets by Gambara and Corsi) alter both real actions in war and textual representations of it? These questions collectively ask *how*, not *if*, women's texts on war were able to shape the larger Renaissance discourse about war. The sheer quantity of martial verse by women makes their importance to the study of war rhetoric a foregone conclusion, despite the neglect of women writers by military historians. Perhaps our best evidence that women's voices in war attracted special attention is the strange moment in Italian literary history when a sixteenth-century editor chose to falsely attribute war poems to female pseudonyms.

The Fabbrianesi

In 1564 and 1580 Giovanni Andrea Gilio published several sonnets by a group of women, all of whom had purportedly lived in the fourteenth century and were from Fabriano. There has been much scholarly debate suggesting that Gilio published fraudulent sonnets out of an attempt to elevate the prestige of this town in the Marche region. He has been accused of publishing sixteenth-century sonnets under the fourteenth-century names of Livia Chiavello, Leonora Genga, and Ortensia di Guglielmo da Fabriano.[15] What makes this story even more interesting is that, later in the seventeenth century, two more apocryphal fourteenth-century women poets from the Marche region were said to be correspondents of this female coterie, Elisabetta Trebbiani and Giustina Levi Perotti. It is striking that three of the women (Genga, Chiavello, and Ortensia) write about (or were said to have written about) war. Moreover, Elisabetta Trebbiani is said to have gone armed into battle alongside her husband and to have defended him when he was attacked.[16]

Eleonora Genga is credited with one sonnet that praises the virtues of women. The poem "Tacete, o maschi, a dir che la natura" (Stop decrying, oh men, that nature) tells men that their honour pales when compared to that of women, and an entire tercet is dedicated to the ability of women to fight and rule.

> Sanno le donne maneggiar le spade,
> Sanno regger gl'imperi, e sanno ancora
> Trovar il cammin dritto in Elicona. (9–11)

(They know how to manage swords. They know how to rule an empire, and they also know how to find the straight path to Helicon.)

Ortensia di Guglielmo, on the other hand, is said to be addressing Pope Gregory XI in Avignon in the sonnet "Ecco Signor la greggia tua d'intorno" (Behold, Lord, your flock around you). The first quatrain begins,

Ecco Signor la greggia tua d'intorno
Cinta di lupi a divorarla intenti;
Ecco tutti gl'onor d'Italia spenti;
Poiche fa altrove il gran Pastor soggiorno. (Gilio, *Topica* 76)

(Behold, Lord, your flock around you.
Circled by wolves intent on devouring it.
Behold all the honours of Italy spent.
Since the great shepherd lives elsewhere.)

The poet sees Italy as having lost its honour, and she calls on the pope to defend his flock that is about to be devoured by wolves. It is the same sentiment that one finds in the writings of Catherine of Siena to the same pope. Yet where the pseudo-Ortensia merely longs for the day when the pope will "levar tanti lamenti" (relieve so many laments), we will see below that Catherine actually calls the pope to task, telling him to "act like a man" and fulfil his responsibilities. Finally, it is the sonnet attributed to Livia Chiavello that fully addresses the notion of a war-torn Italy. This poem resembles many sixteenth-century texts by women, and perhaps for this reason this is the sonnet that has alerted many scholars to its possibly fraudulent authorship.[17] Regardless of the veracity of the author identification, the sonnet is noteworthy for its ambivalent praise of war, couched within a plaint of peace.

Veggio di sangue human tutte le strade
D'Italia piene, il qual per tutto corre:
E disdegnoso e reo Marte discorre,
Lance porgendo ogn'hor, saette, e spade.
Quindi convien, ch'in lungo esilio vade
Fuggendo Astrea con le compagne, a porre
L'albergo, ond'al gran mal nulla soccorre,
E l'honor prisco, e l'ornamento cade.

> Ma se disio di vera Gloria accende
> L'Italico valor, rivolga l'arme
> Contra colui, che 'l Christianesmo sface.
> Contra se stesso ogn'un più tosto s'arme;
> Perchè quel Dio, ch'in su la croce pende,
> Dio di guerra non è, ma Dio di pace. (Gilio, *Topica* 77)

(I see human blood running through all the streets of Italy, and disdainful and wicked Mars passes, always wielding lances, arrows, and swords. Thus Astrea is forced into long exile, fleeing with her companions, to make her home elsewhere, so she offers no shelter against this great evil, and past honours and splendours fall.

But if the desire for true glory ignites Italian valour, let it turn arms against the one who is undoing Christianity; or rather let everyone turn his arms against himself, because that God who hangs on the cross is not the God of war but the God of peace.)

The sonnet begins with a graphic image of streets that are like rivers of blood, streets where lances, arrows, and swords are in continual movement, and it ends as one would expect, with a call to war's end, finishing with the reminder that God is a god not of war but of peace: "Dio di guerra non è, ma Dio di pace." Yet in the first tercet, there is a moment that is hardly peace-loving. The poet calls Italy to arms in war against non-Christians. If Italians desire glory, then they should turn their arms against those who try to "undo" ("sface") Christianity. Chiavello hinges the rhyming words "pace" and "sface" to show that those who undo the faith are those truly at odds with peace, and thus she dismantles, albeit briefly, the binary of war and peace, creating instead a binary of peace versus infidels (those who undo Christianity). She also turns to the same discourse that coloured Corsi and Gambara's poems on war – that one may achieve honour through war. In Chiavello's figuration, the prize is, however, a Christian valour, a pervasive if perverse justification of violence that we will see repeated throughout the sixteenth-century anti-Turkish writings.

Chiavello's poem is thus full of ambivalence, calling for peace while concurrently praising the glory of war. This sonnet, possibly written by a man but attributed to a woman, foreshadows our discussion of four remaining authors who exhibit the same conflict with regards to war. These women – Caterina da Siena, Laura Terracina, Chiara Matraini, and Isabella Cervoni – will glorify peace but will also praise men for fighting or chide them into battle by withholding their praise, empowering themselves as judges in the system of masculine military honour.

Catherine of Siena (1347–1380)

The best-known medieval woman writer to critique the actions of men is Catherine of Siena. Even a cursory reading of her nearly four hundred extant letters reveals an unmistakable frankness and boldness with the kings, queens, and pope of her time, especially given her bourgeois origins as the twenty-third daughter of a dyer.[18] Her scolding or praising is part of a general strategy that Catherine employs to persuade her addressees to bend to her wishes, conflating the sacred and the political, often identifying herself with the Virgin or Christ.[19] Such power depends on Catherine's ability to manage a complex conflation of religious devotion, extreme physical acts of suffering, keen manipulation of reputation, and simple determination.[20] The fact that Catherine could wield power on an international level suggests an almost unbelievable shift in social class due to fame, a fame evidenced by her renowned correspondents and later by her inclusion in the panoply of saints.

There would be two hagiographies of Catherine following her death, but Catherine's unusual circumstance is how she won praise during her own lifetime. Thomas Luongo argues that Catherine's power is in part possible due to the "'feminized' religious culture in the later Middle Ages" where "men sought feminine images of Christ and female holy authorities [like Catherine] because of their distance from ordinary male experience."[21] Thus, in a time when Christianity and specifically Christ became identified with the feminine, important men gathered around Catherine in a "famiglia" (as she called them), in part because of the general appeal of her feminine social role as a mother. In turn, as Luongo explains, Catherine was able to capitalize on this situation and exert power through this feminine role. Though Luongo's analysis rightly addresses the appeal of Catherine's feminine role in what he sees as an increasingly feminine culture, he fails to consider how Catherine also establishes power through her scurrilous attacks on effeminate and/or wayward men. Her critiques of men may thus also be seen as attempts to bring men *closer to* rather than *away from* "ordinary male experience." The more she encourages men to "act like men," the more she constructs her own reputation as a woman deserving of respect.

Specifically, when Catherine writes to the ruling men of the world to discuss warfare, she invokes typically secular themes of the manly soldier, honourable knight, negligent husband, and absent father.[22] She wraps such images of secular masculinity in her own Christian agenda, and then employs an authority that Tylus traces to Catherine's account of the Canaanite woman of Matthew's Gospel (Matthew 15:21–8). In Matthew's Gospel, the Canaanite woman insists that Jesus hear her plea, and she yells out to him to listen to her. In Catherine's interpretation of this story (letter 69) as Tylus reads it, Jesus admires the Canaanite woman's faith and persistence and then confers on the woman (and Catherine and proleptically on her followers) "an embodiment of authority."[23] With this authority, perceived as hers through analogy to the Canaanite woman, Catherine can thus boldly write to men and women of power. She adopts the biblical character's desperate intensity and insists on being heard. It is relevant to this study that, in texts on warfare, Catherine may embody the Canaanite woman's authority but quickly expands her position by threatening men's masculinity if they ignore her.

Examples of gender shaming in her letters are numerous, but one famous letter to a military *condottiere* confronts the issue of warfare directly. In 1375, she writes to Captain John Hawkwood to encourage him to leave his mercenary pursuits and fight for the pope's crusade against the Turks.[24] By the time of her letter to Hawkwood, she has been lauded as performing miracles and is undoubtedly Italy's most famous religious woman.[25] Indeed, it is precisely this period in Catherine's life (her sojourn in Pisa) that has been argued to be the pivotal moment in her expansion of fame and power.[26] She is thus presumably seeking to use not only her God-granted authority as the faithful servant but also her worldly renown to influence Hawkwood to change the course of events.

Contrary to what one might expect from a female religious zealot, she does not ask the captain to lay down his arms. Instead, she begs him to stop fighting Christians and "andar contro a' cani infedeli" (go against the dog infidels).[27] Catherine's ultimate goal is peace within Italy, and as Luongo states, for Catherine, peace in Italy was inextricably linked to the crusade and the return of the pope to Rome (Luongo 81). Thus, it is no surprise that she asks for both peace and war in the same breath, and her rhetorical innovation is the means by which she will collapse both of these notions into a medieval *exemplum* of masculinity, an *exemplum* that she will use to influence the captain who was to receive her letter.

Catherine's letter to Hawkwood was delivered by an embassy of three men dressed as penitents; yet according to contemporary sources, one of the envoys was a Burgundian soldier who was reputedly a man of "'bad character'" but "'very effective at negotiations'" (quoted in Caferro 166). By sending her letter via this morally questionable negotiator, William Caferro argues, "Catherine appears to have intended to negotiate with Hawkwood on his own terms" (166).[28] To Caferro's argument, I would add that not only her envoy but also her epistolary language engage Hawkwood in his own game. Instead of citing biblical passages and images as she does to other addressees, she invokes the tradition of chivalric honour and all that it implies in the formation of medieval manhood: "Scrivo … con desiderio di vedervi vero figliuolo e cavaliere di Cristo, sì e per siffatto modo, che desideriate mille volte, se tanto bisognasse, dare la vita in servizio del dolce e buono Gesù" (I long to see you such a true son and knight of Christ that you would want to give your life a thousand times, if so much were necessary, in the service of the good gentle Jesus) (*Lettere*, Tommaseo ed., II, 328; *Letters* 80).[29] Thus Catherine requests that she see Hawkwood act as a true son and knight of Christ, "cavaliere di Cristo," a term that not only invokes the trope of the *miles Christi* (soldier of Christ) but more importantly addresses this actual knight ("cavaliere") of the Hundred Year's War.[30]

Two years before Catherine's letter, Pope Gregory XI wrote to Hawkwood to praise him for having led the papal troops to a victory against the Visconti. The Pope had hired Hawkwood after having previously been his enemy, and in this letter of 1373 adulates Hawkwood as "obedient to the Roman Church" and a "warrior of Christ, athlete of God and faithful Christian knight" (quoted in Caferro 159).[31] In her letter, Catherine implicitly calls into question Hawkwood's right to receive such Christian and chivalric praise. Though she may not have known of the Pope's letter directly, she demonstrates that she was very informed of matters between the Pope and Hawkwood,[32] and in this letter, we see her making a sort of corrective of the Pope's assessment. For, although Gregory was glad to have Hawkwood as his hired captain and is quick to equate service to the Papal States as being a "warrior of Christ," apparently Catherine, two years later, imagines a "true knight of Christ" as being much different.

The reality of Hawkwood's career is, in fact, one that would not have pleased Catherine. During Hawkwood's campaign from 1375 to 1377, he and his enormous army threatened to march on cities if they did not pay him what were extraordinary amounts of money (Caferro 164, 339). Hawkwood could request such large payments because he had established both a large fighting force and a brilliantly crafted reputation for brutality.[33] When Catherine heard of the arrival of Hawkwood's army in Prato, en route to her native Siena, she took cause to intervene and rewrite the terms of chivalrous warfare.

Catherine's letter, in her typical way, seeks to change a person's behaviour by using a corrective *exemplum*, which is in turn followed by the Christian threat of eternal damnation. In this case, she invokes the noble figuration of the knight, "cavaliere." She then places the representation of this ideal (as she has envisaged it) next to Hawkwood's career "al servizio e al soldo del demonio" (in the devil's service and pay) (T329, N80). Hawkwood was by title a "cavaliere" and, as Caferro reminds us, was in truth "no more or less" of a knight than the other men who roamed medieval Europe (9). Despite the acts of his comrades in arms, Catherine singles out Hawkwood as not measuring up to her interpretation of the ideal knight. *Her* knight battles for Christ, not for the highest-paying prince, and he should "desideriate mille volte, se tanto bisognasse, dare la vita" (be ready to give [his life] for him a thousand times) (T328, N80). The sacrifice of one's life for God, an act that she herself was famously enacting through self-imposed starvation, was, in her terms, an act that was expected of a "vero cavaliere" (true knight). By telling Hawkwood to risk death, I posit that she is suggesting that she is more chivalric than he.[34]

Catherine's request that Hawkwood risk his life for a higher cause also intersects with one of the pillars of masculinity – namely that willing sacrifice of life in war or in other heroic moments is a defining aspect of masculine construction.[35] As the anthropologist David Gilmore states in his seminal work on masculinity, it is not that men are naturally "more brave than women" but that they have inherited cultural expectations to "confront danger as a means of showing valor" (122). Concerning warfare and fighting, he explains that the phenomenon of men (not women) fighting and dying in battle is in part explained by the underlying societal discourse suggesting that men are simply "more expendable" than women (121). Gilmore's thoughts are generative even when considering the late Middle Ages. Sacrifice of life for a higher cause does circulate in the discourse of medieval manhood, and it certainly seems that the effectiveness of Catherine's letter to Hawkwood is due to a gender ideology much like the one Gilmore describes, where proving manhood also implies courageously facing death.

Facing death is only one means of proving masculinity before women and God. If men fail in their military masculinity, Catherine implies that she is specifically vested with the power to enforce a change. We thus might make an addendum to Tylus's notion of authority and the Canaanite woman. When speaking of matters of war, Catherine is doubly invested with power. Not only is she the embodiment of Christ's will because of her faith and persistence, she is also granted the power given to all women; she can demand protection from men as a member of the vulnerable sex. Indeed, like women before and after her, Catherine writes not only from her faith but from her gender, and implies that women, rightfully deserving of men's protection, are the ones who can best police men's masculinity.[36]

Catherine seeks to control Hawkwood's gender performance by invoking exempla of ideal masculinity that were taken from Christian texts or the more metaphorical text of contemporary culture. In a similar vein, she writes to Pope Gregory XI, her extolled "father" and guide, and urges him to be a good *husband*, since he has neglected his bride, the church, by allowing her to be "stripped" in public by paid soldiers (*Letters* II, 61; Tommaseo ed. 206).[37] She also invokes further chivalric imagery and urges Gregory to be a "champion," since he has abandoned her and his people. In other instances, Catherine will drop metaphors altogether, simply prodding men to act "manly." Writing again to Gregory, she instructs him to "Siatemi un uomo virile, non timoroso" (act like a virile man, not a coward) (T 247), N II, 63). In this last example, Catherine drops the use of exempla and, in a certain sense, sheds her reliance on the authority of others. She speaks with her own gender-policing authority, one that presumably comes from her sex more than her role as a servant of Christ. Her text, indeed, resembles the language of other women, not the least of whom was the virago-cum-Lombard-princess Sichelgaita, who called out "Halt! Be men!" to troops if she saw them deserting.[38] In the case of Catherine, however, this language is all the more striking as it comes from the pen of one of history's most famous female saints.

Laura Terracina (1519–1577)

Nearly two hundred years after Catherine, Laura Bacio Terracina, the Neapolitan daughter of a noble courtier, wrote poetry of praise and critique to warring captains in hopes of influencing the terms of war. Although she never exercised the international influence of Catherine, she was the most prolific published woman writer of the Cinquecento, with sixteen editions of her poetry having gone to press by 1566.[39] She exchanged sonnets with the leading poets and rulers of her time, and she was inducted into the short-lived Neapolitan literary academy of the "Incogniti" in 1545.[40] Her readership swelled after her first book of numerous encomiastic poems, and it was through such laudatory poems (more than a hundred written to women) that Terracina's fame was constructed (Jaffe 167). Unlike most of her female author contemporaries, who hailed from more established families, Terracina was very much engaged in the publication of her own texts. Interestingly, as Virginia Cox has eloquently argued, it was Terracina's marginal status in the Neapolitan social classes that necessitated her self-fashioning in print and enabled her to take an active role in the presses.[41] The printing press thus provided an otherwise marginalized Terracina with an instrument to build both her reputation and her sphere of influence. Yet the presses benefited from her writings as well: she was a major figure in the marketing phenomenon described by Diana Robin, where women's images and names on frontispieces were employed to sell books (*Publishing* 56). Robin specifically looks to the book design of Laura Terracina's *Quinte rime* to argue that presses showcased women in the hope of a "working reciprocity," wherein women would gain fame from having their names blazoned on frontispieces and publishers would enjoy the benefits of bestsellers. And it is in this environment of a nascent celebrity print culture that Terracina would use her status as a best-selling woman author, specifically in her texts about warfare, to remind men of their masculine duties.

Terracina's oeuvre includes eight volumes of poetry, published between 1548 and 1567, as well as an unpublished ninth book in manuscript (Shemek, *Ladies Errant* 127–9). Of these works, her third and eighth books are two discrete *discorsi* on the *Orlando furioso*.[42] In the preface to her third book, *Il discorso della S. Laura Terracina sopra il principio di tutti i canti di Orlando Furioso*, she includes a poem to Ludovico Dolce, the sixteenth-century editor and sometime literary agent, in which she demonstrates her exceptional position in regard to the gendering of war. Terracina highlights her uniqueness as a woman writing about war, a matter that is complicated by the fact that we specifically know that she is not the only woman to do so. In her poem to Dolce, Terracina asks for "pardon" for her "virile" language: "E se la lingua mia fu sì virile / Perdon vi chieggio …" (*Discorso*, Canto XIV, p 23v).[43] In Canto XIV of the *Discorso*, she again addresses the matter of war as a virile subject not suitable for women. The canto, which praises Pope Julius III as a warring prince, asks if her amorous poetic style can speak of anger and hate, if her feminine wisdom can follow the path of Mars, and if her pen can be virile enough to continue without a guide.

A che condutto il mio amoroso stile
A parlar d'ira, e ragionar di morte,
Come potrà l'ingegno feminile
Seguir di Marte il fier camin sì forte?
Sarà la pen(n)a mia tanto virile,
che voglia a ciò resister senza scorte. (XIV.1.1–6)

(To what end will my amorous style lead, / as it speaks of anger and tells of death? / How can feminine wisdom / Follow the proud path of Mars so strong? / Will my pen be virile enough / that I may endure without a guide?)

She raises questions that do not merely rehearse the inability topos, but rather insist on the uniqueness of a woman writing about a man's game. Terracina recalls the dominant gender ideologies that restrict women's participation in war – specifically, the matter that women are not to write about it. Women poets, she suggests, are relegated to appropriate themes of love, and Terracina slyly inscribes herself in this discourse, discussing her "amoroso stile" and "ingegno feminile."[44] Yet Terracina's *Discorso* is assuredly not written with "amoroso stile." It makes social critiques of various contemporary groups, including courtiers, captains, and unfaithful men and women. Furthermore, this feminine posture of vulnerability is contrasted with the masculine role of protector as emphasized by the rhyming words of "forte" and "scorte," an effective reminder that women need strong men to guide them, while the woman poet is without a guide as she ventures into the masculine world of war, both real and poetic.

Terracina thus curiously writes herself out of the binary she has created; she is the lone brave female author who is also the vulnerable object in need of men's defence. Feminist theory about war has, in fact, noted how women and specifically women's war poetry are "implicated in both the war system and the gender system" and may be responsible for perpetuating war myths rather than altering them (Cooper xv; see also Sears 23–5). Terracina retells the age-old story of the vulnerable woman and heroic man, essentializing the role of the helpless woman in the face of violence. Her rhetorical strategy, however, is an empowering one, allowing her to be heard over the devastation of war – first by arguing that women *are* in fact present in warfare, and second by requesting that the terms of war be redrawn.

She tackles the notion that war is only a man's business by demonstrating that she is a sentient being, viscerally experiencing the effects of violence. In a uniquely literary line of argument, she uses Ariosto's text as a vehicle to place herself physically in the midst of battle, where her phenomenological experience of war is articulated through the reading process. Reading Ariosto's poem, she states that her senses are overwhelmed when she *hears* the city of Paris crying ("Mi par di udir Parigi in grido, e in pianto") (XIV.2 .1). She continues by noting that she *feels* that Mars is angry ("Già sento irato il valoroso Marte") (XIV.2.1); she *feels* her heart languishing in fear ("mi sento il cor languido e infranto") (XIV.2.5); and she *sees* the great fire of the city ("Veggio in Parigi fuoco di grand'arte") (XIV.3.5). Terracina's frightened response to the *Orlando furioso* is engendered by the fantastic projection of herself into the violent text. She experiences the poetic war intimately, a reaction that, as Michael Murrin has reminded us, was common among Ariosto's contemporaries.[45] The Saracens have attacked Paris, and she describes how no soldiers can be found to fight off their troops. This female presence in battle is again a way for the author to recall the notion that women depend on male heroes; displacing the battlefield onto the book between her hands, Terracina describes how she searches nervously through the text for *paladini* to save the Christian city of Paris. She finishes the canto with a fear that she will be injured, "E credo, che nel fin rimarrò offesa," for she has begun this open discussion of war, a matter which does not pertain to women, or, literally, in her words, a matter that women do not *feel:* "Che 'l sesso feminil d'arme non sente" (That the female sex do not feel about arms).[46] Her statement is a curious one, since she has clearly shown how women *do* feel ("sente") war: hearing, feeling, and seeing the devastation of Paris under attack. Her argument is a conspicuously specious one, but it serves to establish the terms for her next canto, where she calls on her rights as a vulnerable woman to redraw the terms of war.

The next canto, canto XV, is dedicated to cardinals and bloody captains ("Ali Cardinali et Sanguinosi Capitani") and is a commentary on the wars contemporary to Terracina. The canto argues that men, not women, have called for war and that therefore women should be spared.

The soldier who has killed women leaves other men as daughterless fathers and in effect collects unholy "trophies of dresses and skirts."

> Ma, che colpa di questo hanno i figliuoli,
> Et tanti vecchi, e tante afflitte donne,
> Che de l'altrui fallir patiscon duoli?
> Qual pensier è, che tanto vi disdonne,
> Che di noi fate i nostri padri soli
> Lasciando empii trofei di veste, e gonne? (XV.2.1–6)

> (But what fault is this of children / and the aged, and so many afflicted women / who endure the pains of another's defeat? / What thought so overtakes you / that you deprive our fathers of us, / leaving behind unholy trophies of dresses and skirts?) (quoted in Shemek, *Ladies Errant* 149).

According to Terracina, men kill women futilely in their pursuit of fame, despite the fact that women are innocent in war. Terracina's protest then raises the stakes by calling for change, seeking to redefine the terms of praiseworthy warfare. Gazing back at the previous canto, in which she had insisted on women's vulnerability, canto XV describes the current wars as heinous battles where men do not protect but kill women, and her invective against military captains is precisely at odds with what the epic poet is supposed to do for fighting men. She is immortalizing the captains not for their honour but for their cruelty and impiety. In respect of the terms that she has established regarding masculinity and war, men have failed in their gender role as women's protectors, and she sees it as her role to praise or vituperate them accordingly.

In her most innovative rhetorical move, the author explores ways that captains might receive her praise, primarily by reconsidering the way in which victory in battle is established. Like most of Terracina's *Discorso,* this canto is in dialogue with Ariosto's text, and here she is commenting specifically on *Orlando furioso* XV, where the poet praises those captains who win battles with little bloodshed among their *own* men.[47] As a corrective to Ariosto, Terracina asks if it would not be more honourable to allow the enemy to flee. Her call for effective change implies that she could author a different sort of poem, a praise of captains, if they were to reconsider the way in which victory is established.

Non saria assai miglior, dare al nimico
Luoco, ch'ei fuggi possa, & vincitore
Rimaner de l'impresa, e de l'amico,
Et haver fra l'esercito l'honore? (XV.2.1–4)

(Would it not be much better to give to the enemy / Passage, so that he may flee, and thus you remain / Victor of the battle and of the friend / And maintain honour among the army?)

Her questions about the conduct of war lead Shemek to state that Terracina "asks the same questions women have always asked from their position on the margins of men's wars. Is there no glory in letting one's opponent live? Is there no conflict between religious devotion and the military ravages perpetrated by the faithful?" (Shemek, *Ladies Errant* 149). And while Shemek is right to point to Terracina's outrage at war, we must remember that, throughout her *Discorso*, the poet also glorifies war, praising Emperor Charles V and his Spanish captains, who, she hopes, will vanquish the French and the Turks. To reconcile these two positions on peace and war, we might return to Shemek's observation. It may be that "the margins of men's wars" represent a potentially (and counter-intuitively) empowered position for women. Because of her sex, Terracina may call on gender paradigms established precisely by the Christianized epic, where women are the vulnerable sex to be protected from evil. She effectively deploys her gender and her faith to call upon rulers, not in lamentations for peace but rather to conduct war according to her own desires.

Hor voi che del governo havete cura
D'un fier, d'un bel esercito honorato
Oprate ogni valor, con sua misura
Acciò di palma cinto & adornato
Sia il crin di Marte, e la sua man sì dura
Che si può ben lodare e haversi grato. (XV.7.1–5)

(Now you who have the charge of / a proud and decorated army within your care, / enact every valorous deed with moderation / so that the head of Mars may be crowned / and adorned with palms and his hand be strong, / so that he may be praised and thanked).

Terracina's politics of violence will not end war, but they redraw the lines of honourable warfare. Again using the topos of praise, she states, "one can praise" ("si può ben lodare") the army that uses "moderation" ("misura"). When we consider these two cantos together, they seem to confirm that war is the duty of men (male heroes saving Paris), while arguing that killing should be avoided, especially the killing of women. But this inherent contradiction necessarily perpetuates the gendering of war and consequently perpetuates the tragedies she presumably wishes to stop. Terracina thus provides one of the most vivid examples of Olivia Sears's theory that women poets, "whether as defenders or opponents of war ... remain partly responsible for the perpetuation of war as long as they accept the gender systems which make war thinkable and feasible" (24). It is hard to understand how Terracina envisaged an honourable war without the killing that is concomitant to victory.[48] Her *Discorso* thus presents an impossible paradox that praises the very acts it undercuts; what is remarkable, however, is that, within this paradox, there is the irrefutable voice of a woman who will not stand silent at the margins of the master text.

While the rhetoric of the *Discorso* is likely "partly responsible for the perpetuation of war," when we turn to Terracina's sonnets, we find a different perspective that is more productive for peace, at least within Italy and the Spanish viceregency where Terracina lived. In the sonnets, she continues to maintain the notion that fighting is the duty of men, but she complicates this onus by outlining her own just cause for war, a war that ideally happens outside Italy and unites Christians. Terracina's notions of just war are articulated in her sonnets to Pope Paul IV (r. 1555–9), where war with the Turks will receive her praise, while war in Italy is cause for vituperation.[49]

The fear of Turkish invasion is a common theme in Terracina's verse and reflects a pervasive sentiment among Italians during the Cinquecento.[50] Furthermore, Terracina was influenced by a specifically Spanish discourse of noble masculinity, which, at least in the court of Charles V and his Neapolitan viceregency, is characterized by aristocratic men's duty to protect female subjects from the Turkish threat.[51] When Terracina perceives Pope Paul IV (Giovanni Pietro Carafa), her fellow Neapolitan, to be failing in these duties as leader and protector of women, she takes up the pen to admonish him. In her *Seste rime*, Terracina composes several sonnets in which she boldly criticizes him for his passivity towards the Turks in hopes of coercing him into action. The compositions are also shrewdly pro-Spanish, for Terracina likely knew that Paul was not merely avoiding the Turkish threat but actively supporting the Franco-Turkish alliance to remove the Spanish from Italy.[52] She addresses the Pope in several epistolary sonnets, frequently veiling her language in metaphors of duty, as in "Pastor di Christo, e de la santa chiesa," where she asks how he could ignore his enemy even though it is his duty as a shepherd to protect his flock.

> Pastor di Christo, e de la santa chiesa
> come non scacci il tuo crudel nemico,
> che divora tua gregge, appar d'un Lico,
> essendo tu costretto à tor l'impresa? (*Seste rime* 22–3).
>
> (Shepherd of Christ and of his holy church / why do you not chase away the cruel enemy / who is devouring your flock, just like a Lycus, / since the one obligated to complete the task is you?)

The flock of Christ's shepherd is being devoured by the Turkish enemy, but the Pope is not chasing away the predator, a duty to which he, like any shepherd, is "costretto." The "shepherd" is hardly an innovative papal metaphor, but it is important to note that there is a tradition in adopting the shepherd metaphor when asking popes to wage war, as Catherine of Siena had famously done with Gregory XI or as Ariosto (Terracina's muse) himself did in his own attempts to urge Leo X to take up a new crusade. Moreover, as Ascoli has argued, the shepherd metaphor is used by Ariosto to criticize, however indirectly, contemporary papal military endeavours.[53] Terracina, on the other hand, directly censures her papal dedicatee by likening him not only to a shepherd but to Lycus (Lico), the Theban king from Euripides' *Antiope* who abuses his niece Antiope and forces her to abandon her twin sons. In the myth as Euripides tells it, the two sons are found by a shepherd and raised into adulthood, when they wreak vengeance on Lycus by killing his wife and deposing him. Yet good and evil in Terracina's poem are not so easily identifiable. In Terracina's sonnet, ambiguous syntax raises the question "Who is Lycus?"[54] If Paul IV is the cruel Lycus, he will ultimately be avenged. If instead Lycus is the "nemico," the enemy Turks, Paul can play the role of the benevolent *pastore* who rescues and raises the abandoned sons. The multiplicity of narratives as well as the vague structure of Terracina's poem offer the Pope a chance to choose his role – cruel and neglectful king or nurturing shepherd – and her advice here is unambiguous.[55] She tells Paul to raise his hand, not for letters and papal negotiations but for war: "Deh manda fuora la tua forte mano, / non con inchiostro, e carta, ma con arme" (Then send out your strong hand, / not with ink and paper, but with arms).[56]

Initiating war will gain Pope Paul IV the praise of Terracina and potentially fame for posterity, but only if this war is fought in foreign lands and against the Turkish or Protestant threats. Her critique of the Pope's territorial wars within Italy is in fact the focus of another sonnet dedicated to Paul IV, "Non hà guari, che al ciel vidi immortali," where she sees Italy in arms, "'l cor mi trema in tempi tali / vedere in volta, e 'n Arme Italia" (*Seste rime* 22, 5–6) (my heart trembles in times such as these, to see Italy toppled and in arms) and thus fears the wrath of God. She condemns the holy temple ("santo tempio") for its wars, and hopes to correct the Pope's actions by using the motif of a mirror of virtue. In the final tercet, she tells Paul to hold in front of him the mirror of the two popes who preceded him, Clement VII and Paul III, and to remember the war and the peace that these men brought to Italy respectively.

Siavi specchio, e memoria, & vivo esempio
la pace, & la gran guerra, che à noi diero
il terzo Paolo, e 'l settimo Clemente. (12–14)

(Let this be a mirror and memory and living example for you: / the peace and great war they gave us / the third Paul and the seventh Clement.)

Paul can ostensibly choose (as he did with Lycus and the shepherd) whether he will be another Clement VII or another Paul III, and in so choosing, determine his place in history. In Terracina's brief history of the papacy, Paul III brought peace and Clement VII "gran guerra," notably a war at home with the Spanish/Habsburg Empire. Thus, the image of Clement VII is to serve as a "memory" and "living example" of a failed pope, one whose wavering loyalties led to the devastating Sack of Rome. Paul III, on the other hand, had also promoted war, but he did so abroad with Protestant German princes. Within Italy he brought peace through a consensus with Charles V, and thus he wins Terracina's praise as a peaceable pope. Her poetics of war reflect a rather humble politics, one that demonstrates an opposition to wars in her own backyard while promoting violence abroad.[57]

Moreover, Terracina, like so many poets of her time, perceives the war with the Turks as doubly efficacious, conveniently taking the killing far from her homeland as well as uniting the deepening factions that mark her times. In her last poem to Paul IV, "Non poteva capir mai nel mio ingegno" ("I could never understand"), she perceives war to be an ecumenical force: it should be fought "acciò ch' una fe' habbiamo" (so that we will have one faith).[58] In this call to Christian war, Terracina resembles her predecessor, Catherine of Siena, where both women, one living during the Great Schism, the other during the Counter-Reformation, saw war against the Turks as a mode to reconcile Christians. And like Catherine, whose letters beckoning popes to a new crusade were published in 1500 by Manuzio, Terracina combines a discourse of Christian righteousness and temporal responsibility to urge the shepherd Paul IV to snuff out the Turks.

> Tu dunque, almo Pastor, sacrato e degno
> struggi il gran turco – hormai fiero e audace –
> con l'ardita tua man forte e vivace,
> per soffogar tant'odio e tanto sdegno. (5–8)
>
> (Oh you divine, sacred and worthy Shepherd, / destroy the great Turk – now so proud and unyielding – / with your courageous strong and alert hand / to extinguish so much hate and disdain.)

Her desire to see the Pope in battle is unequivocal and the "ardita man" that will "soffogar" the enemy certainly seems distant from the poet of the *Discorsi* who had asked that soldiers allow the enemy to escape.

Not only will war bring the Pope honour, it will also confer masculine identity on him. She tells him, "This is the way to show who you are" ("Questa è la via per dimostrar chi sei") (9). Courage at arms is, after all, part of the chivalric ethos so beloved by Terracina, and is the hallmark of masculinity. Thus, if the Pope fights the Turks, he proves himself both as spiritual leader and as a man, and he will ultimately achieve the "honour of the Christian people," ("l'honor de la cristiana seta") (14). Effectively, the Neapolitan woman from the minor nobility counsels the Pope that his private gender identity is constitutive of his public function as leader of Christendom.

That this humble poet could hope the Pope would listen to her advice is telling. She had gained a modicum of renown (precisely through poems that praised men as the rightful protectors of women). Finally, a matter to which I now turn, she saw women writers as having a particularly influential voice in the construction of men's wartime fame.

Chiara Matraini (1515–1604)

Six years after Laura Terracina's *Discorso* was published, the first book by Chiara Matraini was printed in her home city of Lucca.[59] Matraini's

Rime e prosa (1555) is best known as a *canzoniere* of nearly one hundred poems detailing in great part her love for and loss of Bartolomeo Graziani.[60] The contemporary legend goes that the widowed Matraini had bewitched the married Graziani and thus was responsible for their illicit affair. The primary account of the events (recorded by a relative of the betrayed wife), tells us that Graziani was murdered and Matraini virtually shamed out of the city of Lucca.[61] After the tumultuous years that led to the first book of verse, Matraini did not publish again for nearly thirty years, and with this publication, *Meditationi spirituali*, began her definitive shift to more spiritual topics.[62] Thus a scandalous love triangle, lyric love poetry, religious verse, and a few letters are generally accepted as the literary legacy of Matraini. Yet, Matraini finds herself in my study for a work that has thus far been relatively neglected, her "Oration in Praise of the Art of War."

Following the ninety-nine poems found in her volume of 1555 are two prose texts: the first an epistolary treatise on the defence of love, and the second the "Oratione in lode dell'arte della guerra." These chapters, printed in Roman typeface, mark a generic and visual contrast with the nearly one hundred poems (in italic) that precede them.[63] Furthermore, the "Oratione," set in a larger typeface than any other text in the volume, curiously draws attention from the letter and poetry that precede and follow it. The book was thus an expensive production, containing at least three sets of fonts whose format was clearly meant to guide the reader from love poetry in italics, to prose in roman type, and finally to the presumably most important text, a humanist oration on war. Despite the book design and marketing strategies of the printer, Busdrago, Matraini immediately received acclaim for her poems rather than her prose. In 1556, just as the ink was drying from the publication of her first volume, her entire lyric *canzoniere* was reprinted by the famous Venetian publisher Giolito in a poetic anthology, which by definition excluded the oration. Her poems and letters would be edited, altered, and published twice more in the sixteenth century (1595, 1597), yet the oration was not published again.[64] This is not to say, however, that Matraini stops writing about war, for in these later editions she publishes a letter to the noblewoman Maria Cardona (1509–1563, Marchioness of Palude, Countess of Avellino; poet and musician) on the superiority of learning over arms – "Dimostra di quanto maggiore eccellenza siano le scienze che le armi" (Demonstrating that learning is of much greater excellence than arms) (*Rime e lettere* 126–33). Although the texts – one in praise of war, the other in praise of learning above war – might seem at odds with one another, they are grounded in different traditions: the former, an oration given to young men who are facing an impending military threat, the latter clearly part of the humanist debate about arms and letters. The oration in praise of war, in fact, curiously confirms the letter's argument that learning is superior to arms, as it too begins by placing the study of philosophy above all other pursuits. Nonetheless, the apparent contradiction between the two texts has led Daniela Marcheschi to argue that Matraini's two texts on arms signify a change in ideological position, a result of spiritual maturation influenced by the strong reform currents in Lucca.[65] In Matraini's words – echoing Ochino, Valdes, Erasmus, and Varchi – the arms of faith conquer all enemies:

> Quelli adunque saranno buonissimi e valorosi guerrieri e degni del vero onore, i quali seguendo le scienze migliori si spoglieranno dell'ambizioni, dell'odio, della rapina e vanagloria di questo mondo e di tutti gl'immoderati loro affetti e desideri, e s'armeranno di fede, di giustizia, di carità e di tutti gli abiti virtuosi, e supereranno, con queste potentissime armi, i loro interni ed esteriori nemici. (*Rime e lettere* 132)
>
> (Therefore those warriors, who following the wisest counsel, divest themselves of ambition, hate, theft and vainglory of this world and of all immoderate affects and desires, will be excellent and valorous and worthy of true honour. They will arm themselves in faith, justice, charity and all other virtuous clothing, and they will surpass with these most powerful arms both their internal and external enemies.)[66]

Yet if these are the words of one woman to another, long after the wars of imperial expansion in Tuscany and the Battle of Lepanto, how different they are from the oration written in the time of Lucca's struggle to maintain independence in Tuscany and protect her reputation as a city open to ecclesiastical reform.[67]

The lack of attention given to the oration on war by both its sixteenth-century contemporaries and moderns alike suggests a cultural discomfort with a woman's text that praises war. It is, to my knowledge, the only oration or treatise praising war written by a woman in the Italian Renaissance.[68] It bears the markings of a vernacular humanist treatise: Latinate syntax, frequent classical citations, and complex rhetorical strategies – all unsurprising elements given Matraini's acquaintance with Aonio Palerio, the Greek and Latin professor whose letters are published alongside her poems. Yet her oration differs from the prose of other women humanists writing on war such as Laura Cereta, who laments the brutal effects of war, finding only futile devastation and death (Cereta 169–70).

Matraini's text is instead an unapologetic treatise on the glories of war, and it is also a persuasive exhortation to take up arms. The oration is addressed to "Academic gentlemen" ("signori Academici") (99), students of poetry and philosophy, but the details of both the academy and the possible delivery of the oration unfortunately remain unknown.[69]

Matraini, like Terracina, immediately acknowledges the uniqueness of having a woman address the topic of war. But unlike Terracina, Matraini states that there is a moral imperative for her to communicate her thoughts on the virtues of war. Her argument is grounded in the process of reading the ancients for moral and rhetorical guidance. And specifically from her reading, she tells us that she has concluded that the art of arms is the most "healthy," "honourable," and "holy" ("salutifera, onorevole, santa") pursuit for men after philosophy (100). She validates the defensive use of the military arts, stating that they are necessary for the security of oneself, one's friends, and the *patria*, "when reason and necessity demand it" ("quando che la ragione e la necessità ne costringa") (100). Her rhetoric is thus meant to persuade the audience that arms are honourable; more importantly, she will ultimately ask her audience of men to fight.

Similar praises of the military were, as John R. Hale suggests, delivered throughout the Cinquecento "to persuade men to stop despising the trade of arms" (*Renaissance War* 365). Hale's valuable study suggests that in republics "it took special crisis and special pleading" to persuade citizens to take up arms (365). In 1528, when Florence faced the siege of the last republic, Pandolfini argued that arms were superior to all other studies and virtues: "Questa è la virtù della disciplina militare, la quale supera tutte le altre scienzie et virtù" (This is the virtue of military arts, that which is above all other knowledge and virtues), and Luigi Alamanni spoke of the "glorioso et salutevole campo delle armi" (glorious and beneficial field of arms) (quoted in Hale, *Renaissance War* 365).[70] Thus, in language that echoes both Pandolfini and Alamanni before her, Matraini praises the honour, virtue, and rationality of war, all humanist touchstones of persuasive discourse. The approach would have been particularly effective given Matraini's audience, which she states was a philosophical and literary academy, although she gives us no indication of the specifics of this academy or the crisis at hand.[71] In any case, her language does seem to reflect Hale's description of the "special pleading" that marks the orations used in republics by parties seeking to encourage freemen to fight. For, like the Florentine statesmen in the decades before her, she focuses her argument on the social utility of war and to this Renaissance patriotism adds the promise of fame. War benefits the republic and the individual. The military arts (with philosophy) are the most expedient means by which a man may change his social status and achieve glory and reputation.

> Ma poscia se doppo lei [filosofia] nella lodata e bella militare scienza giustamente l'uomo si essercita, quasi da luogo basso e oscuro levandosi, non solo con superbo trionfo se con onorata vittoria de gli avversari suoi ritorna, in alto e sublime seggio tra noi mortali si vede alzare, ma tra le stelle ancora, col nome suo talvolta, tra gli più rari ed eccelsi semidei si sente con eterna lode di sé meritamente porre. (*Rime e lettere* 101)[72]

> (But then if, after learning philosophy, man applies himself in the lovely and praised military science, and if he returns with decorated victory over his adversaries, he thereby raises himself from an obscure and lowly place not only to the highest and sublime throne that lies among us mortals, but all the way to the stars. And his name will sometimes be heard among the most rare and excellent demigods, and he will receive well-deserved and eternal praise.)

Matraini's oration rehearses the epic notion of combat as a method to gain fame and immortality, whereby men can elevate their name "from an obscure and lowly place" to be counted among the stars and become, if not gods, "demigods." But Matraini is tentative at best about men's unchecked pursuit of personal glory, and she restricts men's behaviour by providing examples of captains whose acts conform to her version of correct warfare. She cites military *cavalieri* of classical antiquity who were motivated by virtuous notions of homeland and state security such as Marcus Curius Dentatus and Lucius Cincinnatus, men who denounced absolute power and who valued "virtù" and "povertà" (102). By proposing these specific classical examples, she is not merely demonstrating her erudition but is setting out her parameters of an ideology of correct masculine behaviour in war, the pursuit of fame motivated by *patria* and not economic greed. She thus places herself in a symbiotic relationship with soldiers by reminding them that their fame depends on her written/spoken word, while Matraini's own reputation as an effective orator depends on the willingness of these men to imitate her examples. Just as the fighter hopes to have his name lifted "among the stars," so too the poet who praises warriors, as Sannazaro also wrote, is carried "into the stars" (Sannazaro, *Elegy I*, 101; quoted in Quint, *Origin and Originality* 44). Immortal fame and praise are within reach for the men of the academy and for the poet offering her services, but all parties must cooperate.

Matraini suggests that men who wish to be better captains can find guidance in the written biographies of famous men, "vite de gli illustri uomini" (102), and clearly she is including her own text within this bibliography. Her oration calls to mind the words of Francesco Burlamacchi, Lucca's "freedom fighter," who claimed that he sought to overthrow Medici control of Tuscany after reading the biographies found in Plutarch's *Parallel Lives* (Hewlett 148–52). Matraini's oration in praise of war calls on this Lucchese humanist phenomenon to situate *writing* on the praise of war as a valuable historical force; and, as we will see, Matraini shows that women's writing is the most effective means to lift a man's name among the stars or cast it in shame.[73]

Shame and praise will, in fact, become the binary conceptual categories of the remainder of her oration. Beginning with the grand concept of empires and moving to the particular of the very members of the academy, she contrasts those states that have become glorious by honouring war with those that have been reduced to ruin and shame through military neglect. When considering those states that have flourished, she notes how their success has often been due to their "molto saggi ed esperti capitani" (wise and expert captains) who were able to "infiammar gli animi de' lor soldati innanzi al congresso della tremenda battaglia con efficace pronunzia, con potenti ragioni e bellissime lodi de le virtù loro" (inflame the spirits of their soldiers before the rally of tremendous battle with effective speaking, powerful reasoning and beautiful praises of their virtue) (103). Her captains are great orators, who, like the poet herself, master language, philosophy, and the rhetoric of praise in order to inflame the hearts of men. Specifically, Matraini argues, these captains must use their orations to "invite" men to fight and promise them "riches, honour, liberty and glory" (104). But these captains must also explain that if soldiers "quando da timore vinti cedessero, che la vergogna, il danno, la perdita e servitù di sé come di tutto l'esercito ne riporteriano" (succumb to fear, they will bring shame, ruin, defeat and personal servitude as well as the servitude of the whole army) (104).

Matraini cites the counsel of Cicero, who advises captains to use speech over silence: "E certo è che quando la ben pronunziata eloquenza prudentemente sia usata, ella è molto più giovevole, come solea dir Cicerone, che la tacita e speculativa contemplazione" (And it is certain that when well-delivered eloquence is prudently used, it is much more useful, as Cicero would say, than silent and speculative contemplation) (104). Her formulation of Cicero's maxim could be taken from any number of sources (*De oficiis*, *De oratore*, the first Catilinian), but is more likely a broad reference to the standard humanist interpretation of the Ciceronian philosophy of the *vita activa*.[74] Notably, it is here that the "Oratione" makes an interesting referential shift, pointing not only to the bravery of the ancients but to the author herself. For when she advises war captains to overcome silence for the good of the homeland, she reminds the listener not just of Cicero but of herself, who in her opening remarks explains that she has been moved to speak: "per esser donna, e accettabil fosse, non ho voluto, quasi da vilissima pigrizia oppressa, biasmevolmente star pertinace" (I did not want to shamefully remain obstinate [in silence], oppressed by cowardly laziness, though as a woman it would be acceptable) (99–100). Traversing gendered prescriptions of feminine silence, she states that, although as a woman it would be "accettabil" to remain silent, she has been motivated by necessity to speak.[75] Thus, Matraini fashions herself as a new feminine version of Cicero – possibly a more cautious one, for she avoids transgressing her title of "gentildonna lucchese" by filtering her commentary on war through ventriloquized speeches of historical war generals.

Significantly, Matriaini's rhetorical technique changes near the final quarter of the text, when she no longer employs male historical characters as her mouthpiece but instead becomes herself the orator before the army of academics. Using the second person plural for the first time since her opening remarks, she asks her audience if they will fear death in battle if the necessity arises – if peace is threatened: "Temerete voi in così fatti casi la morte?" (Will you fear in such cases death?) (106). In damning words, she warns men of the result of timidity and temerity: "pazza cosa sarebbe, anzi inumana e bestiale, temerariamente venire alle mani con esso l'astuto nemico" (It would be crazy, even inhuman and bestial to deliver yourself recklessly into the hands of the clever enemy) (107). Her oration thus shifts from an academic summary of the classical episodes of captains and the art of war into an exhilarating battle cry, marking a generic move from an oration to an exhortation. Matraini exhorts her philosophizing soldiers, both praising their virtue and threatening them with shame, all in hopes of inflaming young hearts to war:

> Volete, giovani pieni di vigorose forze, dimostrare di portare ne' petti vostri i cuori pieni di vilissimo e sconvenevole timore, se quelle che femine sono, esse virilmente l'animo altero nel seno loro intrepidamente portano? (106)
>
> (Oh young men full of vigorous strength, do you want to show that you carry cowardly and harmful fear in your hearts, when those who are women fearlessly carry a proud and manly soul in their breast?)

What is evident from the passage above is that the academy is being castigated rather than praised for a (potential) gender failing. Matraini's words, which equate the fear of death with pusillanimity and effeminacy, are recurrent in the Renaissance discourse around warfare;[76] but when they issue forth from the pen of a woman poet, the stakes are necessarily higher. Failing to perform manhood before women is to be doubly shamed. Just as with Laura Terracina in her *Discorso,* Matraini will evoke a woman's right to demand men's protection, and it is no accident that her most stinging image is the fateful example of how Queen Rome was reduced to a poor handmaiden because of men's negligence: "Ah lassa!, di così gran regina divenne povera e vergognosa ancella" (108). In feminine solidarity, Matraini takes up the case of Queen Rome and reminds men of what becomes of women when they neglect their militant duties.

Isabella Cervoni (c. 1576–after 1600)

As we have seen, women's praise of arms and masculinity by the end of the sixteenth century comprises a large textual corpus that struggles to situate the discourses of war and peace in a binary that never seems to adequately accommodate the complexities of the human condition. This false binary is at the centre of our final text by a woman author, a fascinating pamphlet written at the close of the sixteenth century, a text that is a sort of culmination of many of the discourses previously found in other works throughout the Cinquecento. The *Orazione della Signora Isabella Cervoni da Colle al … Papa Clemente Ottavo, sopra l'impresa di Ferrara* (Oration of the Signora Isabella Cervoni da Colle to … Pope Clement VIII about the taking of Ferrara) is part of a flurry of publications from the pen of a young woman in the small Tuscan town of Colle Val D'Elsa. Her works were addressed to the most influential rulers of the times, King Henry IV and Queen Maria de' Medici of France and Pope Clement VIII; and in one instance she issues a general plea to all Christian princes of Europe. Specifically, her oration to Clement VIII addresses the events of 1597–8 after the Pope's successful seizure of Ferrara. When Ferrara's ruler, Alfonso II d'Este, died with no heirs, Clement declared the duchy to be an empty fief and claimed Ferrara and her lands as part of the Papal States. In order to support his claim against the pretender to the title, Cesare D'Este, Clement quickly raised a very large army and threatened attack. As Cesare realized the futility of his resistance to the Pope's large army, he and the remaining D'Este moved their estate to Modena, leaving Ferrara under a non-Este ruler for the first time in four centuries.[77]

Cervoni's oration begins with echoes of women writers previously discussed. She says that she has heard the negative gossip about the Pope's capture of Ferrara and decides she can no longer remain silent. Like Chiara Matraini, Cervoni must put pen to paper, but like pious Catherine, she uses highly self-reflexive language to explain that she writes what the spirit has told her, "mi son raccolta in me medesima, e sentendomi spirata, … metter penna in carta … per dirne quello, che mi dettava lo spirito" (100r) (I have gathered my thoughts in myself, and feeling myself inspired … have put pen to paper … in order to describe what the spirit has told me).[78] The oration then continues for another twenty-four pages, and outlines a history of wars, those that were fought well and those ending in disaster. At the centre of the praise of success and condemnation of failure is of course the political coup that has just been carried out by Pope Clement.

The work, written when Cervoni was in her early twenties, references the author's gender on several counts. She calls herself a "semplice fanciulla di tenera età" (simple girl of tender age) and explains that she had to battle reason and wisdom in order to write to the pope.[79] Cervoni is concerned with the reception of her work, since it is, "diversa da la natura e qualità d'una semplice Verginella" (100v) (different from the nature and quality of a simple young virgin). She suggestively notes that readers might find an exceptional quality to her writing "marvelling" at her work as well as being "stupefied" by it.[80] Cervoni's discussion of her audience betrays her knowledge of the discourse of exceptional women, particularly those involved with warfare: "stupefied" and "marvelling" are precisely the terms that Petrarch had used when he described his reaction to the armed virago Maria of Pozzuoli, and as we will see in subsequent chapters, not only Petrarch but male authors of the sixteenth century repeat these terms again and again when praising women in war. Cervoni is not herself an armed virago, but she predicts this reaction as she has taken up arms of a different sort. She has put away her "needle" and "spindle" to take up the pen and engage in deliberative rhetoric ("genere deliberativo") and discuss war.

The oration, moreover, provides a curious example of a woman justifying why she can write of war. Cervoni explains that as a woman she is not experienced in war, and she fears that she might be interrupted as was Phormio, the orator who, after giving a speech on warfare, was shamed by Hannibal for his lack of firsthand experience.[81] In response, the "donzella semplice" of twenty-two years of age claims she will not be Phormio, because she only wishes to praise the Pope, not instruct him about war.

> Forse interverrà a me, come a quel Formione, che essendo Filosofo e non soldato, volle insegnar l'arte militare a uno espertissimo, e valorosissimo Capitano, qual fu Annibale. Ma io non imito qui Formione, perché l'intenzion mia è di discorrer sopra la guerra con laude de la Santità V. se ben Donzella semplice, e pura. (100v)
>
> (Perhaps one will interrupt me as happened to Phormio, being a philosopher and not a soldier, he wanted to teach the military arts to an expert, valorous captain, who happened to be Hannibal. But I do not imitate Phormio because my intention is to discuss war by praising Your Holiness even if I am a simple and pure damsel)

The claim is of course a disingenuous one, as the balance of the oration will in fact parse the proper and improper conduct of war, telling when one should wage war and when one should wait.

Cervoni reveals her source for the oration to be the "Storie" of Brother Aitone Armeno, known to us as the *History of the Tartars* (1306), written by Hayton (He'tum) of Armenia, a noble general. The manuscript, *La flor des estoires d'Orient*, was originally dictated in French and almost immediately translated into a Latin text that was presented to Pope Clement V (r. 1305–14). The book contains the geography of Asia, the history of the Mongols, and a military history of Muslims and concludes with guidance to Pope Clement V on how to launch a crusade.[82] Cervoni cites Hayton by providing his conditions for when one should begin war (e.g., just cause, adequate resources, etc.), adding her own terms as well as commentary. Not only is she clearly going beyond her stated scope by instructing the Pope about proper wartime strategy, she also brings a solemn realism to the oration by discussing the tragic results of war, a tragedy regardless of who wins:

> Guasti e danni nel paese tuo, e d'altri; rovini d'edifizii; morti nel combattere; assassinamenti di strade, homicidii, rapine, violenze … E quel ch'è peggio, occasioni infiniti a la dannazion de l'anime humane. (101r–v)
>
> (Wreckage and spoils in both your land and others; ruins of buildings, deaths in battle; assassinations in the street, homicides, rape, violence … And what is worse, infinite opportunities for the damnation of the human soul.)

In fact, her oration, beginning as it does with disastrous losses and the warning of eternal damnation of souls, seems more like a cautionary tale than a text in praise of war. She states that war is useless if the conquered land is destroyed in the process, and then gives many examples of wars that ended badly, each tale containing a stamp of admonition: King Saul who waged war without prudence, King Bardano who was brought to ruin when he attacked at an inopportune time, and Marcus Licinius Crassus, whose avarice led him to do things outside of his dignity and age (a man in his sixties).

The numerous negative examples of war are countered by a slim number of positive examples, an imbalance that suggests that this oration in praise of war may also be its condemnation. There are, nonetheless, examples of virtuous leaders (Charles V, Cosimo I dei Medici) and successful military campaigns. The foremost example of a positive war is, of course, the one that had been avoided, the non-war that prompted the oration, when the present pope, Clement VIII, took over Ferrara. The praise of this bloodless conflict, however, is as unusual as its circumstances. In particular, the praise of Clement is tainted by the counter *exempla* that precede it. Take, for example, the story mentioned above in which Marcus Licinius Crassus was said to have lost his dignity by conducting war when he was over the age of sixty. One wonders why Cervoni would have specified Crassus's age when Pope Clement

VIII was himself sixty-one when he threatened his attack on Ferrara. Furthermore, when she attempts to match Clement's military action with the conditions of Hayton, she does not say that Clement had followed Hayton's advice but rather that one should think it to be so. Her rhetoric is notable: "one must hold sure" ("si deve tener per certo"), "one must believe" ("si deve credere"), and "one has to think" ("si ha da pensar") that such a man of learning would have ensured that he had taken all the necessary strategic precautions (110r). Although she is praising Clement for the outcome of the event, we are not certain that Clement followed the guidance of advisers, or if this is simply what one must assume to be true.

Despite her subtle stab at Clement's age and her more overt critiques of the damages of war, Cervoni's oration is still one that was meant to praise the pontiff, and she likely expected a positive reaction, as her last words ask for the Pope's patronage: "mi fosse così la fortuna favorevole nel procacciarmi un mecenate, e foste Voi quegli, spererei far tal progresso ne le lettere" (112v) (were fortune so favourable to me in brokering a patron, and were You to be that person, I would hope to make such advancement in letters). She also implicitly complimented the Pope's style of conquest by providing a martial tale that mirrored Clement's own actions. She tells how Giovanni Comneno, emperor of Constantinople, on his return from victory over the Persians, entered his city by placing an effigy of the Virgin Mary on a richly decorated carriage, drawn by four white horses, while he humbly walked in front carrying a cross (107v). Clement's own entry into the city of Ferrara on 8 May 1598 involved a sumptuous retinue, where the *Corpus Domini* was carried on a crystal urn covered by a canopy and borne by a white horse. This comparison, however, might also cloak a critique of papal splendour. Unlike Emperor Comneno, Clement did not walk humbly behind the holy sacrament but rather was seated on a *sedia gestatoria,* dressed in pontifical costume, and carried on the shoulders of eight horses, under a *baldacchino* carried by eight men. The lavish affair cost the Pope an astounding 150,000 *scudi.*[83]

In her final pages of this ambivalent oration we find the author asking the Pope to bend to her wishes. Cervoni makes a typical complaint in her call to arms against the "Gran Turco" who had assaulted Christian Europe, and she calls the Pope to arms within her discourse of the "utility" of war. She repeatedly states how "useful" it is to avoid war, and she particularly focuses on how it was most "useful" that the Pope did not spill blood in the war for Ferrara. Nonetheless, she is very clear that a war against the Turks would be "utilizzima" (110v). Despite the somewhat unsurprising call for a war against Islam, the passage is remarkable for the way in which a "semplice Verginella" finds a way to insert herself into a discourse of a division of labour, or in her own words, worldly "utility." As women were not – at least in Cervoni's world view – fighting, they were able to write about fighting. By hammering home the concept of what is and is not useful in war, Cervoni was able to remind Clement that fighting was, in fact, the way that men made themselves useful. Cervoni's positive *exempla,* combined with negative critiques, served as a tool to communicate to Clement that his legacy was, in part, controlled by a simple virgin from Colle Val D'Elsa.

Conclusion

The writings of Catherine, Terracina, Matraini, and Cervoni share a common reflexive strategy of turning to their gender as the origin of their rhetorical strength. They emphasize their uniqueness as women who write of war; and they emphasize their right, as defined by the discursive construct of women, to demand that men perform a correct masculinity. The influence women exercised through such rhetoric is formidable, and it did not go unnoticed by their Renaissance male contemporaries.

The effect of women's writings on contemporary war efforts is still to be determined. We do know that they had a substantial effect on the rhetoric about war, when we consider that Catherine of Siena's letters were gathered and published in 1500 by the noted humanist publisher Aldus Manutius, to move armies into action. In his dedicatory letter to the 1500 edition of Catherine's letters, Aldus claims to bring these unknown epistles to light because they "exhortano al ben fare" (exhort to good works) those who read them.[84] Aldus is specifically interested in the thematic content of the letters, which are written to exhort the pontiffs of Catherine's time to take up the sword against the Turks.[85] As Aldus reflects on Catherine's letters to popes asking that they wage war on the Turks, he finds in them a contemporary relevance: "one would think that they were written to the Pontiffs of our own times, rather than Caterina's" (quoted in Tylus, "Caterina da Siena"). Aldus also perceived an expediency in publishing Catherine's letters; a woman's words and her image on the frontispiece could do more to change the current military situation than reprinting another Latin text of military heroism.

The Aldine edition of Catherine marks a crossroads between male-authored texts that praise women and female-authored texts that praise men for their acts in war. Moreover, it sets the stage for the following chapters, which will focus on the generic production of men praising women in war. We might think of the crossroads between these two types of "praise of women" as ultimately tracing a figure eight; Catherine, like all of the women discussed in this chapter, was able to praise or chide men precisely because of the status and praise she had gained from her writings, which had themselves praised heroes and damned unmanly men. It is a recursive cycle of praise that serves both sexes, and yet one that perpetuates the gendering of war, if not the perpetuation of war itself.

4 Classical and Christian Models of Warring Women: From Plutarch to Boccaccio

The remaining chapters explore biographical narratives of women in war. Accounts of women in the context of war include the bravery of women fighters, the leadership of women regents, the vulnerability of women citizens, the personification of bellicose cities as women, and the identification of these same cities with a cadre of elite women.[1] Many women, particularly those known as "illustrious women" in the literary parlance of the sixteenth century, would become common characters in accounts of attack strategies, siege defences, or military violence.

Illustrious women were components in the historiographical framework that was used by authors to tell stories about the present and past. For example, Vincenzo Calmeta's *Istoria della varietà e della fortuna de' tempi suoi in XII libri distinta* ("History of the Vicissitudes and of the Fortune of His Times in Twelve Distinct Books"),[2] a book now lost to time, is one whose footprints point to how women were part of the sixteenth-century "war story." The *Istoria* is only known to us by the transcription of its table of contents, which is an index of its twelve books inscribed in a manuscript found today in the royal library of Saragossa.[3] From this table of contents we know that the *Istoria* included a fifty-year history of Europe and a collection of tales of illustrious women. The index opens with the name of Mohammed II, conqueror of Constantinople in 1453, and ends with the descent of Louis XII into Italy in 1502, six years before the author's death.[4] Calmeta's text purportedly chronicles the battles, sacks, and "betrayal of contemporary Italy" over eleven books; but the final, twelfth book is curiously anomalous (Finotti 123). It is a collection of biographies of famous contemporary women, presenting, as Cecil Grayson calls it, "una specie di galleria di ritratti delle donne più famose del tempo" (a sort of gallery of portraits of the most famous women of the day) (Finotti 123).[5] And it is this last book that provides a mystery or, more precisely, prompts our investigation to learn the missing narrative that explains how a gallery of famous women came to be part of a history of contemporary wars. Specifically, this index of illustrious ladies indicates the unusual or uniquely Renaissance aspect of the praise of women within the epistemology of war.

This central role of illustrious women is nowhere more obvious than in the genre of literature that included compilations of women's lives. Calmeta's twelfth book of illustrious women would have fitted into this genre, one that had already enjoyed much cachet within Italy for more than a hundred years. Of the Italian texts that narrated the lives of exceptional women and war, the best-known example is from the fourteenth century, Giovanni Boccaccio's compendium *De mulieribus claris* (*On Famous Women*) (c.1361). The lengthy tome inspired translators and imitators in the fifteenth and sixteenth centuries to create catalogues of women's lives, and thus functions as the principal, if not singular, origin text of a loose generic category of "praise of women" literature.[6] In this genre of "praise of women" literature, authors often augmented previous texts or simply reformulated the same stories under different women's names. And most texts, if not all, include tales of women and war.

The next chapters look at Boccaccio's *architext* and several other compendiums of women's lives as well as examples of poetry, letters, and dialogues that praised women and war. In recognition of the centrality of Boccaccio's text, I have anchored each chapter with a version of Boccaccio's *Famous Women*. The chapters will move in a loose chronological fashion; the current chapter looks at classical sources through the fourteenth-century text written by Boccaccio himself; chapter 5 considers the 1547 (reprinted 1558) Italian translation and augmentation of *Famous Women* by Giuseppe Betussi; and the last chapter discusses the 1596 republication of Betussi's translation, which included many additional biographies of women by Betussi and the new editor, Francesco Serdonati. As we consider these iterations of Boccaccio as well as other works that praise women and war, it should become evident that the fifteenth and sixteenth centuries were a unique literary moment in the history of the war story. At a time when epics were peppered with women warriors, writers were flaunting illustrious women as the protagonists of a history peppered with real wars. To understand this moment, we seek a narrative that seems unlikely, one not dissimilar to the text from Vincenzo Calmeta's lost book. Between the history of Italy's battles and the histories of famous women there must have been a good story, and to discover it, we begin, as with all things humanist, in Greece.

Plutarch's *Mulierum virtutes*

Men had been writing biographies of exceptional women with some frequency from the Hellenistic period through the Second Sophistic (60–230 CE).[7] Most of these compendia are now lost, and what has survived in extant literature are typically brief catalogues of heroines such as those found in Hesiod, Homer, and Virgil.[8] Fortunately, the primary classical source for the collections of illustrious women that are so typical in the Renaissance is still available to us. It is the twenty-seven stories of women – revised, recounted, and translated throughout the Renaissance – written by the Second Sophistic writer Plutarch (46–120 CE).[9]

Plutarch's stories would, according to Stephen Kolsky, become "common currency" during the Italian Renaissance after their publication in a Latin translation in 1485, and would act as a source text for the compendia of the late fifteenth and sixteenth centuries (Kolsky, *The Genealogy* 42).[10] Found in the great compilation of Plutarch's works commonly called the *Moralia,* the biographies, known to us today as *On the Bravery of Women* or *The Virtues of Women* (*De mulierum virtutibus* or *Mulierum virtutes*), are an extraordinary text that describes the actions of women in a context of war – women who are praised for their *andreia,* "bravery" or "manliness."[11] Even the most perfunctory look at the stories shows the variety of women's wartime roles: the Lycian women are able to curb the tyrant Bellerophon's rage when men's tactics had been ineffective; the Persian women hike up their skirts and ask their husbands where they are running when they try to retreat from Cyrus; the Chian women revile their husbands, who are ready to lay down their arms in defeat; an anonymous Cumaean woman inspires her comrades to revolution by claiming that the only real man among the Cumaeans is the tyrant Aristodemus; and the Melian women as well as the women of Salmantica conceal weapons in their garments in order to aid their men in revolt.

Plutarch's stories of women will be repeatedly retold in the pro-woman texts of the sixteenth century, and most scholars of the Renaissance likely recognize many of the above listed women from the masterpieces of the sixteenth century. In Castiglione's *Courtier,* for example, Giuliano de' Medici recounts Plutarch's versions of brave women (without citing his source): the Sabine women (3.29), the women of Chios (3.32), and the Persian women (3.32). Torquato Tasso, in his *Discorso della virtù feminile e donnesca,* also gives his nod to Plutarch by claiming that Plutarch and Plato are the nexus of a pro-woman philosophical tradition.[12] Though the essay does not recount Plutarch's individual tales, it does invoke the Greek author's name no less than three times, and it specifically places the writings of courageous women in a Renaissance *querelle* context, calling Plutarch's *Mulierum virtutes* "l'operetta che egli scrisse delle *Donne illustri*" (54) (little book that he wrote about *Illustrious Women*). Tasso effectively establishes Plutarch, not Boccaccio, as the founder of the genre that praises illustrious women, and yet Tasso also surely noted how his own list of illustrious women differed from Plutarch's. Indeed, the list of noble, illustrious ladies (e.g., Catherine de' Medici, Maria of Austria, Elizabeth Tudor) that ends Tasso's essay could not be more distinct from Plutarch's women.

Plutarch's brave women were acting in large groups that typically hailed from the common citizenry. The sixteenth-century "rediscovery" of Plutarch prompted an increasing popularity in artistic and literary depictions of such communities of brave women.[13] The reintroduction of groups of women (rather than singular women) into the "praise of women" literature carried with it narrative and epistemological consequences. One such change was that women as a sex were depicted as having a common experience, and consequently, both Plutrarch and sixteenth-century writers told stories of groups of women in war as part of a critique of larger social ills. The Plutarchan text not only modelled communities of non-noble women, it also offered a new implementation of female exemplarity: one that offered a credible chance for emulation to all women. In addition, Plutarch's tales pointed to social problems as well as exceptional female behaviour. His communities of competent "brave women" acted in feminine solidarity, often in response to men's dereliction. On the other hand, epic poetry portrayed marvellous and anomalous heroines (epitomized in Virgil's Camilla and later iterations by Ludovico Ariosto, Torquato Tasso, and Curzio Gonzaga) as exceptional, and thus praised *certain* women's potential while concurrently confirming men's more militant superiority. The Plutarchan women differ as well from most of the Boccaccian heroines, who are mainly singular women discussed at length below, just as they differ from communities of Amazons, who, though they could often trace their beginnings to the negligence of men, were clearly not seeking to protect the stability of a bi-gendered society. Plutarch's legacy is distinct from heroic poetry and from medieval biography in emphasizing women's ability as a sex to perform bravery, to police masculinity (using the mechanism of shame), to pacify militant men, and to resolve men's wartime problems through ingenuity.

Another legacy of Plutarch, admittedly less kind to women's history, is his argument that women's fame but not their bodies should be made public. In the dedicatory letter to the *Mulierum virtutes,* Plutarch addressed Clea, the priestess of Delphi, stating that he finds sympathy in the teachings of Gorgias, who said, "not the form but the fame of a woman should be known to many" ("Bravery" 475).[14] The difficulty women faced in upholding their reputations while at the same time being visible to public scrutiny is of course a theme that will find its apex in texts such as *The Courtier,* long after the writings of Plutarch. And yet, already in the *Mulierum virtutes,* women are placed in a curious predicament where, again and again, their success during times of war is often dependent on the display and use of their bodies. Regarding Plutarch's *Mulierum virtutes,* McInerney argues that Plutarch places women's bodies at the centre of their performances of virtue, stating that "the virtue of women is inseparable from their bodies and the range of behaviors, taboos, and restrictions that are focused on the body, summed up in the notion of shame (*aidôs*)" (328). Women raise their skirts, hide weapons in their garments, and physically place themselves on the battlefield between enemies. In this figuration, there is an irony; women demonstrate exceptional bravery in war by gesturing to their bodies; yet these very bodies are confined and restricted by the praise that makes them famous. Most simply, the tales do not risk breaking rules of decorum, as they describe women who had lived several centuries before Plutarch. Moreover, the author splits the narrated lives of women and men from their bodies in an artful use of analogy. He states that these "lives" are a commodity that can be compared as one compares art: "is it not possible to learn better the similarity and the difference between the virtues of men and women … by putting lives beside lives and actions beside actions, like great works of art?" ("Bravery of Women" 477).[15] In Plutarch's configuration, this is a collection of stories – a collection of artefacts – not a collection of persons.

The paradox of praiseworthy women performing a public and possibly transgressive act that gestures to the body (such as lifting one's skirt) raises issues of imitation and emulation. It would be perilous for women's reputations to imitate such tales. The stories could, however, be used as manuals of courage, particularly for men. Indeed, the stories were the source for a book written to that end. Polyaenus, a Macedonian author of the second century CE, wrote eight books on wartime strategies composed mainly of stories of famous generals. The eighth book of the *Stratagemata,* however, is an assembly of stories based on Plutarch's women (from the *Moralia* and from his *Parallel Lives*), and is often called the *Strategies of Women.*[16] Polyaenus dedicated the entire work to Marcus Aurelius and his brother, Lucius Verus, so that the co-emperors might learn tactics of war from previous war generals and, most interestingly, from Plutarch's women.

The text is provocative and raises the question of why an author would include women's actions in a manual for (male) war generals. One possible reason that Polyaenus and others would find Plutarch's tales useful as didactic literature is that they enact a psychological transference of shame. Men who read of the shaming of non-militant men might consequently experience a similar reaction. The stories recount plots where women "correct" men's behaviour. They shame cowardly husbands so that they will fight, or they arbitrate peace during men's conflicts that they perceive to be without just cause. Women thus alter the acts of men not by taking up arms – unlike epic heroines – but through more rhetorical interventions. One of the most lasting examples is Veturia (a.k.a. Volumnia), the mother of Coriolanus.[17] Though not the subject of one of the stories in the *Mulierum virtutes,* Veturia is described in Plutarch's more famous work, the *Parallel Lives* (ch. 33) as well as Livy's *History of Rome* (II.39.1–40.12), Valerius Maximus's *Memorable Deeds and Sayings* (V.2.1a), and Polyaenus's *Stratagems of Women* (ch. 25). In these ancient accounts, just as in a later Shakespearian form, the mother leads a band of women to the battlefield to challenge her son either to stop his attack or to kill her first. Livy, and Plutarch after him, make of Veturia a browbeating character who shames her son into peace by asking him to reconsider his attack on a city wherein lived his mother, wife, and children.[18]

In ways that differ subtly from Veturia's lament, two other groups of women in Plutarch's texts stopped wars by placing themselves in the midst of battle – the Sabine women (*Parallel Lives,* "Life of Romulus") and the Celtic women of the *Mulierum virtutes* (ch. 6). As Plutarch writes the story, the Sabine women come between two armies, putting themselves between their own Sabine fathers and their Roman husbands. The women stop the fighting with lamentations, and proceed with shaming barbs and sharp caustic argumentation. The women state that since their fathers had not saved them while they were virgins, the fathers had no right to kill their new husbands. The Sabine women argue that both sides should feel bonded by their new grandchildren, and if the war is fought in the name of protecting women, they ask for the fighting to desist, for they should not wish to return to their Sabine homes as widowed mothers, which they equate to being "captives." Plutarch's and Livy's (*History of Rome*, I.9–13)[19] versions of the Sabine story differ in important ways. While Livy's women apologize for having caused the war and ask for pity from the men (I.13), Plutarch's women instead focus on the ineffectiveness of the Sabine men who did not save them while they were virgins. Plutarch thus counters the trope that women are the cause of conflict (a recurrent theme from Homer to Machiavelli) and suggests that women's action in war is necessitated by men's inaction or deficiency.

The act of shaming men rather than imploring their pity is a hallmark of Plutarch's women. There were certainly classical precursors, such as Aristophanes' *Lysistrata*, and this dynamic was then appropriated by sixteenth-century writers, particularly in the tales of Tuscan women of Francesco Serdonati (as discussed in chapter 6).[20] But Plutarch is also one of the most important models for espousing women's diplomatic abilities during warfare. In his tale of the Celtic women ("On the Bravery of Women" ch. 6), they, like the Sabines and Coriolanus's mother, put "themselves between the armed forces." Notably, the Celtic women established peace through negotiation: "[they discussed] the controversies, arbitrated and decided them with such irreproachable fairness that a wondrous friendship of all towards all was brought about between both States and families" ("Bravery of Women" 493). Plutarch's representation of women who had lived three hundred years before him thus depicts a scenario where women "deliberated" policies and strategies, an act usually within the purview of men. Moreover, the Celtic women maintained authority after the war's end. As a result of their diplomatic skills, the Celtic men "continued to consult with the women in regard to war and peace, and to decide through them any disputed matters in their relations with their allies" ("Bravery of Women" 493). According to Plutarch, the Celtic women's authority continued for at least another century, for in a treaty with Hannibal (284–183 BCE), it was stated that any complaint by the Carthaginians against the Celts was to be judged by Celtic women. When sixteenth-century writers revived these Plutarchan tales, they were thus choosing stories that emphasized the lasting consequences of women's interventions in politics and war.

Alongside Plutarch's intervening peacemakers, the women who share the most fortune in the Renaissance are those who urged men into battle. I would argue that these women, rather than the armed viragos, are the most recurring illustrious women in war described in the sixteenth century. Not only Plutarch's stories are translated or recounted by authors such as Castiglione; even tales of contemporary women that presumably have nothing to do with Plutarch seem to be updated versions of his classical exemplars. Two sixteenth-century standards that are taken from Plutarch are the Phocian (ch. II) and Persian (ch. V) women. The Phocian women (cited in the Renaissance texts of Vives and Marinella, and others)[21] agreed to burn themselves alive if their men were to be defeated, while the Persian women (famously cited in Castiglione 3.32) greeted their retreating husbands by lifting their skirts and humiliating them, asking if they wished to return to the wombs from which they were born.[22] According to Plutarch, both events led to victory, and both were commemorated in perpetuity, the first by a festival and the second by a tradition that required any Persian king entering the city to offer each woman a gold coin.

The Persian and Phocian women's acts of virtue, along with many others in the *Mulierum virtutes*, are actions taken, as Sarah B. Pomeroy states about Plutarch's praise of women in general, when men are "inadequate" or "flawed," and, Pomeroy adds, after such action these women would return to more domestic concerns (147–8). I have much affinity with the former point, and this compensatory role of militant women will be a recurrent *topos* throughout the following chapters. However, Pomeroy's claim that the women returned to their previous lives after exceptional actions in war requires a slight revision. Though women may have returned to domestic concerns after battles, it appears that the traditions and laws that are established because of women's actions during war suggest something other than a return to the status quo. In the case of the Celtic women, they retain the right to serve as judges, and in the majority of the episodes, women's acts are memorialized in traditions, monuments, or festivals (e.g., the tradition of giving Persian women gold coins [V], the equestrian statue of Cloelia [XIV], and the annual festival of Elaphebolia [II]). Although these monuments and traditions celebrating women's acts during wartime often do not improve women's conditions directly, they do serve as reminders of women's potential to subvert the rule of order. My own study will indeed focus on such artefacts. The statues erected and the gold coins circulated to celebrate militant women were tangible signposts in the larger *discourse* of women in war, and this discourse certainly continued long after the actions of these brave women. In my study of literary narrations of women in war, we must consider that, like the statues and temples erected to honour courageous women, the texts of Plutarch themselves become a literary monument of women's competencies in war. They were indeed generative in perpetuating a discourse of gender and war far beyond the limited notion of celebrating brave women. In the sixteenth century, the interpretation of these tales created a tension between the emboldening of real women to action and the counter-effect of emboldening men to assert themselves as the militant sex. It was this tension of exemplarity and emulation that made the praise-of-women genre culturally relevant.

Perhaps also because of this tension, Plutarch's tales of women and war held a strong appeal to the writers of the Cinquecento. There were, after all, other tales of more warlike women throughout ancient literature. Examples not only of legendary Amazons but of historical women, such as those found in Ammianus Marcellinus's discussion of strong and threatening Celtic/Gaulic armed women, were available to the Renaissance compilers of women's lives.[23] Although there are a multitude of reasons why Plutarch was referenced more than other authors, one might hypothesize that Plutarch appealed to the Italians of the Renaissance because of a dynamic that resonated between the era of the author and that of the sixteenth-century reader. About one hundred years before Plutarch, Greek culture had been maligned by the Romans under Augustus as "pernicious and emasculating," and Cicero specifically criticized Greek orators, to whom he owed his greatest debt, as effeminate and disengaged when compared to virile, battle-experienced Romans (McLeod 19).[24] Yet in Plutarch's lifetime, perhaps when Greece no longer posed a threat to the establishment of a Roman identity, Greek men of culture and Greek thought in general were more readily absorbed into the empire (Jones, *Plutarch* 138). Glenda McLeod suggests that there is a possible connection between the colonizing of this culturally prominent culture and the penning of Plutarch's tales of brave women: "It's tantalizing to think that Plutarch writes about the unrecognized talents of his heroines at the very time when Rome began to recognize the talents of the 'effeminate' Greeks" (19). McLeod seems to imply that a humiliated and colonized culture may see the advantage in promoting the virtue of women. I argue that it is this situation that will become equally relevant as we move to the sixteenth century. For as the sixteenth century comes to its close and the status of Italy's occupation by the empire is no longer in question, we shall see that the lives of Plutarch's women will become one of the paradigms of choice, providing, as they did, icons of how those on the margins of authority effect real change.

In leaving the ancient texts of Plutarch and Livy for the Middle Ages, it is important to note that this study has covered only the two most prominent literary legacies of the ancients, epic viragos (discussed in chapter 2) and communities of intervening women of Plutarch and Livy. Though there were others, these models were to offer the most significant competing literary types of women in war. Just how these literary types play out in the literature of the sixteenth century may be one of the more fascinating questions as we approach an era that struggled with integrating an ancient past with a burgeoning Christian culture, a culture with its own tales of women and war: Christian female knights, biblical women (e.g., Judith, Jael, Esther), and women martyrs as described in numerous hagiographies.[25]

Matilda of Canossa

Over the past several decades, historians have opened the archives to recuperate stories of medieval women warriors. One of the first studies of this sort was Megan McLaughlin's article "The Woman Warrior: Gender, Warfare and Society in Medieval Europe," which showed that chronicles provided accounts of many medieval women warriors.[26] Among the historical warring women cited by McLaughlin are bands of Danish women who dressed as men and carried swords, the Lombard princess Sichelgaita who battled men with a spear at the siege of Durazzo, and, of course, the "faithful soldier of St. Peter," Matilda of Canossa (1046–1115).[27]

Matilda of Canossa was perhaps the first Italian woman to gain renown for her actions in war. She reigned over a vast region of northern and central Italy and commanded armies during the Investiture Contest, the significant conflict that was to determine whether the pope or the emperor would invest bishops with their titles and associated land holdings. Matilda provided significant military support for Pope Gregory VII in his continual struggle against Henry IV, the German king and later emperor; and as David J. Hay has shown, she proved to be even more formidable after the Pope's death, rallying reformer troops and forcing Henry back to the Alps in 1091–2.[28]

Matilda gained fame in her own life and was remembered throughout the Middle Ages and the Renaissance as a woman of both Catholic devotion and exceptional fortitude. Donizone's *Vita Mathildis* is a medieval literary encomium that praises her military exploits,[29] and we find biographies of Matilda in many catalogues of illustrious women in the fifteenth and sixteenth centuries, such as those written by Agostino Strozzi, Sabadino degli Arienti, Cornelio Lanci, and Francesco Serdonati.[30] She was also the subject of lengthier fifteenth- and sixteenth-century *vitae* written by Battista Panetti, Silvano Razzi, and Domenico Mellini.[31]

The Renaissance biographies focused on her virtue as a defender of the church, and they often bolstered her fame as a Christian heroine by identifying her with the Matilda of Dante's earthly paradise (*Purgatorio* XXVIII–XXXIII). Her inclusion in the pantheon of illustrious women was associated both with her role in the Catholic church and with her acts of militancy, but the biographies typically avoided detailed descriptions of her militant acts. For example, Francesco Serdonati's biography states that she was with an army, but it does not describe her actions in further detail: "andò … con grosso esercito contra Ruberto Guiscardo" (she went … with a great army against Robert Guiscard) or "presò più volte l'armi contra principi potentissimi" (she took arms against most powerful princes on several occasions).[32]

In addition to these Renaissance biographies describing a militant Matilda, there was also a local attempt (especially around the ancestral lands of Canossa) to emphasize her warrior status.[33] By the fifteenth century a small tablet was added to Matilda's tomb in which she was compared to Mars and Penthesilea. And in a much later artistic representation, Paolo Farinetti painted Matilda's tomb portrait in 1587 with the countess riding astride a horse, "like a man," furthering her praise as an "invicta virago" (unconquered virago) (Holman 641).[34]

In her own lifetime, Matilda was the object of much propaganda both favouring and censuring her militancy. David J. Hay's recent book on Matilda's military exploits demonstrates the important change since Virgil wrote of Camilla and Plutarch of his brave women – that is, the advent (or expansion, in the case of Plutarch) of Christianity. Not only was Matilda fighting on behalf of the pope, she was also commanding armies in a cultural context that was codifying Christian notions on warfare and women's comportment (in and out of arms). Matilda's lengthy engagement in war incited passionate responses on both sides. Those who wrote against Matilda's militancy were able to found their arguments on long-held notions of women's frailty and their appropriate roles as subjects rather than rulers. Polemicists writing in favour of Matilda were doubly challenged as they sought to justify religious war as well as a woman commander. In a commentary on the *Song of Songs,* John of Mantua addresses Matilda, asking how she could *not* fight given that the empire was "prepar[ing] the way for the heresy of the Antichrist": "Therefore, servant and bride of truth, when you see dissension arise, will you hesitate to prevent it through your counsel and arms?"[35] John tells Matilda to fight as a Catholic soldier (*miles Catholica)* and even promises that, if she continues to fight "manfully," she is promised beatification: "And so now, Catholic soldier, press upon and impede this dissension ... if you persevere as manfully as you have begun against this heresy that serves the Antichrist, not only will you be fortunate, but you will be forever beatified" (Hay 209). This *virago Catholica* was compared to Esther, Judith, Deborah, Penthesilea, and Mars, and each of these comparisons was used by both her supporters and her detractors.[36] Interesting, if not ironic, is the fact that her supporters had to confront the misogynistic Christian writings that they themselves had disseminated, especially regarding the notion of a woman at arms.

Although medieval detractors and supporters alike called Matilda a warrior, Matilda never became the *sine qua non* example of a woman warrior or commander. For these figures, Renaissance writers would often turn to fictional women such as Camilla and Penthesilea, or the later examples of Joan of Arc and Isabel of Aragon. We might ask why Matilda did not become the emblem for female militancy in Renaissance Italy, and likewise why she has not received more fame even in our own modern day. Matilda's somewhat tepid status as a virago in modern scholarship may be due to our own cultural biases about militant women. In scholarly works as well as mainstream film, television, and literature, female combatants who wielded weapons and wore armour have become the symbols of female militancy. Those who commanded troops have simply been less popular. Moreover, there is a lack of consensus among scholars about what it means to be a woman combatant. McLaughlin, in her seminal article on women warriors, states that we should be cautious when making distinctions between commanders and fighters, since this distinction was not often made for men. Nonetheless, in her own list of women warriors, she excludes, for example, women who only planned battles. As she states, "the decisive test [for a warrior] would seem to be whether someone was present at the battlefield and involved in a battle to a significant degree, not the number of blows she struck" (196). David Hay, on the other hand, defines the term differently, and cautions us not to call all people on the battlefield warriors (9). He notes that although the term *miles* was applied to a wide range of individuals, from the common foot soldier to an emperor who never saw combat, such a term might actually obfuscate the distinctions between the acts performed by these people. For example, he argues that the military function that Matilda performed was quite exceptional and was that of a true military commander.[37] Appearing on a battlefield and making inspirational speeches, for Hay, is to act as a figurehead, but to do these acts in addition to strategizing battle is to be a general. In sum, both Hay and McLaughlin would call Matilda a "warrior" and a "commander." She was far more than a figurehead, and for both scholars the question of her use of armour or weapons is inconsequential.

I will also address the early modern distinction between woman "warrior" and "commander," but I will do so from a more literary lens. The focus here is not to determine whether women did or did not kill or strategize on battlefields but rather how the rhetorical variances between "the warrior" and "the commander" became fossilized in a culture increasingly devoted to praising "illustrious women."

Petrarch's Armed Virago: Maria of Pozzuoli

One historical Italian woman who did garner some fame in the Renaissance for her militancy was Maria of Pozzuoli, an armed soldier who is known to us because of a letter by none other than the great Italian lyric poet Petrarch.[38] His letter to Cardinal Giovanni Colonna (23 November 1343) betrays an ambivalence towards cultural tenets, wherein a warrior woman is at once gender transgressor and praiseworthy *exemplum* of womanly virtues. In the letter, Maria is the "most remarkable" person that Petrarch has encountered in his day's journey, which has included visits to the ruins of great Roman antiquity. Her description begins as yet another encomium of feminine chastity, as Petrarch proclaims her possession of the "merit of virginity" appropriate to her name (52).[39] Maria's exemplary virginity is then augmented since, even though she spends her time around men, "the general opinion holds that she has never suffered any attaint to her chastity, whether in jest or earnest" (52).[40] Petrarch's praise is complicated by the fact that it places her within a social context that highlights her feminine gender, regardless of her obvious attempts to transgress her prescriptive gender roles. Petrarch's letter exposes how Maria is vulnerable to "public opinion" while also implying that joking or "jest" might tarnish her reputation as much as men's sincere flirtations.[41] In sum, Maria seems to be a woman like any other, who is defined by her sexuality and dependent on the good name given her by "general opinion."

Maria, however, is exemplary not only for her chastity but also for her ability to perform masculinity. Petrarch's letter turns to remark at length on her gender-bending, where her body is "military rather than maidenly" and her "appearance and endeavor that of a strong man" (52).[42] Moreover she garners Petrarch's respect by identifying herself with the objects that are coded as masculine rather than feminine: "She cares not for charms but for arms; not for arts and crafts but for darts and shafts" (52–3).[43] Because appearing as a man is not a sufficient means of acquiring masculinity (even for men), Maria is also asked to perform her masculinity through a competition of strength, where she hurls heavy objects farther than other "real" men, thus legitimizing her praise. The competition enacts traditional rites of masculine performance, but instead of inducting Maria into a group of men who celebrate their strength, her victory over the male competitors only highlights a femininity that she cannot shed. The mere fact that a woman wins a contest causes a sort of masculinity crisis where, after seeing her great ability, Petrarch remains downcast and "ashamed" (53).

We hear little about Maria's wartime practices beyond sparse comments on her military bravery and that she fights in an "inherited local war" (53). Given the brevity with which Petrarch describes her reason for fighting, we realize that the letter is not praising Maria's political motivation or virtuous dedication to a *patria*. Nor does it seem that Petrarch is actually praising Maria as an exemplary warrior. His account differs greatly from later ones that detail her role in defending the city from attacking Aragonese forces and from pirates.[44] Petrarch's focus is not on patriotic duty or military prowess but instead on gender bending; he is "amazed" at the gender transgression of a "heavily armed" woman, an amazement that McLaughlin indicates as typical of descriptions of post-twelfth-century women warriors (195). Although Maria is at first mistaken by Petrarch for a man, she is made the object of a gaze that mimics the lyric gaze, focusing on her teeth, arms, and face, all aspects that the author notes are unlike those of other women. The lyric gaze, codified by this very author, is one that genders its object as feminine, bound to a discourse of chastity, and subjects the woman to containment by the male observer/author.[45] The erotic force behind such a gaze is first expressed as marvel. The description of Maria in fact begins with Petrarch's musing on all things marvellous: "Of all the wonders of God, 'who alone doeth great wonders,' he has made nothing on earth more marvellous than man" and the most "remarkable" of these creatures is "a mighty woman of Pozzuoli," Maria.[46] As his description continues, it becomes apparent that Petrarch marvels not that women may contribute to societal military needs but instead that a woman might be able to perform manliness, here in the form of military tasks, thus challenging men's claim to dominance. It is notable that Petrarch contains the threat that Maria poses to men by situating the maiden warrior within a literary and geographical exotic context. He claims that, after having met Maria, he can now believe not only in the stories of the Amazons but in Virgil's Camilla, who was born not far from Pozzuoli (54).[47] Whether young women of Petrarch's genteel daily life could negotiate arms and virginal reputations remains a matter outside the debate.

Like most biographies of illustrious women by male authors, there is a dark underside to Petrarch's praise. After Maria defeats men in the stone-tossing competition, the shamed Petrarch and his male companions leave in wonder, and he contemplates the day's events: "So we left, hardly believing our eyes, thinking we must have been victims of an illusion" (53).[48] The threat of a potential gender (and power) reversal is tempered by Petrarch's consolatory remarks that close the anecdote, casting the entire event into the realm of illusion, where men are "victims" of a woman's deceit. Men are, interestingly, emasculated not only by a woman's ability to outdo them in arms but also by a woman's ability to enchant them into believing they have been outdone. Maria is uniquely praised and condemned for both transgressing and enacting her gender. She represents a host of ambivalent traits: she is chaste, militarily virile, and cunningly feminine. And despite this emphasis on the feminine, the text is quite openly reaching out to male readers, readers who are both consoled and shamed. Though they are protected from any real fear of being overthrown by women, men are reminded of their duty to outperform women.

Petrarch's description of Maria will become a standard fixture in the biographies of illustrious women, and she is one of the most important medieval examples of a historical, sword-bearing woman warrior.[49] Characterized as armed and in battle, Maria is a combatant, a *bellatrix* (to use Petrarch's word), and thus might suggest a different category from the woman "commander" embodied by Matilda.[50] As a *bellatrix,* Maria could serve as a model for later Renaissance depictions of warrior maidens, a notion suggested by Pio Rajna, who opined that Maria was a possible source for the appearance of armed viragos in Boiardo's and Ariosto's romances. Rajna, however, was quick to advocate for more literary sources, from the Amazon queens to Camilla, and the lesser-known Galiziella, the first virago of Italian romance.[51] Rajna briefly raises the problematic relationship between historical women and literary representation, though only to suggest that Amazons had long been in the fantastic consciousness of writers. We might expand on the issue that Rajna only mentions by discussing how authors reconciled the class difference between a living Maria and the noble heroines of romance or, similarly, how they reconciled a historical Maria with the historical biographies of illustrious warring women of the sixteenth-century courts. At the root of the problem lies the very same debate that began Plutarch's *On the Bravery of Women*, the relationship between women's persons and their fame.

Boccaccio's *De mulieribus claris*

Some twenty years after Petrarch's letter marvelling at Maria of Pozzuoli, the towering Italian medieval figure Giovanni Boccaccio wrote a compendium of "famous" women's biographies that includes neither Maria of Pozzuoli nor Matilda of Canossa. It is hard to overstate the impact of Boccaccio's *De mulieribus claris* (*On Famous Women*), typically hailed as originating the literary genre of female biographies that flourishes in the fifteenth and sixteenth centuries (which will ultimately recoup both Matilda and Maria).[52] The work, much larger than Plutarch's compilation of women's lives, comprises biographies of 106 women, primarily from antiquity, as well as a handful of medieval women. In further contrast with Plutarch, all but two of the stories tell of singular figures (rather than communities of women) who have achieved fame for their virtuous or notorious acts.[53] Plutarch's *On the Bravery of Women* was likely not known to Boccaccio, but he did have other literary precedents on which to model his work. Most importantly, Boccaccio would have known of Petrarch's list of illustrious women through a letter of 1358 as well as a compendium of biographies of men in his *Lives of Famous Men* (*De viris illustribus*).[54] Despite the existence of such precedents, Boccaccio's text was a literary novelty, emphasizing secular women's actions in the emerging humanist discourse. Though Boccaccio was aware of the originality of his text, it is unlikely that he could have ever predicted the impact his work would have:

more than one hundred codices of the various Latin redactions are still extant; it was translated quickly into European vernaculars; and it inspired later imitations throughout Italy, Spain, France, Poland, and England.[55] The *De mulieribus claris* is, as Kolsky states, the "architext" for more than three centuries of women's biographies.[56]

The biographies of *Famous Women* include stories of twelve militant women and at least ten others who are otherwise involved in military actions.[57] Militarism, fortitude, and strength are not consistently positive or negative qualities across these twenty-two biographies. Rather it is arguable that the morality of Boccaccio's militant women is conditioned by contexts such as marital status, ambition, and sexual mores. These contexts make it difficult to identify a cohesive commentary on women's use of arms. While scholars such as Stephen Kolsky, Pamela Benson, and Constance Jordan have noted a general inconsistency in Boccaccio's presentation of such powerful and militant women, Margaret Franklin instead argues that his book presents a cohesive message: Boccaccio's women protagonists are praised for being political, powerful, and even militant as long as they exercise this power within parameters that do not challenge men's right to title, position, and dominance.[58] Thus, a queen whose husband is slain might be praised for taking up arms (e.g., the Amazon queens Marpesia [XI] and Lampedo [XII]), while a queen who holds on to her rule for too long, not ceding power to her son, will be cause for derision (e.g., Agrippina [XCII]).

Following Franklin's thesis, Coriolanus's mother, Veturia (LV), was deserving of praise since she was not ambitious but rather followed the orders of the Roman people to intervene in the attack on Rome. Veturia's intervention was required "since the men of the commonwealth seemed unable to defend it by force of arms" (*Famous Women,* LV, 225). In the context of militancy, however, Veturia's story is quite unexpected, for it exposes that even non-combatant women pose a threat to male dominance, and moreover that even peaceable women might be associated with a failed martial masculinity.

After several military attempts to halt Coriolanus from attacking his own city of Rome, Veturia is begged by the women of Rome to stop her son. Convinced that there is no other way to avoid the siege, the aged woman takes her daughter-in-law and grandchildren with her to the army camp to plead with her son. Boccaccio's account of the famous event nearly triples the length of Veturia's speech as found in Livy. She not only states that Coriolanus is betraying his *patria* but also reminds him of her maternal role in conceiving, bearing, and raising him in this very homeland: "Do you recognize this country you see before you? Indeed you do. But in case you do not, this is the land where you were conceived, where you were born, where you were raised through my efforts" (*Famous Women*, LV, 227). Moreover, Boccaccio's Veturia is not merely the mouthpiece of the Roman people; she also demonstrates an agency in her shaming rhetoric: "She had left Rome as a suppliant but, now that she was actually in the enemy's camp, she *became a scold*. Strength awoke in her feeble breast" (*Famous Women* LV, 225, 227; emphasis added). The transformation from a lamenting and pitiable woman, a notably "feeble" position, to one of angered scolding "strength" proves to be effective.[59] Coriolanus famously calls off his attack on Rome, and Veturia becomes the heroine of the story and the protectress of the Roman people.

With the conclusion of the plot, Boccaccio elaborates for several pages on the aftermath of Veturia's and Coriolanus's encounter. One effect was that women were allowed to wear elaborate ornaments, a practice previously forbidden by law. Boccaccio then focuses his commentary and ire on female ornament. He argues that women's jewels and clothing bring ruin to masculine wealth and reverse the hierarchy of the sexes. He states that men "become paupers through the loss of their ancestral inheritance while women become rich gaining it; deserving women are honored, but so are ignoble ones. All this has brought many disadvantages to men and many advantages to women" (*Famous Women*, LV, 229). Veturia's story becomes, in Boccaccio's hands, a vehicle not only to condemn feminine ornament but also to associate it with women's intervention in the martial matters of men. Although Rome may have been spared the sword of Coriolanus, the result of allowing a woman to be the instrument of that peace is to subjugate men to women. And not only patriarchal dominance but men's masculine identity are put into question by the consequences of Veturia's actions: "But what is there to say? This is a woman's world, and men have become womanish" (*Famous Women*, LV, 229).

Boccaccio's narrator does not hesitate to lay the reversal of a gendered hierarchy on the shoulders of Veturia, stating that, "If Rome's liberty had not been saved by her pleas, I would curse Veturia for the haughtiness that women have assumed as a result of her actions" (*Famous Women*, LV, 231). And yet, the sophisticated author could not have missed the fact that that the dominance of women and the "effeminization" of men was modelled in the story of Veturia itself, where a woman scolds a military commander into a position of weakness and oblivion. The "words, groanings, and prayers" of Veturia and her cohort of women were more powerful than the arms of men who had tried to stop Coriolanus and, moreover, were ultimately stronger than the general himself. After hearing his mother's words, Coriolanus embraced his family and "withdrew from Rome" (229).

Such a cautionary tale of female power, where women's courageous acts incur the subjugation of men, is likely more expected in tales of combatant women. It is, after all, inherent (though admittedly in a much different way) in the Amazon legends in which armed women exclude men from their society, kill their male offspring, and defeat male enemies. Veturia's tale extends this feminine threat to non-combatant peaceable women, and it cannot help but make us think of Boccaccio's near contemporary, Catherine of Siena, the intervening woman discussed at length in chapter 3, who shamed men into peace and war with her own pleas. In Boccaccio's *Famous Women,* just as with Catherine's own letters, female actions are often bound to male inaction or failure, and as Franklin argues, in Boccaccio "the dual threat of male decline and female ascendancy are two sides of the same coin" (43).

This two-sided rhetoric of praise and blame is the bad penny that surfaces throughout tales of women and war long before and well after the age of Boccaccio. Yet, Boccaccio's use of this rhetoric is of a distinct tone. Other texts that praise women during war typically emphasize how women's actions are symptomatic of masculine lack: that is, men's negligence often requires women's exceptional behaviour. In Boccaccio's Veturia, there is a more vexing dynamic at work. The actual praise of women, here embodied in Rome's laws that honoured women, instigates the effeminizing of men. It is a troubling conundrum, since so too could Boccaccio's own praise of women create a situation where women were given ascendancy over men and thus recreate the situation that Boccaccio himself condemned in the Roman senate. Indeed, there is an irony when we consider that a cautionary tale about how the praise of women can effeminize men is found in a book that is in great part in praise of women.

To be clear, in the story of Veturia, Boccaccio does not suggest that an exceptional woman might reverse the hierarchy of the sexes but rather that, when one extends praise from a singular exceptional woman to *all* women, the effect is to debase men. In order to deflect the chance that the book of *Famous Women* could replicate the laws of the Roman senate and engender a shift in real-world politics, Boccaccio turns to diverse tactics of containment. He vilifies exceptional women for moral deficit, and he highlights the peculiar contexts of the stories, making them extreme cases far from ordinary experience.

Given the effort made to contain peaceable women such as Veturia, it should be no surprise that Boccaccio's presentation of *combatant* women is even more complex. These women warriors have been the subject of some critical attention, and frequently the women warriors of Boccaccio are credited for their role in forming artistic representations of warring women as well as the armed maidens of epic.[60] As we turn to the representation of women warriors in Boccaccio and other biographical literature, it is helpful to recognize scholarly studies that have focused specifically on them. One of the first books devoted entirely to armed women in Italian Renaissance literature is Margaret Tomalin's *The Fortunes of the Warrior Heroine in Italian Literature* (1982), wherein she includes a short chapter on Boccaccio's *De mulieribus claris.*[61] Tomalin's work offers many provocative if uneven readings of literary warring women as well as providing brief mention of historical women warriors. On the other hand, Lillian S. Robinson's *Monstrous Regiment: The Lady Knight in Sixteenth Century Epic* (1985), a near contemporary of Tomalin's work, offers a more balanced analysis of women warriors in epic. Regrettably, she does not discuss Boccaccio's role in the literary tradition. More recently, Frédérique Verrier and Cecilia Latella have offered comprehensive readings of women warriors in Boccaccio, philosophical tracts, and epic poetry.[62] Cecilia Latella, in particular, crafts a sophisticated analysis of lengthy passages of Boccaccio's *Teseida* and *De mulieribus claris* to argue for the centrality of both works in the representation of women warriors throughout Renaissance literature.[63]

Boccaccio's Female Combatants: To Be or Not to Be

Scholars of Boccaccio's *Famous Women* have overwhelmingly stated that the women in these tales were not meant to be imitated by female readers.[64] Boccaccio himself forecloses the imitation of his famous women in the commentary that concludes each biography. At the close of most stories, there are extradiegetic moments where a narrator provides a brief moral interpretation of the preceding action and then offers suggestions to readers regarding their own lives.[65] The voice that comments on contemporary behaviour is, in Kolsky's view, a second distinct narrator, the voice of the Christian present. This Christian commentator, as Kolsky states, provides a "sermon" wherein "certainty is restored to the text and women are generally put back in their place."[66] Thus, we return to the complex question of imitation and didactic intention. When women read stories of warrior women, how were they supposed to apply the lessons of our *famous* viragos, if not through combat? An explanation may be found in the story of Sulpicia (LXXXV).

At the end of the story of the devoted wife Sulpicia, the commentator states that in moments of unpleasant circumstances, wives should stand by their spouses with courage. In a gendered revision of militancy, the commentator states that giving up luxury and facing poverty are women's "military service," and are the feminine version of fighting for "fame and glory."

> When changed circumstances demand it, [women] must, alongside their husbands, endure toil, suffer exile, bear poverty, and face danger bravely: the woman who refuses does not know how to be a wife. *This is the military service that brings distinction to women; these are their battles, these their victories and their glorious triumphs.* To have overcome ease and luxury and petty domesticity with virtue, constancy, and purity of heart: this is how women win perpetual fame and glory. (*Famous Women,* LXXXV, 353, emphasis mine)

The displacement of women's "battles" from the field of combat onto a domestic space of poverty is to make female militancy into a metaphor, where warfare is discomfort and combat a courageous attitude. The narrator extols the Christian virtue of spousal devotion and constancy, and he implies that militancy, typically understood as armed combat, is not for women. To follow this narrator's advice would mean that one reads of courageous women in battle as one reads an allegory. Warrior women, despite the historical framework in which they are depicted, are but symbols for feminine virtues that have little to do with war. A *famous* woman could courageously wield a sword against her foes, just as the women of Florence could courageously face the slings and arrows of outrageous domestic fortune.

The narrator most clearly lays out this process of imitation and interpretation in the tale of the famous epic woman warrior Camilla (XXXIX). Camilla is not to be read as a warrior woman, nor even as a model of physical or mental fortitude, but as a model of chastity. Boccaccio's life of Camilla tells of her tendency to hunt and her later participation in the Trojan War; but when the narrator addresses young girls who might be the readers, the emphasis is of quite another spirit:

> I wish that the girls of our time would consider Camilla's example. When they imagine this mature and self-possessed young woman wearing a quiver and running freely through the open fields, forests, and the lairs of animals, constantly curbing wanton desire with its enticements, refusing the pleasures and luxury of elaborate food and drink, and steadfastly rejecting not only the embraces but even the conversation of young men of her own age – when they have imagined this, let them learn from her example the proper demeanor in their parent's home, in churches, and in theaters where many onlookers and the most severe judges of conduct assemble. (*Famous Women* 78)

The above passage not only removes any discussion of war, it shifts Camilla's fame away from her militaristic ability to that of chastity and refusal of urban luxury. In her reading of the passage, Franklin suggests that this commentary on Camilla exemplifies how Boccaccio wants women to imitate "virtues rather than deeds of his heroines"; praise of Camilla, in Boccaccio's hands, is not an inspiration for women to take up arms but rather "an allegory of feminine chastity tied to contemporary cultural practices" (Franklin 67). The female emulator of Camilla is also circumscribed by a limited physical space. Boccaccio effectively moves women warriors from the battlefield to the "parent's home" as well as the public spaces of "churches," and "theaters" where the "most severe judges of conduct assemble."[67] Thus, the narrator fulfils the sort of reading he had suggested above in the passage on Sulpicia. Women's "military service" is the daily battle of the complex urban existence. The most limiting aspect of the narrated commentary is that it effectively restricts not only girls' physical actions but their mental breadth as well, as the narrator wishes girls to contemplate Camilla's successful avoidance of men's sexual attention, clearly the less notable aspect of her story. He leaves aside the question of what would happen if girls also were to admire Camilla's sword instead.

Just because Boccaccio asks his readers to interpret armed women as if they were metaphors of other virtues does not mean that readers could not have read armed women to be examples of what they are – women warriors. The text does not completely expunge the militant aspect of viragos, nor, I would suggest, does the author wish to negate this aspect of his protagonists. Much of the rhetorical force of the stories actually depends on the discourse of women fighting. At times, he asks the reader to imagine a *combatant woman*, not merely a symbolic or metaphorical combatant woman. For example, the fact that the Amazons are said to remove the right breast of young girls "so that it would not grow and hinder them in the use of the bow during adult life" clearly brings with it a message of feminine sacrifice but also an implicit commentary about women's bodies in combat. The author asks us to conceive of the possibility of women's militancy in real, non-symbolic, terms. In effect, the reader is to imagine a real woman warrior; yet at the same time the author diverts such a possibility through symbol, metaphor, and moral condemnation.

The most cohesive example of this paradox is found in the vignettes of Amazon stories (XI–XII, XIX–XX, XXXII). The first two stories are tales of successful queens, Marpesia and Lampedo, who become Amazons after their husbands have been killed. We are not told how the royal women were transformed from presumably typical aristocratic wives into trained warriors, but the story does discuss how these women organized their society so that future girls would become warriors. Boccaccio particularly notes that women warriors were created by changing the way that girls were raised:

> Their concerns, however, were different from our own vis-à-vis the upbringing of girls. The distaff, workbaskets, and other womanly tasks were set aside; through hunting, running, horse-taming, martial exercises, continuous practice in archery, and similar pursuits, the Amazons hardened the young girls and prepared them to acquire a man's strength. (*Famous Women*, XI–XII, 53)

The story thus suggests a real-world potential where custom, not nature, determines the destiny of women in the military.

Taken on their own, biographies XI–XII might suggest a potential for women in war. However, the Amazon biographies that follow (Orithya and Antiope XIX and XX) instead tell the stories of two Amazon co-queens who were defeated. In these stories, Hercules easily defeats the "confused" and "careless" Amazons, commanded by Antiope (XIX–XX, 85). During the attack on the women, Theseus, a member of Hercules' troops, seizes Antiope's sisters Hippolyta and Menalippe. The attack occurs while Orithya is away, and the Queen, upon hearing of the defeat and kidnap of Hippolyta and Menalippe, attempts to seek revenge on Greece. Orithya's attack on the Greeks fails because of "dissension" among her allies. She is not killed, however. After the war is over, she and Menalippe are "returned" to their kingdoms. What becomes of the warring queens once they are returned to their conquered kingdom is unknown, for the narrator claims to "not remember having found any evidence" (XIX–XX, 85).

The story is problematic on several counts. The biography of Orithya begins by telling us that she was "primarily famous" for her "perpetual virginity" and that she was also known for military prowess. Chastity is presented as more memorable and/or praiseworthy than arms. Furthermore, the account of her life continues to dismiss her ability at arms, as it avoids any description of Orithya in battle – as wielding weapons or killing enemies. Instead, the story provides a description of what are more aptly defined as actions of female commanders. Both Orithya and Antiope are not depicted with arms; rather their bodies and reputations are kept out of the bloody fray. By emphasizing the role of commander over that of warrior, the stories effectively stress the women's failures; Orithya and Antiope lost their battles because of dissension and carelessness among their troops. Military prowess in these women seems inconsequential.

Although these women could hardly be seen as positive examples of generals, their stories establish certain tropes for later biographies of successful commanders. The woman in war who is described as brave and strong but who is never depicted in the act of killing or even with a sword in hand becomes a popular sixteenth-century paradigm for praising noble women of the Middle Ages and Renaissance. To avoid a story that might tarnish the reputations of real women (a consideration that was clearly not at issue in stories of legendary Amazon queens), later authors typically discussed the bloody realities of war in biographies of women of the lower classes rather than the viragos of the nobility. Indeed, as the biographies of noble women became more *historical* (i.e., describing historical figures), they also became more *legendary* – flaunting names of ancient heroines with bloated praise of abstract qualities such as spirit and courage while eschewing displays of slaughter by the women. We can, for example, compare Boccaccio's Hypsicratea, who had to accustom herself to the horrors of war, with the later tale of the Duchess of Florence, Eleonora di Toledo, who was hailed as the "new Hypsicratea," accompanying her husband on his campaigns. Though Duchess Eleonora was brave of spirit, no mention is made of killing ever occurring in her presence and certainly not by her own hand.[68]

To briefly finish with Boccaccio's story of Orithya, we note that the tale alludes to the life of a woman warrior *post bellum,* the role of a virago once the battle has ended. The narrator suggests that Orithya is lost to historical oblivion once she returns to a land that may or may not have been hers to rule. So too is Menalippe, the sister of Antiope and Hippolyta, when she is returned to the defeated and conquered Amazon kingdom. This plot resolution of course raises the question of what becomes of warrior women when they no longer fight. If these women were once a threat to social norms, they seem to be tamed by narrative resolution. This was not the case in one of Boccaccio's earlier works, the *Teseida* (*The Theseid* or *Book of Theseus*).

The story of Menalippe, Hippolyta, Antiope, and Theseus is recounted quite differently in Boccaccio's earlier heroic poem the *Teseida,* where the Amazon queens both marry Greeks.[69] The poem, composed between 1339 and 1340, recounts the story of the war between Theseus and the Amazons. This poem posits that militancy in women may or may not be a temporary phase. Women warriors, including the great Hippolyta herself, are shown to be swayed from their militant tendencies by the force of love. In the *Teseida,* we read that the women of Scythia murder their husbands, sons, and male relatives in rebellion against male oppression. The women then continue their violence against men by killing sailors who approach their coastlines. Theseus declares war on the Amazons in order to avenge their treatment of men. When Theseus launches his attacks, the Amazon queen Hippolyta exhorts her women not to feel guilt for their past cruelty to men. She reminds them that the reason they killed men to begin with was that they had not respected women. Their husbands had treated them as if they were the spawn "of monsters or oak trees" (I.29, *Book of Theseus* 25).

Although Hippolyta provides an explanation for the origins of the Amazon realm, she is somewhat distanced from the history of its violence. She was a virgin when the great massacre occurred (and thus had no husband to kill), and she is only depicted in her royal domestic space, never on the battlefield.[70] The characterization of Hippolyta as the intelligent, shrewd, young, and beautiful commander who never personally participates in combat is one that should strike us as a departure from the epic virago model. Despite the fact that Boccaccio was composing what he claims will be the first epic in the vernacular (XII, 84), he chooses a heroine notably different from Virgil's Camilla.

Unlike the failed Antiope and Orithya of *On Famous Women,* Hippolyta is an effective commander. When Theseus's troops attack the Amazon shores, the women quickly take the upper hand. It is only when Theseus himself joins the fight that the battle turns to favour the Greeks.[71] Facing potential defeat, the women secure themselves inside a fortress, which Theseus then prepares to attack by digging underground tunnels. In the meantime, Hippolyta commences a fascinating exchange of letters with Theseus, wherein she attempts to dissuade him from besieging her realm. As her weapon of persuasion, Hippolyta shames Theseus for an inappropriate performance of masculine militancy. She plays to conventional attitudes of gender by suggesting that women are naturally inferior to men, and that to defeat an army of women is cause for blame rather than praise.

> Tu non hai fatto come cavaliere
> Che contro a par piglia debita guerra,
> ma come disleale uom barattiere
> subitamente assalisti mia terra,
> e come vile e cattivo guerriere
> mai non pensasti, se 'l mio cor non erra,
> che 'l guerreggiar con donne e aver vittoria
> del vincitor è più biasmo che gloria. (Boccaccio, *Teseida* I.104)[72]

> (You have not behaved like a knight who takes up a just war against an equal. But like some treacherous cheat, you have suddenly assailed my country, and like a shameful and wicked warrior, you never considered, if my heart is not mistaken, that to make war on women and win victory is more to the shame than to the glory of the victor.) (*The Book of Theseus* 40)

To Hippolyta's accusations, Theseus responds that he is holding the Amazons accountable for their cruelty and that he must conduct war as any good army does, taking advantage of the situation so that he may win.[73] The ever-practical (and gender self-deprecating) Hippolyta surrenders. She persuades her fellow Amazons that the women have no chance of winning as they have angered the gods (particularly Venus and Mars) and because they are mere "females" in battle with the great "Duke of Athens."[74] Indeed, Hippolyta confirms the necessity of male protection by stating that "Se di ciascuna qui fosse il marito, / fratel, figliuolo o padre che fu morto / da tutte noi, non saria stato ardito / Teseo mai d'appressarsi al nostro porto" (I.116, vv 3–6) (If the husband, brother, son, or father we each killed were here now, Theseus would never have dared to enter our harbor) (*The Book of Theseus* 42).

Theseus accepts the women's surrender and upon seeing the beautiful Hippolyta falls in love with her, so that the peace negotiations include a marriage between the two commanders.

The marriage not only brings peace between Greece and the Amazons; it also marks the end of female militancy. Hippolyta is placed into a newly feminine role, as are all of the other women. In Boccaccio's words, they return to "what they were before." The women's faces change, their voices soften, and their bodies turn from wielding weapons to exhibiting grace:

> Le donne avevan cambiati sembianti,
> ponendo in terra l'arme rugginose,
> e tornate eran quali eran davanti,
> belle, leggiadre, fresche e graziose;
> e ora in lieti motti e dolci canti
> mutate avean le voci rigogliose,
> e' passi avevan piccioli tornati,
> che pria nell'armi grandi erano stati. (*Teseida* I.132)

> (The ladies had altered their appearance as they placed their weapons on the ground and returned to the way they used to be: beautiful, charming, fresh, and graceful. Now with blithe movements and sweet songs they transformed their hearty voices; and their steps, which had been great strides before when they were bearing arms, became small again.) (*The Book of Theseus* 145)

This striking "return" to a previous state of maidenhood demarcates the period of Amazon rule as a phase of militancy in the otherwise delicate life of women. This phase is what Latella will liken to a metaphor for adolescence and an "Amazon intermission" ("intervallo amazzonico") (200). Yet, to my eye, this intermission seems to be presented less like adolescence than a malady (distorted faces, voices, and bodies), a condition that possibly has no cure. The reversal of militancy is a thorny topic, for even though the women may no longer perform militancy, the memory of past experience remains. For this reason, they are not as "they were before." They have lived the experience of armed militancy. Not only are these women's bodies possibly altered, but so too are their lives. They have been trained in horseback, arms, and hunting.

The text suggests that a graceful woman with a complex history may have been more alluring than a typical maiden. In an almost haunting reference to a past history of spousal murder, Boccaccio tells that "Molte altre donne a greci cavalieri / si sposarono allora lietamente, / e per signor li preser volontieri, / com'avean gli altri avuti primamente" (I. 135 vv 1–4) (Then many other women happily married the Greek knights and willingly took them for their lords as they had done the former ones) (*The Book of Theseus* 46). The poem tells of widows remarrying, but in this case, they had killed their previous husbands. The narrator indeed confirms that the marriage was a cause for some anxiety on the part of the grooms. The men insisted the women sign a prenuptial agreement wherein the women promised "con iuramenti santissimi e veri / lor promettendo che, al lor vivente, / nella prima follia non tornerieno / e che lor cari sempre mai avrieno" (I.135 vv 5–8) (with most sacred true vows that they would never return to their folly as long as they lived, and that they would always hold their husbands dear) (*The Book of Theseus* 46).

As the ex-Amazon becomes the erotic object, we question whether it is her Petrarchan qualities ("belle, leggiadre, fresche e graziose") that make her an object of erotic desire or her militant past. The erotic mechanism of the *Teseida*'s ex-Amazons-turned-lovers brings us back to Boccaccio's later work, *Famous Women*. As noted earlier, there are three vignettes of Amazon queen biographies in the compendium. They begin with two accounts of strong militant women (Marpesia and Lampedo XI–XII), which are followed by tales of the two queens of Scythia, who were successful in battle until Hercules and Theseus famously defeated them (Orithya and Antiope XIX–XX), and conclude with the final Amazon queen biography, of Penthesilea (XXXII), which is in some ways a concluding statement on Amazon militancy. It not only closes the vignettes of Amazon biographies, it mediates the tales of legendary Amazon queens and the reader reception of these seemingly disparate stories.

The biography of Penthesilea (XXXII) is considerably longer than those of the previous Amazon queens. It explains how she began to practise arms, why she chose to fight, how men responded to a warrior woman, and finally, how the commentator wishes men and women to interpret such a story. The description of Penthesilea resembles those of the later heroines of epic in that it begins by emphasizing her noble lineage and beauty. Her beauty is, however, seen as incompatible with militancy: Penthesilea "scorned" her beauty and "overcame the softness of her woman's body."

Her development into a soldier included wearing armour, covering her "tresses" with a helmet, and riding horses "like a soldier" (*Famous Women* 129). Unlike the steadfast virgin Camilla, Penthesilea is then said to fall in love with Hector because of his military prowess. This love, fuelled by his reputation long before she ever sees Hector, is then qualified by her desire to have a child fathered by a fighter as great as Hector. The story is suggestive not so much for the notion that a man's prowess was an attractive quality in the game of love but rather because of Penthesilea's belief that women, too, could be attractive for their military skills: "Penthesilea wished to please Hector with her skill in combat rather than by her beauty" (131). And thus she fought bravely in the most dangerous of situations. It is a scenario not unlike historical (and even epic) accounts of men who are said to fight bravely before their beloveds (male and female), but it is highly unusual that a woman believed men's desire for women might be inspired by military action. Notably, Boccaccio does not portray Hector as swooning for the Amazon queen, but he does suggest that Hector would seek out Penthesilea so that he might admire her fighting prowess.

This erotic element makes Penthesilea's story unlike those of other viragos in *Famous Women*. Although a woman's military competency is said to be attractive to a man, it is important to stress that the biography begins by emphasizing Penthesilea's conventional beauty. An ugly yet highly skilled Penthesilea would likely have produced a much different story. Moreover, if, as Boccaccio states, Penthesilea's "beauty" is hidden beneath a suit of armour, he surely also implies that she is beautiful *because* of her armour as well.[75] After all, Hector's attention is first caught by her military prowess not her beautiful tresses and gentle face. The erotic tale of a warrior falling in love with the Amazon's face and hair is the story of Penthesilea and Achilles, a tale that is significantly not mentioned in the Boccaccian version.[76] Boccaccio instead tells the story of Penthesilea and Hector, one in which a man admires a woman's martial prowess. Thus, Boccaccio sets the stage for the sixteenth-century dynamics of a rapport like that of Tasso's Clorinda and Tancredi.

The commentary that concludes the Penthesilea story provides a guide to help men comprehend female militancy. The narrator delivers a message not to put "women in their place" but rather to shame men.[77] This narrator expresses a desire that Penthesilea's biography should not make us marvel at a woman warrior but should instead remind us that women can perform virile acts just as men can become cowardly:

> Some may marvel at the fact that there are women, however well armed, who dare fight against men. But admiration will cease if we remember that practical experience can change natural dispositions. Through practice, Penthesilea and women like her became much more manly in arms than those born male who have been changed into women – or helmeted hares – by idleness and love of pleasure. (*Famous Women* 131)

The male reader is like Hector, watching the deeds of an exceptional woman and admiring her skill. How the reader fares in a comparison to Hector, however, is what the narrator puts at issue.

The commentary also raises a question of two ideal readers, possibly split by their gender. If, as Franklin and Kolsky suggest, the female reader was to believe that militant women were metaphorical symbols of strength and virtue and not, in fact, meant to inspire women to rise "fully armed from the *palazzi of* Trecento Florence" (Franklin 8), then somehow the male reader was meant to believe something different. In order to be shamed by such a story, the male reader was supposed to believe that women warriors were indeed a threatening reality – not that women were likely to raise an Amazon army but that they *could* and *would* do so if men did not resume their activities as the warrior sex.

As another hypothesis, Boccaccio may have hoped not that men would read the stories one way and women another, but rather that, with each story's close, male and female readers would be as the male warriors and ex-Amazons of Hippolyta's troops in the *Teseida*. The women would be again "how they were before," "belle, leggiadre, fresche e graziose" maidens, yet now with a knowledge of women's capabilities. Male readers were likewise meant to love these beautiful maidens, but also to be aware and even wary of a potential that lurked beneath a veneer of poetic conceit. Such a state might create enough anxiety among men to motivate them to retain dominance and yet respect women for their ability to return at any time to being the militant sex.

Gender Switching: Beyond *Famous Women*

My reading of ex-Amazons and anxious male warriors is a tale of how Boccaccio might have wished the world to be. In his commentary on

Penthesilea, he confirms instead what was a more anxious vision, that the world was slipping into a state where women were in the ascendancy and men defeated. The arming of women, he reminds us, is a reversal of power told through gender metamorphosis. Women partially "overcome" their sex while men are prone to a gender slippage, wherein they *become* women or hares: "Through practice, Penthesilea and women like her became much more manly in arms than those born male who have been changed into women – or helmeted hares – by idleness and love of pleasure."[78] Penthesilea "and women like her" fill the pages of *Famous Women.* These women scorn beauty, manipulate their bodies, and even teach themselves to witness the horrors of war and accompany their husbands throughout their military campaigns. The Boccaccian text establishes a paradigm that contrasts each sex's relation to militancy; women *overcome* femininity, and men *become* women. Moreover, we will see this model resonate throughout the Cinquecento. The Venetian diarist Girolamo Priuli easily calls men who are defeated in battle "women" and "whores," and Machiavelli writes that the French begin their battles as men and finish as women because they fear death and fight like cowards.[79] In effect, these texts tell us that masculinity and even maleness must be performed in battle in order for men to lay claim to their gender. Much like the men of the tale of Penthesilea, men are "changed into women" if they do not adequately perform militancy. On the other hand, the gender/war paradigm differs for women, where warriors like Penthesilea perform masculinity on the battlefield so that they might "overcome" the feminine. The difference between overcoming one's sex and actually becoming the opposite sex is significant; for in the former, one is still presumably beholden to the restrictions or constructs of the original sex.

If we consider our original medieval Italian virago, Matilda of Canossa, we see that this very issue is taken up in the propaganda surrounding her life. David Hay describes how Christian writers such as the author of Matilda's *Vita*, Donizone, found it easier to explain women's bravery in terms of manliness rather than by expanding the definition of femininity to encompass virtues that were contrary to the patristic Christian teachings. In Hay's words, "[t]ransformation was easier to explain than contradiction" (212). Accordingly, Matilda had been fashioned as an "honorary man" by stating that she too had "'overcom[e] her sex'" (212). I would revise Hay's analysis to suggest that "transformation" is likely not the right word, or at least to consider that these gender transformations are incomplete ones.

Though Donizone's Matilda and Boccaccio's Penthesilea may "overcome" their fears, they cannot avoid the social condemnations that criticize their acts as causally linked to their feminine gender. For example, the manly Matilda is accused of committing war out of "'female rage'" (Hay 204). It is a contradiction that is in fact created by the rhetorical technique of gender ambiguity, for even when women are said to be or appear to be men, they are nonetheless inscribed in a discourse of femininity that binds women to a position of disempowerment that is always firmly under the control of patriarchy.

Conclusion

In the wake of Petrarch and Boccaccio, we move into a time when texts about women and war become much more common. The next chapter analyses works from the late fifteenth and early sixteenth centuries, that critical moment when Vincenzo Calmeta wrote the *Istoria,* the mysterious book mentioned at the beginning of this chapter. It should quickly become apparent that when Calmeta concluded his narrative of Europe's wars with a book of illustrious women, he was participating in a tradition that Boccaccio and Petrarch had established.

The remaining chapters question how these tales of illustrious women change as we move across the centuries. The sixteenth century brought with it the Italian Wars and decades of invasions that left the peninsula vulnerable to occupying foreign forces. These invasions incited new discourses of war where the stakes of correct gender performance were raised to reflect nothing short of state security. Italy was conceptualized as the effeminized and defeated penetrated body, and the war rhetoric that mobilized forces around this body both condemned the effeminized Italian male and sought to effeminize the enemy.[80] Our goal will be to understand just how women were represented in these discourses of resistance and defeat.

5 The Noble Warrior Woman (1440–1550)

Of Arms and Ladies

Social class had an important effect on the encomia of women in war. Competitions of strength and prowess, such as those discussed in Petrarch's letter about the virago Maria of Pozzuoli, would have generated little praise for elite women.[1] Biographies of noble ladies in war, unlike those describing low-born women, emphasized feminine decorum in addition to courage. Such acclaim required a precarious poetry; consequently, when historical noble viragos were praised, they were rarely depicted as bearing arms.[2] John C. McLucas has already observed that class influenced the ways in which women in Castiglione's *Cortegiano* were depicted when he noted that women combatants in the book are described as of a lowly state ("di basso grado") (III.36), while the queens praised in warfare are engaged in "non participatory surveillance" (37). The sword-wielding peasant woman is different from the wise noblewoman commander. Such a division is drawn out in metaphorical and even mythological terms by Vincenzo Sigonio, who in his *La difesa per le donne* (*Defence for Women*) explains that the goddess Bellona is a passionate warrior while Minerva is a prudent strategist:

> fosse tra loro questa differenza, che Minerva mostrasse l'accorto provedimento, il buon governo e il saggio consiglio che usano i prudenti e valorosi capitani nel guerreggiare, e Bellona l'uccisioni, il furore, la strage e la rovina che nei fatti d'armi si vegono. (145)

> (there was between them this difference: that Minerva would demonstrate the wise measure, good government, and sage counsel that prudent and

valorous captains use in the art of war, while Bellona showed the slaughter, furor, carnage, and ruin that one finds in deeds of arms.)

Minerva, a member of the most royal triad of deities, the Capitoline triad (along with King Jupiter and Queen Juno), is likened to a "valorous captain," while the lower-ranking goddess Bellona demonstrates the massacres that one sees on battlefields. The separate professions of woman commander and woman warrior, personified in Sigonio's descriptions of the mythological Minerva and Bellona, delineate a division of class that we will also find reflected in texts that praise historical women. It is, however, not a consistent distinction, and it will be particularly blurred as we shuttle between fiction and history.

This chapter takes up the representation of female militancy in praises of historical women in texts dating roughly but not exclusively from the mid-fifteenth to the mid-sixteenth century. At issue are both the interimplication of class and genre and the question of the imitation of female exemplars. I begin by discussing noblewomen's power to police war activity through observation and surveillance, and I will conclude the chapter with a study of the biographies of women who are more actively involved with war, women who are portrayed as victims, combatants, or commanders. These final stories hail from the 1547 translation and expansion of Giovanni Boccaccio's Latin compendium of famous women. Thus, through their association with Boccaccio's text, they form part of what I argue is the core of the illustrious-women genre in the Italian Renaissance.

Theatre of War

A recurrent literary *leitmotiv* in descriptions of women and war is the actively vigilant woman. Unlike the figures of the historical Maria of Pozzuoli or the fictional Bradamante, this model of woman was particularly suited for emulation by the female patriciate. A woman of noble rank, physically present at the battlefield, and usually in a prominent position above the fighting, passes judgment on the men below.

The gaze of women from afar is by no means a modern topos in literature. Among the most important examples from the Western canon are Helen and Andromache atop the walls of Troy and the women who watched the crucifixion of Christ.[3] These stories arguably establish "women who watch" as central figures in the memorialization of death and lament. In *Iliad* III, Helen is called to watch the battle of Paris and Menelaus. This narrative focuses not on Helen's observations of her husband Paris as much as her conversation with her father-in-law, Priam, a conversation in which she identifies the enemy Greek soldiers on the field. In a later episode from *Iliad* XXII, the gaze of a different woman, Andromache, is directed solely on her beloved Hector. The miserable Andromache gazes in horror as Achilles drags Hector's dead body round the walls of Troy.

These ancient scenes of women watching men are echoed in Renaissance praises of women discussed below, but most of the texts I discuss describe a more active female gaze than the mournful observations of Andromache or the women at the cross. The Renaissance women discussed below are presented as watching men fight in order to ensure manliness, courage, and victory. They incite a reaction in the male hero by triggering a sense of shame (or the fear of being shamed). Using the power of the female gaze, women are given a role in the salutary function of shame, thus exercising their ability to ensure victory.

The power of the gaze to enact the mechanism of shame is well discussed in modern criticism and has roots in both Plato and Aristotle.[4] In his *Symposium,* Plato explains that the gaze of a beloved motivates nobility and heroic acts in war. Phaedrus states that the lover is ashamed to be seen by his beloved doing cowardly things, and thus he argues that armies should be composed of lovers and beloveds, since "they would hold back from anything disgraceful and compete for honour in each other's eyes" (178e).[5] The Platonic example is notably one where beloved and lover are both men, a fact that is meaningful, since both parties, as Phaedrus explains in his discussion of Achilles, are capable of fighting in war (179–180a).[6] Renaissance epic poets, in particular Tasso, also portrayed scenes of male beloved/friendly warriors, but these couples, instead of ensuring victory in war, often highlighted the dangers and pitfalls of same-sex attraction.[7] There were, however, positive, notably heterosexual, models of the warrior and beloved. Leaving the well-known figurations of warrior couples aside for a moment (e.g., Ruggiero/Bradamante and Rinaldo/Clorinda), we see below how the Renaissance praise-of-women genre effectively alters the Platonic figuration of a beloved spectator from male beloved to female.

For Plato, the inspiration to heroic acts is determined more by the power of the onlooker than the virtue of the hero himself, a dynamic well rehearsed in modern theory.[8] The question of *who* is watching is also at the centre of Aristotle's explanation of shame in the *Rhetoric*. The Stagirite's writings on shame appear in various places, most notably in the *Nicomachean Ethics* (IV, 9) and the *Rhetoric* (II, 6), but it is in the *Rhetoric* where he explains that shame occurs when one is watched by "a person you respect," and that the type of shame experienced differs if one is observed by strangers or friends. Notably, both Aristotle and Plato give primacy to the gaze in shame, and Aristotle reminds us of the proverb that "Shame sits in the eyes."

In both Plato and Aristotle gender is central to the discussion of honour and shame.[9] It is thus interesting that the Renaissance writers who take up the issue of the surveillance of men in battle choose women to be the principal onlookers, not only as the lamenting victims (like those showcased in Homer and the Bible) but as the protagonists in a dynamic that alters the battle. The staging of the event may even be said to be a hallmark of the Middle Ages and Renaissance. It enacts a spectatorship where women praise or criticize performances, and in this theatre of war, men compete for the favour of their female audience.

The spectacularization of war is of course not limited to dynamics of shame. Leo Braudy's sweeping work on masculinity and war, from chivalry to the terrorist attacks of 11 September 2001, highlights another function of the gaze, the importance of making virtue a public matter in war, a publicness that often needs an audience, an audience that he will argue may be real or imagined. Braudy argues that battle is the key moment when the sense of personal honour is transmitted into a public social fact (Braudy 56–62): "it is preeminently in war that men make themselves men in the eyes of other men and in their own" (56). The soldier is performing a "fantasy of acting honorably in front of an audience" in order to garner a reputation (56). And he must avoid shame before the gazing public, an audience, that as Braudy states, might "even be an imagined one" (57). Braudy insists on the dichotomy between the personal sense of honour and the need for public validation of honour through observed acts. The gaze of other men is necessary for a masculine warrior's reputation; but also, he explains, in medieval displays of literary knighthood and chivalry, the audience was often female. In chivalric tales, knights fought before maidens, and in tournaments and jousts men performed before audiences of women who gazed on their public performances of honour.

In her book on medieval masculinity, Ruth Mazo Karras problematizes these knightly tournaments before the gaze of women. She adopts the pun "mail bonding" to argue that while women were essential to the discourse that surrounded chivalric masculinity, the competition that played out between knights was performed with the end goal of impressing other men (20–66). Her nuanced discussion does not subtract women from the triangulation; rather, she exposes the male anxieties that lie within the large corpus of chivalric literature that claims that men fight for and before the love and gaze of women.[10] Women's love ostensibly incited men's prowess, and men who succeeded in military matters were erotically desirable. Thus, as Karras argues, men's prowess and women's love "existed in a sort of symbiotic relationship" where "the man's success in deeds of arms obliged the woman to love him, and her love spurred him to further deeds not only by inspiring him but also by supporting him financially" (54).

As Karras makes evident, much of the display of men's prowess was in courtly tournaments, a spectacle clearly attended by women. Women could also guarantee men's military valour in their absence by giving men tokens to carry into battle, thus providing a material substitute for the otherwise scrutinizing female gaze.[11] Fighting on the battlefield provided fewer possibilities for theatricality or spectatorship than were available in tournament games. Therefore, the recurrent notion of visualized war in literary texts and historical chronicles should raise an eyebrow, especially given the difficulty of creating an audience, especially an audience that includes women. On the battlefield, how might we reconcile Braudy's notion of an audience for honour, "even an imagined one," with Karras's observations on the role of women in homosocial wartime bonding?

In no place is the issue of a gendered spectatorship in war more complex than in Baldassare Castiglione's *Book of the Courtier.* Castiglione, among the most adept Renaissance theorizers of spectatorship, lays bare the process by which a soldier might create an audience for his military performance. In Book II of the *Courtier*, the speaker Federico Fregoso explains how a soldier should ensure his observance and thus garner praise.

> Pur sotto la nostra regola si potrà ancor intendere, che ritrovandosi il cortegiano nella scaramuzza o fatto d'arme o battaglia di terra o in altre cose tali, dee discretamente procurar di appartarsi dalla moltitudine e quelle cose segnalate ed ardite che ha da fare, farle con minor compagnia che po ed al conspetto de tutti i più nobili ed estimati omini che siano nell'esercito, e massimamente alla presenzia e, se possibil è, inanzi agli occhi proprii del suo re o di quel signore a cui serve; perché in vero è ben conveniente valersi delle cose ben fatte. (II.8)

> (Yet you may also take it to be implied in our rule that whenever the Courtier chances to be engaged in a skirmish or an action or a battle in the field, or the like, he should discreetly withdraw from the crowd, and do the outstanding and daring things that he has to do in as small a company as possible and in the sight of all the noblest and most respected men in the army, and especially in the presence of and, if possible, before the very eyes of his king or the prince he is serving; for it is well indeed to make all one can of things well done.) (*Courtier* 72)

Federico uses this description of the man on the battlefield as an example of *sprezzatura*. And not surprisingly, the advice he gives the courtier at arms is fraught with the ambivalence that typifies Castiglione's book as a whole; in this case, discreet withdrawal is meant to make a man less discreet. Ultimately, the soldier is to perform his military duty under the watch of a gazing (male) public so that he might receive reward. The episode exemplifies the necessity of spectatorship for the recognition of honourable deeds, but it also chillingly highlights the self-serving motives of soldiers. Federico's comments here and elsewhere imply that a courtier should, in fact, never risk his life unless he is observed, for the only reason a courtier fights is to gain honour and praise. Federico complicates this spectatorship of militancy by then likening such real battle experience to jousts and tournaments, situations in which a courtier should "strive to be … elegant and handsome" (II.8; 73) in order to attract the attention of women. The fighting man who was discreetly withdrawing so as to be observed better by men is, at the tournaments, ostensibly turning his thoughts to women.

In Federico's discussion, women are given to be acutely concerned with men's performance of military *sprezzatura* as mediated by games, and yet they are absent from the battles where they might directly scrutinize men's military performance. Thus, the summation of Federico's speech suggests that women are meant to judge men's ability at simulating war through ludic performance, while men scrutinize "real" war. In both cases, a gazing public is necessary to ensure honourable acts. Women, in this idyllic paradigm, are far from the gruesome battlefield because their sensibilities are meant to be incompatible with the gore of war.[12]

Women watching men pretend play at war fits nicely with the text's courtly frame, wherein the duchess and her attendants gaze on male courtiers who comically banter about politics while circumventing real discussions on tyranny. In my reading of the *Courtier*, however, such rhetorical play also allows for the potential for real change. For example, in Book III, the Magnifico praises famous women from antiquity who were often directly involved in warfare, either as warriors or as bold orators who verbally shamed their husbands into fighting (e.g., the women of Chios and Persia) (III.32). These stories of women of classical times who shame men are potentially used to mobilize gender as a means to shore up masculinity among the audience and readers of such texts.[13] The tales of such famous women suggest how women might assume an active role in the construction of military masculinity and, specifically, that women might incite a change in the political and military situation of contemporary Italy.

Castiglione's female *exempla* are from a host of classical sources, including Plutarch's *Mulierum virtutes,* discussed in the previous chapter.[14] In Plutarch, the Persian women greet their retreating men outside the city walls, lift up their skirts, and shame them by asking the men if they intend to flee back into the womb. In the *Courtier,* instead, the story is revised with courtly decorum as Castiglione removes the vulgar gesture from the tale, limiting their act to a verbal assault.[15] Clearly, such a retelling fits the program of decorum that characterizes the text, but it also would bring these classical stories closer to the realm of imitable behaviour for the Urbino noblewomen. I suggest that these stories of famous women were retold not necessarily so that they would be imitated by Castiglione's female contemporaries but rather so that they might serve the purpose of literary monuments. The stories of women doing brave acts in war would recall and even honour the potential of feminine power. For, while it is unlikely that Castiglione expected Emilia Pia and Elisabetta Gonzaga to imitate the women of Chios or Persia, he might have hoped that the narration of such stories would have mobilized men into action by erecting a narrative reminder of the potential of women in war.

How the ladies of the Urbino court received such a story would depend on questions of class. If on the one hand, tales of Persian townswomen were quite distant from these women's experiences, on the other, the anecdotes of peers, women of the court, would have resonated as recognizably familiar. Castiglione's model of a *courtly* heroine in war is the exemplary figure of Queen Isabella of Spain.

In two separate moments, Castiglione describes the Spanish queen as inspiring troops in victory. In the first episode, Isabella is praised as a competent ruler in arms, and to her is given the sole responsibility for Spain's victory over the Moors in Granada. Her rule was so "divine" that she was able to "make every man do what he was supposed to do" (III.35; 174), and this influence over men, even when these men are "in secret," suggests the power of surveillance over behaviour, a power that is enforceable even when the authoritative gaze is not physically present. It is the mere possibility of Isabella's observation that polices her realm, and it is this internalization of surveillance that will then continue to function after her death. In fact, the people of Spain, according to Castiglione, are so motivated by both "love and fear" of the dead queen, that "it almost seems that they expect her to be watching them from heaven, and think she might praise or blame them from up there" (III.35; 174). According to Castiglione, this policing mechanism is what made her troops successful in Granada during her lifetime and what motivates Spain's captains after her death.

In the second episode, the military captain Cesare Gonzaga recasts the victory of Spanish forces in Granada in a slightly different scenario. In this retelling of the event, Gonzaga explains that Isabella and her maids of honour would accompany the soldiers to the battlefield so that Isabella could wield what John C. McLucas calls her "ultimate weapon," her presence.[16] The presence of Isabella and her maids at the battlefield is depicted in historical sources, including the *epistolario* of Pedro Mártir de Anglería,[17] but it is Castiglione who dramatizes the union of love and war, stating that women would converse with their beloved soldiers until they came upon the enemy. When the couples separated, the women became audience and inspiration for the fighting men:

> poi, pigliando licenzia ciascun dalla sua, in presenzia loro andavano ad incontrar gli nimici con quell'animo feroce che dava loro amore, e 'l desiderio di far conoscere alle sue signore che erano servite da omini valorosi; onde molte volte trovaronsi pochissimi cavalieri spagnoli mettere in fuga ed alla morte infinito numero di Mori, mercé delle gentili ed amate donne. (III.51)

> (then each would take leave of his own lady; and, with the ladies looking on, they would go forth to meet the enemy with the fierce spirit that love gave them, and with the desire to show their ladies that they were served by men of valor; hence, a very small band of Spanish cavaliers was often seen to put a host of Moors to flight and death, thanks to the gentle and beloved ladies.) (*Courtier* 188–9)

Castiglione's description of Isabella's contribution to the war effort differs slightly from that in an earlier text, likely the first Italian praise of Isabella during the war of Granada, Sabadino degli Arienti's *Gynevera de le clare donne* and his separate "Elogio di Isabella" (c. 1493).[18] Like Castiglione, Arienti suggests that Isabella followed Ferdinand near the battlegrounds. In his "Elogio," he states that her contribution was to "inflame" the king, "not as Hypsicratea had done, dressed as a man," but by providing five hundred wagons of medicinal herbs and by staying in the camps with her many virgins and praying for the success of the king's troops.[19] Arienti makes explicit what Castiglione only implies: noblewomen are not meant to don armour and enter into combat. Moreover, Arienti describes Isabella within the established feminine roles of nurse and pious wife. It is a description that differs from both episodes of the *Courtier*, where she functions as an agent of the loving gaze that can encourage but also critique the acts of fighting men.

If Castiglione's first episode told of an imagined and deceased Isabella who gazed on men's actions, the second example (in which she and her maids approached the battlefield) is more problematic. In a situation that parallels Plato's discussion of the beloved in war, Castiglione brings women physically to the battle and argues an unequivocal purpose for women's presence in war.[20] It is a moment that conflates the battlefield and the tournament in interesting ways. While, in an earlier moment, Federico had gendered the audiences of "real war" as masculine and those of games as feminine, here, in Castiglione's account (in the speaker of Cesare Gonzaga), the two spaces are noticeably blended. The audience of war is now a female one, and in Granada it includes the Queen. Gonzaga's account of the victory at Granada not only opens a space for female agency in warfare, it provides an imitable role for the ladies of the Urbino court – most importantly the duchess – giving these women both opportunity and responsibility in the military future of Italy.

We can see that the configuration of women at the battlefield became entrenched in the utopic vision of Tommaso Campanella's *City of the Sun* (*Città del sole*) (1602), written about eighty years after the *Courtier*. In Campanella's fabled land of Atlantis, women and young boys both come to the battlefield: in certain cases, women are allowed to fight in a city's defence (as they did in Thomas More's *Utopia*), and boys are to be trained to be accustomed to blood. Women and children are also said to provide comfort to the men when they come back from the front lines, and most notably, the women and children inspire the men to fight courageously:

> Soleno portar seco una squadra di fanciulli a cavallo per imparar la guerra, ed incarnarsi, come lupicini al sangue; e nei pericoli si ritirano, e molte donne con loro. E dopo la battaglia esse donne e fanciulli fanno carezze alli guerrieri ... per mostrarsi valenti alle donne e figli loro, fanno gran prove. Nell'assalti, chi prima saglie il muro ha dopo in onore una corona di gramigna con applause militari delle donne e fanciulli. (Campanella, *Città* [1981] 72)

> (Customarily, they also have a squadron of boys, mounted on horseback, to habituate themselves, like whelps, to the sight of blood. In time of danger, these are ordered to withdraw, as are also the women. When the battle is over, the boys and the women comfort the warriors ... To show their worth before eyewitnesses, the warriors display extraordinary courage. The first to scale the walls in an assault is afterwards honored with a crown of couch grass and the applause of the assembled women and boys.) (*Città* [1981] 74)

Castiglione's appropriation of the Platonic trope of Phaedrus watching men at war is thus rewritten again in Campanella's Counter-Reformation reworking of Plato's utopic *Republic*. Campanella goes on to explain the darker side of this coin, where the first to retreat is condemned to death: "chi fu il primo a fuggire non può scampare la morte" (72) (The first to flee cannot escape death) (74). In Atlantis, the crime is reported by a "poeta o istorico" (poet or historian) to the prince who then doles out the punishment, thus excising the women from their role of battle-gazers.

Battista Sforza Montefeltro (1446–1472)

In Urbino, the same city where the *Courtier* was set, we find a historical precedent for women's surveillance of men's military prowess or cowardliness. In one episode of a poem that commemorates the life and death of the Countess of Urbino, Battista Sforza, we are told how, as a nineteen-year-old wife, she accompanied her husband, Federico da Montefeltro, to the battlefield during his long siege of Fano in 1463.[21] The poem, "La canzone de vita et morte" of Battista Countess of Urbino was composed by Ser Gaugello de la Pergola, a court poet who wrote several works on the ruling couple.[22] In the *canzone*, the poet describes the young woman as so enlivened by the ongoing battle that she went to the battleground to observe the fight:

Questa Madonna fo animosa tanto
Che venne in campo per voler vedere
Quello armeggiar chese facea tamanto. (ch. III, vv 19–21, p 19)

(This lady was so spirited that she came to the battlefield out of the desire to watch that fighting that was happening so grandly.)

The poem resembles other contemporary descriptions of Battista that describe her curiosity about arms. For example, in 1462, her tutor, Martino Filetico, wrote a dialogue that featured the teenaged Battista and her brother, Costanzo, as the primary interlocutors in three days of discussions.[23] In the dialogue, Battista is notably interested in the study of military arts as well as more practical concerns such as helping prepare artillery ("bombarda").[24] This interest in military matters is then turned to viewing war in de la Pergola's poem. Battista's physical presence at the battlefield, observing the soldiers, suggests Battista's role in the victory of the Urbino forces.[25] De la Pergola writes that not only did Battista want to watch the fighting, but also, much like Helen who identified the Greek soldiers in *Iliad* III, she recognized and observed the soldiers on the field. In the fifteenth-century poem, the young woman goes beyond Helen's function of informing men of the participants in battle. She notes who died and who was injured, who fled and who was captured.

Vedeva tucto 'l dì scaramucciare:
Chi era morto et chi vedea ferito
Et chi vedea fuggire et chi legare. (ch. 3, vv 25–7, p 19)

(She saw all the skirmishing: who was dead, who was wounded, and she saw who fled and who was taken prisoner.)

In this description, Battista records battlefield behaviour. One thinks of the many other ways de la Pergola could have described the arrival of the young woman on the battlefield. For example, Battista could have simply admired the valorous manoeuvres of her *condottiere* husband, or watched the flames, swords, and lances with fear and trepidation.

Instead, de la Pergola describes how she focused on the soldiers' acts of praiseworthy courage and shameful retreat. The Countess, in effect, provided the method by which men were able to claim their honourable or tarnished reputations. She was particularly suited for this role as she had a formidable memory. Her memory was praised as surpassing even that of Themistocles, who knew all the citizens of his city by name.[26]

Battista's watching from above the siege at Fano may be called a loving gaze, yet it may also be deemed, in more cynical terms, a surveillance that ensures men's courageous performance. She provides the audience that Castiglione explained was imperative to a courtier, as he "discreetly" issued from the fray of battle in order to make his heroism seen. De la Pergola's poem not only presents an illustrious woman with interests in martial matters, it problematizes women's endearing company as playing a role in the efficacy of war as well as providing historical witness to fame and humiliation.[27]

Federico da Montefeltro undoubtedly was aware of the ways in which Battista's presence might influence his realm. According to de la Pergola, after the siege and defeat of Fano, Federico asked that Battista follow him into the city:

> Volse el signor che Madonna cintrasse
> Et fo ben recevuta lietamente
> Per che pareva ben chel meritasse. (ch. 3, vv 31–3, p 19)

> (The lord wished that the lady enter the city. And she was received happily because it seemed that she well merited it.)

The passage demonstrates that the wife's physical presence in matters of war is not limited to gazing at and scrutinizing masculinity. In this case, the entrance of Battista alongside her husband might have altered the reception of Federico in the city. It shifted what would have been a triumphal march of a military conqueror into a procession of a courtly couple, performing what was possibly a more generative vision of a humanist ruling dynasty.

In sum, Battista could gaze on troops just as she could become the object of the gaze of her subjects. And finally, both of these functions were part of the role of a faithful consort. After the couple entered the defeated Fano, Battista returned to the palatial court of Urbino.[28] At home, she awaited the return of her husband as "clean and fresh as a pretty ruby," a phrase that rings of erotic and material exchange that complicates de la Pergola's description of the noble bride.

> Et lietamente se torno ad Urbino
> Aspectar la tornata del signore,
> Pulita et fresca commo um bel rubino. (ch. 3, vv 52–4, p 20)
>
> (And happily, clean and fresh as a pretty ruby, she returned to Urbino to wait for the return of her lord.)

In de la Pergola's praise, Battista effectively performs several feminine roles that might otherwise have seemed incompatible: female beloved, guarantor of martial prowess, and benign ruler.

Eleonora d'Aragona (1450–1493)

A contemporary of Battista Sforza, Eleonora d'Aragona also used her position as female consort to the Duke of Ferrara, Ercole I d'Este, to rouse a military response. Yet, unlike Battista or the *damas* of Isabella's court, Eleonora influenced matters of war through a command of words not glances. In two very different moments, the Duchess employed the discourse of *patria* in order to secure the loyalty of the people to the Duke of Ferrara. Both occasions occurred during the sustained war between Venice and Ferrara (1482–4), where the Duchess was faced with the grim prospects of losing both her husband and her realm at the same time. Like all of the women considered in this chapter, she was the subject of a literary text that praised her acts. What specifically draws our interest to Eleonora is her ability to redirect the discourse of power away from her female body and onto the Duke, even in his absence.

In May and June of 1482, Venice was besieging the town of Ficarolo. According to Marin Sanudo's *Le vite dei dogi*, Duke Ercole I, "considerando la ruina li venia adosso, hessendo reduto in Castel Vechio, nel suo palazo gravemente si amaloe" (1.265) (considering the ruin that was to come, having been led back to the Castel Vecchio, fell gravely ill in his palace). In response, Eleonora shrewdly sought, via public sermons, to raise morale among the people of Ferrara.[29]

Eleonora's acts come near the end of the Venice-Ferrara war (also known as the Salt War), when Venice had already conquered some Ferrarese holdings.[30] When the prospects for a Venetian victory at Ficarolo seemed imminent, and with the Duke ill in bed, Eleonora was left to govern, along with the Ferrarese war council.[31] In Sanudo's account of the historical moment, the Duchess took action not because she was rightful joint ruler but rather, as he states, because necessity had prompted her. Sanudo's Venetian bias is clear throughout the text, yet he demonstrates admiration for the Ferrarese duchess, a woman of "greatest wisdom" ("grandissimo inzegno"). When Eleonora was faced with impending war, Sanudo states that she does not call on princes or generals for support; rather, she turns to a Bolognese hermit.[32] At her request, the man preached eight sermons in the cathedral of Ferrara, motivating the Ferrarese to redouble their efforts through his effective rhetoric of patriotism and xenophobia.

The hermit spoke to a full house, telling them to bear the trials of war and maintain loyalty to the Este (Sanudo 1.265). Importantly, he also instilled in his audience a fear of Venetians, thus counteracting any possible apprehensions of the Ferrarese about their own ailing leader. The preacher threatened that if the Ferrarese were to lose, the Venetians intended to steal their possessions and exile them to Cyprus or Crete.[33] Sanudo adds the fascinating comment that the hermit was not the author of these sermons but rather the mouthpiece of the Duchess herself: "E tutto diceva quello che madama Duchessa li diceva dovesse dir" (1.265) (And he said all that the Madame Duchess told him he had to say).

After proclaiming the abilities of the Duchess, the narrator concludes the episode with a conservative turn, suggesting that women are simply not fit for a man's game. Sanudo tells that on a certain day, the Duchess wished for an armada to defeat the Venetians, and so the hermit preached that people should accompany him onto the battlefields with standards bearing a cross and the image of the Madonna. Ferrara's war captain, the "wise" Duke of Urbino, hearing the "uproar on the field" and angered from the "madness" of it all, sent the priest back to the city and told him to explain to the Duchess that the Venetians were not in need of conversion; instead, the Ferrarese needed money, artillery, and men in order to send the enemy away, quoting Federico da Montefeltro: "*Pater*, Venitiani non sonno inspiritadi, dite a madama che bisogna danari, artellarie, et zente a dichazar li inimici de dove i sonno" (1.266) (Father, Venetians are not moved by the spirit. What we need is money, artillery, and people to move the enemies from where they are). Sanudo thus ultimately portrays Eleonora and the church as idealistic dilettantes in war, unaware of the realities and needs of battle, particularly when compared to the "wise" war general Federico of Urbino.

Other texts depict Eleonora as a master of war discourse, swaying public opinion and action through her crafted words, gestures, and spectacle. Just four months after the hermit preached on matters of war in Ferrara's cathedral, the Duchess of Ferrara again saw the need to rally her people, this time in person, around her ailing and immobile husband. Bernardino Zambotti's *Diario Ferrarese* details the critical moment of November 1482 when Ferrara itself faced the threat of a Venetian siege (116–21). Upon hearing that Venetian troops had crossed the Po River, Eleonora called members of the war council, together with a number of other men, to the garden of her palace (118). According to the chronicler, Eleonora greeted the men with "honest tears" ("pianto honesto"), and yet her speech, which is transcribed by Zambotti, is one not of fearful desperation but of spirited resolve. In her address, she explains that the Duke has requested her to speak on his behalf, as he is ill in bed. She states that the Duke has sent her to give an "exhortation," encouraging the men to remain loyal to the D'Este even though the enemy has crossed the river and is at Ferrara's city walls (118). Acting as a war orator, she assures her people that with their "valorous spirits" ("animi valoroxi"), Ferrara can defeat the enemy.

Eleonora's speech remarkably echoes the Boccaccian *exempla* of appropriate female leadership, which, as Margaret Franklin explains, justifies women's power only if the woman leader defers to legitimate male rule.[34] Eleonora, like Boccaccio's famous heroines, is resolute in the face of destruction, but only, we are told, because her husband, the rightful ruler, has given her a mandate to speak. Furthermore, she does not claim that a woman is capable of defending the state; rather, she repeats the cultural truism that power and protection are the provenance of male rulers. The impending danger, according to Eleonora, would not have come to pass had her husband not been ill: "E quando lo duca mio non fosse sta' amalato, potiti essere certo che non haveressemo a questa hora tanto danno" (118) (And if the duke my husband were not ill, you could be certain that we would not have danger in this moment).

Finally, upon the assertion that she might be hiding the fact that the Duke was not ill but dead, Eleonora shrewdly decides to invite the crowd to see the Duke: "Expectati chè farò lo vederìti" (118) (Wait so that I will let you all see him!). She throws open the doors to the Duke's chamber so that the men might enter and speak with their lord. The theatricality of the moment reveals the Duke, frail, barely able to open his eyes, and immobile, but alive. The fear of a woman's threat to legitimate power is apparently assuaged by the presence of the Duke, as the men of Ferrara pass through his chamber touching him and even attempting to re-enter the room.[35] We can see that, despite the presence of an inspiring and vibrant Eleonora, it is the the Duke's body, limp and all but lifeless, that is the fetishized locus of power. Eleonora, or at least the version of her who comes to us through these narrations, understood such dynamics. The actions and words of the rousing moment belong to Eleonora, not her husband, and thus I argue that the body of the Duke is a proxy for or displacement of Eleonora's rule, not the reverse, as one might presume. That is, much like the hermit discussed above, a man who "repeated" the words *she* told him, the Duke embodied phallic authority, but both men were ultimately the instruments of the wise Duchess.[36]

Eleonora in the Compilations of *Illustrious Women*

After Eleonora d'Aragona's death, her actions became the source material for the biographies of famous women, much like those that circulated in her court while she was alive.[37] It is a scenario that demonstrates that women could read tales of illustrious women with hopes of one day being added to the pantheon of women worthies themselves. And this happened precisely when Giacomo Filippo Foresti's monumental *De plurimis claris* (1497), dedicated to Eleonora's sister Beatrice, included a biography of Eleonora only four years after her death. Foresti's biography of Eleonora is then the source for Giuseppe Betussi when he includes her as part of his fifty biographies appended to the vernacular translation of Boccaccio's *De mulieribus claris*.[38] Betussi's edition, published in 1545 and again in a more circulated edition of 1547, is aptly titled (in translation) *Book of Giovanni Boccaccio of Illustrious Women, Translated by Mister Giuseppe Betussi with an Addition Made by Him of Famous Women from the Time of Mister Giovanni until Our Own Days*.[39]

Betussi's entry on Eleonora repeats much of Foresti's entry and is at times a translation of this earlier and lengthier text. Betussi glosses over much of Foresti's language on the moral virtue of Eleonora and instead makes the centrepiece of the biography her oration of 1482 during the Ferrara-Venice war. In contrast to the Zambotti Ferrarese chronicle discussed above, Foresti and Betussi after him depict the Duchess as agent and prime motivator of historical change.[40] She is not sent by her husband to speak by mandate, but rather consults God and then takes the situation under her own control. In Betussi's version:

> havendo il Senato Vinitiano fatto un'essercito contra lui e toltoli molte castella, saccheggiando e trascorrendo tutto il territorio Ferrarese di forte, che per essere infermo il Duca tutta la città incominciava a temere, la Duchessa Leonora essendo com'era di grand'animo non percio si smarri niente, ma prima ricorsa a Dio e poi chiamati a consiglio con gran fede e speranza tutti i suoi cittadini … (171v)

> (The Venetian Senate, having formed an army against him [Duke Ercole d'Este], had overrun and sacked the entire Ferrarese territory and had taken many castles from him. As the Duke was very ill, the entire city began to fear. The Duchess Leonora, being as she was of great spirit, was not at all deterred. First she appealed to God and then called together all of her citizens with great faith and hope …)[41]

Furthermore, Betussi emphasizes that it was precisely the Duchess's words that inspired men to take up arms, and through her came an eventual peace: "con queste e altre simili parole, la saggia donna, operò di sorte, che il popolo incitato a pigliar l'armi, e a difendere il suo signore" (189r) (with these and other similar words, the wise woman applied herself, so that she incited the people to take up arms and defend their lord); and "per mezzo di questa Leonora, le cose incominciarono a ritornare di turbate tranquille, e quiete" (189v) (by means of Eleonora, things began to return from trouble to tranquility and quiet).

Giuseppe Betussi's Translation of Boccaccio's *On Famous Women*

Giuseppe Betussi (1512–1573) was a celebrated writer in his own time, whose literary productions included many translations from Latin (including the above-mentioned translation of Boccaccio's *Famous Women*) as well as many original pro-woman works such as *La Leonora, ragionamento sopra la vera bellezza* (1557) and a dialogue contemplating the honour of Giovanna d'Aragona, *Le imagini del tempio di Giovanna d'Aragona* (1556), a work that notably contained a collection of verses on Giovanna by many poets. Along with working under famous patrons such as Gian Luigi Vitelli and Count Collaltino di Collalto (the same Collaltino as the one made famous by the poet Gaspara Stampa), he formed personal and intellectual relationships with several notable authors of his time as well as with illustrious women such as Vittoria Colonna, Giovanna d'Aragona, and Leonora Ravoira-Falletti.[42] Thus, his translation and expansion of Boccaccio's *Famous Women* was not just an isolated project but a product of Betussi's lifelong interest in the illustrious women of his time.

Given his history of praising contemporary women, it is scarcely a surprise that Betussi's *additione* of the fifty biographies marks a striking break with the Boccaccian model. Unlike Boccaccio's, Betussi's text describes women from recent history and offers exclusively positive praise. Moreover, at the time Betussi was translating Boccaccio's text and adding his own *additione*, he was working in a growing genre of biographies of famous women.[43] In the discussion below, we will see how Betussi sought to establish the rules of this genre, including the most basic question of the language of the text and the imitability of tales.

Betussi's book is the vernacular translation of Boccaccio, a translation that he justifies in gendered terms. In the dedicatory letter to Camilla Pallavicina, he writes that he translated or "rendered" ("ridotto") the Latin work of Boccaccio into the vernacular so that it might have a larger reading audience, and particularly a feminine readership, as most women did not know Latin: "Imperoche la maggior parte non è capace della lingua latina" (iiv) (since the majority [of women] is not capable in the Latin language). In this democratization of literature, he wishes for women readers to know how women of the past "per sangue volendo vivere immortali" (want[ed] with all their heart to live eternally), so that these readers might be inspired to emulate their predecessors and find immortality themselves: "Et le presenti considerando i meriti delle passate … se si conosceranno (secondo i gradi) eguali a queste, saranno certissime di non morir gia mai" (iiv-iiir) (And those present women, considering the merits of past women … if they learn to be equal to these [according to class], they will be certain to never die).

Betussi advises women to imitate the lives that they find in the biographies.[44] His book thus makes clear a didactic impulse that Boccaccio's original text had obfuscated. Boccaccio's *Famous Women* told female readers that they might imitate the stories of illustrious women, but since he had also included women of ill repute among his stories, he warned his addressee to be discerning: "As on entering a garden you extend your ivory hands towards the flowers, leaving aside the thorns, so in this case relegate to one side offensive matters and gather what is praiseworthy" (2).[45] Betussi of course includes the "thorns" of Boccaccio's text in his translation, but in his original addition of fifty women, there are only stories of positive exemplars.

Betussi's *additione* includes tales of women participating in war in various roles, each of which provided differing challenges to women who might seek to emulate their examples. Learned ladies such as Isotta Nogarola are often presented vis-à-vis their relation to war, praised as writing exhortations to Christian princes against the Turks (170r). There are also queens who, though not fighting in wars themselves, were affected by their husbands' militant conduct. Take, for example, Isabella of Naples, who kept her city in peace during her husband's frequent absences because he "only cared for war" (171v). But there were others who pushed more extreme limits of gendered wartime behaviour. Commanders such as Queen Margherita of England led an army out of love for her husband after he was taken prisoner. Margherita attacked enemy troops and had their general decapitated. She continued to fight until she had her husband returned "sano et salvo" (safe and sound). Her actions, Betussi explains,

> mostrò quanto grandi fossero nel suo petto le forze del maritale amore, non havendo tema di pericolo alcuno ne rispetto alcuno alla qualità ne al sesso suo, che senza altra consideratione per amore del preso Re entrò sotto grandissimo pericolo donna, che per lo piu sono timide, che forse ardito guerriero non havrebbe fatto. (162v)
>
> (demonstrated how great were the forces of marital love in her breast. Not having any fear of danger, neither in respect to degree or her sex, she entered into great danger without any hesitation, and for love of the captured king, a woman [who typically are timid], perhaps did what a courageous warrior would not.)

These three biographies reveal a substantial range of women's acts during war, acts that were sufficiently exceptional as to justify placing them in Betussi's catalogue of women. These and all women are presented in a positive light, as the author states that he will write of "illustrious" women, not women who had made themselves "famous" through ignoble acts. He defines "illustrious" ladies as those who have performed worthy deeds, either by "ennobling" themselves or, if already noble, by "augmenting the splendour of their family tree."[46] Indeed, Betussi reflects on the word "illustrious" at several points in the text.[47] In his biography of Queen Isabella of Spain he states that "illustrious" women are "educated and learned," while in the tale of Violentina Genovese, we discover that *illustre* defines women who are "either of noble blood joined with virtuous works, or from the beauty of the spirit or from some other worthy act." [48]

The emphasis placed on nobility (either of spirit or of blood) might help explain why only three of Betussi's fifty women are of low birth. Notably, of these peasant women, all three are involved in warfare. Joan of Arc (ch. 8), rises from her occupation as a shepherd girl to lead the French army, and Bona Lombarda (ch. 15), mistress to a knight, dresses as a man and accompanies him in battle. She is only made his wife and "acquires" nobility once she fights to have him released from prison.[49] Much of the plot of these two biographies is borrowed from Foresti (who had taken the stories from Arienti before him).[50] The last of the non-noble women, however, is not to be found in Foresti or Arienti, and it is interesting that this tale presents a different sort of female valour during war. In the story of "Una Giovanetta contadinella del territorio Padovano" (A Young Farm Girl from Padua), Betussi effectively places female chastity in counterpoint to male sexual aggression in a wartime context.

Chapter 33 of Betussi's catalogue tells about an anonymous Paduan peasant girl whose experience in men's wars is one of victim rather than armed virago. During the siege of Padua by imperial troops (15 September 1509), a beautiful young girl who was fleeing the encroaching enemy troops found herself surrounded by a group of Venetian/Paduan (not enemy) soldiers who threatened to take her by force.[51] The soldiers could not be stopped by reason, since, "in simili travagli le leggi tacciono, la ragione dorme, e i ministri di quella attendono ad altro" (181r) (in similar situations, laws are silent, reason sleeps and the counselors of rule attend to other matters). Thus, the girl was left without protection (of laws or arms) and surrounded by aggressive soldiers. She is praised by Betussi as showing resolve and intelligence, for "seppe adoprarsi" (181r) (she knew how to handle herself), and in response to the men's threats, she threw herself into the river, drowning in order to save her "immaculato" (immaculate) body. People attempted to rescue her, but she refused so that she not be returned into the hands of the soldiers. And though her body was buried "ignobly" alongside the river, Betussi tells us it was "degno di vivere per sempre nelle menti delle donne illustri" (181r) (worthy of living eternally in the minds of illustrious women).

This act of virtue from a common woman stands in contrast, Betussi states, to the noblewomen "nate, nodrite e allevate ne i reali palagi" (180v) (born, raised and nurtured in royal palaces) who lost the title of "illustrious" through dishonourable acts.[52] While women and girls throwing themselves in a river to avoid rape is a shockingly recurrent image in sixteenth-century praises of women,[53] in this case, the Paduan girl becomes the symbol of an honour that, I would argue, involves a critique not only of noblewomen but also men's behaviour in wartime. Not only is this girl unable to seek protection from the men who were supposed to protect her, there are no laws or courts of justice that might defend her (since, during war, men and laws "attend to other matters," 181r). Moreover, the body of the young girl is *immaculate* – integral and not defiled. The adjective, laden with Marian imagery, also provides a contrast between the young girl and the body of the Venetian territory and more generally Italy itself, both of which had been subject to foreign invasion and occupation. Indeed, the import of Betussi's story is that the future of Italy depends on the expulsion of the Hapsburgs. The siege of Padua was for Betussi a symbol of Italian sovereignty, as the defeat of the Hapsburgs was fundamental to the Venetian Republic and the "gloria, sostegno, e riputazione di tutto 'l mondo, non che d'Italia" (180v) (glory, foundation, and reputation of all the world, not only Italy).

In a matter of only four months (July–September 1509), Venice had lost and regained Padua and was now facing a siege for control of the city once again.[54] The *immaculato* body of the virgin peasant girl was thus symbolic of a pre-calamitous, perhaps even prelapsarian, summer, and in her case, such integrity was ultimately preserved only through the sacrifice of her life. Her sacrifice raised her to the ranks of "illustrious women," and she was immortalized. But such praise of a low-born woman was also a critique of men and women of the illustrious class. In this story, noblewomen had lost their noble status through dishonourable acts, and noblemen had simply failed in their duty to protect the *terraferma.* For Betussi, the title "noble" and the status "illustrious" could be granted or revoked, and thus Betussi's text is repeatedly crafted to persuade readers to behave in wartime according to his prescriptions.

Betussi's discussions of "nobility" and "illustrious" extend beyond the long-standing debate about nobility of deed and nobility of blood, precisely because these labels are negotiated with differing social rules of feminine decorum in warfare. Describing a learned woman, an artistic woman, and a warring woman as "illustrious" could be a precarious business. Moreover, to label a combatant woman as both "illustrious" and "noble" challenged notions of feminine virtue as well as the customary norms of the upper-class woman. Betussi recognizes such concerns when he discusses the matter of imitation by his readers. He reminds women readers not to confuse *all* exemplary behaviour as appropriate for imitation; exemplars should be followed "according to class" ("secondo i gradi"). Indeed, the descriptions of Joan of Arc's and Bona Lombarda's militaristic bodies not only indicate their exceptionality as warriors but also mark them as women of the middling or lower classes. In fact, Betussi, following Foresti and Arienti, emphasizes the point that Bona Lombarda is of the lowest social status, saying that she is a "donna di vile e bassa origine e nacque di poverissimi e ignobili parenti" (172v) (woman of vile and low origin and born of the poorest and most ignoble relations). Her inclusion in the list of illustrious women, he tells us, is because she "acquired" nobility with her brave spirit, "col proprio animo acquistata chiarissima nobiltà" (with her own spirit she acquired a most famous nobility). Had she been born not of *ignobili* but *nobili* relations, would her acts have seemed virtuous or immodest?

The physical descriptions of women of the lower class were also notably different from descriptions of their noble counterparts. Arienti describes Bona Lombarda (Bona de Vultulina, ch. 20) as "bruta, nera, picola, ma molto viva, combatendo virilmente per ioco cum li altri guardatori de bestie" (181) (ugly, black, small, but very alive, fighting manfully at games with the other animal keepers), and she was a woman who fought "da guerriero" (as a warrior).[55] Similarly, Betussi characterizes Joan of Arc as "di volto rozzo" (of a brutish face), and he will as well emphasize her physicality in war, fighting with a sword and on horseback.[56] These descriptions stand in contrast to those of upper-class woman in war who are described as beautiful and possessing strong characters rather than strong bodies.[57]

The praise of historical noblewomen in war – not described as physically strong, armed, or wielding swords in battle – draws a patent contrast with literary characters such as Ariosto's heroines Marfisa and Bradamante. This pattern is also true in its converse. Female peasant viragos, a staple if small ingredient of the historical genres, were hardly to be found in epic poetry. If we have established a working rule – that historical noblewomen were always portrayed as beautiful yet unarmed, and that peasant women could be both unattractive and armed – there were, of course, exceptions to this rule. There are rare cases of noblewomen who were also praised as combatants in biographical and historical texts. Two of these noblewomen in particular, Orsina Visconti and Caterina Sforza, provide fascinating examples of differing social receptions accorded to sword-wielding noblewomen.

The most important fifteenth-century writers of women's biographies, Arienti and Foresti, described the noblewoman Ursina Vesconte de li Torelli (Orsina Visconti) as a commander and armed and in battle. On the other hand, the most famous Italian virago, Caterina Sforza, was not described as an armed warrior in texts about illustrious women but was so described in certain historical texts. The literary fortunes of the legends of these two women are as fascinating as their biographies themselves. Ursina Vesconte reappeared as an epic version of herself in Betussi's 1547 addition to Boccaccio, while Caterina Sforza, more famous and more problematic, had her first biography published by Filippo Foresti when she was only thirty-three; she would have to await the 1596 edition to be included in the bound appendix to Boccaccio's famous ladies.[58]

Caterina Sforza (1463–1509)

Caterina Sforza, illegitimate daughter of the Duke of Milan, Galeazzo Sforza, and wife of Girolamo Riario, Lord of Imola and Forlì, was given the monikers "virago" and the "tigress of Forlì" in her own day.[59] She commanded troops, rode on horseback, commissioned fortifications, and was famed for having worn armour and used arms.[60] Her first grand militant act was likely in 1484 when the twenty-one-year-old Caterina and her husband attempted to control the outcome of the papal conclave. While her husband was camped with his army outside Rome, Caterina, though heavily pregnant, went on to occupy Castel Sant'Angelo.[61] From the fortress she ordered soldiers to position their cannons at the entrance to the Vatican in order to ensure that any election would favour the Riarios.[62] Indeed, in what is still the most exhaustive biography of Sforza, the nineteenth-century scholar Pier Desiderio Pasolini argues that it is this moment in Castel Sant'Angelo that marks the beginning of the more militant and arguably more notable phase of her life (I.150).

Actions such as the ones above are why Caterina Sforza has been the subject of scholarly studies as well as fiction, film, television, and even video games.[63] She is Italy's best-known virago, and yet we still know little about how Caterina fits within a larger context of Renaissance illustrious militant women. Considered in this context, it may be that the commonplace that Caterina was a "masculine" heroine actually misses the emphasis placed on her femininity, a discourse imperative to her success in navigating the gendering of war.[64]

Foresti's Biography of Caterina Sforza

The first biography of Caterina Sforza is found in the 1497 *De plurimus claris selectisque mulieribus*, a compendium of biographies of illustrious women by Jacopo Filippo Foresti based loosely on the model of Boccaccio's *De mulieribus claris.*[65] Twenty years after Foresti's biography, Machiavelli wrote of Caterina in several works, but as Frédérique Verrier has pointed out, it was Machiavelli's *Discourses* along with Foresti's biography that came to define the literary fortune of Caterina (Verrier, *Caterina* 36).[66]

Foresti's biography, published when Caterina was thirty-three, skips her early years and begins with the way she became regent of Forlì and Imola, the cities where she effectively served as ruler for twelve years. Foresti's story thus starts in 1488 when conspirators entered her palace, killed her husband, stripped him naked, and threw him to an angry crowd, all under, as Foresti says, the "pretext of liberty" (f. 160). Foresti casts Caterina as a pitiful victim of the conspiracy as she and her children are taken prisoner. He calls her an "adolescentula" (she was twenty-five, to be precise), and he depicts her as vulnerable and despondent: "seeing herself to be without aid … she fell into great sadness of spirit and was consumed the whole night in tears."[67] The next day, according to Foresti, Caterina was brought before the conspirators and told that not only did the assassins no longer wish for the Riarios to reign but that they would "erase her and all of her family from the face of the earth" (f. 160). It is clear that the reader is meant to sympathize with a young, vulnerable, and woeful Caterina who was a victim of violent circumstance. She was a tearful mother and widow, and she was made all the more pitiful by the portrayal of the bloodthirsty men who surrounded her.

Foresti depicts Caterina as shifting into a more resolute figure when he explains that, in the face of this misfortune, she quickly found her strength and showed herself to be an able and shrewd ruler who could make swift decisions. He states that since Caterina had a "fiery spirit," she "gave the world a great and singular example of prudence and constancy … ensuring that no harm would ever happen to her or to her children" (f. 160). Foresti then tells how Caterina entered the castle of Ravaldino under the pretence of negotiating for it to be handed over to the conspirators. In order to ensure her actions, she left her children as hostage and, in the biographer's words, entered the castle and "rejected feminine tears as would a man, and she started to demonstrate her prudence and greatness of spirit against the incensed and mad crowd" (f. 160).[68]

Those of us familiar with Machiavelli's more famous description of the event might at this point expect a theatrical moment where the countess stands atop the castle walls and addresses her enemies face to face. In his account of the same conspiracy, found in the *Discourses*, Machiavelli states that Caterina came to the ramparts of the castle and faced her enemies who threatened to kill her children: "E per mostrare che de' suoi figliuoli non si curava, mostrò loro le membra genitali, dicendo che aveva ancora il modo a rifarne" (And to show that she did not care about her children, she uncovered to them her genital members, saying that she still had the means for producing more children).[69] As Machiavelli tells the story, the gesture of lifting her clothing to expose herself (known in Greek as the *anasyrmos*), is followed by Caterina's defeat of the conspirators; he just does not make clear the connection between the two. After recounting the retort at Ravaldino, Machiavelli simply states that the conspirators were sent into "perpetual exile," since they had made an error by not killing the heirs of the assassinated Duke.[70] With no explanation of the causal relationship between this theatrical moment and Sforza's victory over her enemies, we are left with a story not of wartime strategy but of a rhetorical act that might or might not have had a real consequence. There has been no lack of interpretations of this moment, with portrayals of Caterina ranging from the Medusa to the ideal Prince.[71] Whatever one's interpretive take on Caterina's gesture and retort, all will recognize that Machiavelli's narration of events abruptly stops with the *anasyrmos.* The battle is won, and the reader is left with an impression of a strong female character, if not an understanding of the conspiracy of 1488.

Foresti instead tells of a less dramatic but certainly more likely scenario. Rather than exposing herself at the ramparts of Ravaldino, he explains that Caterina immediately started writing letters to Milan and

Bologna in search of military reinforcements. In his account, she then ordered artillery to be shot from the walls, an act that, according to Foresti, was necessary not only to "control the castle, but also in order to destroy the entire city, if the people either did not calm themselves or if they didn't return her children" (f. 160). Her success therefore hinged on the promise of the arrival of the Duke of Milan's troops as well as her own artillery shells firing overhead.

There is of course no way of knowing what actually happened at the fortress of Ravaldino. The scholar Julia Hairston has divided the various accounts of the event into two categories, what she calls the "historical record" (reports of local chroniclers) and the "canonical record" (the literary tale that was made famous by Machiavelli, particularly the version found in his *Discourses*) ("Skirting" 693). Referring to the historical record, we note that the local accounts of the episode do not describe Sforza as coming to the walls of the fortress.[72] The Forlivese chroniclers Leone Cobelli and Andrea Bernardi both state that Caterina stayed inside her quarters, and in a moment that could have been a source for Machiavelli, Giovanni Corbizzi, a correspondent to Lorenzo de' Medici, wrote that Caterina told those who asked her to come to the walls that she was already pregnant with a child and that she had the "means to make more" (Cobelli 327; Bernardi 1.240).[73] Sforza's nineteenth-century biographer, Pier Desiderio Pasolini, was convinced that the person who came to the ramparts was not Caterina but the castellan, Tommaso Feo, and that in the moment of the threat of assassination of her children, "la fiera contessa non era spaventevole, ma spaventata" (vol. 1, 235) (the brave countess was not frightening, but frightened).

As we have seen, Foresti's account of the 1488 conspiracy is much closer to the "historical record," while we have no idea of its relation to historical events. After recounting the victory over the conspirators, he then goes on for several pages to discuss Caterina's success at retaining her lands, her bloody vengeance on the conspirators (which he defines as just), her incredible beauty, and her education of her children. Foresti also praises her wartime strategy during the invasion of Charles VIII in 1494, in which she made alliances with the Florentines, the pope, and King Ferdinand of Naples. In this matter, she was exceptional for her sex. He states that, "though it is typical for the majority of women to not keep their promises," Caterina decided to suffer the consequences of the French enemy rather than not respect her treaties (f. 161). The biography, published in 1497, ends while Caterina is still ruling – an occupation at which she excels. Foresti, in a claim that might be surprising to scholars familiar with Machiavelli, states that what makes her a most capable governor is her parental spirit: "her spirit, one that preserves the nature of a parent" ("genitoris") (f. 161).

In Foresti's biography, the description of Caterina follows a conventional narration of a historical noble virago in war. She is portrayed as noble, beautiful, and shrewd. As in other biographies of noblewomen in war, she is not said to bear weapons, wear armour, or personally kill any enemies. Moreover, her militant actions are limited to a command of words: Caterina writes letters and, perhaps more significantly in terms of gendered behaviour, commands her troops to fire artillery. This command of spoken and written language places Caterina in the cadre of other illustrious women of the Quattrocento, women who, as Virginia Cox has explained, were praised for public speaking in moments of war.[74] As we have seen above, Foresti himself tells of Eleonora d'Aragona who delivered speeches during Venetian attacks on Ferrara, and he also writes about Caterina's own grandmother, Bianca Maria Visconti Sforza, who delivered orations. Foresti's biography of Bianca Maria, like those of many of the women in his book, is an adaptation of Arienti's earlier work in Italian, and, with specific reference to Bianca Maria, both Arienti and Foresti tell us that she was inspirational in times of war. Arienti's description of Bianca Maria is particularly interesting, as he says that she would go out among her husband's troops on horseback and urge them to fight with "virili parole de affectione piene" (Arienti 268) (manly words full of affection).

In this depiction, Bianca Maria was a negotiator of gender, filling her virile words with affection and effectively bridging the Aristotelian gap between masculine courage and maternal love. The division between maternal women and warring men was articulated perhaps most memorably in the early twentieth century by Benito Mussolini, who made the famous analogy "La guerra sta all'uomo come la maternità alla donna" (War is to men as motherhood is to women) (quoted in Spackman 22).[75] In terms that are perhaps more progressive than Mussolini's, Arienti and Foresti allowed for a more flexible or blended gender performance of militant heroism. Instead of making Bianca Maria and Caterina Sforza into masculine avatars in women's bodies, Arienti and Foresti bring an entirely new concept of militancy to the battlefield. Bianca Maria exhibited "manly words filled with affection," and Caterina suppressed tears "like a man" while enacting violence and governing from the subjective position of a mother.

Foresti's characterization of Caterina clearly stands in opposition to Machiavelli's depiction of Caterina as lifting her skirt atop the ramparts "per mostrare che de' suoi figliuoli non si curava" (to show that she did not care about her children), but it also should make us question how we use the word "masculine" in our descriptions of Sforza. After all, the maternal role, albeit a protective one, situates her within a discourse that might even be called emblematically feminine. Rather than emphasizing Caterina's masculinity, Foresti reminds the reader of the putative discourse of femininity and explains that Sforza is bound to her sex, regardless of her acts of militancy. Foresti's observation that she is unlike other women because she keeps promises underscores her exceptional status while simultaneously undermining her sex. His praise is indeed ambivalent, as he states it is a "miracle" that Caterina keeps her word (f. 161). More significantly, he also reminds the reader that Caterina, as a woman, is not allowed to rule in her own name. Because Caterina is a widow and regent for her young son, Foresti compares her to the legendary queen Semiramis (f. 161), a fellow widow who ruled effectively after her husband's death but also a woman who was famed in Dante and Boccaccio for her licentious sexual behaviour.

Finally, Caterina is also marked as feminine in the several occurrences of her recorded speech. There are in fact a striking number of letters and histories that claim to quote the Countess as speaking during violent times in pithy statements. For example, in 1484 when Caterina famously took control of Castel Sant'Angelo after the death of Pope Sixtus IV, a correspondent wrote to Lorenzo de' Medici that when a messenger was sent to negotiate the surrender of Castel Sant'Angelo with Caterina, she responded, "Ah costui vuol giuocar meco a ricatto di cervello! Egli non sa bene che io ho il cervello del duca Galeazzo e sono fantastica come lui" (Ah, this one wants to play at a battle of wits! He doesn't know that I have the mind of Duke Galeazzo and I am as sharp as he).[76] These are, as Sforza's biographer Elizabeth Lev states, the first recorded spoken words we have of Caterina's (92), and as Lev also points out, they are strikingly different from the decorous and dutiful voice found in the extant epistles written by the Countess before this date.[77] As a second example, a chronicler in Forlì, Leone Cobelli, tells us that when a conspirator held a lance to Caterina's chest, she responded "quietamente" (calmly) that she could not be frightened, as she was the daughter of Galeazzo Sforza: "O Iacomo da Ronco non me far paura: fatti mi poi fare, ma paura no: perché io fui figliuola d'uno che non aveva paura" (Oh Iacomo da Ronco you don't scare me. Acts you can do to me but frighten me, no. Because I am the daughter of one who knew no fear).[78] And of course the most famous reported speech of Caterina Sforza was that reported by Machiavelli, where she faced her enemies who held her children captive, lifted her skirt, pointed to her genitals, and said she had the means to make more children. It is what Verrier has called a "bilingual" Caterina, speaking with word and gesture in the face of power (*Caterina* 74).

These brazen retorts in moments of extreme danger are clearly part of what has attracted so many people to the legend of Caterina Sforza. It bears remembering that such speech was obviously subject to revision, and in fact it is highly unlikely that these statements would have been heard by most of the writers who transcribed them. Nonetheless, we can analyse their content for the impact they have had on her legend as an illustrious virago. In these brief speeches, Caterina almost always remarked both on her gender and on her exceptional status as a daughter or mother. Concluding her speech to Iacomo da Ronco, whose lance (*partisana*) was pressed to her chest, Caterina underscores her sex and the fragility of women in wartime. She states, "Avete morto el mio signore, potete bene ammazzare me che so' una donna" (You have killed my lord [husband], you can as well kill me that I am a woman) (quoted in Pasolini I.218).

Caterina's speeches, like those of Eleonora d'Aragona, continually point to her gender. Moreover, the act of speaking itself highlights the physical presence of a woman – historically a locus of vulnerability – in a masculine arena of war. Thus, by both nature and design, these speeches were paradoxes. She was in effect reversing the notion that women were ineffectual in war, but she often did so by drawing attention to her sex. This was, as we know, a practised strategy of Caterina, even in written correspondence. In one letter, an example of what we know were her own words, she depicts herself not in a brazen flash of courage but rather in a pitiable state of vulnerability; when fearing the attack of Charles VIII, she wrote: "La Guerra non fa per donne et putti come sono miei Fioli" (War is not made for women and babies, which my children are) (To Ludovico Sforza, 27 August 1498, cited in Pasolini II.364). What is intriguing about her statement is not only that it is penned by Italy's most famous warring virago but that it is written in a request for armed reinforcements. Contrary to what her words might suggest, war was indeed an arena in which women could succeed; but as Caterina shows, success often required invoking the ideology of the unwarlike nature of women.

The Lament and Defeat of Caterina

This evocation of the binary of virago/vulnerable woman is exemplified in the contemporary poem *Il lamento di Caterina Sforza* (c. 1500) by Marsilio Compagnoni.[79] The *Lament of Caterina Sforza,* typical of this genre, is ostensibly recorded speech, for it ventriloquizes the subject in first-person verse. Caterina, the speaker of the text, presents herself in a pitiable state, declaring herself to be an abandoned and vulnerable woman. The poem is situated not in the victorious context of the 1488 conspiracy at Ravaldino discussed above, but rather in that of the siege of 1499–1500 by Cesare Borgia and his French army, where Caterina was ultimately defeated, captured, and imprisoned. The poem begins:

Ascolta questa sconsolata
Catherina da forlivo
Che ho gran guerra nel confino;

Senza ajuto abandonata
Io non vegio alcun signore
Ch'a cavalo monti armato
E poi mostri suo vigore
Per diffendere il mio stato.
Tuto el mondo è spaventato
Come senton gridar Franza;
E d'Italia la possanza
Par che sia profundata.
    Scolta questa sconsolata
    Catherina da forlivo

(Hear the inconsolable Caterina of Forlì.

That I have a great war at my borders. Without help and abandoned, I don't see any lord armed and mounted on a horse, showing his vigour to defend my state. The whole world is frightened as they hear the cries of France. And the strength of Italy seems to be sunken.

Hear the inconsolable Caterina of Forlì.)

Like the authors (Chiara Matraini, Laura Terracina, and others) discussed in chapter 3, the ventriloquized Caterina asks for men to take up her cause. But unlike the above-mentioned women poets, Caterina requests aid from the point of view of a female combatant. She exhorts men to fight because she too will fight, preferring death in battle, even risking torture:

> non me pesa di morire
> Morendo in mia rocha forte,
> Pur che possa far languire
> Miei nemici a sangue e morte,
> Con le mie bombarde acorte
> Ch'io ho piantate atorno atorno,
> Ma terome note e zorno
> Se io dovesse esser squartata.

> (It worries me not to die. Dying in my fortress, while I might make my enemies languish in blood and death, with my ready artillery that I planted all around them. But I will hold out night and day even if I must be quartered.)

She is a woman who is in the middle of the enemy's attack, and she exhorts her listeners to help her. Her suffering is common to all of Italy. If they do not intervene now, all of the dukes and great lords will pay the consequences:

> Io vo' perder per bataglia
> E morire con honore,
> Ma 'l me dole ben d'Italia
> D'ogni duca e gran signore.
> Non se acorgon de l'errore
> Io son posta in meza al foco
> Convien a lor mundar el loco
> Se non fan bona pensata.

> (I want to lose by battle and to die with honour. But mine is also the suffering of all of Italy, of every duke and great lord. They do not realize their error, and I am placed in the middle of the flame. They need to purge this place, if not they will have to think well about what is to come.)

She continues to exhort the lords of Italy to fight Cesare Borgia and the French, and she does so by asking that they join her on the battlefield, where she herself will come armed:

aiutar nostri vicini
e observar la libertade
e mantenir nostri confini, etc.
...
io verrò, io stessa, armata.[80]

([come] to help our neighbours and witness liberty and maintain our borders, etc.
I will come, myself, armed.)

Caterina is simultaneously abandoned and armed, and her presence is meant to mobilize men into fulfilling their militant duties. The shame of cowardly men who surrounded the virile Caterina became a *topos* in writings that praise her militancy. Machiavelli himself, in his *Art of War,* compared her "great undertaking" to the "shameful" acts of the men who did not know how to guard the fortress against Cesare Borgia.[81] Isabella d'Este famously stated that, "se Franzosi biasimano la viltà de li homeni, almeno debbono laudare lo ardire e valore de le donne italiane" (If the French mock the timidity of Italian men, they should at least praise the ardour and valour of Italian women).[82] Guicciardini used the defeat of Caterina Sforza as a means of suggesting that men and women had exchanged gendered traits: "Essendo tra tanti difensori ripieni d'animo femminile ella sola di animo virile, furano presto ... espugnate dal Valentino" (Being between so many defenders filled with feminine spirit and only she with a manly heart, they [Caterina's troops] were quickly ... stormed by Valentino).[83] And finally, Piero Parenti will go so far as to suggest that Caterina's bravery tricked the French into thinking she was a man and that the male soldiers were so cowardly that the enemies thought they were women:

> Madonna rifuggì nella rocca e gagliardamente si difendeva, talché uscì un motto che quando crederono e' Franzesi avere a fare con uomini trovorono donna, quando ebbono a fare con donne trovorono uomini. (quoted in Verrier *Caterina,* 51)
>
> (Madonna Caterina took refuge in the castle and bravely defended herself, so much so that there began a saying: that when the French believed they were encountering men they found a woman, and when they thought they were dealing with women they found men.)

The *topos* of the militant masculine woman who is surrounded by non-masculine or effeminate men is, as we have seen, recurrent within the genre of illustrious women. Specifically in regard to Caterina, Verrier reads this dynamic (found in Guicciardini, Parenti, and Machiavelli's *Art of War*) as perpetuating the regressive theme of the virile woman who emasculates men, a classical trope that she traces to Hercules and Omphale (58).[84] I would instead argue that while the "threat" of virile women who emasculate men is a typical trope in literature about war (e.g., Ariosto's Alcina or Tasso's Armida), the legends and histories of Caterina Sforza do not seem to invoke such a relationship. Instead, the above-cited authors present Caterina as taking up arms *because* of men's demonstrated pusillanimity. The men were "effeminate" before Caterina demonstrated her "virility." The sequence is important. Caterina does not emasculate men; rather, effeminate men have required her to compensate for them. Contemporary authors were attentive to this message, as they demonstrated an anxiety about Italian militancy in general.

If the desire was to present Caterina as a foil to ineffective male soldiers, it is interesting that neither the authors of Caterina's biographies nor the historians (e.g., Machiavelli, Guicciardini, and Parenti) depict Caterina as armed. Although there are texts that describe how Sforza wore armour, used weapons, and even wounded enemy soldiers,[85] these aspects do not become part of her literary legend. Not even Machiavelli chose to offer us a sword-wielding, armour-wearing Italian version of Joan of Arc. Instead, we are left with a virago who, ironically, becomes better known for her audacious speech and gesture than for her prowess as a commander or combatant.

Caterina's life and deeds are fascinating and quite remarkable from many points of view; ironically, however, this fossilized *legend* of Caterina Sforza is not all that impressive in terms of wartime militancy. She is best known for the 1488 *anasyrma* atop the castle of Ravaldino, which ended in a victory over conspirators, and for the 1500 defeat by Cesare Borgia, when she was imprisoned and taken to Rome. These two events, however, do effectively communicate, through a synchronic semiotic structure, the Machiavellian *topos* of criticizing the dereliction of men's militancy in Italy. The solitary woman, exposing her genitals atop a city wall while facing what is possibly a mass of male onlookers, provides an unforgettable image of a woman whose public strength stands in contrast to the conspiring men who are gathered below. Though the *anasyrma* cannot be read as bringing about a consequential victory, I argue that it creates an image in which Caterina physically points to her femininity not to defeat the enemy but to mobilize men around her into action. The same gesture in Plutarch was meant to have this same effect. If we read the gesture forward towards the defeat of 1500, the image of the exceptional Caterina makes the men around her seem all the more unexceptional.

The Legend beyond Machiavelli

As we know, the legend of Caterina does not end with her defeat in 1500. Once in Borgia's custody, she was held for several days before being taken to Rome for her imprisonment in Castel Sant'Angelo, and several texts circulated that discuss her possible rape by Borgia during her imprisonment, while some texts even obliquely allude to a highly doubtful mutual romantic encounter.[86] The historical reality of the rape of women in war cannot be overstated, and it is a repugnant *topos* that finds its way into the celebration of illustrious women in war in shocking forms. We recall for example the above-discussed virgin who threw herself into the river to avoid the shame of sexual violence, or perhaps the figure of the Roman Lucretia, who in her suicide sought a military vengeance for her violated body. However, for a multitude of reasons, possibly related to decorum and social class, this episode of Caterina's sexual violation is typically missing from her sixteenth-century encomia.

What does figure centrally in the encomia, instead, is Caterina's role as co-founder of what would become one of Italy's most famous families. Her secret romance (and possible marriage to) Giovanni di Pierfrancesco de' Medici (1467–1498) produced the famous war captain Giovanni (commonly known as Giovanni of the black bands) (1498–1526), father of Cosimo de' Medici, the future Grand Duke of Tuscany.[87] Caterina Sforza would thus be celebrated in the foundation stories of the dukes of Tuscany as one of the *capostipite* of the ducal line. Francesco Serdonati makes this genealogical line central in his biography of Caterina, and Vasari included her portrait (1555–62) in the decorative program of the Palazzo Vecchio after the Medici dukes made the palace their home.[88] The fortune of Caterina was thus not limited to her military defiance and her likely invented gesture at Ravaldino. As the Vasari portrait demonstrates, for example, there was a concerted effort by the Medici to assimilate Caterina into a Medicean heritage; she was not depicted with the baton of a ruler (as she had been in Foresti's illustrated biography) as the ex-Countess of Forlì, but instead was shown dressed in the widow's veil, mourning not her dead Riario spouse but her Medici husband.

Figure 5.1 Unknown artist, *Portrait of Caterina Sforza*. Woodcut from Jacopo Filippo Foresti. *De plurimis selectisque mulieribus*, Ferrara, 1497. Getty Research Institute, Los Angeles (2964-860)

The historical acts of Caterina Sforza raise the issue of the relationship between the literary virago and historical examples of militant women. There has been a trend in scholarship that relates literary viragos to the proliferation of real women who exercised power in the political and military realm. Beatrice Collina, for example, has claimed that the viragos of fifteenth-century epic poetry enabled Caterina and other Quattrocento women to identify with strong female literary characters. As Collina argues, the historical emergence of women such as Caterina concurrently with depictions of literary viragos is not mere chance.[89] Such a theory is appealing in that it empowers literature with a salutary and even feminist cultural role. While my own study engages

Figure 5.2 Giorgio Vasari and workshop, *Portrait of Caterina Sforza*, c. 1559. Palazzo Vecchio, Florence. Photo credit: Alinari/Art Resource, NY

in this inquiry, I resist the claim that one sort of woman produced the other. The risk of such a conclusion is that it obfuscates the differences between historical and fictional women viragos, and it does not take into account that the *representations* of historical women – which were undoubtedly influenced by literature – reflect highly stylized versions of historical events that were not always historically accurate.

Indeed, it may be more generative to discuss the reciprocity between the *texts* that represented historical and fictional viragos rather than seek to know how texts influenced real women. Julia Hairston provides an example of this sort of scholarship by tracing the episode of Caterina Sforza at Ravaldino across a hundred years of literary representations. After Caterina's appearance in various chronicles, letters, and the anthology of Foresti, she reappeared in Francesco Serdonati's 1596 large anthology of women, *Donne illustri* (the topic of the next chapter), as well as in Traiano Boccalini's *Ragguagli di Parnaso e pietra di paragone politico: Centuria I* (1612).

As Hairston explains, Serdonati's narration reflects certain literary trends from the illustrious-woman genre, and it defines Caterina's acts at Ravaldino in terms of her status rather than in terms of feminine decorum (692). The sixteenth-century writer Serdonati attempts to resituate the legend of Caterina within a new concept of illustrious women. He retells the Ravaldino *anasyrma* story, but he invokes God and avoids the mention of Caterina's genitals:

> E dicendo essi [the conspirators] che ucciderebbono i figliuoli; ella per levar loro la speranza, che la tenerezza de' figliuoli la dovesse indurre a far cosa indegna di sé, s'alzò alquanto i panni dinanzi, e disse, che ringraziava Iddio che non eran guaste le forme da farne degli altri.
>
> (And when they [the conspirators] said that they would kill her children, she, in order to dash their hopes that tenderness for her children would induce her to do something unworthy of her, she lifted some of her garments in front, and said that she thanked God that her mold to make others was not broken.)[90]

Serdonati's version of the story also carves out a new morality of illustrious women in combat. The truly "unworthy" (*indegna*) act would have been to relinquish her title, not (he implies), the lifting of her skirt. Giving the *anasyrma* episode a strategic motive, Serdonati continues by incorporating Foresti's biography, creating a hybrid of two principal source texts. He states that Caterina proceeded to fire on the conspirators, "la cui risposta accompagnata con tanta bravura di parole, e di fatti perché s'apparecchiò alla difesa, e faceva di continuo sparare artiglierie sopra nimici" (Serdonati 1596, 590) (Caterina's response was accompanied with much bravura of words but also of deeds because she prepared for the defence and had the artillery continually fire on the enemy).

Sixteen years after Serdonati's publication, Traiano Boccalini used the legend of Caterina to bring the question of women's actions in war out in the open. Boccalini's *Ragguagli di Parnaso* is an imagined trial of Caterina before the judge Apollo, in which male judges debate whether to place Caterina in Parnassus for her bold method of maintaining her realm or to condemn her for her gesture of lifting her skirt and showing her genitals. The resulting verdict is that a noble and public woman was obliged to demonstrate "virility" and thus could not be held to the same standards as ordinary women, and that, moreover, she had indeed (re)produced illustriously, as she was the mother of Giovanni de' Medici and grandmother of Cosimo I (Boccalini 120–1).[91] It reflects just how much the praise-of-women genre had changed since Boccaccio lauded the warrior Camilla not for her skill at arms but for her chaste behaviour; it also highlights how distant the legend of a historical virago might be from the noble viragos of epic and romance. Caterina is a brave political ruler who is (possibly) a warrior in times when male warriors are not sufficient. Fictional heroines, on the other hand, coexist with male warriors. They are armed, kill, engage in battles, and are not found lifting their garments in order to protect their realms.

Orsina Visconti, the Possible Source for Bradamante

If Caterina Sforza's legend had little to do with literary viragos, the tale of another woman, Orsina Visconti, provides a closer analogue to epic warrior maidens. Betussi translates and amends the *vita* of the noble Orsina Visconti that he found in his sources, Arienti (ch. 21) and Foresti (ch. 156). Orsina stands apart from Betussi's collection of decorous noblewomen, as she is described quite vividly as armed and even bloodthirsty in a battle to save the castle Guastella on 17 March 1426. Her unique narrative dates at least back to Arienti, the original source for her appearance in the genre. In Arienti, Ursina Vesconte de li Torelli is a "virago," practised in arms and a capable horsewoman ("a le volte lei usò munificentia de arme et de cavali," 195). Nonetheless, she has more conventional virtues as well: she is a religious woman who has helped poor women marry; she has no tolerance for "li usurari et le femine lasive" (usurers and lascivious women, 195), and she is an ideal household manager, "virtuous" in the office that pertains to women – handiwork and household governance.[92] What follows this rather generic praise of Orsina, however, is a striking depiction of her participation in war.

While her husband was in Milan, an army was sent by Venice to attack her lands. As the Venetian "Schiavoni" were heading to Guastella, Orsina, who was ten miles away, rallied an army to defeat the enemy. Arienti records her speech in which she asks her subjects, her "brothers and sons" ("figlioli et fratelli mei") to fight for love of Filippo (the Duke of Milan), of Guido (her husband, the Count of Guastella), and of herself. Her speech is effective, as her "virile and affectionate words" inspire every listener to fight: "Ogni homo, a le virile et affectionate parole de la donna, resposeno essere tutti disposti et parati al suo volere" (198) (To the affectionate and virile words of the woman, every man responded to be disposed and amenable to her will). And though her words echo those of other women viragos in Arienti's collection, and might even make us think of Eleonora d'Aragona, the tale of Orsina will show itself to be cut from a different cloth.[93] She does not merely inspire men to fight but dons sword and armour to put herself in the midst of combat. After her speech, Orsina lights the artillery ("bombarda"), dons a helmet and gloves, and mounts her horse. Armed and ready for combat, she gives a second speech in which she declares, "Io non me spogliarò l'arme, nè me coprirò de veli il capo, fin non habia spezato li inimici" (198–9) (I will never take off my arms, nor cover my head in veils until I have destroyed the enemy). She is a *rara avis,* perhaps the first armed and fighting virago in the genre of Renaissance biographies of illustrious women. And it is notable that the account suggests an intriguing gender shift from decorous noblewoman to transgressive virago. This shift, however, derives from patriotic duty rather than *natural* desire. As implied in her words, Orsina would prefer to be "'womanly," veiled, and unarmed, but she is sacrificing her right to a feminine gender script for the good of the state.

Arienti tells us that Orsina, like Queen Semiramis who rescued Babylon, jumped to action when necessity demanded it.[94] Without delay, she mounted her horse, wielded her sword, and rushed to battle. She was undoubtedly in the fray of the battle where five hundred enemies were killed:

> incominciò cum fiera invasione ad combatere cum l'armata inimica; et quilli de la terra, rinfrancati de animo et de forza, aiutarono la valorosa donna per tal modo, che l'armata fu rota et spezata tutta, et furono morti circa cinquecento Schiavoni. (200)

> (she began with a courageous advance to combat the armed enemy; and the troops from Guastella, their spirits and force reassured, helped the valorous woman in such a way that the enemy battalion was broken and completely divided. There were around five hundred Schiavoni dead.)

Arienti underscores not only Orsina's bravery but the danger of battle by noting that her own men were also killed in great numbers, so that the "rocks were made red." The deaths on both sides add a realistic flavour of danger to the description, while the language of the battle scene (e.g., "emperor at arms" and surrounded by the enemy "three times") echoes the formula of Virgilian epic:

> Lei se adoperava come uno imperatore de arme, inanimando li suoi ad ferire li inimici, et fu veduta circa tre volte infra li inimici. *Et quasi fu opinione* che se inquinasse le proprie mane nel schiavone sangue, perché de quello era scaturita sopra l'arme, et sopra la curta camura de panno celestre. (200–1, emphasis mine)

> (She manoeuvered like an emperor of arms, animating her troops to wound the enemy, and she was seen about three times amidst the enemies. And it was *nearly believed* that she had tainted her own hands with the blood of the Schiavoni, because their blood had spewed out over her arms and over her short mantle of light blue cloth.)

Despite her exceptional valour and her victory over the Venetian Schiavoni, Orsina cannot slough off the conventions of gender. In the midst of praise, there is still doubt surrounding the most graphic details – the bloodying of "her own hands." Notably, it was "*almost* believed" or literally "*almost* the opinion" that she had "tainted her hands" with enemy blood. The language used by the author subtly skirts the issue of Orsina's role in killing. This authorial ambivalence is also apparent in the moment when he states that Orsina's presence in the battle resulted in the killing of enemies. The author states that Orsina joined her troops and "furono morti circa cinquecento Schiavoni" (there were around five hundred Schiavoni dead). The passive construction allows Orsina to be associated with victory and simultaneously to maintain some distance from actual killing. Arienti depicts Orsina as going undeniably further than Giovanna Bentivoglio, who was described as a woman commander: "[she] inspired men to taint their hands in enemy blood" (121). Orsina is a woman warrior, and possibly a killer. She took to the battlefield, going far beyond the limits approached by other women in the biographies, and yet Arienti still seems compelled to contain her within a proper feminine script. The episode concludes with several allusions to her more conventional post-bellum life. After the battle, her husband praises her "feminine spirit"; she has three children (all of whom are excellent at arms, including her daughter); and most importantly, she finishes her life as a "fidele cristiana" (203) (faithful Christian woman).[95] Her Christian virtue, continual prayers, and supplication for forgiveness of her sins are, Arienti tells us, what distinguish her from Boccaccio's Semiramis and merit her inclusion in the compendium of illustrious women.[96]

The exceptional narration of Orsina that appeared in Arienti's 1491 manuscript found its fortune in print, like most of Arienti's text, first in a published Latin adaptation by Foresti (1497) and then in a vernacular reworking by Betussi in his 1547 translation of Boccaccio. Aside from her presence in these early catalogues of women, Orsina's story remains one of the few accounts of a historical noblewoman warrior combatant. It is thus understandable why Pio Rajna singled out Orsina as a potential source for Ariosto's depiction of Marfisa and Bradamante (Rajna 49).

If one looks at this legacy of Orsina within the catalogues of famous women, it seems that, rather than breaking the barriers of the rhetorical conventions of praising women during warfare, the exceptional tale remains just that, an exception. Moreover, its translation from vernacular to Latin and back into the vernacular involves a process of translating the body of Orsina into an *illustrious* woman during an age that had read the eroticized tales of viragos such as Bradamante. Compare Arienti's tale, which makes no mention of Orsina's person, to Betussi's statement – published decades after the *Orlando furioso* – that Orsina "fu donna assai bella, non punto inferiore a quelle che per ciò hanno acquistato eterno nome" (146v) (was a very beautiful woman, no less than those who have gained eternal fame for this quality). Furthermore, before Betussi recounts the story of her courageous acts on the battlefield, he emphasizes the way women gain the status "illustrious": "Operò continuamente degne cose d'una donna illustre, vivendo sempre con buone opere, e miglior nome, in grazia del marito, e de' suoi sudditi" (146v) (She continually performed deeds worthy of an illustrious woman, living always with good acts and a good name, in the grace of her husband and of her subjects). Orsina, for Betussi, is a woman of virtue whose tale is the stuff of legend, but her tale is also one that is very close to fiction: "Di questa donna valorosa donna si potrebbono scrivere assaissime cose, e *quasi incredibili*" (146v, emphasis mine) (Of this valorous woman one could write so many things, and they are *almost unbelievable*). And finally, her story, like so many of Betussi's tales, illustrates the vices of men. Betussi adds to Arienti's original description that Orsina could not tolerate "gli huomini lascivi, e di vili costumi" (146v) (lascivious men as well as those with shameful habits). She, like other illustrious women, was not only a woman hero but a standard by which to judge shameful men.

Women Intermediaries in Betussi

If Orsina is exceptional, a quasi-fictional yet quasi-historical mirror of the woman warrior canonized by Boiardo and Ariosto, the majority of Betussi's women in war, especially those he does not take from Arienti and Foresti, are more representative of standard sixteenth-century female roles: suicidal victims, steadfast wives, and, finally, a number of pacifist intermediaries. Unlike the Plutarchan women discussed in the previous chapter, the intermediaries of Betussi's wars are not villagers protecting their husbands but regents advising their royal sons.[97] Women such as Anna Marchesana of Monferrato (also known as Anne of Alençon [1492–1562]) in his chapter 38 prevented war by providing a maternal role to her entire people. This story of Anna, as in so many of the later chapters of Betussi's compendium, may represent a more authentic mid-century *vita,* as her tale is not taken from the collections of Foresti or Arienti.[98] Betussi's entry on Anna does not discuss the troubled and troubling times depicted in her other biographies, but rather tells of her magnanimity. She both inherited and performed nobility, and thus she is the noble analogue to the Paduan suicide; both were illustrious women who performed nobility according to their class.[99] Betussi explains that the noble marquise demonstrated her class-specific virtue by ruling with "magnanimity." Her rule was so just

> ch'alcuno non sarebbe stato che più tosto non si fosse contentato d'essere suddito a lei, che ritrovarsi di sua libertà: perché sempre si è dimostrata madre et sorella loro. In tutte le guerre, che sono state nel Piemonte, sempre le terre sue quanto maggiormente si è potuto sono state rispettate. (192r)
>
> (that one would always rather be her subject than have his freedom, because she had always shown herself to be their mother and sister. In all the wars that took place in Piedmont, her lands were always respected, as much as was possible.)

The love of a female sovereign for her subjects is defined in familial terms; and most importantly, such a bond acts as a protective shield ("always were her lands respected") against the perils of war, arguably creating an inviolable body of the state. Like Castiglione's portrait of Isabella of Spain, Betussi's depiction of Anna creates a unifying bond between herself and her subjects; however, in contrast with the *Courtier's* obsessive focus on the gaze, the tale of Anna of Monferrato broadens the roles of women rulers, suggesting that their generous and just *acts*, not merely their surveilling gaze, have a profound effect on war.

The Ideal Virago of the Mid-Cinquecento

If Betussi presents Anna of Monferrato as the ideal peaceful ruler, he also gives us the ideal virago in Queen Maria of Hungary (in his chapter 39). Her portrait, like Anna's, is not taken from previous sources such as Arienti or Foresti, and thus represents a fully realized mid-century version of a noble virago. Betussi's narrative depicts the delicate compromise between the commander and warrior, recognizing the physical stress of war on her person while maintaining her decorous reputation.

The famous sister of Emperor Charles V, Maria of Hungary fled to Flanders in 1526 after her husband was killed by the Turks between Buda and Belgrade. Betussi writes that Maria had an "animo guerriero" (warrior spirit), was physically able to withstand the elements, and gloried in the command of armies.[100] Betussi's lengthy description of her military skills finishes with a regret that Maria actually highlights the failings of men, "men in name only," who are "cowardly," "effeminate," and "pusillanimous." This painful reminder of the faltering of the male sex, however, should only bolster women's glory:

> Ma quanto piu di ciò mi doglio, tanto maggiore è la gloria delle donne, che possono vedere per molte vie crescere la dignità loro, udendo una donna sofficiente à reggere uno esercito, metterlo all'ordine, conoscere il tempo di combattere, l'occasion di ritirarsi, animosamente romper gl'inimici, e togliendo anch'ella delle rotte, per ciò non punto smarrirsi, ma cercar di rifarsi. (193)
>
> (But the more I complain about that, the greater is the glory of women, who can see in many ways the growth of their own dignity, hearing how a woman is able to rule an army, put it in order, know when to attack, when to withdraw, robustly defeat the enemy, and even if she experiences defeat, she does not lose spirit for it, but seeks to rally.)

Betussi's description of Maria of Hungary actually takes much from Petrarch's own characterization of a different Maria, the peasant from Pozzuoli. Both women were able to withstand the rain and cold, and both women are characterized as not bothering with "womanly" concerns. But unlike Petrarch's Maria of Pozzuoli, Maria of Hungary did not seek to "overcome" her nature. Rather, as Betussi argues, her "great spirit" ("grand'animo") was given her by nature. Notably, even though Betussi explains Maria's incredible resistance to cold or heat as resembling that of a "private soldier," he does not dare portray her body as masculine, as Petrarch described his Maria. Maria of Hungary thus remains within certain bounds of feminine decorum: her body is physically present on the battlefield but far from the rhetorical scrutiny that described the manly characteristics of Bona Lombarda, Joan of Arc, or Maria of Pozzuoli. And even her acts in war are always those of a great commander, for, like Matilda of Canossa, Maria is not described as wielding weapons.

Finally, Maria's tale, like all the stories in Betussi's "addition," is meant to be a didactic one. In this capacity, the story brings us back to Boccaccio's original text, the one that Betussi himself translates in the same binding. Like Boccaccio's tale of Penthesilea, the story of Maria of Hungary is a stinging condemnation of a lack of manhood. Betussi, like so many of his contemporaries, describes men both as changing gender and as being debased to the status of rabbits, the common symbol of cowardliness: these men are "men only in name, and in effect not pusillanimous women, but vile and cowardly rabbits" (193v). Unlike Boccaccio, however, Betussi overtly states that the subject of his tale is meant to be imitated by women. He states that women can increase their own "dignity" by hearing of how this woman "led an army, put it in order, knew when to attack ..." Not only her virtues of intelligence and fortitude but even her acts would serve as examples for the women who hear this story, if, Betussi claims, women "con gli occhi vedessero quello che a pena accenno" (193v) (could see with their own eyes that which he has just shown).[101]

The story of Maria of Hungary during warfare accordingly marks a great shift in the praise-of-women-in war genre from its beginnings in Boccaccio. Where Boccaccio's Camilla was meant to be imitated as a model of chastity, Betussi's Maria of Hungary provides an imitable model of a different sort for women of the upper classes. They can act with bravery, lead battles, and effectively change the course of wars; and most importantly, their actions may include offensive as well as defensive reactions to the threat of invasion. Finally, they may perform militaristic deeds without risking their womanly status as virtuous and "illustrious." Where Betussi opened opportunities to women, he also began an overt exploration of the relation of class and gender in warfare. How these questions of class and women's agency played out in the second half of the century is the focus of the final chapter.

6 The Fame of Women and the Infamy of Men in the Age of Warring Queens (1550–1600)

> Shee may read (seeing at this present they are translated) besides the bookes of Holy Scriptures, (which sufficiently set downe that which belongeth to the ornament of the minde) the workes of Plutarch written touching women of renowme, who in times past lived in the world: and that which many long time after, and Boccace himselfe have written, with other Authors that lived in our time: and shall read if it may be done in faire pictures and painted tables, which with great efficacie moove the mindes of children that are tender and delicate. By this reading she shall find not onely wordes, which not being garnished with examples, profite much to that age, but also the notable actions and glorious enterprises of famous & renowmed women, where with shee may increase the notable vertues by nature liberally bestowed upon her.
>
> Giovanni Michele Bruto (c. 1550–1594)[1]

When compared to the previous fifty years, the second half of the sixteenth century witnessed a reduction of bloodshed within Italy, while the rest of Europe reeled under the violence of the religious wars.[2] The treaty of Cateau-Cambrésis (1559) ended the Hapsburg-Valois wars or so-called Italian Wars with the supremacy, if at times contested, of Spain in Italy.[3] In these relatively more peaceful times, transalpine events greatly influenced the discourse of women and war. In Paris, a daughter of Florence, Catherine de' Medici, became Queen of France when her husband, Henry II, ascended to the throne in 1547. She was widowed by 1559 and was queen mother to her son Francis II until 1560, regent of her second son, Charles IX, until 1563 (and advised him until his death in 1574), and acted as adviser for her third son, Henry III, until the end of her life.[4] Her thirty-year reign as regent and/or adviser for her three sons was famously characterized by civil and religious wars, and she is documented as taking strategic command of the royal army, a role that included a visit to Rouen's battlefield in 1562.[5] In England, there were three reigning queens within a relatively short period: Jane Grey, Mary Tudor, and Elizabeth Tudor. Elizabeth, like Catherine de' Medici in France, was locked in war and, like the French monarch, is believed to have made a foray onto the battlefield, notably when she delivered the oft-quoted oration at Tilbury in 1588.[6] Elizabeth's forty-five year rule (1558–1603) made its mark on the Italian consciousness; unsurprisingly, both she and Catherine would find their biographies included in Italian texts of illustrious women.

How Catherine and Elizabeth, reigning from two of Europe's most important thrones, might have influenced Italian literature – just as Isabella of Spain had done a century before – has been somewhat overlooked by literary critics and social historians.[7] This chapter briefly addresses the literature on warfare that was written to or about these two queens. The focus of the chapter, however, is the question of how these queens served as the backdrop for the illustrious-women genre that flourished in a time when great women were leading by example.

Catherine and Maria de' Medici

Catherine de' Medici would undoubtedly have been familiar with the genre of works about illustrious women. French women aristocrats had long received works that celebrated illustrious women's virtue,[8] and Catherine herself was meant to receive a set of tapestries wherein she was shown as Queen Artemisia.[9] In the libraries owned by and accessible to Catherine, there would have been Boccaccio's *De mulieribus claris* as well as other catalogues of women's lives, such as the *Donne illustri* by Niccolò Martelli (1498–1555), a work that the author says he presented to Catherine.[10] And it is likely that the texts and tapestries, along with other gifts depicting examples of illustrious women, were part of the instructional program for young gentlewomen.[11]

The importance of the discourse surrounding the virtue and abilities of women was certainly not limited to Catherine's youth, and such a matter would arguably become more critical as she progressed from her role of marginalized spouse to *de facto* ruler of France. The preponderance of books praising strong women in the sixteenth century may indeed be linked in complex ways with the ascendancy of women such as Catherine, Elizabeth, and Mary of Austria to Europe's thrones.[12]

These women were personally engaged in the management of the discourse of feminine virtue, and one of their primary tools was undoubtedly the production of literary texts. Catherine specifically would receive and/or commission many books on the virtues of women, such as the *Fort inexpugnable de l'honneur du sexe feminine* by François de Billon (1555).[13] She was also the inspiration for many Italian works of praise: Pietro Aretino wrote his *Ternali* for her (1551); Bernardo Tasso, Bernardo Capello, and Agostino Cacci wrote poetry in praise of her; and Gaspara Stampa wrote a laudatory sonnet to both King Henry II and Queen Catherine, published posthumously in Stampa's *Rime* of 1554.[14] This Italian-language literature written in praise of Catherine was in great part a result of patronage networks, often involving Italian exiles (*fuorusciti*) at her court, such as her official Italian poets, Luigi Alammani and Bartolomeo Delbene, both of whom unsurprisingly dedicated many works to the Queen.[15]

Before Catherine herself was included in the biographies of illustrious ladies, she figured in the literary context of war in various ways, and the bias of representations of Catherine and war, both during and after her lifetime, was largely dependent on the religious sympathies of the artist. Despite Catherine's efforts to bring peace to France (especially in dealing with her son Henry III and son-in-law the King of Navarre),[16] Catherine garnered infamy as "the evil Italian Queen," responsible for the St Bartholomew's Day massacre.[17] The most damning contemporary condemnation of Catherine (the queen mother at the time) was Catherine's first biography, *Discours merveilleux de la vie, actions et deportemens de Catherine de Médicis, Royne mere* (1574/5), a work likely written by a Huguenot and one that focused on her "Italian" deceptiveness.[18] The Italian origin of the Medici queen and more generally the Italian community in France were often held responsible for France's problems. In Renaud de Beaune's writings of 1588, the Italians were deemed responsible for the "discord in France," and Catherine herself, far from attempting to reconcile religious factions, was said to "impede" peace.[19] To discuss the xenophobia that Catherine met is also, necessarily, to discuss her sex. That is, the matter that precipitated the "Italian question" in the first place is the Renaissance reality of foreign brides who often married into foreign ruling houses, and these marriages often resulted in situations whereby the discourses of misogyny and xenophobia became superimposed onto the female consort herself.[20] Indeed, as I argue below, the "illustrious-women" literature written in the late sixteenth century addressed the difficulties faced by foreign brides, giving them suggestions on how to negotiate such concerns.

Catherine herself spent a lifetime balancing plural identities. As daughter of Lorenzo di Piero de' Medici (1492–1512) and French noblewoman Madeleine de la Tour d'Auvergne, she was characterized simultaneously as the progeny of a common banker, an heiress of immense wealth, and the daughter of a French line that traced itself back to St Louis. She was also characterized as both the nurturing mother and the scheming assassin. With regard to the discourse of power and war, these characterizations could be used to malign as well as praise her. In contrast to the Protestant texts that excoriated the Queen as wicked, bloodthirsty, and trained in the deceptions of Machiavelli, a biography by Nicolas Houle (1562) compared her to Artemisia and praised her for her "courage" and "valour."[21] While militancy might be the vice of women in the eyes of some critics, it was an "illustrious" trait for others. If the Protestant histories viewed Catherine's strength as vicious or cruel, many Italian texts such as Cornelio Lanci's catalogue of women extolled Catherine's strength in putting down the Huguenot rebellions.[22] Moreover, Francesco Serdonati made her rule during the Wars of Religion the centrepiece of his compendium of illustrious women. These accounts of female regency notwithstanding, what is fascinating in terms of Catherine's impact on the Italian literary scene is the way in which she was implored by Italian writers to engage in warfare, specifically as an ally against the wars of imperial expansion in Tuscany. Letters and verse written by men and women beseeched her to send armies to protect and "liberate" her ancestral land.

Catherine was asked to intervene in Italian conflicts that were ongoing with the Hapsburg Empire and with France. Her place at the French court was particularly complex given the relations between France and Florence, complications that had become strained even before Catherine's husband, Henry II (ruled 1547–59), ascended to the throne.[23] When the war of Florence and Siena erupted (1554–5), it effectively placed Catherine (aligned with Siena) at war against her cousin Cosimo de' Medici (aligned with the Hapsburg Empire).[24] The Florentine expansion into Siena and its resulting siege of the city inspired many to write to France in complaint, not against Catherine but rather seeking her support in defeating Cosimo. One of the best-known poems, written in 1553 before the Florentine siege of Siena, is the *canzone* "Venite all'ombra de' gran gigli d'oro" by Annibale Caro (1507–1566), a poet working for the Farnese cardinal in Rome and a critic of the imperial and Tuscan hold on Italy.[25] In the poem, King Henry II is praised as both the conqueror of the emperor, "vincitore di Augusto invitto" (conqueror of undefeated Augustus), and as the war general who turns his face towards justice while war (Bellona) and discord (Iri) are at his back (vv 48–51).[26] When the poem addresses Catherine directly, the political implications become more localized, moving from abstract anti-imperial language to direct anti-Medicean tones (here Medici is understood as the cadet branch of the family headed by Cosimo I de' Medici). Catherine, a member of the main Medici branch, is addressed as the "gran Giuno" (great Juno) (v. 60). She has an "alma inviolata e pura" (pure and untouched soul), and is said to be happy and certain in her husband's love. Furthermore, the Queen has given Florence and all of Italy hope for liberation:

E fu nostra ventura,
e providenza del superno Iddio,
ch'in sí gran regno, a sí gran re t'unio,
perché del suo splendore e del tuo seme
risorgesse la speme
della tua Flora e dell'Italia tutta. (vv 67–72).

(And it was our fortune
and providence of eternal God,
who has united you in such a great kingdom and to such a great king,
so that from his splendour and from your seed,
might revive the hope
of your Flora and of all Italy)

Catherine's "seed" of Medici blood combined with Henry's "splendour" will save the peninsula that has become both "serva e distrutta" (servant and destroyed) and is awaiting its freedom –"salute e libertà n'attende" (life and liberty it awaits) – from the yoke of imperial and Medicean occupation.

Caro's poem anchors its hope on the Queen's ability to join her consort in one kingdom due to his great love for her: "gode dell'amor suo, lieta e sicura" (you delight in his love, happy and secure) (v 62). The irony of these words, given Henry's well-known affair with Diane de Poitiers, was immediately noted by Caro's contemporaries, and yet Caro's writing placed his hopes in Catherine's effectiveness in spousal intercession.[27] The act of writing to women in the hope that these female addressees would in turn influence their husbands is quite common in the history of Italian letters, especially in the context of Medici women.[28] How spouses were to intervene was of course a delicate matter of balancing social expectations of gender with the exercise of personal agency. It is no surprise that the methods of Catherine's interventions with her husband were criticized as taunting by some English authors, and as one scholar suggests, Catherine was used as a counter-example to warn Elizabeth I of how not to act as a female ruler.[29]

Such interest in Catherine's own spousal influence over Henry is further developed in the verses written to the Queen by the gifted writer Virginia Martini Casolani Salvi, a Sienese exile in Rome. Virginia Salvi has recently received increased critical attention, particularly by Virginia Cox and Konrad Eisenbichler.[30] Eisenbichler both disambiguates Virginia Martini Casolani Salvi's identity from that of her namesake and sister-in-law, Virginia Luti Salvi, and also explains her antagonistic history with the imperial government of Siena, including her own arrest and trial – an arrest precipitated by her political poetry.[31] Virginia Salvi clearly did not write to Catherine de' Medici as a social peer, yet the two women did share a mutual acquaintance, Piero Strozzi. The Salvi family had befriended the pro-French Florentine expatriate Piero Strozzi when he visited Siena in 1538, and Catherine had a long-time family connection with the Strozzi: Piero Strozzi's mother, Clarice, had helped raise Catherine de' Medici after she was orphaned; Piero's father helped fund Catherine's dowry, and perhaps more importantly, Piero himself had lived under the protection of Catherine de' Medici in 1533 and would later be one of her favourites, chosen as the marshal of the French army in Tuscany.

With this context in mind, it is less surprising that Virginia Salvi, a political woman who had direct connections with Piero Strozzi, the Queen's cousin, addressed two poems to Catherine, speaking to her as a Florentine who should take pity on Tuscany.[32] In a sonnet to the Queen, "Afflitti e mesti intorno al alte sponde" (Mournful and downcast beside the high banks), Salvi depicts the great sorrow of the Sienese, which has been caused by the furor and hunger of the empire, represented by the "famelico Augel" (ravenous bird) (quoted and translated in Eisenbichler, *The Sword and the Pen* 195–6). Salvi's sonnet seeks to appeal to the Queen's loyalty to her Tuscan origins by saying that not only Siena but Florence herself feels the sorrow of the times, for Flora cries even more than those Sienese who weep along the Tiber: "Piange, Reina mia, la vostra Flora / Piu' di tutt'altre mesta" (Your Flora, my Queen, is also weeping, / More sorrowful than the rest) (195; translation 196).

The poem is a call to action, for it is Catherine, according to Salvi, who has the power to console Flora's pain and whose "glances" are powerful enough to chase away her sorrow: "son possenti / I vostri rai far, che di duol non mora" (but your glances / Have the power to let her not die of grief) (195; translation slightly altered 196). The conceit, one exploited repeatedly by Petrarch, suggests that a woman's "rai" (rays/glances) can relieve the pain of the poet. Yet Salvi alters this erotic conceit. The Queen is to alleviate the pain of Florence; but unlike Petrarch's lover, who could console the poet by merely acknowledging him, it is unclear how these glances of the Queen would benefit Florence.

We might thus read Salvi's sonnet alongside her *canzone*, also written to Catherine and addressing her with a more explicit request. Written after the siege of Siena, the *canzone* "L'ardente amor, la pura, e viva fede" (The burning love, the pure and lively faith) (Domenichi, 199–202; quoted and translated in Eisenbichler, *The Sword and the Pen* 263–7) requests Catherine's intercession by asking her to persuade her husband to send assistance to Siena. Like the sonnet, this work tells of the "nemico augel" (enemy bird) that now has preyed on Siena with weapons: "Col suo artiglio n'havesse a forza presi" (it had captured them forcefully with its claws) (263; translation 266). The *canzone* employs further imagery to appeal to Catherine, such as the figure of the nurturing mother, an image that Catherine herself would invest much time in developing.[33] Expanding the avian analogy, Salvi describes Catherine as the good mother whose dear children are taken from their "nido" (nest) by a "belva" (beast) (which is repeatedly called a bird), so that the children have turned to the mother in their need:

A Voi, come a pia madre, i cari figli,
Che da belva crudele
Sian del amato nido tratti fuore,
Venghiamo, offesi da rapaci artigli
Del empio, e infedele
Augel, cagion del nostro aspro dolore. (263, vv 23–8)

(You, as to a merciful mother, your dear children,
who have been forced from their beloved nest
by a cruel beast
come, injured by the rapacious claws
of the pitiless and unfaithful
bird, the source of our bitter pain.) (266)

Salvi's poems seek aid in war from a powerful woman, and thus they offer a counterpoint to the poem she wrote to Catherine's husband, King Henry II, in which she uses a chiding tone to remind him that if he does not intervene in Siena's time of need, his "Real cortesia" (Royal courtesy) will diminish.[34] Moreover, when Salvi writes to Catherine, she clearly could not have recourse to the shaming mechanism of inadequate masculinity as had Catherine of Siena, Laura Terracina, and Chiara Matraini as discussed in chapter 3. Instead, she invokes rather conventional feminine imagery – family and the metaphorical domestic space (here represented as a nest) – in order to appeal to a woman in war.[35] Salvi's poetry to Catherine de' Medici also adopts a Petrarchan eroticism in which she subtly interpolates the Queen in an erotic schema that is meant to incite war.

The *canzone* figures a sequential exchange of pathos and desire, where the first response is pity, and this sentiment is then to be transferred into an erotic mode that might persuade the King. Salvi writes that the Queen would feel "pietade" (pity) for the Sienese if she were to see them:

Ben so che per pietade io vedrei il viso
Vostro di pianto molle
Se vi fosser presenti i martir nostri
E 'l duol v'avrebbe amaramente anciso
Quando il nemico volle
A forza darne in prede a fieri mostri. (264, vv 34–9)

(I know well that I would see your face, out of pity
wet with tears, if our sufferings were reported to you
and you would have died of grief
when the enemy wanted
to give us, by force, to wild monsters.) (266)

The pity inspired by this sight is then meant to move Catherine to action. She is to "rekindle" the King's "desire" to take up arms:

Nel regal cor del vostro alto Consorte
Di nuovo raccendete
Quel bel desio di liberare altrui
Dal giogo, che ne da perpetua morte. (265, vv 67–70)

(In the royal heart of your highest consort,
rekindle again
that fair desire to free other people
from the yoke that gives them perpetual death.) (267)

Salvi shrewdly refers to Henry as "consort" not king, emphasizing the intimate and erotic relationship between the pair. Moreover, the words "raccendere" (rekindle) and "desio" (desire) are typical in the erotic lyric canon, and they may possibly explain how her "glances," the Queen's weapons in Salvi's earlier sonnet, might be able to salve the pain of Florence and Siena. Through her relationship as consort and specifically through her skilful use of glances, Catherine can bring effective change to the war, as Salvi again tells her: "Che Voi sola potete / Troncare al fier nemico i lacci sui" (And You alone will be able / to stop the fierce enemy's looting) (265; translation 267).

We have no knowledge of whether Catherine responded to Salvi's poetry, but we do know that she did attempt to persuade her consort and later her sons to intervene in Italian affairs. It is interesting that a second Tuscan woman also wrote to a different queen of France to instruct her on how to exert her will within the construct of marriage. Indeed, nearly fifty years after Salvi, Isabella Cervoni wrote to the second Medici queen of France, Maria de' Medici, writing verse on how the new bride might use her powers of persuasion on the king, and that through such spousal influence she might become an illustrious woman.[36]

Isabella Cervoni's home of Colle Val D'Elsa was not far from Salvi's Siena, and she addressed a *canzone* to Maria de' Medici that praised her beauty, eyes, soul, and intellect.[37] In her "Canzone in laude di Madama Maria de' Medici," Cervoni then tells Maria that she will be called into "quelle bande … [di] Donne sagge" (69v) (those great bands … [of] wise women), particularly those women who advised their husbands.[38] Whereas Salvi had been seeking an immediate response by Catherine, Cervoni writes to the Queen in a more didactic tone, telling her of the long historical tradition of influential wives. Her poem offers a mini-catalogue of illustrious women, telling brief stories of ancient and medieval queens such as Placida and Clotilda. Like Plutarch she praises the Romans and then moves on to praise the Greeks and Gauls who asked their women's advice in times of war and peace:

Costume appresso i Greci ancor fu usato
Di voler nel governo, e ne' perigli
De le Donne il parer, che sempre piacque.
Nè a' Galli usar de le lor Donne spiaque
I saggi, e pii consigli;
Se trattar si dovea di guerra o pace. (70r)

(The custom, which was always beloved, was still used by the Greeks, who wanted the opinion of women in their government and in times of danger. Nor was it unwelcome by the Gauls to use the sage and pious counsel of their women, when they needed to speak of war or peace.)

After illustrating how wives had exerted agency throughout history, Cervoni makes a list of the wealth of Maria's legacy: arms, knights, temples, arches, and cities, as well as duchies and safe maritime passages. The aggregate of these items is what Maria brings with her to the marriage. Cervoni argues that this legacy of arms, knights, temples, and so on, is her cultural dowry. Specifically, Cervoni says that these items are the "beauties" and "virtues" of the Queen: "Queste son Donna le bellezze vostre / Le virtù vostre, le vostre grandezze; / Ch' a la Francia portate hoggi con Voi" (70v) (These are your beauties / your virtues, your greatness / that with you today you take to France). And, Cervoni explains, a wife must make use of all of these virtues. The poet revises the notion of feminine beauty and focuses on the "grazia" (grace) that Maria brings with her from the majesty of the Grand Duchy of Florence. Maria's qualities will make her even more beautiful to her husband than Esther was to Ahasuerus, notably a comparison with yet another persuasive wife:

D'Ester la grazia a vile
Tenuto havria Assuer, se' visto havesse
Pur'una volta Voi; nel cui bel viso
L'alma Natura espresse
La grazia, che fa in terra un Paradiso. (70v)

(Ahasuerus would have found the grace of Esther to be vile were he to have gazed but once upon you, in whose face noble Nature expresses the grace that makes on earth a Paradise.)

And finally, Maria will make the French her subjects not with the sword but with this powerful beauty and grace:

Attende Voi, che non con foco, o spada
Tutti i Galli farete a voi soggetti.
A vostri amici ferirete i petti
Per ciascuna contrada
Con la bellezza vostra, e con la grazia. (70v)

(You will see that you will make all Gauls your subjects, not with fire or sword. You will wound the breasts of your friends throughout the land with your beauty and grace.)

Cervoni's letter may not request that Maria de' Medici engage in warfare, but it does suggest that the new bride encompasses all of the triumph and glory that war has brought to the realm of Tuscany. Moreover, the bride is beautiful specifically because of these glories, and this, says Cervoni, is her greatest weapon: the one that will wound the hearts of the French and make them her subjects.

Elizabeth I, Queen of England

When Isabella Cervoni wrote her verses to Maria de' Medici, another queen reigned to the north, a woman who famously did not take a husband and thus influenced government and warfare without recourse to spousal intervention. When Elizabeth came to the head of England's realm she was already versed in Latin and Italian as well as in the Italian literary canon. She would also have been cognizant of the Italian literary tradition of illustrious women, as she would likely have been familiar with Boccaccio's *De mulieribus claris* (*Famous Women*).[39] There is no lack of scholarship to substantiate the claim that Tudor England embraced Italian culture with enthusiasm (though an enthusiasm sometimes fraught with ambivalence), and the influence of Italian political philosophy on Elizabeth's rule is likewise a matter of scholarly interest. But as Keir Elam has noted, almost all studies regarding early modern Italy and England have "concerned the importing or reception of a 'model' culture," so that the dialogue between the two countries has seemed "exclusively unilateral."[40] The influence of English culture, specifically during the long and stable rule of Elizabeth, did have an impact on Italy, and the extent to which she might have changed the landscape of the Italian *querelles des femmes* is still to be understood.

One very apparent influence of Elizabeth on Italian literature is that her name is added to certain catalogues and biographies of illustrious women. Bernardo Tasso, for example, includes her in a list of women whom he recommends to his female warrior protagonist Mirinda in the *Amadigi* (1560). The poem, published two years after Elizabeth ascended to the throne, states that Elizabeth is "d'infinito valor, d'animo invitto" (*Amadigi*, XI, 31) (of infinite valour, of unvanquished spirit). Nonetheless, Elizabeth's name is also notably missing from other compendia of biographies, no doubt because of her Protestantism and excommunication in 1570, in which she was denounced as a "heretic and favourer of heretics."[41]

This absence of Elizabeth from some catalogues of famous women is as telling as her inclusion in others. For example, in Cornelio Lanci's encyclopedic *Esempi della virtu' delle donne* (1590) there is no mention of Elizabeth, while Mary Tudor, Elizabeth's half-sister and a Catholic, is praised for having led her army into London and taken the throne over her sister's wishes (172). Again, in a reflection of partisan leanings, Elizabeth is featured prominently in another Italian text published a year later, *Le vite delle donne illustri del Regno dell'Inghilterra et del Regno di Scotia* (1591), written by Petruccio Ubaldini.[42] When he wrote the text, Ubaldini was residing in England and was occasionally employed by the Elizabethan court, and thus this text of illustrious English and Scottish women is one example of a text that transmitted culture from England to Italy.[43] The influence of the work in Italy was nearly immediate, as Ubaldini's biographies were mined as a source for an Italian compendium of illustrious women published by Francesco Serdonati in Florence in 1596. Though Ubalidini's work is cited throughout Serdonati's anthology, there is no biography of Elizabeth in his text.

Elizabeth was a sticking point for Italian writers who praised powerful and militant women. She was fabulously involved with successful martial endeavours such as the defeat of the Spanish Armada, yet her Protestantism sat uncomfortably in praises of virtuous ladies. Scipione Mercurio, for example, points to Elizabeth as proof that women can perform "military virtues." He states that though she was the ruler of a "little realm," she was able to humiliate Philip of Austria's army: "rompendogli le armate, deprendandogli le ricche Flotte delle Indie, & insultandogli continuamente con le sue armate vittoriose le Riviere della superba Spagna" (4) (breaking the armada, taking from him the riches of the fleet of the Indies, and continually insulting him with her victories off the shores of haughty Spain).[44] But, as Mercurio is also quick to protest, her religion was an impediment to her fame: "a qual grado di gloria sarebbe giunta, se all'invitto animo suo havesse aggiunto lo splendore della Chiesa Cattolica" (4) (what level of glory would have been achieved if to her undefeated spirit she had added the splendour of the Catholic Church!). Similarly, Torquato Tasso, in his treatise *Il discorso della virtù feminile e donnesca,* expresses his discomfort with and admiration of Elizabeth. After extolling a list of women rulers, he awkwardly includes Elizabeth while omitting her name: "Né la presente reina d'Inghilterra deve con silenzio esser trapassata, perché se bene la nostra malvagia fortuna vuol ch'ella sia dalla Chiesa separata, nondimeno l'eroiche virtù dell'animo" (8) (Neither should we pass over the present Queen of England in silence, because even though our bad fortune wishes that she from the Church be separated, she is not so from heroic virtues and spirit).

The Feminine Virtue of Militant Women

Tasso's treatise, discussed at length in chapter 1 of this book, presents a theory of women's virtue that identifies nobly born women as inherently illustrious and even "heroic." The work was published in 1580, roughly thirty years after Giuseppe Betussi published his *Donne illustri,* the translation of Boccaccio's *Famous Women.* Both Betussi and Tasso developed theories of illustrious women, and both discussed women in the context of war. Betussi advocated that women, regardless of class, could be "illustrious" by demonstrating active displays of agency, often in politics or warfare, and Tasso extolled the heroic potential of noblewomen while suggesting that lesser-born women were not suited for such illustrious roles. Yet, as I argue above, Tasso states that noblewomen could choose not to perform great acts and nonetheless be called "heroic." For Tasso, illustrious and heroic women could merely live decorously in palaces of grandeur.[45]

Much has been made of Tasso's attempt to reconcile Aristotelian notions of women's deficiencies with a Neoplatonic view of women's abilities in government and the military. Maria Luisa Doglio implies that Tasso's acknowledgment of women's ability to reign and command was necessitated by women such as Catherine and Elizabeth, who were living examples of female competency.[46] I share Doglio's view of the influence of historical women rulers on literature; Tasso himself carefully lists several of them. However, Doglio's assessment of Tasso misses his neglect of historical evidence of virtuous acts by lowborn women. Thirty years before Tasso, Betussi's text emphasized acts in war as a way for women to gain fame, and he argued for such social mobility by providing a handful of historical examples of lowborn women who became "illustrious" through their military competency.[47] Tasso's theory of thirty years later restricted women's behaviour by limiting heroic acts to noblewomen. If, as Doglio suggests, Tasso's praise of noblewomen was a "necessary" recognition of historical figures such as queens Catherine and Elizabeth, it simultaneously ignored the previously documented historical heroism of common women.

The genre of compendia of illustrious women was mindfully engaged in a process of recuperating women's history and crafting a new verisimilar historiography of women and war. Moreover, the genre, once typified by catalogues of ancient and mythical women such as those found in Boccaccio's *Famous Women,* was transforming into anthologies of tales of *living* illustrious women as well as lowborn viragos such as Bona Lombarda. As we approach the end of the century, the status and temporal proximity of viragos (e.g., Catherine, Elizabeth, among others) become recurrent elements in the genre. Such biographies of living or recently deceased heroic women demand a different hermeneutic process than the stories of mythological or ancient heroines as presented by Boccaccio. Living powerful queens were incontrovertible proof of women's abilities, and they provided a material foundation that could ground even those mythological tales in a realm of possibility. As the sixteenth century marched on, compendia of *donne illustri* referenced the heroic acts of women that were already known to readers. I am not claiming that these anthologies of biographies were "histories" in the modern or even Renaissance sense of the word, but rather that they *presented* themselves as histories while at the same time recuperating the multiple literary conventions of representations of women and war. Perhaps the most perplexing part of this genre is that, just as historical representations became quite literary, they also became self-conscious about historical convention. For example, when biographies recounted the deeds of noble *historical* women, these women were not depicted as physically strong or as killing their enemies. This representation stood in obvious contrast to the very literary trope of depicting contemporary epic and fictional women as sword-swinging viragos such as Bradamante and Marfisa.

I will claim with some caution that this rule (e.g., not representing noble historical women as armed) and other modes of representing historical women and war undergo a shift at the very end of the century with Francesco Serdonati's 1596 edition of Boccaccio's *Famous Women*. There is no doubt that I will have missed many innovative texts that predate Serdonati, and I, too, have already cited cases of noblewomen who have been portrayed in arms. Nonetheless, Serdonati, if not entirely novel, changes the discourse of women and war by presenting large numbers of women who are not entirely conventional. The most noticeable change Serdonati made was to broaden the range of women he described in warfare. Instead of limiting himself to singular heroines, he included several communities of contemporary women who fought courageously in war. Moreover, he also described noblewomen, though typically not living contemporaries, as armed and killing. And finally, the author was particularly interested in celebrating Italian women, particularly Tuscan women. Thus, Serdonati's project created a book that exhibited a certain patriotism, an approach taken by previous texts (e.g., *Laude di donne bolognesi* [1514]). Unlike the authors of these earlier sixteenth-century anthologies, however, Serdonati praised Tuscany and to some extent Italy as a land of courageous women in war. In this manner, he prefigures nationalistic wartime books found during the Risorgimento and Fascist eras.[48]

Francesco Serdonati (c.1540 Florence – c.1603 Rome?) and Illustrious Women[49]

Francesco Serdonati's edition of Betussi's translation of Boccaccio's *Famous Women* is actually a compendium of several books.[50] In 1596 Serdonati reprinted Betussi's 1547 translation of Boccaccio and added his own biographies to those already appended to the book. Thus, the new book contained three editions: the translation of Boccaccio's *Famous Women*, Betussi's addition of 50 contemporary biographies, and another whopping 120 biographies written by Serdonati himself, all of which are introduced by the essay "On the Perfection of Women," an essay that thoroughly addresses the ability of women in warfare, discussed at length in the first chapter of this book. As the book's title suggests, the works of Betussi and Serdonati are "additions" ("giunte") that follow the translation of Boccaccio's master text: *Libro di M. Giovanni Boccaccio delle donne illustri. Tradotto di Latino in volgare per M. Giuseppe Betussi, con una giunta fatta dal medesimo, d'altre donne famose, e un'altra nuova giunta fatta per M. Francesco Serdonati d'altre donne illustri. Antiche e moderne.*[51] The novelty of the work is that, despite the title, these new biographies resist and rewrite the Boccaccian paradigm of famous women while addressing the matter of "heroic" birthright that was discussed by Tasso.

Serdonati's project, anthologizing Boccaccio and Betussi, was an attempt to establish itself as the new bestseller in what had become a very popular literary industry – compendia of illustrious women. Serdonati's was not the only illustrious-women compendium that told of women and war. For example, Scipione Vasoli's *La gloriosa eccellenza delle donne e d'amore* (1573) contained short entries on women who, through love of their husbands, were instrumental in conducting or stopping war. In Vasoli's text, we find the stories of Coriolanus's mother and the Sabine women, where the author emphasizes that the virtue of women can bring peace: "per la prudenza, e virtu' delle Donne si spantosa guerra si mutò in continua pace" (91) (through prudence and virtue of women such a frightful war was transformed into continual peace). In a different work, Cornelio Lanci's *Esempi della virtu' delle donne, ne' quali si vede la bellezza delle vergini, maritate, e vedove* (1590), the entries are presented in thematic sections, and the longest section by far is dedicated primarily to women in times of war, generically called "Women who are strong in everything" ("forte in ciascuna cosa"). In this subdivision of strong women, there are an impressive 117 entries, including the usual suspects of Bona Lombarda, Maria di Pozzuolo, Catherine de' Medici, and Mary (but no Elizabeth) Tudor, as compared to only 11 women in the section on "Women who bring peace to men" ("pacificarono gl'huomini"). Tomaso Garzoni's *Le vite delle donne illustri della scrittura sacra* (1586) focused on holy women, and occasionally the author narrates the lives of women who demonstrated courage in the face of violence or who showed "ardimento virile" (virile courage), as in the case of Judith (153).[52] And all of these works find their apex in the mega-collections of Pierpaolo Ribera, *865 donne illustri antiche e moderne* (1609) and Silvano Razzi's *Delle vite delle donne illustri per santità raccolte dal p. abate don S. R. camaldolese,* a six-volume set published from 1597 to 1606 offering biographies of illustrious saintly women in the calendar order of their celebration days.[53]

As with any generic development, new authors brought innovation and sought individual recognition. Serdonati's publisher, Giunti, made certain that the reader was aware of the novelty of the 1596 edition of Boccaccio by printing the title page and subsequent divider pages in large roman font, announcing Betussi's and Serdonati's contributions with colophon and all.[54] This visual signifier cued the reader to prepare for the shift in content from author to author. As we have stated above, Betussi's additions were distinguished from Boccaccio's entries in describing praiseworthy contemporary women and focusing on the notion of nobility. Serdonati, on the other hand, provided biographies of ancient, mythological, and contemporary women. I will further argue that Serdonati's concern was not with the illustrious/noble quality of militancy but rather with the *function* of women's militancy in Italy's arena of wars and foreign occupation.

Serdonati's final *giunta* of 120 biographies contains narratives that include accounts of legendary Amazons, peasant women combatants, Old Testament women in the midst of violence, and almost contemporaneous accounts of women in the context of sixteenth-century wars. In 66 tales (or nearly two-thirds of Serdonati's addition), we find stories that highlight women who are praised for heroic acts during war. This figure is striking because it suggests that heroism in warfare is not just one way but rather the primary way of entering into the pantheon of illustrious women. Another important innovation by Serdonati is the narration of 18 stories that describe groups of historical women. Though it has not been noticed in the criticism before, the inclusion of these collectives of women (rather than individual women) distinguishes Serdonati's text from the compilations of Betussi and his predecessors, Foresti and Arienti. Of course, Francesco Serdonati is not the first Italian to write about communities of famous women. Boccaccio himself had recounted the stories of two groups, the wives of the Cimbrians (ch. 80) and the wives of the Minyans (ch. 31). The former killed themselves rather than be dishonoured in prison, and the latter sacrificed themselves to save their husbands so that the men in turn might slay their captors.[55] Following Boccaccio's monumental work, writers such as Laura Cereta (1469–1499) repeated the tales of the wives of the Cimbrians and Minyans in her own catalogue of illustrious women in the fifteenth century.[56] And outside the compilations of illustrious women, tales circulated that described battalions of Sienese women fortifying the walls of the city before a siege by Florence in the 1550s.[57] What sets Serdonati's women apart from all of these communities of women, however, is that the women in his compilation are armed fighters.

The armed communities of women found in Serdonati are active participants in warfare and at times shame men for their militant dereliction.

Thus, they share a certain spirit with the women described in Plutarch's *On the Bravery of Women*. Plutarch's text, as discussed above, was often cited and circulated after its translation into Latin in 1485.[58] Indeed, Plutarch's *Bravery of Women* as well as his *Parallel Lives* are mined by Serdonati himself for his biographies of illustrious women. Most notably, he virtually translates Plutarch's "Women of Melii," a community of women who hid daggers under their dresses and assisted their husbands' successful revolt.[59] Through his numerous citations of Plutarch, Serdonati was engaged in the general trend of recuperating the Greek author, but he was as well selecting certain examples of Plutarch that he felt should be included in what was becoming the Italian canon of "illustrious women."[60] In my view, Serdonati included specific stories in his book to create an intratextual tapestry of women in war, where ancient tales would inform the reading of contemporary biographies.

We might take a pair of stories, the ancient story of the "Spartan Women" (509) and the Renaissance tale of "The Women of Diu" (603), as an example of an intratextual reading. In Serdonati's tale of the "Spartan Women," a story borrowed from Plutarch's "Life of Pyrrhus," men's conceptions of women in war are confounded by women's bravery. With the threat of an impending siege by Pyrrhus, the all-male council of Sparta, the Gerousia, decided to send the Spartan women out of the city for their safety. The noblewoman Archidamia then entered the Gerousia, sword in hand, and spoke on behalf of Spartan women, saying that the women did not wish to outlive their *patria*. The women were allowed to stay within the city, and many of them aided the men in digging a trench so that they might rest during battle. The men ultimately drove off the enemy, and Sparta was victorious. Serdonati then provides a Renaissance analogue to this story in the tale of "The Women of Diu." In 1548 when Mohamed, king of Cambay (Khambhat), besieged the Portuguese fort of Diu, the castellan wanted to send the women, here called "bocche disutili" (useless mouths), out of the fortress for their safety. According to Serdonati, the matrons of the city did not want to abandon their husbands, and they were allowed to stay within the city for the siege. Some women of "animo virile" (manly spirit) took picks and fought off men, while others acted as guards at the walls. The Portuguese were victorious against Mohamed.

The story clearly appropriates several elements of Plutarch's tale of the Spartan women. Men believe women to be unfit for fighting, vulnerable to attack, and best protected by sending them outside the city. Women, on the other hand, resist this ideology and practice, and confront men so that they may stay in their homelands. They then are active participants in the battles that lead to victory. Serdonati's story is also a modernization of the ancient one. Ancient Spartans and Molossians are replaced with Christians and Muslims, and, significantly, some of the women go beyond their Greek forerunners; where the Spartan woman Archidamia carried a sword into the council but did not wield it in battle, the Christian women arm themselves with weapons against the Muslim Cambians. Moreover, the story of Diu modernizes the Greek story by emphasizing contemporary attitudes towards women, a cultural context underscored by the popular terminology "bocche inutile" (useless mouths). The term was a rather common moniker given to certain groups of people in siege warfare. They were "useless" as they were not combatants, and they were "mouths" that reduced food rations. What is fascinating in the tale of the "Women of Diu" is that the arc of the story is not only that these "useless mouths" show themselves to be courageous women who are instrumental in the victory, but that men undergo a change of attitude and recognize the error of categorizing women as liabilities. The victory of the Portuguese against Mohamed provokes the male leader of Diu to "riconoscer la salvezza di quel luogo dall'arditezza, e dalla prudenza delle donne" (605) (recognize the safety of that place was due to the spirit and prudence of women). The women's courageous actions thus not only contributed to the victory but also triggered a learning process on the part of the men.

Serdonati's tales of communities of women often blend historical narration with extradiegetic commentary about gender polemics, and thus these stories of female militant communities can also serve as editorials for a change in gendered war practices. For example, the tale of the "Hungarian Women" provides numerous commentaries on warcraft. Serdonati states that when the Turks invaded Hungary, the Hungarian women killed many invaders and were also killed by them during a battle that lasted for forty days. With graphic descriptions, Serdonati depicts armed women in battle. An anonymous woman decapitated two soldiers with one swipe of a scythe, and another woman watched as her mother was killed by a rock thrown at her head. She then took the bloody stone from her dead mother's body and hurled it down on the attacking soldiers, killing several of them. With anecdotes such as these, it is no surprise that Serdonati characterizes the victory of the Hungarians over the Turks as due to the bravery of both women and men, a victory that he clearly portrays as a result of the sexes fighting together. He then compares this example of men's and women's courage to a defeat that was caused by the gender failures of Christian men. Serdonati concludes his story of the Hungarian women with the following comment on a seemingly unrelated event:

> Se paragonerai queste [Ungare] donne co' soldati che questo presente anno 1594 furono posti a guardia dell'Isola di Comar presso Iaverino, dirai che queste fossero huomini, e soldati e questi del presente anno femmine vili. (605–6).

> (If you will compare these [Hungarian] women to the soldiers who this present year of 1594 were placed on guard on the Island of Comar near Iaverino, you will say that these women were men, and the soldiers of this present year were cowardly females.)

The biography's conclusion shows how the victorious Hungarian women stand as a symbol of the failings of the men in Comar, but it also offers a problematic assessment of gender, as it calls men who act uncourageously in war "cowardly females." In a story that advocates for the effectiveness of women in combat, Serdonati also advocates an opposing view by perpetuating the notion that war is gendered as male and cowardly behaviour is by definition female. The "Hungarian Women" story thus reveals how deeply ingrained the universal gendering of war is, and how even the most pro-woman texts participate in the very discourse they proclaim to resist.

Nonetheless, stories such as the "Hungarian Women" are apparent examples of militant women enacting an effect on the outcome of war. And just as the male characters of Serdonati's stories learned that women are not merely "useless mouths," so too could the *stories* of militant women change the hearts and minds of readers. The author contrasts the victorious Hungarian women to the defeated Island of Comar; Comar notably lacked women combatants. The victory of women in one war is meant to emphasize the shame of the retreat of cowardly men in a far-off location. The attentive reader would see that the author had provided a strategy for victory that placed not just women but the *stories* of illustrious women on the front lines. It would seem that the author hopes that stories of armed women might correct men's "cowardly" behaviour in order to stave off defeat.

The story of "Marulla donzella di Metellino" (Marulla, the damsel of Metellino) (580) stages exactly how the actions of brave women could bring real and tangible changes in the ways men fought wars. In Serdonati's version of Marulla's biography, when the Turkish fleet was besieging the land of Coccino on the island of Metellino, the noble damsel Marulla saw her father killed by the enemy.[61] Realizing that her people were losing the fight, "non si diede alle lagrime, o lamenti, ma a guisa di franco guerriero imbracciato lo scudo del padre, e presa in mano la spada si mise nella prima scheria, e combattendo francamente ributtò con vera virtù i nimici" (she did not give herself over to tears or laments, but took the guise of a brave warrior. Putting on her father's shield and taking his sword in hand, she went to the front line and, fighting heartily, she repulsed the enemy with true virtue). Such feminine bravery was not merely cause for celebration; in Serdonati's words, it also indicated inadequacy on the part of men. Seeing Marulla fight incited shame; and, as in many of the Plutarchan tales, this shame was necessary for mobilizing masculine courage and ultimate victory: "che' Coccinesi vergognandosi, ch'una donzella facesse quello, che tutto 'l popolo insieme non havea prima osato di tentare la seguitarono con tanta prontezza, che alla fine cacciarono i Turchi della terra" (580) (the Coccinesi being ashamed that a damsel had done that which the entire people together had not previously dared to attempt, followed her with such fervour, that in the end they chased the Turks from the land).

In this account, Serdonati invokes Plutarch's faith in the power of women to shame men; but again, unlike the women of Plutarch, Serdonati's woman is depicted as armed. In this story, Serdonati arms the noble Marulla, and thus the story recalls the armed viragos of epic poetry, at least in terms of social class. Marulla also stands in contrast to the noble *unarmed* female commanders of historical biographies of past illustrious women. With few exceptions, historical armed viragos were from the lower class, and even these were often contained in a literary convention casting them in the realm of the fantastic.

Serdonati's story of Marulla, a tale borrowed from Sabellico's *Dell'historia vinitiana* (1558) and more famously from Bandello's *Novelle*, 4:18, follows his sources in that he arms a woman who uses a sword effectively.[62] However, while the other sources mention that her father was a great warrior, Serdonati specifies that she is a "nobil donzella" (noble damsel), and thus emphasizes her position. We must be careful not to make too much of Marulla's aristocratic status, as her armed prowess is somewhat tempered by the fact that she is located outside of mainland Europe, in the exotic periphery of the Venetian island territories. This atypical behaviour by a noble woman is possibly tempered by her location at the margins, just as Amazons were always depicted as living beyond the periphery of the "civilized" world. In addition, Marulla (both in the source texts as well as in Serdonati) is returned to a more conventional role at the end of the tale, as she is to marry one of the Venetian soldiers. After the victorious battle at Metellino, Antonio Loredano, the admiral of the Venetian fleet, recognized the bravery of Marulla, and "oltre a gli altri premi le permise che s'eleggesse fra quei soldati un marito a suo modo" (580) (beyond the many other awards, he permitted her to elect a husband of her choice from the soldiers). It is an ambivalent conclusion: the woman who was exceptional among women and men was now returned to the role of wife, as dictated by the patriarchy. Yet the particulars of the situation also bestow an unexpected agency on Marulla.[63] She is given the ability to choose her husband, thus reversing the pervasive dynamic of the woman as prize for martial victory.

In Serdonati's compendium, Marulla is one of several examples of noblewomen who arm themselves. Other armed noblewomen range from Queen Margaret of Anjou (1430–1482), described as killing in the Wars of the Roses (581), to Orietta Doria, widow to the lord of Lesbos, who successfully fought off a Turkish invasion in 1450 (577). In addition to these individually named noblewomen, there are the abovementioned communities of women whose social class is left ambiguous, such as the "matrons" of the Portuguese fort in Diu, who took picks and fought off the invading forces of Mohamed, king of the Indian city of Khambhat (603).

Christine of Lorraine and Serdonati's *Donne illustri*

The great variety of women whom Serdonati describes is particularly notable when we consider that he presented them all as possible models for imitation by the book's dedicatee, Christine of Lorraine, the Grand Duchess of Tuscany. Unlike the Boccaccian text, whose dedicatee seems to be but a furtive choice by the author,[64] Serdonati's work is not merely a casual presentation but one that is crafted with the dedicatee in mind. Francesco Serdonati, a teacher at a public grammar and humanities school, seemed to know the Grand Duchess at least slightly, and his letters demonstrate a fairly frequent correspondence with the Florentine ducal court.[65]

Serdonati's dedication letter to the Grand Duchess places her in a dialectic with the hundreds of women contained in the book, as he instructs her to find in these pages a "vivo specchio" (living mirror) of her illustrious lineage.[66] Although the mirror is a commonplace in moral didactic literature, it is less frequently found in the catalogues of famous women. Serdonati's use of the image seems to point to the personal identity and genealogy of the onlooker.

> Sì come in vivo specchio potrà Vostra Altezza conoscere in questo libro composto dal gran padre della Toscana elequenza, accresciuto poi da huomo conosciuto, e di nuovo da persona intendente arricchito di nobil raccolto d'altri fatti gloriosi di donne Toscane in parte, e altre della sua patria, suo chiarissimo lignaggio. (2v)
>
> (Just as in a living mirror, Your Highness will be able to know your most famous lineage in this book, composed by the great father of Tuscan eloquence, then augmented by a well-known man, and then enriched again by a knowledgeable person with a noble collection of other glorious deeds performed in part by Tuscan women as well as by women from your homeland.)

The text and Christine have parallel lineages of greatness. Boccaccio ("il gran padre della Toscana elequenza") was translated by Betussi ("huomo conosciuto"), and the present book was enriched by Serdonati ("persona intendente"). Likewise, Christine was to read about her own illustrious lineage ("chiarissimo lignaggio"), but this identity is notably fragmented: both Tuscan and French, including glorious *donne toscane* as well as women from her *patria* of France. Christine, after all, was the princess of the house of Lorraine, but she was also the granddaughter of a Tuscan woman, Catherine de' Medici. Her living mirror reflects the portraits of at least 120 women, ranging from the Amazons to contemporary women of the 1590s. Thus, the Grand Duchess was presented with a multitude of possibilities in this looking-glass.

The cross-cultural marriage of France and Tuscany, physically embodied by the Grand Duchess, was woven into the tales of Serdonati's illustrious women, as biographies of Medici consorts and Tuscan peasant women stood comfortably beside descriptions of women of the Lorraine family and other exceptional French noblewomen. This nexus of France and Tuscany, however, was not entirely unproblematic. For instance, in the text, there is a certain domesticity in the Lorraine women, one that is not apparent among the Tuscans. While the Tuscan women are frequently valiant fighters defending against siege warfare or accompanying their husbands to battle, the Lorraine noblewomen are depicted as docile women who enter into cloisters and then seem to disappear from worldly matters.

One reason why the book may present such a disparity between the French and Tuscan women could be that Serdonati was reacting to Florence's anxiety around the presence of a foreign princess. The author could have been seeking to assuage local misgivings about a French grand duchess by presenting Lorraine women as unthreatening pious ladies who founded convents and did not lead controversial lives. Florence, in fact, had a history of xenophobia with regard to Medici consorts. We can think back to Cosimo I's wife, Eleonora di Toledo, who was often vilified for her Spanish origin. The diarist Marucelli called her "una barbara spagnuola et nimica alla patria del suo marito" (a foreign [barbarian] Spaniard and enemy of the homeland of her husband), and a Jesuit contemporary was quoted as saying that she only cared for Spaniards, stating that she "has no affection for anyone from any other nation."[67] The match with Christine of Lorraine was potentially a source of even more discontent than that between Eleonora and Cosimo I. When the Grand Duke of Tuscany, Ferdinando, chose Christine over a daughter of the Spanish imperial house (other proposed brides included the daughter of Charles, the Archduke of Austria, and the daughter of the Duke of Braganza), he was severing a long-standing tie with the empire and re-establishing an alliance with France, an alliance that had been on shaky terms since the 1554–5 Florentine expansionist war against Siena and France.[68]

If the entry of a French noblewoman into the Florentine ruling family was marked by unease, the Serdonati edition of Boccaccio's *Famous Women* offered the unique possibility of crafting an idealized trajectory for the Medici consort, uniting France and Tuscany in a glorious past and productive future. The *donne toscane* mentioned in the dedication letter to Christine included many descriptions of women collectives. These women, like those of the Plutarchan text *Mulierum virtutes*, are identified by their *patria* and as such are quickly identifiable as Tuscan or otherwise. The "Women of Signa," the "Women of the Mugello," the "Women of Foiano," the "Women of Casentino," and the "Women of Colle Val D'Elsa" tell of an undeniable legacy of Tuscan womanhood.[69] Many of the texts read like a brief historical survey of Tuscan women's roles in warfare, in all cases fundamental to the defeat of an invading force. The women of Mugello (560) frightened off invading troops with their blood-curdling screams, and the women of Colle Val d'Elsa (587) fought alongside men to defend their city from an attack by Alfonso, the duke of Calabria, in 1479 and won praise from the Florentine war ministry, I Dieci della Guerra. The women of Casentino (569–71) helped fight off a force of nearly 3,000 marauding German and Hungarian cavalry mercenaries in 1358. The battle was a surprise rebel attack (not a defensive repulsion of a siege), as the men and women villagers hid among the hilltops and threw stones down at the troops led by Amerigo del Cavaletto and Conrad, Count of Lando. Finally, one of the more dramatic stories took place near Florence, where the women of Signa (572) fought off the invading troops of Giovan Galeazzo Visconti in 1396. According to the story, more than 10,000 cavalry and even more infantry descended on Signa, while the Tuscan male troops awaited them in another, wrong, location. Since there were few men in the city, the women dressed as soldiers and took swords in hand to defend the city, until the soldiers left in shame:

> Ma perché non v'erano tante genti, che si postessono scambiare, e rinfrescare, le donne ancora vestitesi da soldati con l'elmo in testa diedono di mano all'arme, e quando fu di mestieri corsono alla muraglia l'ufficio di soldati, si che i nemici non poterono prendere il luogo, e alla fine si partirono con vergogna. (572–3)

> (But because there were not many people that might be used to alternate with and refresh the others, the women therefore dressed as soldiers. With helmets on their head, they gave their hands to arms, and when it was necessary to do the job of soldiers, they ran to the walls, so that the enemies could not take hold of the city, and in the end the troops left in shame.)

This tale offers an impressive visual image of armed women atop city walls witnessing the defeat of the shamed attacking men. The narrative also carries a political message, a modernized and armed revision of a Greek concept: the woman as agent of state security. The historical context of women combatants along with their role as patriotic freedom fighters offered an epistemology of gendered statehood that was likely inspirational, if not groundbreaking, to the new grand duchess. Though it is hard to believe that Christine could have felt a sisterhood with village women so far from her own social standing, she could no doubt recognize that the admirable legacy of Tuscan women had an integral place in the history of her new state.

Serdonati's tales also included other nobler women with ties to Tuscany who would have been more accessible to Christine. For example, she could possibly feel more affinity with the representations, in Serdonati's "living mirror," of exceptional noble consorts in war. Among these women are two figures central to the Medici line, the grandmother and the wife of Cosimo I, Caterina Sforza and Eleonora di Toledo, respectively. Caterina is portrayed as a virago at her fortress, and Eleonora is called a new "Hysicratea," who followed her husband wherever he went in "tempi di guerra" (times of war) and gave him counsel on peace and war.[70] One of the more interesting cases of a noble wife in wartime, especially given the context of Christine as the ideal reader, is Cia Ubaldini, not a Medici wife but a Tuscan noblewoman nonetheless. During the siege of Cesena, Cia bravely defended her husband's city by commanding an army, but she is most praised by Serdonati for making the difficult decision to choose alliance/allegiance to her husband over her father. Cia's father, on the opposing side, uses his paternal authority to tell her to surrender. She responds that, since he had told her to always be obedient to her husband, she is actually following her father's instructions by defending her husband's city:

> Rispose: "Padre mio quando voi mi deste al mio Signore, mi comandaste, che sopra tutte le cose io gli fossi ubidiente, e così ho fatto infino a qui, e'ntendo di fare infino alla morte. Egli m'accomandò questa terra, e disse, che per niuna cagione io l'abbandonassi, o ne facessi alcuna cosa senza la sua presenza, o d'alcuno segreto segno, che m'ha dato. La morte, e ogn'altra cosa curo poco, ov'io ubbidisca i suoi comandamenti." (565)

> (She responded: "My father, when you gave me to my lord, you commanded me that above all things I should be obedient, and so I have been so until this moment, and so I intend to be until death. He entrusted me with this land, and he said that for no reason was I to abandon it. Nor was I to do anything without his presence, unless he gave me a secret signal. I care little for death or other things, thus I obey his commandments.")

The event marks a powerful response by a noblewoman who not only exhibits a courageous spirit and love of her new *patria* in the face of war but also adopts a shrewd strategy for obeying her husband's wishes without sacrificing paternal respect. The relevance of such a tale to Christine of Lorraine's own situation as a daughter to the powerful

Duke of Lorraine might seem peripheral or coincidental were it not for other biographies in the book that issue the same moral message of loyalty to husband over father. These tales all share a common didactic imperative, one that would remind the Grand Duchess of where her loyalty should lie and also provide her with the language she could use with her paternal family if necessary.

When we place these *donne toscane,* warring peasants, and brave noblewomen alongside the illustrious women of the Lorraine family, there appears to be a great discontinuity, a break that is all the more obvious given that the Lorraine biographies are clustered one after the other as if to make a mini-chapter in the history of illustrious women. Positioned as a gallery of women of Lorraine, their stories create a nice textual analogue to the pictorial program that Maria Maddalena, Christine's daughter-in-law, commissioned later at Poggio Imperiale. In a gallery of painted portraits, Maria decorated rooms either with Hapsburg emperors or with women worthies, ancient and modern.[71] But by contrast with the subjects of Maria Maddalena's commission, the ancestors of Christine's father do not seem to be as interesting as the women who surround them.

Before and after the Lorraine biographies there are stories of exceptionally courageous women, particularly in war. Preceding the Lorraines are Queen Fredegund of France, who led 20,000 soldiers; the Longobard women, who placed rotting chickens under their breasts so that they would not be raped by attacking soldiers; and Clotilda, who threw herself on the battlefield and stopped a civil war with her tears. Immediately following the catalogue of Lorraine women is the story of the noblewoman Bundica (Boudica) of Britain, a queen who led (again) 20,000 soldiers against the Romans, and who poisoned herself when she realized that she was defeated. These stories bookend the five Lorraine biographies of Valdruda, Geltruda, Doda, Reinolfa, and Severa of Lorraine. All five are tales of women who became cloistered nuns or abbesses. Moreover, the tale of Doda, Duchess of Lorraine, seems to present her life as an imitation of her husband's rather than of female agency. The story explains that her husband renounced his duchy in order to take the cloth, choosing the contemplative life over one of rule. In response, Doda, "a' parimente seguitando l'esempio del marito, abbandonò il Ducato, e le mondane pompe, e si vestì Monaca nella Città di Treveri" (533) (similarly following the example of her husband, abandoned the Duchy and mundane pomp and clothed herself as a nun in the City of Treveri).[72]

The tale of Doda emphasizes the way in which she follows her husband's actions rather than choosing her own path; more importantly, however, it must have provided a complex message for the young Christine of Lorraine. Christine's life was virtually a reversal of that of Doda. Her husband, Ferdinando de'Medici, had been a cardinal, but in 1587, when his brother Francesco de' Medici died without issue, he returned to Florence to rule. He renounced his cardinal's hat in 1589 so that he might marry Christine. Unlike her ancestor who gave up rule for Christian prayer, Christine's husband gave up his clerical duties so that he might produce an heir, thus figuring Christine in a maternal role rather than a contemplative one.

It is of course conjecture, but one could easily see how Christine might have found Serdonati's accounts of her patronymic foremothers to be less inspirational than tales of many of the other women he describes, particularly those who were depicted as demonstrating heroism in times of exceptional circumstances. To be clear, Serdonati does indicate that some of the Lorraine women were indeed fascinating figures. Geltruda is said to have founded a convent in which women would dress in religious habits in the morning and change into secular clothes after eating, and were even allowed to marry if they chose. Nonetheless, the narrative construction of the Lorraine tales lacks the arc of a story, the tension and climactic structure that is found in other women's biographies. And the Lorraine women (with the exception of Geltruda) are depicted as unengaged with the world, where the "illustrious" Christian life is one marked as contemplative retreat.[73]

If Serdonati provided an unthreatening genealogy of Lorraine women, he countered this with his vivid description of Christine's other, Tuscan, lineage. And not only was Christine Tuscan, she was the direct descendant of the French queen who began this chapter, Catherine de' Medici. Catherine, Christine's grandmother, had played a large role in the life of the young girl, and Serdonati rightly assigns her a detailed biography, the longest of the collection by far (645–55). She is also the only woman of Serdonati's 120 to achieve the lexically unusual epithet of "Eroessa" (Heroess).

Catherine's biography, unsurprisingly, begins with her Medici parentage and then sets out to depict a woman of unsurpassed will and competence during war and conflict. When her husband is away at war, she runs the kingdom with "marvellous prudence" (649). Her abilities are more stringently tested after the death of her husband, when she must quell the plots against her son Charles IX's ascension to the throne

(1561–3). She is depicted as allying herself with noble houses of Europe to defeat the rebellious French princes, and she is shown to personally engage in military activity:

> uscì in campagna, e ritolse loro molte nobil Città, e fortezze, e gli ridusse a combattere presso Parigi, ove furono rotti, e disfatti, e alcuni capi fatti prigioni, e la Reina poi andò a combattere Ave di Grazia data dagli eretici in mano de gli Inglesi, e lo riprese mal grado de difenditori, e rese tutto 'l regno quieto. (650–1)

> (she went out to the countryside and retook from them [heretics] many noble cities and fortresses, and she led them to combat near Paris, where they were broken and undone, and some captains were taken prisoner. The Queen then went to battle against Le Havre, placed into the hands of the English by the heretics, and she retook it in spite of its defenders. She thus rendered the entire kingdom peaceful.)

In closing his entry on Catherine, the author points out that Catherine and Florence had always borne a great love for one another. In Serdonati's version of history, Cosimo I had provided France (under Catherine's rule) with money for its wars, and she had likewise always financed the Florentine convent of Le Murate. Students of Tuscan history would recognize that the author is painting a somewhat rosy picture of a tense Franco-Tuscan relationship. The French crown's heavy financial debts to Florence were matters of political tension, and Catherine had long accused Cosimo of stealing her Florentine properties.[74] Serdonati's text instead resolves these disagreements by suggesting that Catherine loved her *patria* and gave her most valuable gift to the city through her granddaughter, Christine of Lorraine. Serdonati states that, before her death, Catherine wished to give Florence all of her wealth, "benefici," and "fare un favore universale a tutta la Città, e a tutto lo stato, e mostrare l'amore, che li portava" (to do a universal favour for the entire city and state, and to show the love that she bore them). Thus, she sent Christine of Lorraine to wed Ferdinando.

The biography of Catherine closes with her death, and it is followed by one last entry, a brief biography of Christine of Lorraine herself. Serdonati describes Christine's admirable knowledge of letters, history, statecraft, and ruling. Indeed, he calls her ability stupefying: "dico che tale scienza è in lei delle divine, e delle humane lettere, e delle storie principalmente, e tanto senno, e tanta cognizione delle cose di state, e de governi de' popoli, che chiunque n'ha contezza, ne rimane stupefatto" (672) (I say that her knowledge is principally the divine and humane letters and histories, as well as such wisdom and such understanding of the matters of state and of governing people, that whoever learns of it remains stupefied). The passage reminds us of how earlier lowborn women viragos were often described as "stupefying" or "marvels" for their competence in arms. Here, instead, Christine is a marvellous commander. Notably, Serdonati's language does not situate Christine in a fictive realm of unbelievable women but instead places her in a genealogy of illustrious and exceptional women. Indeed, the author states that Christine's great abilities are not surprising when we recall that she was raised and taught by Catherine de' Medici:

> fu allevata, e ammaestrata da Caterina de Medici Reina di Franci sua avola materna, che fu un vero ritratto di prudenza, e di valore, e un chiaro lume delle donne, e da lei fu amata adismisura, si che fu compagna di molti suoi viaggi, partecipe di tutti i pensieri, consapevole di tutti i segreti, di tutte le imprese, e di tutte le cure: onde ella apprese la cognizione di tutte le cose appartenenti al reggere stati, e governar popoli. (672–3)
>
> (she was raised and trained by Catherine de' Medici, Queen of France, her maternal grandmother, who was a true portrait of prudence and valour, a shining beacon among women. Christine was loved by her beyond measure, such that she was her companion on many travels, she was privy to all of her thoughts, knowledgeable of all of her secrets, her undertakings, and her cares. It is from her that Christine gained the understanding of all things pertaining to ruling states and governing people.)

It was thus at Catherine's side that Christine learned the secrets of the Tuscan Queen of France and received what might be called a feminine education on how to govern a state and rule a people. Christine was, in Serdonati's hands, a true living mirror of one of Florence's most splendid daughters.

Despite the encomiastic language of Christine as stupefying, by the time Serdonati had published his book of illustrious women, she had done little in Florence to prove her mettle. Christine had been in Florence only six years at the publication of the book, and her biography has little to say about her actions related to statecraft. Instead, she is praised as humble, pious, and charitable, spending her time visiting monasteries and helping young women in need. In Serdonati's entry,

Christine's most notable act was that she was always the first woman in Florence to obey sumptuary legislation, thus providing a model of modesty and virtue for all women to follow. Finally, the biography and the very lengthy book close with a reference to the future, a hope that Christine's children will have the virtues of both lineages: "degli avoli suoi, nella quale si spera dovere risurgere e rifiorire le virtù dell'uno, e dell'altro lignaggio" (of her forefathers, in which one hopes the virtues of each lineage will be reborn and thrive again).

The biography of Christine of Lorraine and more generally the entire work of the *Donne illustri* of Serdonati are thus directly influenced by the rule of the powerful European monarchs and, most specifically, Catherine de' Medici. The lineage of Christine of Lorraine, however, was also one that was extended through a "living mirror" to the viragos of Tuscany and elsewhere. Christine was still quite a young ruler, and Serdonati suggests that she could fashion herself as she chose, leading armies or quietly retiring to an abbey; her only circumscription was loyalty to the house of Medici.

How Christine (and Maria Maddalena after her) may have incorporated Serdonati's book into their ruling and artistic commissions still awaits study. Suggestively, Christine's life does seem to reflect the incongruities of her 120 images. Just as she ruled as regent, she was devoutly dedicated to the development of the monastery La Crocetta. And especially near the end of her life, she seems to have struggled with exactly which path to choose, a public life as co-regent or a private one in the sanctuary of her Villa La Quiete, in effect, mirroring the very contradictions that had been written for her some forty years earlier.[75]

Conclusion

The *Donne illustri* of Francesco Serdonati marks a sort of apogee of the Boccaccian legacy of illustrious women's biographies in the sixteenth century. Although many compendia describing famous women are written at the century's turn (some dedicated to Christine of Lorraine), none of the works anthologize Boccaccio as Betussi and Serdonati had done.[76] One of the common elements that characterized the biographies of Boccaccio, Betussi, and Serdonati in particular, was the dual purpose of bolstering the position of women while emboldening and/or vituperating men. If a woman were to be praised as a virtuous victim of war or as a courageous participant in combat, it most assuredly signified the dereliction of men. While stories of the militant woman had arguably always been caught in an ambivalent trajectory of purpose, at times circulating to praise exceptional women and at others simply to debase non-militant men, with Serdonati, at the close of the sixteenth century, this representation of the militant woman became increasingly multivalent. Women had demonstrated that they could fight in large numbers and that success in wars depended on rightly understanding women's militant potential. Given the abundance of communities of female militants in Serdonati as well as of armed individual viragos, one might even posit that these tales nudged, if ever so slightly, the division of labour that had made warfare an exclusively masculine endeavour.

The tales of illustrious women in Serdonati – and arguably many of the texts that surrounded Catherine de' Medici and Elizabeth I – also performed another discursive function. These works eschewed ruminations on abstract feminine militancy and described more concrete acts of women in combat, thus raising the discourse of a military and political female potential in the Italian peninsula. The communities of warring women, the armed noblewomen combatants, and, most importantly, the genealogy of historical illustrious women now established through anthologized books of illustrious women suggested something much more tangible than did the legendary women of Boccaccio or even the virile women of Betussi. Women could take up arms and change their world, for other women had already done so.

Conclusion

The last three chapters of this book discuss tales of (pseudo) historical women in a wide array of roles during war: armed citizen soldiers, astute commanders, victims of sexual assault by male troops, and women as guarantors of men's military prowess. Among these illustrious women, we find dozens of female combatants. Thus, the philosophical debate about whether women can fight in combat, the topic of chapter 1, is proved by example. Authors of biographies of armed women confronted the terms of the debate head on, stating that women were capable of showing more courage than men and of "overcoming" the physical weakness of their sex. These armed illustrious women also provided correlative examples to the poetic chivalric viragos discussed in chapter 2. While epic poetry depicted noble, virgin, sword-wielding maidens, the tales of historic illustrious women broadened the scope of armed women to include widows, wives, and commoners. With few exceptions, however, these biographies did not depict nobly born ladies as armed and participating in violence. Thus, there was a gap between the chivalric virago and the historical virago. Some of the more interesting texts regarding women and war indeed sprang from the efforts of critics and moralists who sought to reconcile these two generic types. Finally, we note that historical tales commented not only on women's roles in war (e.g., commander, soldier, victim) but on the obligations of men to protect women. Texts about illustrious women therefore operated like those texts discussed in chapter 3, where women compelled men to engage in combat through shame.

With arguably one or two exceptions, every text discussed in this book affirmed the relationship between masculinity and warfare. Moreover, there is an absence of texts that suggest that women should fight instead of men. Every author considered in this book presented combat as a choice for women, while it remained an obligation for men. Thus, we cannot discuss women and war without raising the matter of men's moral responsibility to fight.

The ideology that men are the warrior sex bound to protect women circumscribed the lives of both men and women. Most obviously, men and boys participated in and were subject to the violence of war regardless of personal desires. There is still much to learn about men and militarism in the period, and my study limits its analysis of masculinity to the pernicious practice of controlling men's behaviour through admonitions about failed military masculinity. This gender shaming commonly took the form of suggestions that certain male behaviour – from playing music to wearing ornate dress – compromised success in warfare.

The social control of women was also influenced by the ideology that framed women in the gendering of war. In the putative belief of women's militancy, they were weak and innocent non-combatants. Much of the literature that argued for women's abilities in war took aim at the confinement of women to domestic life. Texts that argued for women's martial abilities emphasized their potential to contribute to society *outside* the home, away from spinning and weaving and other domestic concerns. Some authors directly critiqued contemporary wartime practices regarding women. These included, among other things, the practice of casting women out of besieged cities as "bocche inutile" (useless mouths).

The discussion has addressed how the gendering of war is represented in the wide array of texts of the period but has not fully answered a question posed at the beginning of this study – why was the Italian sixteenth century so fascinated with texts featuring armed women?[1] I briefly approached an answer by suggesting that there was a pleasure in reading about the "marvellous" and also noted how some texts possibly enjoyed popularity due to the proliferation of powerful women in the contemporary political sphere. For a more complete answer, it is my belief that we must consider the synthesis of how texts of warrior women fit within the debate of women's militancy. Through this lens, we can consider how the armed woman and her role in the war story resonated with readers who experienced decades of war and successive military and political defeat.

Tales of historical militant women were not only fantasy but evidence of how women defeated men. In their victory, they also showed how the weak might overcome the strong, and this was surely a seductive message in an age of autocratic rule and foreign ocupation. Certain authors of the period proclaimed such a possibility explicitly: Ortensio Lando's *Exhortation* (satirically) claimed that armed women had overthrown the patriarchy, and Serdonati commented in his tales of illustrious women that armed women could defeat oppressors when men were unable to do so. We can therefore speculate that stories of militant women became so popular in the sixteenth-century print industry because they embodied, among other things, the power of the weak against the aggressor, the occupied over the occupier. Italians who read tales of courageous female compatriots surely felt a sense of civic pride. And perhaps, at a time when Italy, a land that was long described as the victimized woman,[2] was itself occupied, there was as well a fantasy of the vulnerable woman who rises up and arms herself. Italians not only had a collection of beautiful, sword-bearing epic maidens; they also had Cia Ubaldini, Caterina Sforza, Catherine de' Medici, and the communities of unnamed women who fought at city walls throughout Italy. The readers of these tales could, if inspired, re-enact the life of Marulla, who after seeing her warrior father killed before her eyes, took up the sword and shield of the dead man and fought to victory.

This spirit of empowerment may be why tales were popular, but it did not inspire women to take up arms in any significant numbers. Before we look to history to consider why this might be, we should look to the texts and recall that the tales of armed women are only in part about women. Women were compelled to fight only because of men's dereliction. The tales of illustrious women and war were thus also directed at men – not to inspire a new Marulla but to resuscitate her father, the defeated Italian man. The coherent message these tales provide is that the armed and invigorated man was the best chance to return *misera Italia* to its glorious state.[3]

Finally, there is one last reason why the armed woman might have appealed to readers. It is the inherent irony of her person. If the armed woman simultaneously signified an exceptional woman and an unexceptional man, then she was the warrior that should not have been. Her discursive function could incite men to battle but could also symbolize peace. The presence of an "innocent" on the fields of war caused not only marvel but shock, particularly in some of the bloody and tragic tales of illustrious women. The female figure thus underscored men's dereliction as well as the human atrocity of war – that war, once the rhetoric is stripped away, is but a justification of mass homicide. The armed woman therefore has a potential, perhaps buried in the depths of our psyche, to represent an end of violence and a desired peace.

Notes

Introduction

1 The law 380/1999 was passed on 20 October 1999. Carreiras 98–9; see also Office on Women in the NATO Forces. Women were tangentially included in the armed forces in 1944, when Mussolini's government formed the *Servizio Ausiliario Femminile* (Women's Auxiliary Service).
2 See Farina.
3 Ammendola and Galatino, 104 n11. See also Farina, who argues that public opinion became more pro-women in the armed services during the 1990s because of television coverage of foreign female soldiers (215–22).
4 See Pioppi.
5 On the Pentagon's 2013 decision, see Rogers. See also Miller, who claims that civilian feminists rather than women listed in the military want to see combat opened to women.
6 See Grendler, "Critics."
7 Other scholars who have been sensitive to the matter of women's militancy in the Renaissance include Cox, Robin, Sears, Shemek, and Stoppino.
8 Goldstein finds that war is universally gendered as masculine across cultures and throughout time, 10–19.
9 "Heu miseram sortem, qua nos natura deusve/ esse genus muliebre dedit. Servilius usquam/ est animal nullum, nec probro obiectius omni./ Nos sumus imbelles; nec vis praestantior ulla/ in nobis rationis inest animusque pavore/ semper hebet. Validae vires in corpore nullae." *Sforziad*, Book III, 699–704. Robin provides the original Latin of *The Sforziad* Book III in her appendix to *Filelfo in Milan*, 193.
10 See for example Euripides, *Trojan Women*, where Hecuba laments her state throughout the play; but see in particular her first lament: "Pitiful wives of

Trojan husbands who were once armed with bronze swords, daughters ill wed, brides of death. Join me in my wailing" (42).

11 Lenzi cites contemporary source material describing violations against women in the siege of Piacenza. One chronicle states that, "tutte le donzelle, vergini, maritate, vedove, monache tutte furono svergognate, e stracciate, e mal menate [...] Loro erano svergognate le donne, e figliuole in sua presenza; e quando n'erano ben sazi que' cani giocavano ai dadi una donna coll'altra" (quoted in Lenzi 82).

12 "Hic virgo rapitur; coniunxque pudica / hic spectante viro patitur quodcunque libido / imperet atque furor." Filelfo, *Sforziad,* Book III, 665–7, quoted in Robin, *Filelfo in Milan* 192.

13 The concept of "Beautiful Souls" is borrowed from Hegel's *Phenomenology of the Spirit,* which described men and women. They are defined by a mode of consciousness that allows them to protect "'the appearance of purity by cultivating innocence about the historical course of the world.'" Elshtain, *Women and War* 4.

14 "Mortem dulcedine laudis, / natorumque metu, misera pietate parentum, / coniugis et patriae nimia formidine temnunt." Filelfo, *Sforziad,* Book III, 401–3, quoted in Robin, *Filelfo in Milan* 186.

15 "we have conquered a city won over neither by reason or arms; and we have placed the captive city under our rule. For it lacked nothing it needed to protect itself and to face dangers from its enemies. But God himself, I believe, wished to punish the guilty because they hastily summoned the Venetians, although there was no war and they feared no losses. They, however, subjected themselves to the Venetians like slaves, though Venice sought no such thing – nor were they forced to play the slave to anyone" (translation Robin, *Filelfo* 80); ("Nam si nos vera fateri / convenit, invictam nulla ratione nec armis / vicimus et captam nobis submisimus urbem. / Nil et enim deerat, quo se minus ipsa tueri / posset et adversis se contra offerre periclis. Sed deus ipse reor voluit punier nocentes, / quod nullo nec Marte citi, nec damna verentes / accierint Venetum, cui se nil tale petenti / subicerent servos – nulli servire coacti"), *Sforziad,* Book III, 771–9, quoted in Robin, *Filelfo in Milan* 194–5.

16 On non-combatants in the Middle Ages, see Allmand; see also Illston 42–4.

17 The protection of women was used to justify the 2001 American invasion of Afghanistan. First Lady Laura Bush gave the presidential radio address on 17 November 2001, focusing on the "brutality against women and children by the al-Qaida": see http://www.presidency.ucsb.edu/ws/index.php?pid=24992#axzz1fsys15W0. She later toured with a team of Afghani women across the United States, hailing the valiant efforts of U.S. soldiers in protecting the rights of women. The ensuing public-relations success

allowed First Lady Laura Bush and political propagandists to proclaim "George W. Bush – the W stands for Women." See the feminist challenge to this claim in Ferguson and Marso.

18 Women in siege warfare had been sanctioned in Flavius Vegetius Renatus's fifth-century treatise *De re militari.* Vegetius states that women might use rocks or other projectiles to defend a besieged city (30). On Vegetius in the Middle Ages, see Shrader.

19 Lynn 165. Valerie Eads challenges the notion that women only fight in defence; see "Means, Motive, Opportunity: Medieval Women and the Recourse to Arms," http://deremilitari.org. Much work is still to be done on camp followers. On women's work in the army camps, see Lynn; and Cook. For a somewhat dated but useful brief overview see Hale, *War and Society* 161–2. See also Crim, who comfortably states that "at no time in European history were so many women engaged in warfare – as spies, foragers, artillery personnel, or soldiers – than between 1500 and 1650" (29).

20 Bandello 4.18.751; Serdonati 580.

21 These statistics leave out all references to biblical or mythological women.

22 Pennington and Higham; and Cook.

23 Scholarship on medieval warring women is extensive. A basic starting point is the online annotated bibliography maintained by Valerie Eads: http://bobrowen.com/valerieeads/medievalwomeninwar.html. See also McLaughlin; and Hacker. Verrier's *Les armes de Minerve* is the best monographic study of historical and literary women combatants in Renaissance Italy. Tomalin, *Fortunes,* contains a lengthy study of historical women warriors. See also Verbruggen; and Dufresne.

24 Goldstein 10. Goldstein's book is a careful consideration of the role of gender in warfare and is clearly not written to discount the impact of women in war, including those who fight.

1 The Philosophical History of the Armed Woman

1 On the importance of literary form to representations of women's militancy, see Verrier-Dubard de Gaillarbois, "Pallade e il centauro" 50; Elshtain, *Women and War* 49–50; Schweizer 1–18.

2 See Blythe 244 for a discussion of this passage and the controversy in feminist criticism over the term "weakness."

3 See Filogenio 152, who states that he "cannot easily subscribe himself" to the "mixing and confusion" of women and men in war and public offices. His complaint is not that women are not capable but that they are put at risk of losing their honour because of lascivious men.

4 The first translation of the *Republic* in Latin was in 1402 with a collaboration of Chrysolorus and Uberto Decembrio (Hankins 108). In his own dialogues, Uberto Decembrio says that men should fight while women take care of the house – *De republica libri IV* (c. 1420): "Quodque viri fortes robustique tutele urbis invigilent, quos quidem eorum princeps duxerit eligendos; mulieres autem domus custodie ac familie sancte ac pudice curam agitent" (quoted in Hankins 116).

5 On Pier Candido Decembrio's translations, see Hankins 120. Pier's opinion of women and war is presented in a third-party dialogue, the *Dialogi in Lactantium,* written by Antonio da Rho and discussed in Hankins 151.

6 In his *Calumniator,* Bessarion maintained the equality of men and women and cited Plutarch and Amazons in support of this view. See Hankins 229, n164.

7 After a discussion on the advantages of allowing women to pursue their natural inclinations, including military professions, the commentary provides a medieval anecdote to women bearing arms: "which, many write, was the custom of brave German women" ("quod a foeminis Germanorum fieri solitum, multi scribunt") (Morzillo 218).

8 All English translations are mine unless otherwise noted. When using parenthetical in-text citations, I have listed the source page numbers immediately following the respective language. I have also tried to keep as close as possible to the original text (e.g., diacritical markings, spelling) when transcribing from early modern editions.

9 See Morzillo 190: "Horum tamen officiorum leviora quaeque propter generis imbecillitatem mulieribus tribuenda."

10 All of Fiorimbeni's index entries cover minor points such as women adept at music and medicine, ignoring the lengthier discussion of women at arms. One of the index entries, "Donne molto differente dall'huomo," is particularly problematic because this is actually a sub-argument in the discussion of women in the military.

11 Unless otherwise stated, the Italian text and English translations of Campanella, *La città del sole,* are taken from the 1981 bilingual edition edited by Donno.

12 See Campanella 2008 for a comparison of the 1602 Italian edition and the 1637 Latin edition. According to the editor's note, Gaeta (Caietae) refers to Giacomo di Gaeta, who condemned women's militancy and used the Amazon custom of removing their breast as proof of women's incapacity to fight (63). On Gaeta's description of Amazons, see Di Gaeta 71–5.

13 Donno's English translation has been altered to reflect the literal sense of the Italian.

14 Campanella's source is Botero, *Relationi universali* 1.3.172, who wrote that women of Monopotapa (a.k.a. Monomopotapa) conducted themselves in war much as the Amazons did in the area that is present-day Tanzania and northern Mozambique (Campanella 139, 73n). Campanella adds that men of the period "si effeminano" (effeminize themselves) by calling themselves "Vossignoria"; and in Africa, he shows concern that, beyond just Amazons, there are public bordellos of effeminate men (Campanella 1981, 122–3)

15 Verrier-Dubard de Gaillarbois demonstrates how arms and letters were transgressive fields for women, as they both represented public acts. See Verrier, *Le miroir des Amazones* 108–10. In the introduction to Bandello's novella of the virago Marulla (4:19), the author suggests that women could be apt at both arms and letters if educated to be so. See also Camerata.

16 Camerata 9 (quoted in Verrier, *Le miroir des Amazones* 110).

17 On the Amazonian tribes depicted in travel narratives of European explorers, see Verrier, *Le miroir des Amazones*. See also Schwarz, particularly chapter 2, which provides an excellent study of the metonymical charge of the Amazon quest, a continual search for what is beyond the edges of the map and dependent on the frustration of not ever arriving.

18 "Essendo la donna di molta humidità ripiena, e di pochissimo calore, come vuole Hippocrate, & Aristotele in mile luoghi, e perciò anco più fredda de gli huomini; cosi il fredo, come, l'humido sono atti a farla debole" (Mercurio 2). On classical notions of feminine weakness, see Aristotle, *The Generation of Animals* 1.19.727a, 18–20. For a discussion of Plato's writings on female weakness, see Blythe; and Tuana.

19 For a philological discussion of these traits and what Aristotle meant by the "softness" of women, see Mayhew 102.

20 In what seems to be an attempt to counter Plato's *Republic*, Antonio Brucioli published Aristotle's politics under the name of *Republic*. The book, dedicated to Piero Strozzi (the anti-Medici war captain), also bears a dedicatory preface that implies certain political motivations for the unusual name of the translation: *Gli otto libri della Repubblica che chiamano Politica di Aristotile* (1547). For a detailed discussion of women's place in Aristotle's natural order, see Femenias.

21 The irreconcilability between warfare and the female Aristotelian body is an interpretation that offers a revision of Thomas Laqueur, who stated that there is no causal relationship between the social and the anatomical in Aristotle: "The biological is not, even in principle, the foundation of particular social arrangements" (29).

22 Giovan Battista Gelli's *La Circe* stages dialogues between Ulysses and various people turned into animals who do not wish to return back into human form. In the fifth dialogue, women are grouped into one category and represented by a doe. The doe states that she is just as much a "deer" as the male, and thus she doesn't want to be a woman, as humans do not treat each sex equally: "io son così cerva da quanto il maschio, e vo fuori come fa egli; e non ho tanti dolori nel partorire i miei figliuoli, nè tante noie nello allevargli, come io avrei essendo donna" (Gelli 55).

23 "Nelle Città, & nelle case sono stati divisi secondo la capacità di ciascuno. E perche le donne sono più delicate de gli huomini & hanno a portare il peso della pregnezza, & dare i primi nutrimenti a' figliuoli, & haverne la prima cura: le guali cose ricercano, & lungo tempo, & molta quiete; fu loro meritamente assegnata la casa ..."; "non solo guardia di quello, che i mariti con robustezza loro havessino acquistato fuori, ma anco ritornando eglino a casa stanchi dalle fatiche gli ricogliessino, & ristorassino col mangiar preparato" (Lottini 262–3).

24 Hercole Filogenio has been been identified as both Ercole Marescotti and Fabrizio Beltrami. The author goes on to suggest that this timidity is what makes women imperfect: "Ma l'audacia, e la fortezza sono virtù, e la timidità, e debolezza sono vitii, l'uno del corpo e l'altro dell'animo; segue adunque che l'huomo sia virtuoso, e perfetto, e la Donna sia vitiosa et imperfetta" (Marescotti 12).

25 Garzoni cites Aristotle, Galen, and Isidorus on women's weakness ("Discorso" 237). For a summary of Renaissance thought on women's physical inferiority, see MacLean 15–44. See also De Maio 59–81.

26 "Woman's nature is suited to indoor tasks: as her body is less capable of endurance; as she is more fearful and prone to protect stores. Man's nature is suited to outdoor tasks as his body and mind are more capable of enduring cold and heat, journey and campaigns, and as he is more courageous and able to defend against wrongdoing" (Xenopohon 419–21).

27 See, for example, Alberti, *I libri della famiglia* 257.

28 "Aristotele, nel *Libro degli animali,* disse che, in ogni specie d'animali, le femine sono più molli e mansuete de' maschi ..."; "*mulier,* la cui derivazione, secondo Isidoro, ci significa 'cosa molle'"; and "E cotal mansuetudine della donna è affermata ancora da Galeno, nel commento decimo settimo sopra la quinta particola degli *Aforismi* di Ippocrate" (Garzoni, *Le vite* 237). Later in the treatise he asks, "Ma che dirò della fortezza, dote corporale delle donne?," a question that he follows with a list of warring Amazons, medieval queens, and Old Testament heroines (243).

29 See the introduction by Maria Luisa Doglio for an overview of the history of the misogynist tradition and the development of the treatises of the pro-woman *querelle* (Capra 13–62). It should also be noted that Capra presents a very different version of women's militancy in his *L'anthropologia* 2.21, where he states that stories of women warriors seem to him to be fictions (also discussed in Verrier, *Le miroir des Amazones* 63).

30 Scipione Mercurio: "Aggugnete poi a questo il costume donnesco, che per lo più e otioso, e delitioso, delle quali cose ciascheduna per se a bastante a snervare ogni vigore in Hercole o in Atlante" (2).

31 "Le troppe forze fanno le più volte coloro che sono, temerari" and "Niuna cosa è che più offenda la iustizia che il troppo ardimento e la troppo corporale forza" (*Della eccellenza* 110).

32 On Sichelgaita, see Eads. For an overview on gender and the crusades, see Edgington and Lambert. The source of Sichelgaita is told by the medieval female historian Anna Comnena (1083–1153) who writes of Gaita (Sichelgaita) in the *Alexiad* 147. The story of Eleanor dressed as an Amazon is very likely not historical but one that circulated throughout the Middle Ages. See Owen 148–52, and Purcell 59.

33 On the importance of biblical heroines for the notion of women's "astuzia" in war, see Verrier, *Le miroir des Amazones* 118–19.

34 On Judith and Esther as heroines of war, see Milligan, "Unlikely Heroines." Lodovico Domenichi in his *La nobiltà delle donne* follows his praise of Amazons with the stories of Judith and Esther. Both are praised as women who have saved their nations (23v–24r).

35 I follow the notes of the editors of the modern edition, Varanini 249–50. Excerpt from sermon, n56, of 21 October 1304.

36 Originating in southern France during the late tenth century, the *Pax Dei* movement sought to protect women and others from the violence of wars (Allmand 254).

37 Blythe's study has spurred some scholarly interest in the field, including Illston. For a general note on Plato's reception in the Middle Ages and Renaissance, see Boter; and Hankins.

38 Ptolemy of Lucca, *De regimine principum* 4.5.2: "Amplius autem, corporale exercitium confert foeminis quantum ad vertutem corporis et fortitudinem, sicut in ancillis familiarum et mulieribus rusticanis est manifestum, quia fortiores sunt et saniores. Virtutis autem proprium est quod bonum faciat habentem et opus eius bonum reddat. Si ergo in gymnasiis ac rebus bellicis magis confortatur foeminea virtus, congrue opera bellica videntur eisdem competere." English translation and Latin in Blythe 258.

39 Ptolemy of Lucca's interpretation of the legend is cited by Blythe: one reason for keeping women out of combat "'derives from the ineptitude of women's members for fighting. Aristotle distinguishes, in *On the Generation of Animals,* between males and females in this way since a male has stronger members, arms, hands, nerves, and veins (which results in the production of a rougher voice), buttocks, belly, and other more subtle attributes. Women are just the reverse, so they are more suited for the act of generation, and their breasts for nourishing their offspring – but all of these things impede fighting. It is written that, for this reason, Amazon girls cut off their right breasts and press down their left, so as to not be impeded in shooting arrows'" (quoted in Blythe 262). Otranto Cathedral's famous mosaic floor depicts an Amazon with her breast removed shooting a deer. The image is possibly critical of Amazons, as her prey is recognized as an allegorical symbol of Christ.

40 Verrier traces this intellectualization of the art of war from Polyaenus's *Stratagems,* dedicated to Marcus Aurelius (161–80). On the vast number of treatises that addressed women's militancy, see her *Le miroir des Amazones* 61–125.

41 In Pompeo Colonna, see specifically 217; Lottini, *Avvedimenti civili,* n490, will quickly qualify his statement with a moral premise of household obligation, suggesting that though women may be trained to be in war they should not be; Stefano Guazzo "Dell'honor delle donne"; and Sperone Speroni, "Orazione contra le cortigiane."

42 Guazzo is likely referring to the fable of Lorenzo Astemio (c. 1435–1508), "De vidua et asino veridi" (The Widow and the Green Donkey). In the fable, a widow wishes to marry, but she worries about public opinion. To show her how the opinion of people is fickle and unimportant, a female friend of the widow paints a donkey green, to the amazement of the townspeople. In time, the newness wears off, and the people are no longer interested in the animal. The same, the friend states, will happen if the widow is to take a husband. Lorenzo Astemio, *Fabulae ex graeco in latinum per Laurentium Abstemium virum clarissimum* (Venice 1495).

43 Lodovico Domenichi, *La nobiltà delle donne* (1549) is a reworking of Heinrich Cornelius Agrippa, *De nobilitate et praecellentia foeminei sexus* (1529) and has also been labelled a plagiarism of Domenico Bruni's text *Della difesa delle donne* (see Tessier).

44 "Anchora in cioche si appartiene all'arte della guerra, nel tirar con l'arco con la fromba, co i sassi, nel combatter con le armi a piede & a cavallo nello accamparsi, nell'ordinare le schiere, nel condurre l'essercito, & per dir brievemente, promesso che tutte le arti fussero essercitate parimente da gli huomini & dalle donne."

45 On Amazons in Italian literature and in particular for a helpful discussion of the poem *Amazonida* by Andrea Stagi, see Verrier, *Les Amazones* and *Le miroir des Amazones.*

46 Giovanni Botero (1544–1617), in his *The Reason of State,* says that he refuses to offer his opinion of whether women should be allowed to fight; but he does provide a detailed list of warring Amazons in the New World: "Others too may decide whether women should take part in warfare" (*The Reason of State* 174). This English translation is of the 1598 edition. The section devoted to women at arms and Amazons is not included in the first edition of 1589, which was, regrettably, the text used for the recent Italian edition by Continisio (Botero, *Della ragione di stato*).

47 "fortezza di animo e di corpo e in quel che non vagliano per armeggiare, non è lor mancamento ma di chi dà loro creanza, poiché si è visto chiaro di quelle che sono state già tempo allevate sotto tal disciplina, quanto son riuscite valorose ed esperte" (*Il merito delle donne* 62).

48 The communities of women in the midst of wars figure prominently in *querelle des femmes* literature, particularly after Castiglione cited several Plutarchan examples in his *Cortegiano* (book IV).

49 "Mi pareva forse, perché iersera ne ragionammo d'esser alle mani con questi uominacci e che faccesse una gran ruina e fatto d'arme, tagliandone molti a pezzi e uccidendoli, affanno svegliatami, [...]trovai che tutta questa rimanotta era occorsa tra la mia gattesina ed alcuni valenti soriconi, o topi" (*Il merito delle donne* 73).

50 Marinella's treatise appeared in 1600 and then in 1601 with an additional fifteen chapters and with a slightly altered title: *Le nobiltà, et eccellenze delle donne, et i diffetti e mancamenti de gli huomini* (1600); *La nobiltà et l'eccellenza delle donne, co' diffetti et mancamenti de gli huomini* (1601).

51 "I would like these men to try the experiment of training a good-natured boy and girl of about the same age and intelligence in letters and arms. They would see how much sooner the girl would become expert than the boy and how she would surpass him completely" (*The Nobility* 80).

52 The chapter numbering of Marinella's treatise is irregular, with many chapters having the same number.

53 The original Latin letter is found in "Ad illustrem dominam Bonam Sforciam," in *Puglia Neo-latina,* ed. F. Tateo, M. De Nichelo, and P. Sisto (Bari: Cacucci, 1994), 81–3. Quoted in Cristofaro 2005, 43. My translation.

54 Ammirato's essay, likely dedicated to Christine of Lorraine, is transcribed and edited by Carmela Cristofaro. On the difference between a princess and her subject, see "Alcuni ammaestramenti" 18–19: "considerando quanto sia diverso lo stato delle principesse alle private, non all'ago e

alle tele intenda esser nata, ma, in quanto appartiene a sé, a governare e a regger popoli." This passage is discussed at length in Cristofaro, "Alcuni ammaestramenti" 193–4. On the difference between "femina" and "donna," see also Filogenio 116.

55 Tasso states: "Perciò che la virtù della madre di famiglia sarà la parsimonia, e della donna regia la leggiadria e la delicatura" (*Discorso* 64). All translations from the *Discorso* are mine.

56 See also Cox, *Women's Writing* 171, where it is stated that Tasso effectively "corrects the more idealizing humanistic positions with a dose of Aristotelian 'rigor' and social realism [...] Of course he does so at the expense of women."

57 See *Discorso,* 55–6: "contra Platone conchiude Aristotele che la virtù dell'uomo e della femina non sian la medesima; perciò che la virtù dell'uomo sarà la fortezza e la liberalità, e la virtù della donna la pudicizia." Then, in a defence of Aristotle's notion that female strength is the strength of one who obeys: "Non niego nondimeno che la fortezza non sia virtù feminile ancora, ma non l'assoluta fortezza, ma la fortezza ch'ubidisce, come dice Aristotele" (60).

58 The one exceptional mention of a woman at arms is Maria of Austria (1505–1558), sister of Charles V and the aunt of the dedicatee. Tasso refers to her "executing her offices" of captain and king in wars and government "rinnovo in voi la memoria della gloriosa reina Maria, sorella di Carlo Quinto e di Ferdinando vostro padre, la qual nelle guerre di valorosissimo capitano e nel governo degli Stati di prudentissimo re esercitò gli uffici" (*Discorso* 67–8).

59 "Così fra le donne molte ci nascono d'animo e di virtù eroica, e molte ancora nate di sangue regio, se ben perfettamente non si possono chiamar donne eroiche, molto nondimeno alle donne eroiche s'assomigliano" (*Discorso* 63).

60 Tasso includes several women in his catalogue of nearly twenty women. As Doglio points out, this catalogue echoes Bernardo Tasso's impressive list of illustrious women in canto 11 of his *Amadigi* (1560) as well as Giraldi Cinzio's *Ecatomiti* (1565), 14–25. Ferretti notes that in a manuscript version of the treatise, the list of illustrious women is even longer.

61 Letter to Christine of Lorraine: "In che secondando lo vostra altezza, e come è seco congiunta col corpo, così cercando di congiungersi con l'animo, ho gran campo di rallegrarmi con esso lei che, ricordandosi ella più d'esser principessa che donna, procacci che infino ai diletti e passatempi suoi non sieno difformi dagli studi e dai pensieri del Gran Duca, accompagnandolo alla caccia, e non in scene e in delizie, ma in cavalcare

e in correr lancie procurando che si adoperino i paggi suoi: cosa intesa da me con tanto diletto, perché io non fui presente quando si corse alle stalle, et che il Serenissimo Gran Duca, secondo il solito tenore della sua liberalità, compartì doni et pregi fra essi, et che V. Altezza istessa fece della grazia e dei favori ad alcuno, che le giuro, Madama, di gran lunga ciò che in questo ampliando mi dicessi, rimarrebbe inferiore al vero" (quoted in Cristofaro, *Alcuni ammaestramenti* 105, from Ammirato, "Alcuni ammaestramenti" 381–2).

62 Robinson 117 argues that Ariosto, in the *Orlando furioso*, creates this same doubling effect of the double standard: "the traditional one that demands sexual purity of women but is able to make allowances for the susceptibility of men, and another that requires men to adhere inflexibly to the chivalric epic while permitting women a greater degree of moral innovation."

63 "Consideriam hora queste cose non come le considera il moral Filosofo, ma come dal Politico son considerate" (Tasso, *Discorso* 58). Tasso challenges Aristotle's *Ethics*, which states that "fear" is involuntary and therefore not as shameful as intemperance, the vice for which Aristotle would have men blamed. In Iason Denores's sixteenth-century commentary on Aristotle, "gittar le armi" is listed as the opposite of "fortezza," one of the "great morals": "la fortezza vietando il fuggir nella giornata & abbondar l'ordine nella battaglia & gittar le armi" (11).

64 McClure (2013) 11, 206n, offers an alternative interpretation to my own, where he argues that Tasso describes a more heroic virtue.

65 The efficacy of social control through disgrace is featured in Tasso's *Gerusalemme liberata*, when Rinaldo is shamed for leaving the battlefield to luxuriate in the garden of Armida (canto XVI).

66 See D'Ancona and Bacci 271–2. There is little biographical information about Francesco Serdonati. Alessandro D'Ancona lists Serdonati's birth year as 1537, in Lamole, Florence, while Serdonati is commonly listed as born in 1540.

67 There is no good translation for "donnescamente," since it can mean "ladylike" or, as Serdonati is making clear, "in a commanding manner." All translations from Serdonati are mine.

68 See *Della perfezione* 483–4: "Percioche la felicità humana, se crediamo ad Aristotile, s'acquista con l'operazioni dell'animo fatte secondo la virtù. Se dunque la donna può conseguire la felicità come l'huomo, bisogna confessare, che ella possa fare le medesime operazioni che l'huomo, e perche le perfette operazioni non si posson fare senza le virtù, bisogna anche dire che la donna possa havere le medesime virtù che l'huomo, e per conseg uente essere perfetta come l'huomo."

69 See *Della perfezione* 484: "Percioche le virtù, con le quali s'acquista la felicità, e si fanno tutte l'opere egregie, o, sono nella parte dell'anima ragionevole, come la sapienza, l'intelletto, e la prudenza; overo nella parte appetitiva, e ne costumi come la giustizia, la temperanza, e la fortezza e l'altre a queste simiglianti, e quelle intellettive, queste morali si chiamano, quelle s'imparano, e s'accrescono con la disciplina, con buoni ricordi, e con l'aiuto del maestro, e però hanno bisogno di tempo e d'esperienza ad impararsi."

70 On the debate around the "bocche inutili" during the war of Siena, see Cantagalli 334–5; in Marinella, see canto XVIII, 69–70.

71 On the "advantages" and "disadvantages" of masculinity, see Connell 245–7.

2 The Poetic and the Real: The Chivalric-Epic Commentary of the Armed Woman

1 On the increasingly historical and verisimilar epic, see Murrin. On the negative critiques of gunpowder in literary texts, see Murrin 123–37. On the historical response to gunpowder, see Hale, "Gunpowder."

2 The most extensive study of the warrior woman in Italian Renaissance epic is Stoppino. See also Shemek, *Ladies Errant*; Everson, *Italian Romance*, and "Epic Tradition," with special attention to n73, which provides a bibliography of scholarship on women warriors; Petrocchi; Villoresi; Alhaique Pettinelli; and Günsberg.

3 Works that discuss both the literary developments of the virago and the connections between historical and literary viragos are also numerous: Tomalin; Robinson; Rajna 47–54; and Allaire. Shemek, *Ladies Errant* 86–9, implies that the criticism levelled at the woman warrior of literary romance was a projection of the male anxieties around women regents.

4 "Both in subject matter and form, epic may well be the most exclusively gender coded of all literary genres; so much so that epic and masculinity appear to be almost coterminous" (1). On Schweizer's presumed ignorance of successful Italian female epic authors see Cox, *Preface* 7.

5 See Valeria Andò, who uses this scene to discuss how women were able to insert themselves into the masculine world of war specifically through weaving. On Homer's tempering of the heroic figure, see White 50–8.

6 A. Rossi 116. In *Iliad* 8, when the Trojans are camped near the Achaean camp, Hector sends orders to the city: "'for the boys who are in their first youth and the grey-browed elders to take stations on the god-founded bastions that circle the city; and as for the women, have our wives, each

one in her own house, kindle a great fire'" (8.518–21; quoted in A. Rossi, *Contexts* 116).

7 Blok 145–93 provides a philological study of archaic literary references and particularly the Homeric citation of Amazons.

8 "ci insegna Aristotile nel secondo 'della *Retorica,*' dove dice che, benché la fortezza sia virtù, non sta però bene attribuirla alle femine, ed è stato in ciò riguardevole Omero, ma non già Virgilio con Camilla, né meno l'Ariosto né il Tasso né io con le Marfise, con le Bradamanti, con le Clorinde e con l'Erinta" (Bracciolini 43). See discussion of this passage and Bracciolini more generally in Quint, *Francesco Bracciolini.*

9 On the debate about the effect of Amazons on the gendering of war, see Blok; Arrigoni; Schwarz; Verrier, *Le miroir des Amazones.*

10 After Homer, the story of Penthesilea was expanded. Most memorably, Achilles kills her, unaware that she is a woman. He removes her helmet and falls immediately in love upon seeing her face. Particularly important to the Penthesilea legend is the missing text of *Aethiopis* of Arctinus of Miletus (sixth century BCE) as well as the much later *Posthomerica* by Quintus Smyrnaeus (fourth century CE). See Arrigoni 41–50 for a description of Arctinus and other variants of the Penthesilea story.

11 See Arrigoni 127–60. On the significance of Virgil's Camilla as a female warrior, see Becker.

12 See Connolly on the connection between masculinity, warfare (action), and rhetoric (words) in Virgil and other Roman works.

13 The question of Virgil's source for the character of Camilla is still unresolved. See Arrigoni *passim* for a discussion of possible influences on Virgil. See also Williams 226, note to lines 803f.

14 Dante (*Inf.* I, 106–8; *Inf.* IV, 124); Petrarch (*Triumph of Chastity* and elsewhere); Boccaccio *(De claris mulieribus).* For these and other references see Arrigoni 127–54.

15 Comparisons between Camilla and the Amazons are found in *Aeneid,* book 11: "at medias inter caedes exsultat Amazon" (in the middle of the slaughter the Amazon exulted, 11.648) and "pictis bellantur Amazones armis" (with ornamented weapons the Amazons wage war, 11.660). The relationship of Camilla to the Amazons is one of the central arguments of Arrigoni. She claims that Virgil makes Camilla into a very particular type of Amazon: he doesn't demonstrate contempt for Amazons, as Euripides and Aeschylus do; she is not a barbarian invader; and he differentiates Camilla from other Amazons by giving her a history as a hunter (23).

16 Arrigoni 18 explains how the role of the milk of wild beasts or a savage childhood is common to Harpalyce, Atalante, Camilla, and the Amazons.

These women also share a trajectory of huntress to warrior: "In altre parole, e senza i moralismi moderni: donne guerriere non si nasce, prima bisogna aver praticato la caccia. Ci sono però diversi modi di caccia e non tutte le cacciatrici sono guerriere, soprattutto guerriere riuscite."

17 This passage, particularly the question of the parenthetical phrase "monstrat amor verus patriae, ut videre Camillam," has sparked extensive debate, on which see Arrigoni 117–24, and A. Rossi, *Contexts* 115–24.

18 A. Rossi, *Contexts* 121–2, cites the historical cases of Selinuntian women who fought during an attack by the Carthaginians, as well as a siege of the Spanish city Iluturgi by Scipio. The *Posthomerica* by Quintus Smyrnaeus continues the narration of the Trojan War, and likely drew on the same cyclic sources as Virgil, including Arctinus; see above.

19 Hippodameia is a variant reading for Tisiphone (Quintus 13).

20 *The Trojan Epic* 14. James's translation is slightly altered for clarity.

21 *La Scanderbeide* 58: "Da la Città Pirro sagace in tanto / Non poca aita à quei di fuor procura, / Spoglia ogni donna del femineo manto, / E la fa rivestir maschia armatura: / Può questa mostra nel Tiranno tanto, / Che non da lungi il ver ben raffigura, / Ch'ingannato ne vien dal sesso imbelle, / Com'ei fè la Città con finta pelle" (VI: 41).

22 The scene of the Donne Corciolane is depicted in Serdonati, *Donne illustri* 617. Serdonati lists the *Mambrino Roseo*, book 14, as his source.

23 The *Orlando furioso* was published in three forms during the author's lifetime: 1516, 1521, and 1532. Benson claims that the 1532 edition shows a growth in Ariosto's thought on the defence of women, particularly in the relation of female militancy and marriage (123–6). Unless otherwise noted, English prose translations of Ariosto are Waldman's.

24 In this and the following passage from Ariosto, I have used Shemek's translation over Waldman's, as hers more closely reflects the original (Shemek, *Ladies Errant* 96). All Italian citations of *Orlando furioso* are from the Caretti edition.

25 Trans. Shemek, *Ladies Errant* 97.

26 "Che Bradamante sia, tien fermo e sodo / (che ben l'avea veduta altre fiate) / il signor de la rocca"; "The lord of the castle was quite clear in his mind that this was Bradamante, whom he had seen on previous occasions" (XXXII, 81:5–7), Waldman translation. Though I am indebted to her close reading of this episode, I diverge greatly from Shemek's interpretation of the lord's reaction to Bradamante. Shemek takes the lack of shock to display the "speechlessness" and great amazement of the lord (Shemek, *Ladies Errant* 97).

27 In her analysis of the development of the Bradamante character in pre-Ariostan poetry and prose, Stoppino explains that Bradamante begins as

the daughter of an Arab king, then becomes a fighter among female giant warriors, then the illegitimate daughter of the Christian lord Amone, and finally, in Ariosto, is made both legitimate and Christian.

28 Rajna 42–7 insists that we should not consider female giants and armed maidens in the same category. This is repeated by Grilli 18. Stoppino 56, instead, shows a continuum of female militancy in the heroic tradition, ranging from the giants to Bradamante. De Costa argues that although women warriors are different in typology, they share the trait of inciting female desire.

29 Examples of how "guerriere" have been considered non-women permeate the literature: Grilli 19 distinguishes women warriors from "figure veramente donne"; and Croce, *Storie* 189, states that the epic contains "donne-guerriere e donne realmente donne." Robinson states overtly that they are "not to be taken literally." However, she also suggests that "neither are they purely emblematic" (120). Robinson appeals to the feminine body not to insist on militancy but rather to argue for the incorporation of women in the realm of politics.

30 The revelation of the woman beneath armour is too common to be summarized. The most important examples are Pulci, *Il morgante* III, 17; Boiardo, *Orlando innamorato* III: V, 40; Ariosto, *Orlando furioso* XXXII, 79; Bernardo Tasso, *Amadigi* IV, 27–8. Notably, in Torquato Tasso's *Gerusalemme liberata,* Tancredi is said to have fallen in love with Clorinda while she still was without her helmet: "fuor che la fronte, armata apparse," I, 46, and in canto XXII, after he has delivered his mortal wound, it is when Tancredi removes Clorinda's helmet that he realizes his tragic act. For an insightful discussion on the "revelation" of women in chivalric poetry, see Valeria Finucci's "Introduction" to Fonte, *Tredici canti del Floridoro* (XXXIII).

31 On the power of recursive signifiers to create a unity (such as the identity of a masculine knight) simply through the repeated use of such signifiers, see Žižek. Žižek refers in particular to words such as "God," "country," "party," and "class" as signifiers "without the signified" (99). See also Judith Butler's interpretation of Žižek (189–92).

32 On the Medici use of chivalric imagery, see Randolph (193).

33 The *Stanze* were written to celebrate the victory of Giuliano de' Medici in a tournament held on 29 January 1475 in Piazza Santa Croce in Florence. On the role of Lucrezia Tornabuoni in the revival of chivalric literature and imagery in Renaissance Florence, see Milligan 2011.

34 The fact that a signifier like "knight" could be used to mean its opposite is discussed by Žižek, who states that the "retroactive effect" of naming

allows that an object can become "identical-to-itself even if all its properties have changed" (94).

35 On the appropriation of chivalric symbolism and culture by Renaissance courts, see Scaglione. On the use of armour as cultural symbol, see Springer. Particularly suggestive is Springer's discussion of a statue of Charles V that allows the viewer to remove the armour to see the body below (117–20).

36 I thank Alessandro Carpin for the initial suggestion of armour as a veil.

37 Here I quote Butler in one moment where she concurs with Žižek's identity theory: "What is refused or repudiated in the formation of the subject continues to determine the subject. What remains outside this subject persists as a kind of defining negativity. The subject is, as a result, never coherent and never self-identical precisely because it is founded and, indeed, continually refounded, through a set of defining foreclosures and repressions that constitute the discontinuity and incompletion of the subject" (189). See Butler 198–9 on the discussion of her own interpretation of foreclosure, as well as Lacan and Žižek on foreclosure *(Verwefung)* in identity formation.

38 Robinson argues that, in the *Orlando furioso,* Marfisa is the "epitome of what a knight should be," and thus the fact that this exemplar is a woman actually serves to point to the "absurdity of the ideal," since knighthood is meant to correspond to manly nobility (184).

39 Quoted in Cristofaro, "Alcuni ammaestramenti" 54. I thank Deanna Shemek for assistance with the English translation.

40 Robinson observes that Bradamante is the only knight in the *Orlando furioso* whose military success is reflective of virtue. Bradamante's success is linked to the morality of the event (178). Moreover, Bradamante kills only one opponent in the *Furioso* (Pinabello) and two in the *Innamorato* (Martasino and Daniforte); she otherwise allows her opponents to live after their defeat. Finucci argues that Bradamante's lack of war booty is demonstrative of the author's refusal to attribute masculine prowess to the character (236).

41 Robinson argues that Marfisa's "conduct is so straightforward and her heroism so impressive that the revelation almost never evokes the special shame at being bested by a female that Bradamante's victories inspire" (182).

42 My reading of this episode owes much to Shemek's reading of Bradamante's negotiation of gender, identity, duty, and desire in her confrontation with Rodomonte (*Ladies Errant* 104–8).

43 Ascoli demonstrates how the male warrior and armed maiden are interwoven into the same impenetrable erotic fantasy as the virginal damsel ("Like a Virgin" 142–57).

44 Verrier, *Le miroir des Amazones* 31–41, provides a useful list of examples of warrior women divided by category of virgin, widow, and prostitute. There are cases of viragos who are not virgins in epic and romance: Bradamante will return to fighting once her husband, Ruggiero, is killed, and in the *cantare* of Andrea da Barberino, *L'Aspramonte,* the virago Galiziella fights while married and pregnant (see Stoppino 33–43). Tomalin provides a survey of less-known chivalric texts that include examples of married viragos, particularly in the latter half of the sixteenth century.

45 See Benedetti for the association of the notion of Diana (Artemis) with the women of Tasso's *Gerusalemme liberata.*

46 "Cette virginité était un signe d'exception, le gage sexuel d'une excellence qui pouvait contribuer à justifier une pareille inversion des rôles entre hommes et femmes" (Verrier, *Le miroir des Amazones* 32).

47 For Marulla, see the Introduction in this volume. On the Pisan girl, see the Latin *Carmina* of Castiglione as well as the Italian verse translation by Lodovico Domenichi: "De Viragine Semianimem in muris mater Pisana puellam / Dum fovet, & tenero pectore vulnus hiat, / Nata, tibi has, dixit, taedas, atque hos humenaeos / Haec defensa tuo moenia marte dabunt? / Cui virgo: Haud alias taedas, aliosve hymenaeos / Debuit haec nobis grata reprendere humus. / Hanc ego sola meo servavi sanguine terram: / Haec servata meos terra tegat cineres. / Quod si iterum ad muros accedet gallicus hostis, / Pro patria arma iterum haec ossa cinisque ferent" (Castiglione, *Poesie* 154). Castiglione and Domenichi quoted in Verrier, *Le miroir des Amazones* 32–3. See also Stoppino 18–57, who deals at length with the question of the marriage trope of warrior maidens who fight their suitors and marry the one who can defeat them.

48 A selected list of warrior women raised on the milk of wild beasts includes Marfisa (Ludovico Ariosto); Clorinda (Torquato Tasso); Silveria (Margherita Sarrocchi); and Vittoria (Curzio Gonzaga).

49 Barbaro, quoted in King, "The School" 59. English translation of Barbaro's *On Marriage* can be found in Kohl, Witt, and Wells 220–7 (quotation from 223).

50 Stoppino states that Marfisa is a transliteration of the Amazon Marpesia, but as a character is Boiardo's creation (83). She suggests that Ariosto is revitalizing a genealogy between Marfisa and Boccaccio's Marpesia (75).

51 I thank Stoppino, who in personal correspondence communicated that, though animality had been important for women warriors in fifteenth-century heroic poetry (e.g., the warrior in *Ancroia* has a heart wrapped by four lions), Ariosto is likely the first poet to reintroduce the nursing trope.

52 Stoppino provides an excellent analysis of how categories are "blurred" between the warrior and the warrior bride (81–7). On the other hand, Benson makes a distinct division between the female knights who are "not interested in marriage" and those who "will be wives and who undertake military action only as a means of furthering the interests of husbands and families" (124).

53 Shemek, *Ladies Errant,* challenges the notion of "closure" and argues for a more ambiguous and open interpretation of Bradamante. The extent to which Bradamante is domesticated at the end of Ariosto's *Orlando furioso* is discussed fully in Hairston, "Bradamante"; for a bibliographic history of the debate, see note 3.

54 Moralists were often anxious about women reading chivalric literature. The strongest injunction is from Juan Luís Vives, who suggests that for girls no education would be preferable to a chivalric one: "For such girls [female readers of chivalry] it would have been preferable not only that they had never learned literature but that they had lost their eyes so that they could not read, and their ears so that they could not hear" (74). Also see Cox, "Women as Readers."

55 Andreoli discusses the *cassoni* of Girolamo da Santa Croce (125). Also of note, Francesco d'Este, son of Duke Alfonso I and Lucrezia Borgia, named his two daughters Marfisa and Bradamante.

56 Campigli's comments are in reference to Curzio Gonzaga's epic poem *Fidamante* (quoted in Cox, "Women as Readers" 138). Cox notes that this assumes that Campigli is the author of the *moralità* as well as the *argomenti* to her poem *Flori* (n12). English translation mine.

57 Some authors, such as Boccaccio, Betussi, and Serdonati (addressed in subsequent chapters), will guide women on how to imitate exemplary women. Franklin 8, and Kolsky, *The Ghost* 13, both state that women readers were not meant to imitate the deeds of the famous women of Boccaccio. Caroline McManus discusses how John Harrington (1561–1612), in his English translation of Ariosto, encourages women to read the Bible rather than to imitate Bradamante (77).

58 Moderata Fonte says that statues and texts about honourable men are meant to be inspirations to young men (*The Worth* 229–30), as does Ottaviano in the *Courtier* (4.9).

59 Monluc II:173. On Monluc's complex relation to chivalry during the Italian wars, see Potter 150–82.

60 "Haver sempre l'Ariosto nelle mani e quella parte più sovente legere che d'arme tratta" (Lando 46c).

61 See also Tomalin 47–8, 142–3; Benson 133–4; Piéjus 35–7.

62 Shemek raises a similar question when she notes that critics have systematically read canto 32 with a gender bias (*Ladies Errant* 224, n45).
63 Stoppino discusses how the armed maiden of epic and romance allows men to love masculinity, or in essence love themselves, without rupturing the heterosexual model. Furthermore, the woman warrior allows for alliance with the male competitor: "In the person of the warrior woman, enemy becomes ally, and ally becomes bride" (56).
64 Segre notes how Boiardo and Pulci were attracted to chivalry as a way of life. Ariosto, on the other hand, uses chivalry as a vehicle for relaying contemporary values (17).
65 The *Poetics* had been translated into Latin in 1498 by Giorgio Valla, but it wasn't until the 1540s and the lectures of the Paduan academies that it began to be valued by Italian writers; Javitch 16–17. Tomalin discusses the importance of Segni's translation of 1549 on the Italian epic.
66 On the armed woman in the debate about epic poetry, see Milligan "Unmaking."
67 Translation is Shemek's (*Ladies Errant* 85).
68 The problem of social class and the categorization of the militant woman is dealt with at length in chapters 5 and 6 of the current volume.
69 Shemek suggests that Pigna mistakes Queen Maria for her daughter Margaret, 221, n28.
70 On warrior women fighting on the losing side, see Quilligan 27.
71 On Clorinda in the context of the warrior woman debate, as well as a consideration of Gildippe, Tasso's other warrior maiden, see Milligan, "Unmaking."
72 Finucci, "Maternal Imagination" 72–3; and Benedetti.
73 Allaire suggests that the transvestite women of Pulci's *Morgante,* Ghaldina, Antenisca, and Rosana, who wear armour solely for purposes of disguise or safety in flight, are precursors of Erminia (34).
74 Quint, pointing to Clorinda's origin story, suggests that she could be the knight, the maiden, or the dragon "of religious error itself" (*Epic and Empire* 244).
75 Chiappelli calls Clorinda's militancy a "mask" (*Il conoscitore,* 59–60; 56–7), while Zatti says her armour "represses" her body ("Epic in the Age," 213).
76 On this passage see Latella 543.
77 "molte siate i costumi sono buoni, ma non sono convenienti, come la fortezza a la donna" (Tasso, *Discorsi* 601).
78 For biographical information see Maroi, Montella, Jaffe, Robin *(Publishing Women).* See also chapter 3.
79 The incipit of canto 20 appears in the 1516 edition, while canto 37's exordium to women was added for the final 1532 edition. Benson discusses the two distinct narratorial voices found in cantos 20 and 37, arguing that canto 37 marks a growth in Ariosto's pro-feminist voice (132–8).

80 On the *donne omicide* and Marganorre passages, see Benson 132–48.
81 Isabella Colonna is also briefly mentioned by Ariosto (37, 9). The list of illustrious women found in canto 46 does not praise women as warriors. The exclusion of contemporary women from Ariosto's exordium of women has been discussed at length. See MacCarthy 1–11.
82 On Isabella Colonna see the useful entry in the *Dizionario Biografico degli Italiani:* F. Petrucci, "Isabella Colonna": http://www.treccani.it/enciclopedia/isabella-colonna_(Dizionario-Biografico).
83 There are numerous discrepancies between editions, and there is yet to be a critical edition of her works. My transcriptions are from the 1577 edition of Terracina's *Discorso.* All translations of Terracina are mine unless otherwise noted.
84 Terracina quotes Ariosto in the last line of each of her stanzas. The eighth line is lifted from the first stanza of each canto of Ariosto, and this pattern follows in sequential order. The last stanza of Terracina's canto quotes two verses of Ariosto's, so that the result is that each canto in Terracina has an entirely original introductory stanza with an additional seven stanzas that cite Ariosto.
85 Terracina references Harpalyce and Camilla in 20.6: "S'ode la fama vostra già per tutto / Più assai che d'altre famose donzelle / E del fior vostro ogn'hor si vede il frutto, / Che se'n va col suo odor sino alle stelle. / Non farò de le duo, più chiaro mutto; / Perche si fanno, e leggon l'opre belle, / Ma per le vostre rime, e dotte prose / *Arpalice, e Camilla son famose*"; and regarding Bradamante: "Quanto si legge che fe Bradamante / Di sua persona si gagliarda, e fiera" (20.7.vv1–2); and about Marfisa: "Sol Marfisa, & Anthea fur gratiuse, / *Perche in battaglia erano esperte, & use*" (20.7. vv 7–8). Italicized lines represent those that Terracina lifted from Ariosto.
86 See Cox, *The Prodigious Muse,* for her discussion on the warrior woman in woman-authored epic, particularly chapter 5, on secular narrative.
87 Fonte, *Tredici canti* 61–2.
88 The English translation is taken from Sarrocchi, *Scanderbeide,* an abridged version of the epic by Rinaldina Russell. The translation includes large portions of the Italian text in an appendix, and I have cited this modern edition unless otherwise noted.
89 Cox argues that the heroine in Sarrocchi represents an exceptional woman, while women warriors in other epics represent women's potential more generally ("Women as Readers" 137).
90 The objective of the crusade was to take Jerusalem, but events led the Doge Enrico Dandolo to besiege and conquer Constantinople. For a short description of the political and historical context, as well as a bibliography of the event, see Lazzari 41–5. Translations of *Enrico* are Stampino's.

91 For Laura Lazzari, not only are women warriors' bodies not called weak, they are also desexualized: "perdono ogni connotazione sensuale e non sono percepite quali oggetti del desiderio" (72). Such a desexualization of *guerriere* demonstrates a break with Marinella's sixteenth-century predecessors. See also Lazzari's general discussion on women warriors in Marinella (61–97).

92 See *Il libro della bella donna* 288.

93 See Carmela Cristofaro's discussion of the passage (60–1): "Che se lor dato fosse, a questo nostro / secolo, pien d'onor fallace e vano, / come pingon con l'aco ornate d'ostro, / pugnando, armate gir col brando in mano, / bella materia di purgato inchiostro / non men forse darian che 'l gran Troiano, / del qual cantò Maron tant'altamente/ che 'l suon de la sua gloria ancor si sente" (*Amadigi* 11, 4).

94 "Me' t'era star tra feminile ingegno; / Che cercar tra i guerrier pregio, o vittoria" (*L'Enrico* 522–3).

95 The armed woman and armed girl have resurfaced as a popular trend in the twenty-first century (e.g., Disney animated films, video games). Given the context of an armed service that institutionally includes women, it will be interesting to see whether these media are to have any effect on the gendering of war.

3 Women Writers Demanding Warrior Masculinity: Catherine of Siena, Laura Terracina, Chiara Matraini, and Isabella Cervoni

1 This study seeks to enrich the received perception that women writers wrote primarily in the lyric genre, and even then primarily to discuss love and piety. Cox (*Prodigious Muse)*, Eisenbichler ("Un chant," *The Sword*, and *L'opera)*, and Kirkham have recently shown how women adopted lyric poetry for political and martial themes.

2 Elshtain has identified the influence of competing traditions of the feminine in warfare – including, among others: Plutarch's Spartan mothers, where mothers encourage heroic acts of militarism – as well as the non-combatant "beautiful soul" who is in need of protection by a warrior man. See especially Elshtain, "Reflections," *Women and War*, and "Women and War."

3 Italian and English translations of Colonna are from Cox 2013, 77–82. Vittoria's husband, Francesco D'Avalos, and her father, Fabrizio Colonna, were both imprisoned at the battle of Ravenna in 1512.

4 Vittoria Colonna's time in Ischia was spent in the care of the Duchess of Francavilla, Costanza D'Avalos, Colonna's husband's aunt. On Ischia, D'Avalos and Colonna hosted a coterie of writers and intellectuals. See Robin, *Publishing* 3–8.

5 The women on Ischia, including Vittoria Colonna, plead with Del Vasto to stay on Ischia to protect them from the Venetian fleet. Del Vasto delays his departure out of concern for these women; see Giovio 13. The dialogue is discussed in Zimmermann 86–103.
6 On the trope of abandoned women, see Lipking; Bassanese; and Hagedorn.
7 On the influence of the *Heroides* on Renaissance poetry, see Lipking and Hagedorn. For Stampa's poem 62, see Tylus's translation.
8 On Gambara's life, see Chimenti as well as the biography by Zamboni in Gambara, *Rime e lettere*. On Gambara's poetry relating to war, see Sears 126–60. On Gambara's works and life, see: *Le rime*; Sandal; Pizzagalli; Cox, *Women's Writing*, and *Prodigious Muse*; Jaffe; Kennedy.
9 This provocative reading of the letter is from Chimenti 61.
10 See Gambara's lengthy verse "Quando miro la terra ornata e bella," which critiques men for their worldly pursuits, including creating fortunes and seeking honour on the battlefield. One stanza addresses men on the battlefield: "Questi per aver fama, com'accade, / ne la sua più fiorita e verde etade, / seguendo il periglioso e fiero Marte, / or fra mille saette e mille spade / animoso si caccia; e con quest'arte, / mentre spera di farsi a le contrade / più remote da noi alto e immortale, / casca assai più che un fragil vetro, frale" (vv 57–64; *Rime e lettere* 32).
11 Though there is some disagreement on the dating of the poem, we find Bullock's argument the most salient. He claims that the context of this poem is 1536 when, following the death of Alessandro de' Medici, cardinals Ridolfi, Salviati, and Gatti entered the city to restore liberty to Florence, an attempt that famously failed; see Bullock 1995, 112–13. See also Stortoni 1997, 30–1. Translation mine.
12 On "Italia mia," see chapter 2; see also Sears; Costa-Zalessow 316–31; and Brose.
13 For a detailed account of the life of Girolama Corsi as well as the Spanish surname of her presumed husband (Ramos), see V. Rossi, "Di una rimatrice" 183–219. See also Cox, *Women's Writing* 45–51.
14 Petrucci's sonnet is the incipit in Domenichi and in Bulifon. On Petrucci's sonnet, see Cox, *Lyric Poetry*, 311. On Petrucci as well as other women writers from Siena, often writing about war, see Eisenbichler, *The Sword*.
15 The most thorough examination of the Fabrianesi is provided by the *Dizionario biografico degli Italiani* under the headings "Livia Chiavello" and "Eleonora della Genga." See also Morici 662–95; and Cox, *Women's Writing* 145. Another sixteenth-century author, Ortensio Lando, published works under a woman's pseudonym. On Lando see Ray (*Writing Gender*).

16 Trebbiani is first found in Giovanni Cinelli's *Biblioteca volante,* but her story is then widely repeated by writers known for their praise of women, including Crescimbeni and Bergalli.

17 Critics such as Stoppelli believe that the external force that is seeking to destroy Christianity in verse 11 is more likely the Turkish force of the sixteenth century than one of the fourteenth. However, a fourteenth-century woman writer, Catherine of Siena, asked that a crusade be taken against the infidels, thus complicating the notion that this is a sixteenth-century invention.

18 Catherine's opus includes nearly 380 letters, various orations, and the *Dialogo della divina provvidenza,* a book of meditations written in dialogue with God. All of Catherine's works are available in the original Italian on the CD-ROM *Santa Caterina da Siena, Opera omnia. Testi e concordanze,* ed. F. Sbaffoni (Pistoi, 2002). I have cited Tommaseo 1860, as well as Suzanne Noffke's English translation of the *Letters* 2000. On the vexed issue of Catherine's authorship, see Tylus, *Reclaiming*. For an excellent overview of Catherine scholarship see Muessig, Ferzoco, and Kienzle.

19 Luongo's monograph argues that Catherine finds her authority in a multifaceted identification with the Virgin and Christ. Tylus's article argues that Catherine's "scandalous" and self-proclaimed "humiliating" role of asserting herself in public allows her to "appropriate Christ's blood as ink and make it her own" ("Caterina da Siena" 131).

20 On Catherine's abstention from food and the attention she received because of her self-deprivation, see Bynum; and R. Bell, *Holy Anorexia.*

21 Luongo 14–15.

22 Catherine does not always invoke secular images of men when scolding men for their actions in war. After Breton mercenaries (fighting on the Pope's bankroll) slaughtered 4,000 citizens in Cesena in 1377, Catherine wrote to Pope Gregory XI reminding him that he should value human blood (as Jesus had done) more than lands and territory. On this letter and Catherine's tense reaction to Gregory's return, see Tylus, *Reclaiming* 28–9.

23 Tylus provides a subtle and convincing reading of the two biblical tellings of the Canaanite woman as well as of Catherine's letter that cites the passage, letter 69 (*Reclaiming* 129–32).

24 Catherine's letter to Hawkwood can be found in Tommaseo, ed., vol. II, 327–30, as well as in Noffke's English translation in *Letters,* vol. I, 79–81. The bibliography on John Hawkwood (Giovanni Acuto) is quite extensive, though often owing more to legend than history. For early sources, see the Florentine histories by Leonardo Bruni; Poggio Bracciolini; and Scipione Ammirato. For recent scholarship on Hawkwood see Fowler; Barlozzetti; and Caferro.

25 The anonymous panegyric *Miracoli di Santa Caterina* was written in 1474, one year before her letter to Hawkwood. See R. Bell 38.

26 On Catherine in Pisa, see Tylus, *Reclaiming* 133–5.

27 Hawkwood never went to battle in the crusades (Tommaseo ed., vol. II, 329).

28 Caferro's biography of Hawkwood pays particular attention to Hawkwood's adept ability to negotiate for money by crafting a cruel reputation.

29 Translation for this and all other passages of Catherine's letter are in Noffke, *The Letters of Catherine of Siena*, and will be noted as letter number in Tommaseo (T) and page number in Noffke (N).

30 Although Hawkwood was knighted, it is not known when or by whom he received his title (Caferro 9).

31 From the Archivio Segreto Vaticano, Registri Vaticani, 269, fol. 51r–51v.

32 This same letter states that she has been informed about the captain's pledge to fight in the crusade: "I find it very strange that you should be wanting to make war here after pledging (as I've heard) your willingness to go and die for Christ in this holy crusade" (*Letters* 81).

33 Caferro mentions several stories that circulated regarding Hawkwood's brutality. For example, he famously settled a dispute between two of his corporals who were fighting over which one would rape an attractive young girl by stabbing the girl first (23).

34 Tylus argues that Catherine's use of shame to "highly visible men" is incumbent on Catherine's exposing herself to public scrutiny. Tylus states that, "If women's movement into the public space and 'birthing' of charitable acts allows them to call attention to Christ's scandalous incarnation, men's refusal to enter that space as Caterina defines it marks them as unmanly: as men who are not *virile*" ("Caterina da Siena" 131).

35 On men's military duty and sacrifice of life in battle, see Gilmore; Friedl; as well as the controversial Mansfield. Mansfield attempts to work through the claim that masculinity implies a sacrifice of life, but his argument is weakened by his misogyny. Shin presents an interesting Renaissance corollary in Machiavelli, whose heroines are always presented as less than men since their motives are primarily personal rather than related to higher societal considerations.

36 Women as the arbiters of masculinity are found throughout ancient literature and figure prominently in Plutarch's *Moralia*, in "Sayings of Spartan Women." In a later example, a character in Moderata Fonte's *Worth of Women* states that if men do not follow the models of ideal knights, women are obliged to take up arms, like "Amazons of old," and correct the situation (*Worth* 230); see also chapter 1 of the present study.

37 On these letters to Pope Gregory and the sixty letters that Catherine writes relating to the schism, see Scott.

38 The story of Sichelgaita is found in the *Alexiad* or *Alexias* (c. 1148), written by the world's first acknowledged female historian: "There is a story that Robert's wife Gaita, who used to accompany him on campaigns, like another Pallas, if not a second Athena, seeing the runaways and glaring fiercely at them, shouted in a very loud voice: 'How far will ye run? Halt! Be men!'" (Comnena 147). On Sichelgaita's military exploits, see Eads.

39 For a thorough publication history of Terracina's oeuvre, see Robin, *Publishing* 60–1.

40 For biographical information on Laura Terracina, see Maroi; Montella; Jaffe; Robin; and Cox, *Women's Writing*.

41 Cox challenges Dionisotti's thesis that women's writing was a brief phenomenon of the mid-sixteenth century by arguing that critical attention has overemphasized print culture. Aristocratic women writers, who far outnumbered women writing from the middle classes, did not typically publish except in invited anthologies. On Terracina, see especially *Women's Writing* 80–5.

42 For an excellent discussion on the the *Discorso* see Shemek, *Ladies Errant*, especially 129–38.

43 All citations of the *Discorso* are of the 1577 edition. The edition Shemek consulted contains a spelling variant, "Sarà la penna mia tanto verile" (148). She does not specify which edition she is citing in this case, but she notes the "abundant differences" among editions (*Ladies Errant* 230–1n).

44 Ann Rosalind Jones notes how even modern editions of early modern women poets "downplay women's work in genres other than love poetry" (309).

45 Murrin states that contemporaries, including Lodovico Dolce, compared Ariosto's poetry to painting and stated that they experienced the text as "spectators at a war in progress." Murrin cites Quint's *Epic and Empire*, which notes the classical precedence of Lucan's war writings (81, 282n).

46 "Io temo d'essequir tanta aspra impresa, / Che 'l sesso feminil d'arme non sente, / E credo, che nel fin rimarro offesa, / Poi che il desio, ne l'esser non consente, / Questo dirò, per non far più contesa, / Et acquietar la mia superba mente" (XIV.7.1–5).

47 While the first stanza of *Furioso* XV states that bloody victories often tarnish a captain's reputation, Ariosto will praise his patron for having killed the enemy while saving his own men: "Come vincer si de', ne dimostraste; / ch'uccideste i nemici, e noi salvaste" (XV.2.7–8).

48 I thank Carol Lansing for drawing my attention to the medieval and Renaissance practice of reducing *noble* casualties by capturing opponents in hopes of ransom. Although more research still needs to be done in this area, this practice may not have prevented bloodshed of masses of soldiers. The large numbers of fatalities chronicled in warfare during the sixteenth century suggest that the capture of captains was made possible only by slaughtering many of the troops.

49 Although much of Terracina's biography is unknown, we presume that her views would be in part formed by her acquaintance with men who fought with the Spanish/Habsburg forces. The Neapolitan nobility were subject to imperial rule, and accordingly were often fighting in Italy and Flanders. For relevant studies on militarism and Spanish Italy, see the essay and extensive bibliography in Donati.

50 Turkish troops landed on the beach of Terracina's family's neighbourhood in Chiaia near Naples in 1563, a fact she memorializes in her sonnet "Oh, Crudel moto! Oh, cosa horrenda e fiera." The sonnet is transcribed in Montella, who also provides the context of the invasion at Chiaia (108). Two biographies list her family's villa in Chiaia as her birthplace: Maroi; and Borzelli.

51 For an exemplary text of such a phenomenon, see the sixteenth-century *Castillo inexpugnable* by Fray Gonzalo de Arredondo y Alvarado (Burgos: Juan de Junta, 1528) and the synopsis of the text given by Robert Gaston. The text, which was in the library of Don Pedro Álvarez de Toledo, Spanish Viceroy of Naples, urges Charles V to remember the courageous El Cid and to weep for the abominations committed against Christians by the "filthy" Turks, especially against women. As Gaston notes, in the book there are also female perspectives given of the Turkish threat (164–5).

52 On Carafa's anti-Spanish sentiments and the Carafa war, see Dandelet; and Pastor 14:64–180.

53 In canto XVII, Ariosto invokes Leo X as both lion and shepherd, who must roar and raise his arms to defend his flock from the wolves. See Ascoli's reading detailing how Ariosto indirectly critiques Leo through his use of interlacing structure ("Ariosto's 'Fier Pastor'" 189–224).

54 The referent of the clause "appar d'un Lico" is ambiguous (Paul or the "nemico"), especially given that "appar" is an infinitive rather than a gerund.

55 She reminds the pope that the French king, Henry II, was allying with the Turks to defeat Charles V's control over southern Italy: "Che disegno crudel, che desio vano, / e del Re Franco, che patir vol parme, / che facciano di noi turchi macello" (*Le seste* 23)

56 Terracina's sonnet is also critical of France, which had been allying itself with the Turks to defeat Charles V's hold over Italy; see the preceding note.

57 Terracina's praise of certain popes may also suggest her leanings to papal reform, especially Valdesian reform. See Robin (*Publishing Women*) 61.
58 The sonnet was left unpublished until the modern edition of the *None rime.* See Montella 104.
59 Matraini published prolifically: *Rime e prose di Madonna Chiara Matraini, gentildonna lucchese* (1555); *Lettere di Signora Chiara Matraini, gentildonna lucchese con la prima e seconda parte delle sue rime* (1595); *Lettere di Madonna Chiara Matraini, gentildonna lucchese con la prima e seconda parte delle sue rime* (1597); *Meditationi spirituali* (1581); *Breve discorso sopra la vita e laude della beatiss. Vergine e madre del figliuol di Dio* (1590); *Dialoghi spirituali* (1602). For a critical study of the published and unpublished works, see Giovanna Rabitti's "Introduction" to Matraini, *Rime e lettere*; and Bullock and Palange.
60 Matraini writes 104 poems in the volume. There are 99 poems set in a *canzoniere*, which precedes the prose, and then 8 sonnets (5 by Matraini) exchanged between her and Lodovico Domenichi, Andrea Lori, Giovambattista Giraldi Cinzio, and Lodovico Dolce.
61 See Rabitti's analysis of manuscript sources, including that of Gherardo Sergiusti, the relative of Elizabeth Sergiusti, Graziani's wife ("Linee").
62 Matraini's collections of sonnets that are published in the 1590s are also noticeably more spiritual than her first collection. Maclachlan suggests that, in the poetry of the 1590s, the "angelic man is replaced by the poet's own direct relationship with her salvation" ("The Poetry").
63 The first publication using cursive script is found in the letters of Catherine of Siena, published by Manuzio in September 1500. See Ridolfi 101–5. For the association of typesetting and readership, see Grendler.
64 The ninety-nine poems of Matraini's first edition appear in *Rime di diversi signori napolitani, e d'altri, nuovamente raccolte et impresse: Libro settimo* 68–154. The *Oratione* is not included in the recent English translation of Matraini's works by Elaine Maclachlan, and, to my knowledge, its only reprint since the 1555 edition is in *Rime e prose.*
65 See Marcheschi 41–58 for an analysis of the letter to Cardona and the specific bibliographic citations of reform-minded clerics, editors, and publishers. See also her chapter on Matraini's commissioning of the Sybil in Lucca's Santa Maria Forisportam. The painting depicts Matraini as the Sybil who directs a kneeling emperor/*condottiere* to see the Virgin and Jesus in the sky above. Notably, the painting details the superiority of Christ over worldly matters such as arms.
66 All translations of Matraini are mine.
67 See Hewlett on the cultural openness of Lucca to religious reform.

68 The "Orazione" of Isabella Cervoni, discussed below, is much more ambivalent about war.
69 Sergiusti's account states that Matraini and Graziani had created a sort of "academy" in his house: "Una Accademia ... haveva missa in Casa sua." This, or an established academy in Lucca, could be the setting for the *Oratione.* For Sergiusti, see Rabitti, "Linee" 141, and Jaffe 134n. Also notable is that in her *Dialoghi spirituali* (1602) she dedicates works to an imaginary *Accademia dei Curiosi.*
70 *Archivio Storico Italiano*, ser. I, vol. XV, 351, 346.
71 On the Academy, see note 69. As for political crises in Lucca, there were many in the period just before her publication of the *Rime et prose*, most notably Francesco Burlamacchi's plot to overthrow the Medici in the 1540s.
72 Italian citations of Matraini's "Oratione" are taken from Giovanna Rabiti's modern edition, *Rime e lettere* (Bologna, 1989).
73 See also Matraini's letter to Cardona, in which she states that, although Achilles was lucky to have Homer, many warriors are cast into oblivion (*Rime e lettere* 130–1).
74 See Schmitt and Skinner on Ciceronian thought about silence, action, and virtue. They state that eloquence is used to move others to action, with virtue as the end goal, "not mere erudition" (730). On humanist belief of "thought unexpressed," see Struever 60–1.
75 On gender transgression, see Luckyj.
76 See, for example, Bartolommeo Cavalcanti in his speech to amateur soldiers, telling them to do away with feminine refinement and be more "rough and tough.": "Scacciamo da noi ogni molle pensiero, spogliamoci d'ogni effeminato habito; non le donnesche delicatezze, ma più tosto la militare antica rozzezza a noi giudichiamo convenirsi" (quoted in Hale, *Renaissance War* 365). On the discourse of effeminacy and warfare in the Cinquecento, see Milligan, "The Politics" and "Masculinity."
77 On the devolution of Ferrara to papal control, see Mitchell; and Masetti Zannini.
78 All translations of Cervoni's oration are mine.
79 Cox gives Cervoni's birthdate as around 1576 (*Prodigious Muse* 258).
80 "Sene maraviglierà grandemente"; "stupefatto" (100v).
81 Cicero tells of Hannibal and Phormio in *De oratore* 2.75. Plutarch will recount the story, as does Petrarch in his invective against a physician.
82 See Ghazarian 69–71. Hayton is also cited as a source for a number of stories of illustrious women in Filogenio 185. There were multiple Latin editions throughout the sixteenth century and two Italian translations, in 1559 and 1562 (see Burger xi).
83 For a description of the entry of the Pope as well as a facsimile of contemporary *avvisi* and engravings, see Mitchell 26–8.

84 See Tylus, "Caterina da Siena" 137 for an exceptional reading of this printed edition and its place in a humanist program. This and all citations of Aldus's edition come from Tylus.

85 Tylus, "Caterina da Siena," reminds us that Venice, Aldus's patria, would have felt more vulnerable to Turkish attack than other cities (117).

4 Classical and Christian Models of Warring Women: From Plutarch to Boccaccio

1 Cox, *Women's Writing,* notes that cities were vying to have illustrious women writers to claim as their own (102). I would expand this notion to suggest that cities were often identifying or "branding" themselves with so-called illustrious women of all sorts, not only writers.

2 Calmeta 1959, LXIV. Grayson asks scholars to search for this missing text, as it would provide a historical text by an author who was associated with the key figures of the fifteenth century, in particular Cesare Borgia.

3 The manuscript is found in codex n. 11846 in the library of the Reale Seminario Sacerdotal de San Carlos de Zaragoza (see Calmeta xliii*)*.

4 The index of the book is reprinted in the appendix of Calmeta (118–22). On Calmeta see the introduction to Grayson's edition.

5 The entries of women whose biographies would apparently have been included in the twelfth book are as follows: Giovanna di Voloes, Bianca Maria, Buona di Savoia, Eleanora d'Aragona, Isabella d'Aragona, Beatrice da Este, Isabella da Este, Elisabet da Gonzaga, Costanza [de] D'avalos, Antonia dal Ba[l]zo, La Prefettessa, Emilia Pia, Margarita Pia, Alda Boiarda, Lucrezia da Este, Lucrezia Borgia, Caterina Sforza, Ciancia Principessa, La Duchessa d'Amalfi, Costanza Sforza, Margarita da Trivulzi, Marchesana di Cotrone, Giulia Farnese, Maria Natta, Chiaretta Spinola, Laura Scioppa, Felice della Rovere, Damigella Trivulzi, Ippolita Fieramonte, Giulia da Gambara, Elisabet Colle, Graziosa (I have left the names as they are found in Calmeta 122).

6 On the fortune of the *De mulieribus claris,* see Zaccaria, *Boccaccio narratore;* Kolsky, *The Ghost;* and Franklin.

7 McInerney provides a list of ancient books of famous women: *Biographies of Famous Women* by Charon of Carthage, *Women who were Philosophers or Otherwise Accomplished Something Noteworthy* by Apollonius the Stoic, and the *Account of Deeds Accomplished by the Virtue of Women* by Artemon of Magnesia (326). Another work (not mentioned in McInerney), *Women Intelligent and Courageous in Warfare,* can be found in Westermann 213–18. It contains fourteen sketches of ten non-Greek heroines and four Greeks (quoted in McLeod 19 n18).

8 Hesiod's *Eoiae* and Homer's *Odyssey* provide the earliest Greek catalogues of heroines that have survived. The ancient catalogues of famous women that remain are often merely lists, and McLeod argues that they were not the inspirations for the books of illustrious women found in the Renaissance. The ancient catalogues often cast women as dangerous erotic objects or only in relation to their "heroic sons" (13). On the other hand, Virgil's heroines, found around Dido in the underworld, represent the dangers of erotic desire that Aeneas has left behind (11–18). It should be noted that female protagonists such as Camilla have a far-reaching influence and represent a type that is very different from the "catalogues" of women studied by McLeod.

9 For a study of ancient sources of biographies of famous women, see Stadter.

10 The first published Latin translation in Italy of Plutarch's *On the Bravery of Women* is the 1485 translation by Alamanus Rinucinus, *De virtutibus mulierum*. Beatrice Collina claims that the first Renaissance author to give prominence to the "classic" arguments of Plutarch is Jean Tixier de Révisy, known as Giovanni Ravisio Testore in Italian, in his *De memorabilibus et claris mulieribus* (1521). See Collina, "L'esemplarità" 103–19.

11 McInerney summarizes the history of the "manly woman" in Greek thought, and then argues that "lurking behind the novel figure of the brave and virtuous woman [in Plutarch's *Mulierum virtutes*] is a highly traditional, and restrictive, understanding of womanly virtue" (323).

12 Tasso 1997. For an extended discussion on Tasso's *Discorso*, see chapter 1 of the present volume.

13 For a comprehensive study of Plutarch in the Renaissance see Gallo. Alicia Morales Ortiz's study of Plutarch's *Moralia* in Spain also offers useful information on the fortunes of the text throughout Europe.

14 Plutarch's summation of Thucydides and Gorgias was taken up by Renaissance writers such as Tasso. For recent critical attention given to the Renaissance reception of the debate put forth by Plutarch, see McClure, especially n100.

15 Comparing lives of famous people is a technique Plutarch left unfinished in his *Mulierum virtutes* but exemplified in his famous *Parallel Lives*, a work that contains biographies of Greek and Roman men in couplets to allow for comparison.

16 The text, *Stratagems in War* or *Stratagemata*, was dedicated to Marcus Aurelius (161–80) and Verus (161–9), while the co-emperors were engaged in the Parthian War. Marcus Aurelius is said to have carried the book with him during the Marcomannic war. For a discussion on Polyaenus see Schettino.

17 The mother and wife of Coriolanus in Livy are Veturia and Volumnia, respectively, while Plutarch names them Volumnia and Vergilia. Shakespeare adopts the name of Plutarch's Volumnia for Coriolanus's mother.
18 Livy II.40.7 "Did not your anger fall from you, no matter how hostile and threatening your spirit when you came, as you passed the boundary? Did it not come over you, when Rome lay before your eyes: 'Within those walls are my home and my gods, my mother, my wife, and my children?'" (350).
19 The story of the Sabine women appears in other histories: see Ovid, *Ars amatoria* (1.101–34). On the representation of the Sabine women in Livy, Ovid, and Plutarch see Miles 179–215.
20 Aristophanes' *Lysistrata* was published in Italy in 1516. The play deals with female agency in the face of male incompetence in matters of war and ends with Lysistrata's negotiation of peace via the bodies of women.
21 Vives 184–5; Marinella, *The Nobility* 108.
22 The gesture of women lifting garments is found in various classical texts and is told in both Plutarch's "Sayings of Spartan Women" and the *Mulierum virtutes.* See H. King, "Agnodike" 53–77. Julia L. Hairston provides an excellent analysis of how this classical gesture is then adopted in Machiavelli's account of Caterina Sforza ("Skirting the Issue").
23 Marcellinus states that, "A whole troop of foreigners would not be able to withstand a single Gaul if he called his wife to his assistance, who is usually very strong, and with blue eyes, especially when, swelling her neck, gnashing her teeth, and brandishing her sallow arms of enormous size, she begins to strike blows mingled with kicks, as if they were so many missiles sent from the string of a catapult" (80).
24 On Ciceronian critiques of Greek culture as effeminate, see Zetzel. Analysing a passage from Cicero's *De oratore,* Rebhorn argues that the orator establishes an opposition between the virile, civically engaged Roman orators (experienced in battle and politics) and the Greeks, who are likened to sodomites and slaves (26).
25 On hagiographic literature that shows women's bravery in the face of violence, see Schulenburg 140–50.
26 McLaughlin argues that there was a preponderance of women warriors before the twelfth century, including the medieval St Prospera.
27 McLaughlin 1990, citing Bernold of Constance, *Chronicon* in *Monumenta Germaniae Historica, Scriptores,* vol. 5 (Hanover: Hahn, 1844), 443.

28 Henry IV led his troops to attack Canossa in 1092 but retreated when he realized that Matilda was not present and yet had fortified the castle. He fled to the north of Italy but was prevented from crossing by his enemies' blocking of mountain passes, leaving him virtually imprisoned from 1093 to 1096 (Hay 117–59).

29 The work is actually the second book of a two-part book entitled *De principibus Canunsinis* by Donizo of Canossa. See Donizone modern edition and Italian translation. See also Eads 2003.

30 Renaissance accounts of Matilda in compendia of famous women include Agostino Strozzi, *La defensione delle donne* (I note that Matilda is the only woman from modern history included in his list of brave illustrious women); Sabadino, *Gynevera delle clare donne;* Lanci, *Esempi della virtù delle donne;* and Serdonati, *Delle donne illustri.*

31 For *vitae* of Matilda see Battista Panetti, "De rebus gestis Comitissae Matildis" (c. 1497); Domenico Mellini, *Dell'origine, fatti, costumi, e lodi di Matelda la gran Contessa d'Italia* (1589); Benedetto Luchino, *Cronica della vera origine, et attioni della illustrissima, et famosissima Contessa Matilda* (1592); and Silvano Razzi, *Vita della Contessa Matelda* (1587), dedicated to Don Giovanni Medici. Razzi's *vita* is then included in his encyclopaedic *Vite delle donne illustri per santità,* published in six volumes. Matilda is the first and longest entry of volume five, published in 1602.

32 Serdonati, *Donne illustri* 537. My translations.

33 Matilda enjoyed some fame in Ferrara. The Este – with the help of authors no less important than Boiardo himself – tried to ally themselves with the Countess, claiming that they were her descendants. However, not only were these biographies fantastical, they often were limited to a very local audience; Rizzi, "L'autore."

34 Matilda's representation astride a horse is unlike other representations of women such as Joan of Arc, who was represented as riding sidesaddle in Martial d'Auvergne, *Les vigiles du Roi Charles VII,* 1484, and in Antoine Dufour's *Vie des femmes illustres* (1505). See Hollman 659 n8

35 Quoted in Hay 208.

36 Hay 198–238.

37 Hay addresses the differences between classical and medieval usage of *milites/bellatores* and *imperatores/duces* but notes that some high medieval authors did continue to use the classical distinction (9–10).

38 The letter is found in Petrarch's *Epistolae familiares,* book five, letter 4.

39 "Mariam vocant; singulare illi servate virginitatis decus" (*Le familiari* V.4. 88–9). All English translations of Petrarch's letter of 23 Nov. 1343 are taken from the Bishop edition.

40 This characterization of the woman as vulnerable to public opinion regarding her reputation for chastity regardless of her actions is a precursor to Castiglione's famous passages about women's chastity in his *Cortegiano.*
41 "Nulli unquam tamen, ut constantissima omnium opinio est, vel ioco vel serio rigide mulieris attentata virginitas" (*Le familiari* V.4.90–2).
42 "Corpus illi militare magis quam virgineum, vires corporee probatis militibus optande" (*Le familiari* V.4.93–4).
43 "Non telas illa, sed tela; non acus et specula, sed arcus et spicula meditatur" (*Le familiari* V.4.95–7).
44 See Tixier de Ravisy 196–7; Sigonio 50. See also Di Bonito.
45 The critical literature that deconstructs the subjectivity and gendering of the gaze in Petrarch (typically his lyric) is vast, and owes much to Vickers's seminal essay.
46 Petrarch, *Letters from Petrarch* 52.
47 "michi quidem femine huius aspectus credibiliora efficit quecunque non modo de Amazonibus et famoso illo quondam regno femineo, sed etiam que de bellatricibus italis virginibus traduntur, duce Camilla, cuius inter cuntas celebre nomen est" (*Le familiari* V.4.140–4).
48 "Denique ita inde discessum est, ut, vix oculis fidem dantes, subesse aliquid prestigii putaremus" (*Le familiari* V.4.130–2).
49 Petrarch's story of Maria is featured in Sabadino degli Arienti's *Gynevera del le clare donne;* Francesco Serdonati also includes her in his "addition" to Betussi's translation of Boccaccio's *Donne illustri.*
50 Petrarch uses the word "bellatrix" twice in the letter: letter IV, 5 is titled "Ad eundem, Baiarum descriptio et puteolane femine bellatricis," while the second appearance is at the end of the letter when describing how Maria is like those women warriors of the past, "sed etiam que de bellatricibus italis viginibus traduntur ..." On the manuscript history of the letter titles, see Vittorio Rossi's introduction in vol. I of *Le familiari* (clxi–clxiii).
51 Galiziella is the female combatant of Andrea da Barberino's *Aspramonte* (Rajna 49). See Rajna's entry on "donne guerriere" (46–54), where he argues that figures such as Bradamante and Marfisa are not to be confused with certain literary figures such as the women of early French romances, (e.g., *Tristan de Nanteuil*), who disguised their sex in order to return to their husbands. Nor, he warns, should we confuse these women with "gigantesse," who were also skilled at arms. Rajna argues that historical viragos were possibly influential for Ariosto's choices, though he questions the influence of the real on art. In any case, for Rajna these historical viragos might include Joan of Arc, Maria of Pozzuoli, Bona Lombarda, Caterina Sforza, and an Orsini bride of Guido Torelli.

52 Collina, "L'esemplarità," calls Boccaccio the "founder" ("capostipite") of the genre of *donne illustri* and provides a short analysis of Boccaccio's break from the traditions that preceded him (105–6).

53 The communities of women discussed in Boccaccio include ch. 31, "Wives of the Minyans," and ch. 80, "Wives of the Cimbrians." Both groups are cited by the Quattrocento writer Laura Cereta (70).

54 There is conflicting scholarship on Boccaccio's familiarity with Plutarch. Kolsky presents the most convincing argument that Boccaccio did not know *On the Bravery of Women*. On the importance of Petrarch's 1358 letter to Empress Anna as well as the *De viris illustribus,* see Kolsky, *Genealogy* 39–47 and 190n.

55 Virginia Brown provides concise information on the manuscript history of the text as well as its translations into various languages (Boccaccio, *Famous Women* xi–xxv). See also Branca, *Tradizione* 92–8, as well as *Un secondo* 57–62. The only monograph in Italian dedicated to *De mulieribus* is Filosa.

56 Kolsky, *The Ghost,* approaches the *De mulieribus claris* as "'architext' – that is, as the definitive model for those subsequent writers and compilers who sought to justify famous women" (4).

57 Verrier, *Le miroir,* identifies twenty-two women who are involved in a "military action": Semiramis (II), Marpesia and Lampedo (XI–XII), Hypermnestra (XIV), Hypsipyle (XVI), Orithya and Antiope (XIX–XX), Iole (XXIII), the wives of the Minyans (XXXI), Penthesilea (XXXII), Camilla (XXXIX), Dido (XLII), Tamyris (XLIX), Cloelia (LII), Veturia (LV), Artemisia (XLVII), Busa of Canosa (LXIX), the Wife of Orgiago (LXXIII), Hypsicratea (LXXVIII), the wives of the Cymbrians (LXXX), Triaria (XCVI), and Zenobia (C).

58 Franklin argues that Boccaccio's *Famous Women* presents a "consistent delineation of the parameters of acceptable female authority" (1). She offers a counter-interpretation to Kolsky, Jordan, and Benson, who all read a certain ambiguity or inconsistency in Boccaccio's presentation of women (1–7). Kolsky, *Geneaology,* also provides a contentious reading of the critical tradition of the *De mulieribus claris.* He overturns the feminist criticism of the 1980s and 1990s, which, he claims, places the work in a misogynist straitjacket that does not allow for the nuance in Boccaccio's work.

59 It is notable that Boccaccio is ambivalent about Veturia's "strength." Virginia Brown's translation of the passage "non ante filium vidit quam, pietate patria posita, se succendit in iram" (LV 224) ("[Veturia] put aside patriotic duty and burst into a fit of anger as soon as she saw her son," 225) gives the sense that Veturia allowed emotion to displace her patriotic mission. Although the Latin might be somewhat less damning than Brown's

English translation, it nonetheless does seem that Boccaccio is criticizing Veturia. This is particularly ambivalent, given the moment of rage described in the following sentences as an awakening of "strength" in Veturia's "feeble breast" ("suscitatis in effeto pectore viribus inquit," LV 226).

60 Franklin discusses Boccaccio's influence on the visual tradition of women worthies. She notes that Boccaccio made certain depictions of women "suitable" (15–18).

61 Tomalin's study is characterized by highly biased readings of gender representation.

62 Verrier, an expert on military tracts, offers a fascinating perspective on literary representations of militancy in *Le miroir*. Verrier, *Les armes* illustrates how humanist values included military concerns.

63 Latella does not cite Verrier, though her project covers many of the same texts. Latella presents the intertextual fortune of the woman warrior across Italian, French, English, and Spanish literature.

64 Franklin, Kolsky, Jordan, and Benson all argue that Boccaccio was not suggesting that female readers imitate women. Jordan (1987) articulates the matter of imitation as such: "Each of his portraits of famous women could be said to constitute a negative example, one that discourages rather than encourages emulation. Considered as a totality, the text seems to act as a *concessio,* a refutation of the apparent thesis" (28–9). Kolsky, *Geneaology,* provides a splendid overview of feminist criticism on the pitfalls of female exemplars and imitation of them (181–2 n4).

65 Kolsky, *Genealogy,* suggests that the stories are appended by two distinct voices, a narrator and a commentator, where the narrator is often attentive to the humanist mission of the work, finding multiple sources for stories and accounting for them, while the commentator provides advice for modern times, often with little reference to the stories themselves (134–41). This argument is restated in Kolsky, *The Ghost* 2–4.

66 Kolsky, *Genealogy* 135.

67 Benson suggests that Boccaccio's equating of the theatres and churches of medieval Florence to Camilla's battlefields was a way of providing the contemporary female reader with a practical application of a story of a warring woman: "While we do not normally think of churches, theaters, and parents' homes as being the equivalent of fields, forests, and battlefields, the moral does provide a way of finding some practical connection between the strengths of these ancient women and the challenges that contemporary society actually presents to young women. The physical dangers of wild places are equivalent to the moral dangers social interaction offers to the young ladies of Boccaccio's time" (24).

68 In Serdonati's 1596 addition to the translation of Boccaccio's *Famous Women,* Eleonora di Toledo was said to be a "quasi nuova Issicratea" (657). Her biography differs in important ways from that of Boccaccio's Hypsicratea, as it avoids the exposure to violence as well as any discussion of her changing her appearance to seem more masculine. In both stories, the women do not participate in acts of killing.
69 Branca, *Boccaccio,* mentions Armannino Giudice's *La Fiorita* as a possible source for the *Teseida* (131). See the discussion of the *Teseida* in Latella 191–206.
70 Latella provides a convincing argument that Hippolyta is kept innocent of the violence (196–7). She is moreover described within the conventions of the poetic beloved, using adjectives such as *bella, giovane, costumata,* and *pulcella* (I.25).
71 Theseus shames his troops by suggesting that they are acting like little girls against the Amazons. His action recalls Virgil's Tarchon, who shames his troops for their defeat by Camilla: *Aeneid* XI 720–40.
72 Italian quotations of the *Teseida* are identified by the book, stanza, and verse number. English translations are indicated by the page number in the McCoy edition.
73 Boitani suggests that readers would have been most persuaded by Theseus's argument, as he is presented as the virtuous character (187); Latella suggests that Hippolyta's reasoning is also left in an ambiguous space, where readers might also have agreed with her (199).
74 Latella offers a provocative discussion of this moment in the *Teseida,* suggesting that Hippolyta is actually admitting the failure of the "Amazon experiment" (200).
75 Latella claims that Penthesilea's transvestism and virile behaviour would preclude any fortunate ending or erotic encounter. As proof of this, she notes that all three militant women in Boccaccio who dress as men (Penthesilea, Semiramis, and Hypsicratea) are killed (224). This division does not hold for Penthesilea, since the other Amazons, though it is not expressly stated, were likely understood to be armed. Furthermore, the story of Hypsicratea (LXXVIII) tells of a husband devoted to his cross-dressing wife. Only at the end of his life, when likely neither of the spouses was dressed in battle gear, does he go mad and kill his heirs and her.
76 The Penthesilea legend told in the *Posthomerica* depicts her as being killed by Achilles, who falls madly in love with the woman once he removes her helmet and sees her feminine beauty. See ch. 2.
77 Kolsky, *The Ghost,* argues that the narratives often tell of brave women who "spark a crisis in men" (13).

78 The use of rabbits will be commonly repeated in the Middle Ages and Renaissance to indicate fearful men. See for example, Matraini's *Oratione* on the art of war cited in a previous chapter and Serdonati's biography of Mary, Queen of Hungary: "non maraviglia poi, se si veggiono infiniti huomini, huomini solamente di nome, e negli effetti non pusillanime femmine, ma vili e codardi conigli" (Serdonati, *Donne illustri* 436). See also Tomalin for a discussion on the tension between custom and nature in Boccaccio's *Famous Women* 23–5.

79 Priuli's comments on Venice's "great ruin" and defeat by the League of Cambrai in the battle of Agnadello blames many of the vices of the citizens, including "womanly" sodomites (*Diarii*, t. XXIV, p III, vol. IV 35–6). He states that Italian soldiers fled like women and whores "chome putane et femine" instead of unsheathing their swords (*Diarii*, t. XXIV, p III, vol. IV 54, v 21). Describing the same battle, he states that Venetian soldiers "flee like whores" ("scamponno come putane") at just the name of French soldiers (55, v 21). Perhaps one of Priuli's most quoted passages regarding the Turks is his praise for their courage in overtaking a Venetian galley. He states, "*cum* veritade li Turchi meritavanno honore … Et *cum* veritade li Turchi sono valenthomeni, et li Christiani sonno putane" (*Diarii*, t. XIV, p 3, vol. II 429). For details regarding the event see Tenenti 259. In his *Discourses* 3.36, Machiavelli discusses how Frenchmen who fail in battle "become less than women" (*Discorsi* 510). On effeminacy in Machiavelli, see Milligan, "Masculinity." For a broad bibliography of the political associations of a defeated Italy as feminine, see Shemek, *Ladies Errant* 203 n1.

80 Paula Findlen provides a provocative analysis of how the invaded Italian peninsula was represented as a penetrated body politic (49–108).

5 The Noble Warrior Woman (1440–1550)

1 On Maria of Pozzuoli see chapter 4. Women's exercise was circumscribed in texts such as Castiglione's *Courtier* "circa gli esercizi del corpo, alla donna non si convien armeggiare, cavalcare, giocare alla palla, lottare e molte altre cose che si convengono agli omini" (*Cortegiano* III.7) ("as for bodily exercises, it is not seemly for a woman to handle weapons, ride, play tennis, wrestle, and do many other things that are suited to men") (153).

2 There are rare examples of noblewomen depicted as bearing arms. In addition to those discussed below, Cia Ubaldini and Caterina di Chiaramonte are noblewomen depicted as armed in Serdonati 1596.

3 For a provocative study on what the author calls "women looking from afar" in Homer and the Bible, see D.R. MacDonald, *The Homeric,* especially 143–7.

4 Modern psychological literature on shame raises important questions about how shame is mobilized in different ways across class, race, and gender. For example, in the accessible study of Lehtinen (56–77), the so-called salutary version of shame is placed in contrast to a more pervasive shame felt by women. For a nuanced treatment of shame in Plato as well as a useful bibliography, see Tarnopolsky 468–94.

5 "If there was a mechanism for producing a city or army consisting of lovers and boyfriends, there could be no better form of social organization than this: they would hold back from anything disgraceful and compete for honour in each other's eyes. If even small numbers fought side by side, they could defeat virtually the whole human race" (Plato, *The Symposium* 10).

6 "They [the gods] honoured Achilles … He had the courage to choose to act on behalf of his lover by avenging him: he not only died *for* him but also died *as well* as him, since Patrocles was already dead" (Plato, *The Symposium* 11).

7 Tasso's text will borrow more from Virgil's tragic Euryalus and Nisus dynamic than from Plato's *Phaedrus*. It implicates the male beloved warrior, as Marc Schachter has argued, in a sterile and non-productive role.

8 See Michel Foucault's *Discipline and Punish*.

9 Plato emphasizes that men lovers are more honoured for their sacrifices than are women or boys: "They [the gods] gave higher honour to Achilles than Alcestis" (180b; *The Symposium* 12); and Aristotle shows how to complain of suffering makes a man womanly and shameful: "Now the man who is defective in respect of resistance to the things which most men both resist and resist successfully is soft and effeminate; for effeminacy too is a kind of softness; such a man trails his cloak to avoid the pain of lifting it, and plays the invalid without thinking himself wretched, though the man he imitates is a wretched man" (VII. 7, 1150; Aristotle, *Nicomachean Ethics* 177).

10 Karras argues that men ostensibly fight for the love of women and that they seek to be erotically desirable through their displays of prowess. She cites, among others, Charny, Froissart, La Marche, Chastellain, and *Livres des fais de Bouciquaut*.

11 Karras provides the example of a group of ladies in the English court who fastened a golden ring to the leg of Lord Scales, demanding that he not remove it until he had done battle (55).

12 Women's distaste for gore is exemplified in an anecdote in II.8.73.

13 For a discussion of the stories of brave women in the context of masculinity in the *Courtier*, see Milligan, "The Politics" 361–3.

14 Daniel Javitch's critical edition of the *Courtier* mentions Plutarch, Livy, and Valerius Maximus as being potential sources for the various classical *exempla* (Castiglione, *The Book of the Courtier*). Determining Castiglione's sources awaits more research.
15 See the incisive analysis of this Plutarchan moment in Hairston, "Skirting," and Verrier, *Caterina* 75–84.
16 McLucas provides an analysis of the "non participatory surveillance" provided by Isabella during war. As he states, Isabella's role, as described in book 3, 51, incites men's performance in battle: "she shows her ultimate weapon: her very presence on the battlefield instigates prodigies of male heroics" (37).
17 Quoted in Gáldy 294n.
18 I am indebted to Kolsky's discussion of Arienti's "Elogio di Isabella" (quoted in *Ghost* 99–109).
19 Quoted in Kolsky, *The Ghost* 104, n126: "tu, regina magnanima, adcesa e inflamata per l'onore e triumfo de Cristo, non come Ipsocratea in abito d'omo il suo Mitradate, ma cum il proprio aspecto de la tua sacra Maiestà, cum più de cinquecento carette lo sequitavi e cum aromataria, medicine e commeate e victuarie per le neccessitate del campo in le confine de lo exercito. E ivi residendo per custodia cum le tue dilicate figlie e dame le quale e tu, come la diva Ursia e sue numerose virgene certante per la cristiane fede, oravi Dio che 'l tuo consorte re salvo cum victoria retornasse" (Arienti 37r–38r).
20 The scenario of noble women watching their men fight is dramatically enacted in the war of Siena. During a skirmish between Sienese and Florentine troops outside the Sienese city walls, the Sienese noblewomen were said to have climbed to their towers, assured of seeing a victorious fight, and instead watched all of their men cruelly killed: "Erano in quel giorno tutte le dame sopra le loro alte torri ed anco su la muraglia stessa, credendo vedere una vittoria per loro perpetua; ma per il contrario veddero un miserabile caso" (Montalvo 32).
21 On Battista Sforza see Mazzanti. She was by title "Countess of Urbino" because Federico, an illegitimate son of Guidantonio, did not receive the title of duke until 23 August 1474, from Pope Sixtus IV.
22 The manuscript that contains the poem is part of the famous ducal library now located in the Vatican, codex 692, fondo Vaticano-Urbinate. Given Castiglione's connection to the ducal family, it seems likely that he was familiar with the text.
23 For the dating of the dialogues, see Filetico 27.

24 See Filetico I. 118–41 and II. 7. See also Arienti's entry on Battista: "ella comendava molto la disciplina militare, per la quale dicea se deponevano li cattivi ed acquistavansi li dominii, li regni, che era bella cosa audire, com fondate rasone, in una vergene polcella" (292).

25 On Battista's potential attendance at the battle at Fano, the editor's notes to the poem state that, in the *Cronaca* of Ser Guerriero, Battista went to find the count in Pietracuta in December of 1462. He finds no other accounts of her assisting in the siege and the bombardment of Fano (25 September 1463) (de la Pergola 48n).

26 Battista's brother in the *Iocundissimae disputationes* claims that Battista surpassed Themistocles, who knew all the names of his citizens, and Filetico, her tutor, claimed that the young woman knew all of Virgil by memory (Filetico 91).

27 Benedetto Croce in his *Storie e leggende Napoletane*, cites the *Diarii*, which described how the Queen of Naples, Giovanna, and the Queen Mother, Ippolita Maria Sforza, watched the defeat of French troops in July 1495: "La regina madre e la regina giovinetta trassero allo spettacolo, recandosi a Castellammare a vedere 'questo triumpho de' francesi, che tanto erano prima gagliardi, et hora, voltante fortuna, venuti sí mansueti, che di loro si faceva quello il re voleva'" (quoted in Croce 157).

28 De la Pergola states that Battista stayed with Federico after Fano: "Madonna fe la via de la montagna / Et verso Fossambron piglio el camino / Con sua famiglia et sua compagnia magna" (de la Pergola ch. 3, vv 49–51, p 19).

29 There is no mention of Eleonora's actions in May and June (e.g., to the sickness of the duke or the Bolognese priest she hires) in the Ferrarese chronicles of Ferrarini or Zambotti.

30 On the war of Ferrara, also known as the Salt War, see Mallett. On the siege of Ficarolo see Mantovani.

31 The defence of Ficarolo had become compromised by the fall of defence towers and parts of the walls. Additionally, there was much internal fighting between the Bolognese under Bentivoglio and the Ferrarese league under Federico da Montefeltro. See Mantovani's account of the siege of Ficarolo and his analysis of primary documents, including correspondence between Bentivoglio, Ercole D'Este, and Eleonora.

32 "Et non potendo resister con forze a' Venitiani, benché fusse ajutato el Ducha da la liga – ch'è il Re, Ducha di Milan et Fiorentini – si pensò di far venir uno heremito, di nation bolognese" (Sanudo 1.265).

33 "perché Venitiani haveano deliberato, havendo Ferara, di mandar essi citadini in Cypro, overo in Candia ad habitar, tuorli la roba et le possessione,

et altre parole" (Sanudo 1.265). I thank Holly Hurlburt for her insight that this fear-mongering had some basis in reality, as Venice had been seeking to colonize Cyprus and Crete.

34 Franklin shows how, in numerous biographies, Boccaccio provides negative portrayals of women if they "ultimately seek to govern in their own right rather than as regent for their rightful heir" (35). Furthermore, she shows how Boccaccio's portrayals of powerful women represent cultural ideologies and that those women who are depicted as positive *exempla* all share virtues of chastity, wifely devotion, and deferment to gender superstructures (59).

35 "bixognò aserare li usci, chè tale persona ge tornò doe fiate" (119).

36 Similarly, Eleonora's daughter, Isabella d'Este, explicitly stated that a woman ruler's power depended on at least the presence of a male ruler or heir in the state. In 1510, while Isabella's husband, Francesco, was imprisoned in Venice, she was asked to send her only son, Federico, as a hostage to Rome, thus securing her husband's release and his subsequent loyalty to Venice. Isabella refused to relinquish her nine-year-old son, stating that without a son or husband, she did not "trust in the faithful obedience of her subjects" (16 March 1510): letter "To Ludovico Brognolo in Rome, on the Emperor's request for her son, Federico" (16 March 1510, Mantua). I cite the translation of the letter by Deanna Shemek, provided in personal correspondence. For more information on the period of Isabella's regency, see Luzio.

37 For example, Bartolomeo Goggio's "De laudibus mulierum" was dedicated to Eleonora d'Aragona, and Arienti's *Gynevera* was among the manuscripts kept at the palace library of Duke Ercole I (Zaccaria 519–45).

38 Betussi's debt to Foresti was likely first noted by Giuseppe Zonta, who suggested that he had taken much of his work from Foresti, while Vittorio Zaccaria later simply called Betussi's work "plagiarism," showing that he had in large part copied twenty-three of Foresti's biographies (see Zonta 335; Zaccaria, *Boccaccio* 286–306). See also Nadin Bassani 47–9.

39 The translation by Betussi was published in at least two editions, both in Venice, in 1545 by Andrea Arrivabene and in 1547 by Pietro de Nicolini da Sabbio. I have cited the 1547 edition unless otherwise noted. On Betussi, see: Nadin Bassani; Mutini; Verci; Zonta; and Robin *Publishing* 108–11. On the early translations of Boccaccio's *Famous Women*, see Torretta.

40 Eleonora d'Aragona, chapter 26 (188rv–189rv)

41 All translations of Betussi are mine.

42 For a concise biography of Betussi, see Mutini.

43 For a presentation of fifteenth- and early sixteenth-century praises of illustrious women, see Kolsky, *The Ghost*. Of the authors discussed by Kolsky, Arienti enjoyed great fortune as a result of the later publication of portions of his manuscript *Gynevera de le clare donne*, composed around 1489–90. Critical works on the *Gynevera* and Foresti's *De plurimis claris selectisque mulieribus* (Ferrara: Lorenzo de' Rossi, 1497) are Kolsky, *The Ghost*; Kolsky, *Genealogy*; Franklin; and Benson.

44 Predating Betussi, Agostino Strozzi's *Defensio mulierum* (c. 1501; published as *La defensione della donna d'autore anonimo*, 1876) also suggests that women should imitate stories of illustrious women. Arienti, on the other hand, does not give such advice to his female readers, though they could certainly have used the book for this purpose. Pamela Benson cites a letter from Isabella D'Este, who, after receiving a copy of Arienti's manuscript, states that she will "read it attentively, and … will attempt to follow in the footsteps of those illustrious ladies" (quoted in Benson 41n).

45 "Quin imo perseverans, uti viridarium intrans, eburneas manus, semotis spinarum aculeis, extendis in florem, sic, obscenis sepositis, college laudanda" (4–5).

46 See "Di Violantina Genovese," chapter 23: "contraria al Boccaccio, quelle che io ho conosciuto essere state, ed essere degne d'eterno ricordo le ho voluto obbligare a piu stretto nome, e solamente giudicare nobili e illustri quelle, che operando cosa degna di lode e d'onore da se si sono nobilitate ovvero nobili, hanno accresciuto splendore al ceppo di che sono uscite" (183v).

47 Betussi's discussion of "illustrious" women begs a revision of Beatrice Collina's claim that Torquato Tasso was the "only author that formulated a theory of the illustrious woman" ("L'esemplarità" 107).

48 "Isabel of Spain," chapter 24: "Ebbe quattro figliuole femmine … tutte da lei ammaestrate in quegli studi, che debbono essere propri, e necessari alle donne nobili e Illustri" (Betussi 186r); "Violantina Genovese," chapter 23: "Questo nome d'Illustre, dal principio della presente opera, nelle donne ha incominciato a prender forza, e haver luogo, o dalla nobiltà di sangue congiunta, con l'opere virtuose o le bellezze dell'animo o da alcuna degna operazione" (183r).

49 "col proprio animo acquistata chiarissima nobiltà" (174v). The husband and "knight" of Bona Lombarda/Lombardi (1417–1468) is Pietro Brunoro. He was a mercenary captain who, according to legend, met her while she was minding her flocks in the Valtellina. Her story is widely recounted in contemporary accounts and in the foklore of the Valtellina in Lombardy.

50 Betussi's *Additione* has twenty-three biographies in common with Foresti (Nadin Bassani 48). Also, because Foresti had copied many of Arienti's

tales, it is important to note that these two biographies (Joan of Arc and Bona Lombarda) are also in Arienti.

51 The soldiers who were said to harass the young girl are those who were "typically" guarding the city.

52 "E che si come questa fanciulla si ha acquistato il nome d'Illustre, cosi quelle [noblewomen] l'hanno perduto e lo perdono" (180v).

53 For other sixteenth-century examples of women throwing themselves into rivers, see Castiglione *Cortegiano* (3.47), which mentions two women who drown themselves to avoid shame, and Serdonati's story "Donzella di Valdarno," which includes a poem on the subject by Varchi (Serdonati 598).

54 In 1509 Padua was lost by Venice after Agnadello (June), regained (July), and then besieged again (September). Interestingly, the defeat at Agnadello incited many scathing critiques to be levelled against the "cowardly" Venetian aristocratic troops. Girolamo Priuli called the Venetian men sodomites, whores ("puttane"), and effeminate (64–90 *passim*). On the siege of Padua, Priuli again states that the noble Venetians were effeminate and unable to conduct warfare: "La natura dei nobelli venetti hera molto timida et, *ut ita dicam*, quasi effeminata per non essere consuetti in guere nè in lo exercitio militare" (296–7). On the relations between Venetian nobility and the siege of Padua, see Libby 323–31.

55 In Betussi, the description is softened: "di color nero, di statura piccola, ma molto gagliarda ..." (157r). Notably, she is no longer called "ugly" ("brutta").

56 Here Arienti is more complementary than Betussi. He calls Joan of Arc "bella, de viso brunetto" (103).

57 In her study of warrior maidens in epic poetry, Maggie Günsberg suggests that viragos of the highest classes are described in less detail than those of lower ones (17). However, she contrasts them to the "unfeminine" viragos of history (19), thus missing the distinction of class between women such as Maria of Pozzuoli and women such as Caterina Sforza, who was lauded as beautiful (7–35).

58 Arienti's book of illustrious women unsurprisingly does not include Caterina Sforza. She had not yet performed many of her memorable deeds, as she would have been in her twenties when the manuscript was written. Foresti, who uses Arienti as a source for many stories, thus is the author of the Sforza biography. Beatrice Collina suggests that Foresti may have met Caterina, since he was the prior of the convent of the Agostiniani in Imola and Forlì (79). When Betussi uses Foresti as one of his principal sources for his addition to Boccaccio, it is thus more interesting that he excludes Caterina Sforza (an enemy of the Venetian state and a problematic figure).

59 Caterina is called a "virago" by Marino Sanudo in *I diarii* (2.529). "Tigress" was first used by Lorenzo Giustiniani in 1498 to a Venetian ambassador "quella tygre di la madona di Forlì" and was then reprinted in Sanudo 2.60 (quoted in Pasolini 2. 65).

60 The chronicler Bartolomeo Cerretani describes Caterina as "fierce and cruel with arms in hand" ("con l'arme in mano era fera e crudele," 266). In various sources, she is repeatedly described as galloping on horseback while pregnant. For secondary works on Caterina Sforza, see especially Pasolini. See also Verrier, *Caterina Sforza*; Graziani and Venturelli; Breisach; de Vries, *Caterina Sforza*; Hairston "Skirting"; and Lev. On patronage of fortresses see de Vries 112–17.

61 Pasolini 1.148.

62 Upon Pope Sixtus IV's death, Caterina feared that the next pope would seek retribution for the nefarious deeds of her husband, Girolamo Riario (Sixtus's nephew). On her control of Castel Sant'Angelo, see Pasolini 1.149–58. For a highly biased anti-Sixtus viewpoint of events see Infessura 164–5.

63 De Vries lists several modern representations of Sforza in media, film, and video games: "Caterina Sforza: The Shifting Representation" 180.

64 Modern scholars and Sforza's contemporaries alike called her actions masculine. See de Vries, *Caterina Sforza*, which states that after Caterina's husband was assassinated in 1488, "Caterina shifted her behavior to become more forceful – and more masculine" (38). De Vries goes on to nuance her argument (as does Verrier) to suggest that Caterina negotiated masculine and feminine discourses, using one or the other to her advantage. On how Caterina was at the vanguard of scientific experimentation (understood to be a masculine arena), see Ray 2015.

65 Foresti's Latin is cumbersome and flawed, and I have relied on the generous help offered by Daniela D'Eugenio for my translations. Foresti also includes a history of Caterina in his historical chronicle *Supplementum chronicarum* (first published in 1483 in Latin and then subsequently expanded two times. It was translated into Italian in 1505 and reproduced, edited, and annotated over the century). On Sforza's appearance in the *Supplementum* see Verrier, *Caterina* 37–40.

66 Machiavelli mentions Caterina Sforza in his correspondence and *Prince*, chapter 20; *Discourses*, book 3, ch. 6; *Florentine Histories*, book 8, ch. 34; *The Art of War*, book 7; and *Decannali*.

67 Foresti, "totam noctes illam in lachrymis consumpsit" (she was consumed the whole night in tears) (f 160).

68 "Muliebres lacrimas pro virili a se reiecit, et suam prudentiam, suamque animi magnitudinem contra insanum, furentemque populum demonstrare curavit."

69 Italian original, Machiavelli 1993, 208; translation in Machiavelli 1989, 444. On the *anasyrmos* see Hairston, "Skirting," and Verrier, *Caterina,* a monograph dedicated to the *anasyrmos* in Machiavelli as well as its history and resonance throughout literature. On the unusual use of the plural "le membra genitali" for female genitalia, see Freccero 175–6. Verrier also provides a survey of the texts that alter Machiavelli's lexical formation.

70 "Così costoro, scarsi di consiglio e tardi avvedutisi del loro errore, con uno perpetuo esilio patirono pena della poca prudenza loro" (Machiavelli 1993, 208).

71 Freccero and Verrier (*Caterina*) read Caterina's gesture as a positive sign for women's power and liken it to that of the Medusa. For Freccero, the genital "members" are the members of a body politic that promise a political futurity. Hairston ("Skirting") reads the event as skirting the maternal body, since Caterina could not guarantee that she would be pregnant with a male heir; Spackman provides a focused analysis of various readings of Caterina's gesture. She cites Gramsci in particular, who read Caterina's gesture as a symbol of the commoner overthrowing tyranny. Spackman claims that to see Caterina's gesture as the phallic mother is reassuring to male fantasy and that she is actually more linked to the Medean figure, someone *in addition to* the mother, who cannot be drawn back into the private sphere (20–3).

72 Hairston, "Skirting," offers an insightful reading of the variant texts of the episode at Ravaldino. Hairston credits Machiavelli with the origin of the story of Caterina's gesture of lifting her skirt. Elizabeth Lev mistakenly credits the recounting of the gesture to the correspondence of Galeotto Manfredi to Lorenzo de' Medici, 20 April 1488 (quoted in Lev 278, 10n). There are indeed several contemporary accounts that describe Caterina's actions and whereabouts during the siege of Ravaldino: Corbizzi to Lorenzo de' Medici, 17 April 1488; Giovanni Bentivoglio to Lorenzo de' Medici, 18 April 1488; Migliore Cresci to Lorenzo de' Medici, 17April 1488 (quoted in Pasolini 1.230, 4n); and the Duke of Milan to the King of Hungary (quoted in Pasolini 3, doc. 295). These accounts state that Caterina, in her chambers or in other unspecified locations, made various pronouncements that she was pregnant or had the ability to make more children:

73 The letter of Giovanni Corbizzi to Lorenzo de' Medici was sent from Faenza and is dated 17 April, the same day as the alleged retort: "Madonna non vole uscire: el popullo po bene dire: noi amazeremo vestri figloli: Lei risponde che non se n'ha a fare, che ad ogni modo l'anno atosichati: et che le ne ha uno in corpo et è atta a farne de gl'altri" (quoted in Hairston, "Skirting" 695 18n).

74 Cox "Gender and Eloquence," suggests that we nuance our belief that there was an injunction on women's public speaking in the Quattrocento, since women of the courts were called upon to speak in both ceremonial and urgent moments. Cox points to the context of Ferrara and Bartolomeo Goggio's *De laudibus mulierum* (c. 1487) as well as Ercole de' Roberti's cycle of women worthies.
75 Mussolini's aphorism is frequently attributed to the futurist poet Filippo Tommaso Marinetti, perhaps because of the similar language used by the futurists in their glorification of war, as well as the fact that the quotation was recycled as an epigram in a 1941 book on futurist women, Goretti, *La donna e il futurismo.*
76 Guidantonio Vespucci to Lorenzo de' Medici, 18 August 1484; Florence State Archives, filza 39G (quoted in Pasolini III.100). These statements recall a recurring figuration in biographies of illustrious women. As Virginia Cox points out, Plutarch wrote of how Portia claimed to be worthy, as she was the daughter of Cato, a genealogy that also strengthened her credentials as an orator; see Cox, "Gender and Eloquence" 74.
77 In her early years of marriage, Caterina wrote frequently to her family in Milan of clothing, hunting, and riding, as well as the recommendations of men and women at court; Lev 42–77.
78 Cobelli, *Cronache forlivesi* 321; cited in Pasolini, vol. 1. 218.
79 Compagnon, 1500. For the discussion of the text see Pasolini, vol. 2. 276–81. According to Pasolini, the lament not only reflects the sentiments of Caterina found in her letters, it also reflects words that may have been uttered by her; vol. 2. 276.
80 Cited in Pasolini, vol. 2. 278–9.
81 "Fece dunque, la mala edificata fortezza e la poca prudenza di chi la difendeva, vergogna alla magnanima impresa della contessa; la quale aveva avuto animo ad aspettare uno esercito, il quale né il re di Napoli né il Duca di Milano aveva aspettato" (Machiavelli 1971, 378).
82 Isabella Gonzaga to the Marchese of Mantova; letter 14 January 1500, cited in Pasolini 1897, 71.
83 "Ma essendo tra tanti difensori ripieni d'animo femminile ella sola di animo virile, furono presto, per la viltà de' capitani che v'erano dentro, espugnate dal Valentino. Il quale, considerando più in lei il valore che il sesso, la mandò prigione a Roma, dove fu custodita in Castel Santo Angelo: benché passato di poco uno anno, per intercessione di Ivo di Allegri, ottenne la liberazione" (Guicciardini, *Storie d'Italia* 1971, IV 13.)
84 "Le message subliminal du passage de l'*Art de la guerre* jouait sur le mécanisme psychologique suivant: une femme virile dévirilisait les hommes, comme si un jeu de vases communicant semblait régulait les rapports entre les sexes" (Verrier, *Caterina* 58).

85 "tutto il dì va et esce fuori a la scaramuzza a cavallo armata, in modo che tanta benevolentia pel suo valoroso operare con quelli Signori Francesi, che non la vorríano vincere e tral loro a Forlì non si parla d'altro"; letter of Jacobo Sala (1500), cited in Pasolini 1897, 66. Sanudo states that on 23 November 1499 Caterina had armour made for her and was reported to have wounded some people with her own hand: "Fo ditto, la madona di Forlì si ha fato far curazine … et par habi ferito alcuni di suo man" (Sanudo, *I diarii*, vol. 3, 57). See also, "Ell'era grandde comprexa bella faccia, parlava pocho, portava una vesta di raso tané con braccia dua di strascicho, uno c[i]amperone di velluto nero alla franzese, uno cinto da homo et scharssella piena di duchati d'oro, un falc[i]one a uso di stortta achantto, e tra' soldati o appiè o a chavallo era temuta assai perché quella donna mai conobbe paura et coll'arme in mano era fiera et crudele" (Cerretani 266).

86 Graziani and Venturelli (261) cite several sources that refer to a sexual relation (whether violent or not) between Borgia and Sforza: Sanudo "di zorno e di notte nella sua camera ditta madama, la quale è bellissima donna, con la quale, *judicio omnium*, si deva piacer" (M. Sanuto, *I diarii di Marin Sanuto*, III, x. 86); an anonymous Vatican chronicler says he cannot speak of what happened to Caterina – "Taccio quello che osò fare il Duca Valentino a questa Donna Nobilissima" (cited in Pasolini II, 226–7); Andrea Bernardi speaks of sexual violence as well – "de li ingiustitie nel corpe de la nostra poverina e sfortunata dita Madona, zoè Caterina Sforcia, che era molto formosa del so corpo" (Bernardi I, pt II, 294).

87 Caterina had two significant relationships after the death of Riario, first with Carlo Feo and then with Giovanni di Pierfrancesco de' Medici. Once she lost power, she claimed to have married each of them in secret, legitimizing her children. Her son, Giovanni de' Medici, was never called "delle bande nere" in his lifetime.

88 Serdonati, "Ma ella poi rimaritatasi a Giovanni de medici fu madre del valorosissimo, e famosississimo Signor Giovanni de Medici padre del Gran Duca Cosimo" (591). On the portrait of Sforza in the Palazzo Vecchio, see de Vries, *passim*, and Verrier, *Caterina Sforza* 258–64.

89 Collina ("L'esemplarità") suggests that Boccaccio's, Pulci's, and Boiardo's armed women allowed "un numero notevole di gentildonne di identificarsi finalmente in un modello forte, autorevole e positivo" and "la contemporaneità dell'invenzione letteraria delle guerriere alla vita di Caterina e di altre nobildonne, che al pari di lei esplicarono doti di governanti e combattenti, sono dati di fatto che non possono essere collocati nell'ordine della casualità" (78).

90 Serdonati 1596, 590. Translation is an alteration of Hairston, 692. Hairston quotes a later redacted version of Serdonati that excises the lifting of the garments gesture.
91 See Hairston, "Skirting" 693–4, for an English translation as well as a discussion of how Boccalini incorporates Tasso's theory of a lady's virtue.
92 "Fu virtuosa molto et specialmente in quello, che a le donne apertiene in lo artificio de le mane, et in la prudentia de gubernare la casa et la famiglia cum boni exempli" (196).
93 In an earlier chapter (ch. 10) describing Giovanna Bentivoglio, Arienti tells how Giovanna did something that is "cosa degna in una donna de perpetua memoria in persuadere et armare li amici ad inquinarse le mane nel sangue de li amici" (121) (worthy of a woman of perpetual memory, in that she persuaded and armed her friends to taint their hands in the blood of the enemy) .
94 In the first moment, he draws comparison with the Assyrian queen's martial valour, who in her haste left half of her hair unbraided so that she might get to battle. The second comparison to Semiramis is to show how Orsina did not imitate the queen's sexual mores. See Kolsky, *The Ghost*, which provides a list of all of Arienti's comparisons to Boccaccio in the appendix.
95 The book's praise of virtue is complicated by the fact that it makes a reference to Ginevra Sforza in every chapter, a woman highly criticized in her own time. The emphasis on living a Christian life in Orsina's tale was quite relevant, for although Arienti could not have predicted this, Ginevra Sforza was excommunicated near the end of her life and died dishonoured and buried in a common grave. See the "Introduction" to the 1888 edition of the *Gynevera,* which makes an unapologetic critique of Ginevra and questions the sincerity of Arienti's praise.
96 In the same years that Arienti was writing this work for Ginevra Sforza, Ginevra's son, Ercole Bentivoglio, was engaged to Barbara Torelli, the great-granddaughter of Orsina Visconti of the Torelli; the two were married in 1491. The betrothal of Barbara Torelli to Ercole Bentivoglio likely explains why Orsina's husband's name, Torelli, is prominently included in the title, even though her maiden name, Visconti, would be the more noble.
97 Another example of an intermediary taken from Arienti and Foresti is Margherita of Scotland (1456–1486) (ch. 22), who persuades her son to avoid war by telling him that preserving the realm is just as honourable as expansion.
98 Anna was alive at the time of Betussi's publication. A short biographical account praising Anne of Alençon is found in Lodovico Dolce's *Dialogo della institutione delle donne*. He praises her prowess in war, though he does not provide any historical details. He states that she and her daughter were much loved in their respective principalities (Dolce 80r).

99 "But because of this nobility alone I would not have moved to memorialize her, if she hadn't so much preserved and augmented it with her own valour" ("Ma perché da questa nobiltà sola non mi sarei mosso a far memoria di lei, se molto più col proprio valore non la havesse conservata e accresciuta," Betussi, 191).

100 "in tutte le azioni conuenienti ad animo guerriero, fortemente si è dimostrata. Imperocchè essendo d'animo generoso, mai non si è lasciata vincere ne all'otio, ne alla delicatezza, anzi la dove le altre donne consumano il tempo in piaceri, e nel comandare a donzelle, in donneschi esercizi, costei s'è dilettata, tratta dalla gloria, e dal generoso animo, di spenderlo in comandare ad eserciti, in dare assalti a città, e come generale e capo di guerra, ad opporsi a'nimici. Perchè con verità si può dire costei essere stata quella, che, col consiglio e con le sue forze, abbia mantenuto la guerra di Fiandra, e di tutti quei luoghi: ne contenta solamente d'adoperarsi col consiglio, sempre si è veduta, come vecchio, e ammaestrato soldato, patir quei disconci, andare a quei pericoli, sopportar caldo, e freddo, non temer pioggia ne vento, piu ne meno d'ogni altro minimo e privato soldato. Questo pure e di più, si è veduto a'giorni nostri in questa generosa, e magnanima donna, nella quale non è possibile, che la natura non abbia peccato, auendo a costei dato cosi grand'animo, e maravigliose forze, e'l sesso donnesco. Ma essendo queste delle potenze di natura, non è maraviglia poi, se si veggiono infiniti huomini, huomini solamente di nome, e negli effetti non pusillanime femmine, ma vili e codardi conigli. Certamente a costei così valorosa, e dotata di tanto animo, si conveniva più viril sesso" (Betussi 192r–193v).

101 The printed edition states "a pena accenno," possibly suggesting "appena" (what he has just shown). However, one might also interpret this to mean "a penna accenno," meaning what Betussi has shown "by pen."

6 The Fame of Women and the Infamy of Men in the Age of Warring Queens (1550–1600)

1 Bruto's work, originally titled *Institutione di una fanciulla nata nobilmente,* is available in its trilingual edition on Early English Books Online (EEBO).

2 Mallet and Shaw discuss the legacies of the Italian Wars, 289–312. Even after the close of the Italian Wars, warfare continued to be a gruesome reality for Italians in the late sixteenth century, both on the peninsula and abroad. The Battle of Lepanto (1571), which involved thousands of Italians, shows how warfare at a distance was central to Italians in the latter part of the century.

3 Dandelet argues that after 1559 Spain was "virtually unchallenged in Italy" (57). Levin argues that Spanish control of Italy was continually challenged by Italians themselves.

4 I use the term "queen" to indicate Catherine throughout her life. This term indicates her status as the first lady of France. Catherine lost the title "queen" after her husband's death in 1559, at which time she became the queen mother.

5 For biographies of Catherine de' Medici, see Knecht and Orieux. On Catherine's political strategies, see Crouzet, *Le haut coeur*. On her involvement with the attack on Rouen, in which she is said to have ordered 10,000 cannon shots on the walls of the city and then to have led the troops through the breach, see Orieux 272.

6 Though there is some critical debate (see Frye) on whether Elizabeth actually visited the troops at Tilbury, a convincing argument for her presence has been put forward by Janet Greene. Regardless of Elizabeth's historical activities, the speech was included in a 1623 letter of Leonel Sharp and was published in 1654.

7 Studies on the influence of foreign queens on Italian literature are scanty. Cox has tackled the issue as part of her study of women writers in Italy, but there is as yet no comprehensive study of the matter (see *Women's Writing*). Michael Wyatt briefly addresses the importance of English culture to Italians in his book on Tudor England and Italy (see *The Italian Encounter*, especially 101–16). For the influence of Queen Isabella of Spain on Castiglione, see McLucas.

8 Cynthia J. Brown discusses works of illustrious women that were dedicated to the Queen of France and her sister-in-law in the early sixteenth century.

9 See S.G. Bell, *The Lost Tapestries*. The tapestries were planned for Catherine's regency. They were woven decades later during the reign of Henry IV for his future bride, Marie de' Medici. Bell explains that many female rulers owned tapestries based on De Pizan's work, including Elizabeth I, Anne of Brittany, and Mary Queen of Scots (158–9). For brilliant photographs of the tapestries as well as other art relating to Catherine and Maria de' Medici, see the catalogue of the exhibition on the two queens, *Women in Power: Caterina and Maria de' Medici*, ed. Clarice Innocenti (Florence: Mandragora, 2008).

10 In a dedication to Catherine's lady-in-waiting Maddalena Bonaiuti, Martelli states that he gave Catherine a copy of his *Donne illustri*, which was soon to be published (Martelli *Libro*). It is unclear if this was a catalogue of illustrious women or sonnets to illustrious women as the book was never

published. Catherine would also very likely have had access to Boccaccio's *De mulieribus claris* in Latin or in Italian translation. The 1543 translation of Lucantonio Ridolfi was dedicated to Albizza degli Dei, a family who would provide Catherine with one of her ladies-in-waiting. On Catherine and Boccaccio, see Dialetti. On Ridolfi's translation of *De mulieribus claris* dedicated to Albizza degli Dei, see Picot.

11 On the use of *exempla* in the education of young girls, see Collina "L'esemplarità" 103–20.

12 The reality of strong women rulers has been credited both for the popularity of the praise-of-women genre as well as the backlash that included texts characterized by a nostalgia for a time when women were ruled by men; see Sluhovsky 51.

13 De Billon's *Fort inexpugnable de l'honneur du sexe feminine* was composed in Rome in 1550 and then published in 1555 with a dedicatory epistle to five princesses, including Catherine. For a discussion of this work and other works dedicated to Catherine, see Balsamo.

14 On Catherine's library, see de Conihout and Ract-Madoux, 39–62.

15 On the Italian presence in France see Picot. For a biography of Bartolomeo (Baccio) Del Bene see the introduction of Del Bene's *Un idillio rusticale;* on Alammani see Hauvette. Much less work has been done on the French influence on Italy of the sixteenth century. On this topic, see the final four essays of Fontana.

16 Crouzet, "A Strong Desire," uses Catherine's letters to show her dedication to peace as well as her perception of peace as gendered feminine. See in particular p 114, where Catherine blames the past wars on men's will: "Henceforth, if I am not hindered again, I hope one will know that women have more will to safeguard the kingdom than those who have put it in the state where it is."

17 On the propaganda used against the Queen regarding this event, see Kingdon.

18 Sandberg 2008. On the Queen as Artemisia, see Ffolliott, "Catherine de' Medici," and Innocenti.

19 Cited in Ffolliott, "Exemplarity" 331.

20 Kruse 1995 also connects anti-Italian feeling to the paranoia about powerful women.

21 Nicolas Houel, *Histoire de la royne Arthémise* (Paris: 1562). A sympathetic biography in Italian appears in a compendium by Francesco Serdonati; see the discussion below. Brian Sandberg points out how, in the visual arts, Antoine Caron's works for the royal family (*Homage à la Madone* and his *Education guerrière du prince)* both exalt a feminine role in the learning of military practices (106). See Kruse on legends linking Catherine's actions to Machiavelli's *Prince* (144–5).

22 Lanci 179.
23 Franco-Tuscan relations were strained in both directions. Catherine had inherited considerable properties after the assassination of her half-brother Alessandro de' Medici in 1537, but the privilege of these properties led to a protracted legal battle after Cosimo requested a liquidation of them in 1567. Moreover, Cosimo sought the repayment of debt by the French crown, money that had been lent in the 1560s to finance the military response to the civil wars; see Jensen.
24 The war between Florence and Siena was fought between imperial-Florentine armies and Franco-Sienese forces under the command of Piero Strozzi, a Florentine exile who was protected by Catherine and King Henry II.
25 Caro 91–5. The poem is followed by a long censure by Castelvetro and then a discussion of the responses that Castelvetro's comments inspired. Salvatore Lo Rey argues that the poem must date from between 19 July 1553 and March 1554; see "'Venite all'ombra de' gran gigli d'oro' Retroscena politici di una celebre controversia letteraria (1553–1559)" in Lo Rey 253–94.
26 "Mirate, come placido e severo / è di se stesso e a sè legge e corona. / Vedete Iri e Bellona, / come dietro gli vanno, e Temi avanti, / com'ha la ragion seco, e 'l senno e 'l vero: / bella schiera che mai non l'abbandona. / Udite come tuona/ sopra de'licaoni e de' giganti / Guardate quanti n'ha già domi, e quanti / ne percuote e n'accenna; e con che possa / scuote d'Olimpo e d'Ossa / gli svelti monti, e 'n contro al ciel imposti. / Oh qual fia poi, spento Tifeo l'audace / e i folgori deposti! / quanta il mondo n'avrà letizia e pace!" (46–60).
27 Caro's song was immediately criticized by Castelvetro in what became a famous literary controversy. One of his many points of contention was the reference to the love of Henry for Catherine; Lo Rey.
28 Natalie R. Tomas discusses this phenomenon; see especially her sharp description of letters written to Lucrezia Tornabuoni and Clarice Orsini, 53–5.
29 Mihoko Suzuki explains that Anne Dowriche's *The French Historie* (1598) portrays Catherine as a transgressor for using language that "taunts the king and his 'trustie mates'" for being less manly than she is (182). Suzuki argues that Catherine is shown as "overstepping her bounds" as a counsellor. Notably, I argue that such taunting language is quite common in women's writing to men about war.
30 Eisenbichler, *L'opera*; *The Sword*; "Un chant"; "Poetesse senesi." On Salvi, see also Cox, *Women's Writing*; *ProdigiousMuse*; *Lyric Poetry*.
31 Eisenbichler, *The Sword* 165–77.

32 The poems to the French royals are published in Domenichi's anthology of women writers in 1559 (197–202). Salvi's poetic output was extensive, and she was regarded as one of the best woman poets of her time.

33 On Catherine's development of the image of the devoted mother, see Crawford 2000.

34 The sonnet "Non sia cagion l'altrui maligno impero" ("Let not another's evil rule be reason") is transcribed and translated in Eisenbichler, *The Sword* 262. Eisenbichler notes Salvi's appeal to Henry using the reprimand that Mary, "a higher Lady," expects him to "put his 'courtesy' into action" (198).

35 Catherine of Siena also wrote to women rulers using familial language. She wrote to Giovanna, Queen of Naples, over several years in attempts to garner aid in Pope Gregory XI's crusade against the Turks. See for example the letter of late June 1375 where Catherine tells Giovanna that the church "is a mother who feeds her children at her breast with sweetest life-giving milk," as well as "I want you to be a good daughter" (102). In the letter to Elizabeth of Hungary, the queen mother, she emphasizes her role as mother to her son, the king, as well as telling her to act like "hungry children" and rise up to take what is hers; in Noffke vol. 1, 170.

36 Maria de' Medici, daughter of the Grand Duke and Grand Duchess of Tuscany, Francesco de' Medici and Giovanna d'Austria, married Henry IV in 1600.

37 Cervoni has recently come to critical attention as a result of the efforts of Virginia Cox (see *Women's Writing; The Prodigious Muse; Lyric Poetry*).

38 The *canzone* was published, along with two others directed to the king of France, in *Tre canzoni … in laude de' christianiss[imi] Re, e Regina di Franci, e di Navarra, Enrico Quarto, e Madama Maria de' Medici* (Florence: Giorgio Marescotti, 1600). The poem is bound along with other short poems; page numbers are from National Library of Florence Palatino Collection 12.B.A.6.1.12.

39 Boccaccio's *De mulieribus claris* was translated into English in the mid-sixteenth century by Henry Parker and dedicated to Henry VIII, Elizabeth's father.

40 "Introductory Remarks," in Elam and Cioni 26.

41 The papal bull *Brutum fulmen*, dated 27 April 1570, can be found in an English translation at: http://tudorhistory.org/primary/papalbull.html. Bull and website quoted in Wyatt 136.

42 A much shorter manuscript on six illustrious women was presented to Elizabeth in manuscript in 1577. On Ubaldini and a brief history of the *Vite delle donne illustri* see Wyatt 127.

43 Ubaldini is noted for authoring texts in, or translating texts into, Italian. This practice created an interesting exchange. For example, his account of the Spanish Armada, *Commentario del successo dell'Armata Spagnuola nell'assalir l'Inghilterra l'anno 1588,* was taken from English sources but then translated back into English and printed by the English court. Ubaldini was also responsible for bringing stories of English military prominence into the Italian vernacular (see Rizzi, "English News").

44 "Ma che diremo noi della virtù militare delle donne? E per incominciare ... la Regina di un picciol Regno, in una grad'Isola."

45 Cox, *Women's Writing,* explains that Tasso's representation of women is ambivalent. While sensitive to women writers he also "reshapes the gender conventions of Ariostan romance to give women more ambiguous and less morally positive roles" (168). Cox also details the ways in which Tasso's proscriptions confine literary activity to a "statistically minuscule elite," thus pointing to the diminution of women's literary output at century's end (see especially 194–6).

46 Doglio, "Il Tasso" 16.

47 The differences in the theories of "illustrious women" as presented by Betussi and Tasso should also take into consideration their different life contexts. Betussi, working in the Venetian printing industry, surely differed from Tasso, who penned a more theoretical tract while in the employment of the court of Ferrara.

48 One exemplary "modern" work is Eugenio Comba's *Donne illustri italiane: Proposte ad esempio alle giovinette,* published in Turin in 1872 and in its fourth edition by 1885. The book was republished in the fascist era (1935) with additions of brave women from the First World War. Maura Hametz argues that although fascism idealized the maternal female body, it was also flexible enough to include those women who sacrificed themselves for the nation; Hametz 150–4.

49 Alessandro D'Ancona lists Serdonati's birth year as 1537 in Lamole, Florence, while Serdonati is commonly listed as born in 1540 (D'Ancona and Bacci 271–2). A biographical study on the writer is still needed.

50 There are many exemplars of the text. The presentation copy is likely the one located in Florence's Palatina collection housed at the Biblioteca Nazionale di Firenze 22.2.2.25. Portions of Serdonati's biographies were printed again in the nineteenth century: *Vita di cinque donne illustri italiane* (1869); and *Alcune vite di donne celebri scritte da F.S.* (1872).

51 The paratext of earlier editions is not always included in the Serdonati text. For example, Boccaccio's dedicatory letter is included, but Betussi's letter

to Camilla Pallavicina is not. Betussi's lengthy letter to Collaltino di Collalto, which concludes his book, is also removed in the Serdonati edition.

52 Garzoni, "Discorso."

53 This is not a comprehensive study or list of examples of the "famous women" genre. Many books are excluded, especially those that pertain to women of certain geographic areas.

54 On page 478, the recto of the last story by Betussi, there is a colophon of Giunti 1615: "Per Filippo Giunti MDCXV." The print irregularities of the edition merit more study.

55 Jordan demonstrates how these stories fit within a program of wifely love as advocated by Boccaccio ("Boccaccio's In-Famous" 39–40). Plutarch tells the story of the Minyan wives with some variation, calling them the "Etruscan Women" (ch. 8).

56 Laura Cereta provides a mini-catalogue of illustrious women, including the Minyan and Cimbrian wives, in her letter to Pietro Zecchi (65–72).

57 On the Sienese women during the siege of Siena see Eisenbichler, *The Sword* and McClure, *Parlour Games*.

58 On translation of Plutarch see chapter 4.

59 Serdonati mines various sources of Plutarch for communities of women. Tales taken directly from Plutarch include those about communities (women of the Melii and the Spartan women) as well as singular illustrious women (Policrita as well as Archidamia).

60 Various citations of Plutarch's women had become more common in sixteenth-century discussions of women's virtue. The best-known example of this is Castiglione, who cites Plutarch's brave women in *Courtier* III: 32–3.

61 Bandello, like the historian Marco Antonio Sabellico, places the incident on the island of Lemnos (Bandello, *Novelle* IV: 23; Sabellico, Book X, 485). It is interesting that Serdonati chooses the island of Metellino, as Bandello tells us that the island of Lesbos was called Metellino (Mettelino) II.13. Though it could be a simple mistake, one wonders if Serdonati's variation is intentional.

62 Serdonati lists Sabellico as one of several sources, although his tale differs from Sabellico's version. Bandello's tale of Marulla is introduced with a letter to Giovanna Sanseverina e Castigliona, in which he tells of the ancient women of arms and letters. He mentions modern examples of women of learning but offers an unusual list of contemporary women at arms. He begins by naming a woman warrior, Luzia Stanga, and then tells the story of an unnamed girl, the daughter of the gardener Alessandro Bentivoglio, who used a sword against two kidnappers.

63 Serdonati alters the story as told by Sabellico and Bandello, both of whom tell how Marulla deferred her marriage by stating that she could only choose a husband once she knew what sort of man he was.

64 Boccaccio's dedication letter suggests that he would like to dedicate it to one woman, yet chooses another, and, as Kolsky has shown, the choice of the dedicatee seems to have been made long after the text was completed.

65 Short biographical information on Serdonati is listed in D'Ancona and Bacci, 271–2. See also Francesco Serdonati, *Lettere*. His letters, starting in 1571, are often written from Raugia, and include updates about Turkish military endeavours. After 1602, the letters are written from Rome (Serdonati 1872). The letters often mention his numerous books, many of which were tracts about conducting war. Of note is the letter of 9 May 1608, where he asks that not only the Grand Duke and his son but also the Grand Duchess receive one of the presentation copies of his treatise on war.

66 In 1592(3?), just a few years before Serdonati's text, Ludovico Buti crafted a double portrait of Christine and her father, Duke Charles II of Lorraine, that required a mirror to see both images. It is now housed in the Museo delle scienze of Florence. It was painted on triangular wooden slats so that, standing from below, one could see the image of the Duke while, with the use of a mirror, one could see from above Christine's portrait. Whether Serdonati knew of the portrait is unknown (see Butters).

67 Both texts are cited in Zanrè 13, 16.

68 In the Florence-Siena war of 1554–5, Siena was backed by the French crown, King Henry II and Queen Catherine de' Medici. Contemporary chronicles tell us that, shortly after Ferdinando chose Christine as his bride in early May 1588, two events occurred that might be considered pro-Hapsburg or anti-French. In that same May, groups of men removed the Cappello coats of arms from city buildings and replaced them with those of the Hapsburg house; and at the Bargello, two portraits depicting Piero and Leone Strozzi were ripped to shreds (De' Ricci, *Cronaca* 516). The Strozzi brothers were Florentine *fuorusciti* and had been protected by Catherine de' Medici's court. Additionally, they fought as the captains of the French army against the Florentines during the war with Siena in 1554. To shred these portraits some thirty-five years after the war with Siena had ended and thirty years after the Strozzi's deaths seems much less an act against the long dead army captains than an indirect critique of France and the Grand Duke's choice of a French bride.

69 Each of these localities was part of the Grand Duchy of Tuscany. The Mugello was particularly dear to the Grand Duke's family as it was the ancient home of the Medici family.

70 On Caterina Sforza see chapter 5.

71 See Harness 46–58. The figures of Matilda and Semiramis most clearly represent women's fortitude in warfare.

72 Arnolfo decides to become a desert hermit because "serving God was more noble and honourable than ruling in the world ... and Arnolfo renounced his Duchy" ("considerando essi, che il servire a Dio era cosa molto più nobile, e più meritevole, ch'el dominare al mondo ... Arnolfo rinunziò il Ducato") (532)

73 On the relationship between a narrative arc and history, see White.

74 See Jensen.

75 See Harness.

76 *Della dignità e nobiltà delle donne* (1624–32) of Cristofano Bronzini was also dedicated to Christine of Lorraine. Cox, *Women's Writing*, provides a bibliographic history of Bronzini's monumental work, separate volumes of which were published in 1624, 1625, 1628, and 1632. The fourth volume is dedicated particularly to "Illustrious Women" (*Della virtù e valore delle donne illustri).* The entire work survives in manuscript in the National Library of Florence (Magl. VIII. 1513–38). For further information on Bronzini see Cox, *Women's Writing* 352 n89.

Conclusion

1 Zemon Davis refers to a similar emphasis on women in her influential article "Women on Top." A fascination with female rule arose at the same time that men were asserting new claims on women's property.

2 On the theme of Italy as woman and victim, see Costa-Zalessow.

3 Zemon Davis shows a similar case of how certain seemingly pro-women acts or texts, such as the carnivalesque trope of "women on top," worked less to empower women than to reinforce men's dominance.

Bibliography

Primary Sources

Alberti, Leon Battista. *De commodis litterarum atque incommodis*. Ed. Giovanni Farris. Milan: Marzorati, 1971.

———. *The Family in Renaissance Florence*. Trans. Renée Neu Watkins. Columbia, SC: University of South Carolina Press, 1969.

———. *Libri della famiglia*. Ed. Ruggiero Romano and Alberto Tenenti. Turin: Einaudi, 1994.

———. *The Use and Abuse of Books*. Trans. Renée Neu Watkins. Prospect Heights, IL: Waveland Books, 1999.

Ammirato, Scipione. "Alcuni ammaestramenti per le gran principesse." *Opuscoli del Sig. Scipione Ammirato*, vol. II. Florence: Massi e Landi, 1637.

———.*Orazione di Scipione Ammirato scritta alla nobiltà napoletana confortandola ad andar alla guerra d'Ungheria contra i Turchi*. Florence: Gli Heredi di Iacopo Giunti, 1594.

Antonelli, Pietro Matteo. *Donne illustri del Furioso*. Pesaro: Gli Heredi di Bartolomeo Cesano, 1563.

Antoniano, Silvio. *Dell'educazione cristiana e politica de' figlioli, libri tre*. Milan: Pogliani, 1821.

Aretino, Pietro. *Poesie varie.Vol. 1*. Ed. Giovanni Aquilecchia and Angelo Romano. Rome: Salerno, 1992.

Arienti, Giovanni Sabadino degli. *Gynevera de le clare donne*. Ed. Corrado Ricci and Alberto Bacchi. Bologna: Commissione per i testi di lingua, 1968.

Ariosto, Ludovico. *Orlando furioso*. 2 vols. Ed. Lanfranco Caretti. Turin: Einaudi, 2005.

———. *Orlando furioso*. Trans. Guido Waldman. Oxford: Oxford University Press, 1983.

Aristotle. *Gli otto libri della Republica che chiamono Politica di Aristotile.* Venice: Alessandro Brucioli e fratelli, 1547.

———. *History of Animals: Books 7–10.* Ed. and trans. David M. Balme. Cambridge, MA: Harvard University Press, 1994.

———. *Nicomachean Ethics.* Ed. and trans. David Ross. Oxford: Oxford University Press, 1980. (Reissued 1998)

———. *The Politics of Aristotle.* Ed. and trans. Peter L. Philips Simpson. Chapel Hill, NC: University of North Carolina Press, 1997.

Arredondo y Alvarado, Fray Gonzalo de. *Castillo inexpugnable.* Burgos: Juan de Junta, 1528.

Bandello, Matteo. *Tutte le opere.* Ed. Francesco Flora. Verona: Mondadori, 1952.

Bernardi, Andrea (Novacula). *Cronache forlivesi di A.B. (Novacula) dal 1476 al 1517.* Ed. G. Mazzatinti. Vol. I (1895); vol. II (1897). Bologna: R. Deputazione di Storia Patria, 1897.

Bernold of Constance. "Chronicon." *Monumenta Germaniae historica scriptores.* Vol. 5:443. Hanover: Hahn, 1844.

Betussi, Giuseppe. *Libro di M. Giovanni Boccaccio delle donne illustri, tradotto per Messer Giuseppe Betussi, con una additione fatta dal medesimo delle donne famose dal tempo di M. Giovanni fino ai giorni nostri.* Venice: Andrea Arrivabene, 1545.

———. *Libro di M. Giovanni Boccaccio delle donne illustri, tradotto per Messer Giuseppe Betussi, con una additione fatta dal medesimo delle donne famose dal tempo di M. Giovanni fino ai giorni nostri.* Venice: Pietro de Nicolini da Sabbio, 1547.

Bisticci, Vespasiano. *Libro delle lodi delle donne.* Ed. L. Sorrento. Milan: Società Editrice Dante Alighieri, 1910.

Boccaccio, Giovanni. *The Book of Theseus.* Trans. Bernadette Marie McCoy. New York: Medieval Texts Association, 1974.

———. *Famous Women.* Ed. and trans. Virginia Brown. Cambridge, MA: Harvard University Press, 2001.

———. *Teseida delle nozze d'Emilia.* Milan: Arnoldo Mondadori, 1992.

Boccalini, Traiano. *Ragguagli di Parnaso e pietra di paragone politico.* Venice: Pietro Farri, 1612.

Botero, Giovanni. *Della ragione di stato.* Ed. Chiara Continisio. Rome: Donzelli, 1997.

———. *The Reason of State.* Trans. P.J. Waley and D.P. Waley. New Haven, CT: Yale University Press, 1956.

———. *Relationi universal di Giovanni Botero Benese.* Brescia: Compagnia Bresciana, 1599.

Bracciolini, Francesco. *Lettere sulla poesia.* Ed. Guido Baldassarri. Rome: Bulzoni, 1979.

Bronzini, Cristofano. *Della dignità e nobiltà delle donne.* Florence: Pignoni, 1624–32.

Bruto, Giovanni Michele. *La institutione di una fanciulla nata nobilmente.* Antwerp: Plantin, 1555.

Brutum fulmen. 27 April 1570. English translation available at: http://tudorhistory.org/primary/papalbull.html.

Bulifon, Antonio, ed. *Rime di cinquanta illustri poetesse.* Naples: Antonio Bulifon, 1695.

"Cabala, Mysteries of State." Letters of the Great Ministers of K. James and K. Charles. London: M.M.G. Bedell and T. Collins, 1654.

Calmeta, Vincenzo. *Prose e lettere edite e inedite.* Ed. Cecil Grayson. Bologna: Commissione per i testi di lingua, 1959.

Camerata, Girolamo. *Trattato dell'honor vero et del vero disonore, con tre questioni dove si tratta chi meriti più onore o la donna, o l'huomo o il soldato o il letterato.* Bologna: Alessandro Benacci, 1567.

Campanella, Tommaso. *La città del sole: Dialogo poetico / The City of the Sun: A Poetical Dialogue.* Ed. and trans. Daniel J. Donno. Berkeley: University of California Press, 1981.

———. *La città del sole / Civitas solis.* Ed. and trans. Tonino Tornitore. Turin: Nino Aragno Editore, 2008.

Capra (Capella), Galeazzo Flavio. *L'anthropologia.* Venice: Heredi d'Aldo Romano e Andrea d'Asola, 1533.

———. *Della eccellenza e dignità delle donne.* Ed. Maria Luisa Doglio. 2nd ed. Rome: Bulzoni, 2001.

Caro, Annibal. *Opere.* Ed. Stefano Jacomuzzi. Turin: UTET, 1974.

Castiglione, Baldassarre. *The Book of the Courtier.* Trans. Charles Singleton. Ed. Daniel Javitch. New York: Norton, 2002.

———. *Il libro del cortegiano con una scelta delle opere minori.* Ed. Bruno Maier. 2nd ed. Turin: UTET, 1964.

———. *Poesie volgari, e latine del conte Baldassar Castiglione.* Rome: Niccolò e Mario Pagliarini, 1740.

Caterina da Siena. *Lettere di Caterina da Siena.* 4 vols. Ed. Niccolò Tommaseo. Florence: G. Barbèra, 1860.

———. *Lettere di Caterina da Siena.* Ed. Piero Misciattelli. Siena: Giuntini, 1913.

———. *Letters of Catherine of Siena.* 4 vols. Ed. and trans. Susan Noffke. Tempe: Arizona Center for Medieval and Renaissance Studies, 2000.

———. *Opera omnia. Testi e concordanze.* CD-ROM. Ed. Fausto Sbaffoni. Pistoia: 2002.

Cereta, Laura. *Collected Letters of a Renaissance Feminist.* Ed. and trans. Diana Robin. Chicago: University of Chicago Press, 1997.

Cerretani, Bartolomeo. *Storia fiorentina.* Ed. Giuliana Berti. Florence: Leo S. Olschki Editore, 1994.

Cervoni, Isabella. *Orazione della Signora Isabella Cervoni a Clemente VIII*. Bologna: Battista Bellagamba, 1598.

———. *Tre canzoni … in laude de' christianiss[imi] re, e Regina di Francia, e di Navarra, Enrico Quarto, e Madama Maria de' Medici*. Florence: Giorgio Marescotti, 1600.

Cobelli, Leone. *Cronache forlivesi: Dalla fondazione della città sino all'anno 1498*. Bologna: Regia Tipografia, 1874.

Colonna, Pompeo. "Apologiae mulierum libri II." *Studi e ricerche sull'umanesimo italiano: Testi inediti del XV e XVI secolo*. Ed. Guglielmo Zappacosta. Bergamo: Minerva Italica, 1973.

Colonna, Vittoria. *Rime*. Ed. Alan Bullock. Rome-Bari: Laterza, 1982.

Comnena, Anna. *Alexiad*. Trans. E.R.A. Sewter. Harmondsworth, Middlesex: Penguin, 1969.

Compagnon, Marsilio. *Il lamento di Caterina Sforza*. Venice: Matteo Capcasa, c. 1500.

De Anglería, Pedro Mártir. *Epistolario de Pedro Mártir de Anglería*. Ed. and trans. José López de Toro. Madrid: Gongora, 1953–5.

De Billon, François. *Fort inexpugnable de l'honneur du sexe feminine*. Paris: J.D'Allyer, 1555.

de la Pergola, Gaugello. *De vita et morte illustris. d. Baptistae Sfortiae Comitissae Urbini*. Ed. Adolfo Cinquini. Rome: Tipografia della S.C. de Propoganda Fide, 1905.

de Pisan, Christine. *The Treasure of the City of Ladies*. Trans. Sarah Lawson. Harmondsworth, Middlesex: Penguin, 1985.

de Révisy, Jean Tixier (Giovanni Ravisio Testore). *De memorabilibus et claris mulieribus*. Paris: S. Colinari, 1521.

De' Ricci, Giuliano. *Cronaca: 1532–1606*. Ed. Giuliana Sapori. Naples: Ricciardi, 1972.

Del Bene, Bartolomeo (Baccio). *Un idillio rusticale*. Ed. Nello Tarchiani. Florence: Lumachi, 1903.

del Sera, Beatrice. *Amor di virtù: Commedia in cinque atti (1548)*. Ed. Elissa Weaver. Ravenna: Longo, 1990.

Denores, Iason. *Breve institutione dell'ottima republica: Raccolta in gran parte da tutta la Philosophia di Aristotile … ecc*. Venice: Megietti, 1578.

Di Gaeta, Giacomo. *Ragionamento chiamato l'accademico overo della bellezza*. Ed. Anna Cerbo. Naples: ESI, 1996.

Dolce, Lodovico. *Dialogo della institutione delle donne*. Venice: Giolito de Ferrari, 1547.

Domenichi, Lodovico. *La nobiltà delle donne*. Venice: Gabriel Giolito de' Ferrari, 1549.

Domenichi, Lodovico, ed. *Rime diverse d'alcune nobilissime, et virtuosissime donne*. Lucca: Vincenzo Busdragho, 1559.

Dominici (Banchini), Giovanni. "Governo di cura familiare." *Prosatori volgari del Quattrocento*, 21–4. Milan: Ricciardi, 1955.

Doni, Anton Francesco. *I marmi*. 2 vols. Ed. Ezio Chiòrboli. Bari: Laterza, 1928.

Donizone di Canossa. *Vita di Matilde di Canossa*. Ed. and trans. Paolo Golinelli. Milan: Jaca Books, 2008.

Dowriche, Anne. *The French Historie*. London: Thomas Orwin, 1589.

Equicola. Mario. *De mulieribus – Delle donne*. Ed. and trans. Giuseppe Lucchesini and Pina Totaro. Pisa: Istituti Editoriali e Poligrafici, 2004.

Euripides. "Antiope." *Select Fragmentary Plays*. Ed. and trans. C. Collard, M.J. Cropp, and K.H. Lee. Warminster, PA: Aris and Phillips, 1995.

———.*Trojan Women*. Trans. Diskin Clay. Newburyport, MA: Focus, 2005.

Ferrarini, Girolamo. *Memoriale estense (1476–1489)*. Ed. Primo Griguolo. Rovigo: Minelliana, 2006.

Filelfo, Francesco. *Odes*. Ed. and trans. Diana Robin. Cambridge, MA: Harvard University Press, 2009.

Filetico, Martino. *Iocundissimae disputationes*. Ed. and trans. Guido Arbizzoni. Modena: Franco Cosimo Panini, 1992.

Filogenio, Hercole. *Dell'eccellenza della donna*. Fermo: Sertorio de' Monti, 1589.

Fonte, Moderata (Modesta Pozzo). *Il merito delle donne: Ove chiaramente si scuopre quanto siano elle degne e più perfette de gli uomoini*. Ed. Adriana Chemello. Venice: Editrice Eidos, 1988.

———. *Tredici canti del Floridoro*. Ed. Valeria Finucci. Modena: Mucchi, 1995.

———. *The Worth of Women: Wherein Is Clearly Revealed Their Nobility and Their Superiority to Men*. Ed. and trans. Virginia Cox. Chicago: University of Chicago Press, 1997.

Foresti da Bergamo, Jacopo Filippo. *De plurimis claris selectisque mulieribus*. Ferrara: Lorenzo da Valenza, 1497.

Gambara, Veronica. *Rime e lettere di Veronica Gambara*. Ed. Felice Rizzardi. Brescia: Giammaria Rizzardi, 1759.

———. *Le rime*. Ed. Allan Bullock. Florence: Olschki, 1995.

Garzoni, Tomaso. "Discorso sopra la nobiltà delle donne." *Le vite delle donne illustri della scittura sacra con l'aggiunta delle vite delle donne oscure e laide dell'uno e l'altro testamento. E un discorso in fine sopra la nobiltà delle donne*. Ed. Beatrice Collina. Longo: Ravenna, 1994.

———. *Piazza universale di tutte le professioni*. Ed. Giovanni Battista Bronzini. Florence: Olschki, 1996.

Gelli, Giovan Battista. *La Circe*. Venice: Marc Antonio Bonibelli, 1595.

Giacomo di Gaeta. *Ragionamento chiamato l'accademico overo della bellezza*. Ed. A. Cerbo. Naples: ESI, 1996.

Gilio, Giovanni Andrea. *Due dialoghi*. Camerino: Antonio Giojoso, 1564.

———. *Topica poetica.* Venice: Oratio de' Gobbi, 1580.

Giovio, Paolo. *Notable Men and Women of Our Time.* Ed. and trans. Kenneth Gouwens. Cambridge, MA: Harvard University Press, 2013.

Giraldi Cinzio, Giovanbattista. *Discorso dei romanzi.* Ed. Laura Benedetti, Giuseppe Monorchio, and Enrico Musacchio. Bologna: Milennium, 1999.

Guazzo, Stefano. "Dell'honor delle donne." *Dialoghi piacevoli del signor Stefano Guazzo, gentil'huomo di Casale di Monferrato.* Venice: G.A. Bertano, 1586.

Guicciardini, Francesco. *"Discorso di Logrogno." Republican Realism in Renaissance Florence: Francesco Guicciardini's "Discorso di Logrogno."* Ed. and trans. Athanasios Moulakis. Lanham, MD: Rowman and Littlefield, 1998.

———. *Maxims and Reflections of a Renaissance Statesman (Ricordi).* Trans. Mario Domandi. Gloucester, MA: Harper and Row, 1965.

———. *Ricordi.* Ed. Carlo Varotti. Rome: Carocci, 2013.

———. *Storie d'Italia.* Ed. Silvana Seidel Menchi. Turin: Einaudi, 1971.

Homer. *The Iliad.* Ed. and trans. Herbert Jordan. Norman, OK: University of Oklahoma Press, 2008.

Infessura, Stefano. *Diario della città di Roma.* Ed. Oreste Tommasini. Rome: Forzani e C. Tipografi del Senato, 1890.

Lanci, Cornelio. *Esempi della virtu' delle donne, ne' quali si vede la bellezza delle vergini, maritate, e vedove.* Florence: Francesco Tosi, 1590.

Lando, Ortensio. *Essortatione.* Brescia: Demiano de' Turlini, 1545.

Lanteri, Giacomo. *Della economia.* Venice: Vicenzo Valgrisi, 1560.

The Letters of Abelard and Heloise. Ed. and trans. Betty Radice. Harmondsworth, Middlesex: Penguin, 1974.

Livy. *History of Rome: Books I–II.* Vol. I. Trans. B.O. Foster. Cambridge, MA: Loeb Classical Library, 1919.

Lottini, Giovanni Francesco. *Avvedimenti civili.* Venice: Iacomo Leonzini, 1575.

Luigini, Federigo. "Il libro della bella donna." *Trattati del Cinquecento sulla donna.* Ed. Giuseppe Zonta. Bari: Laterza, 1913.

Machiavelli, Niccolò. *Art of War.* Preface, trans. Allen Gilbert. In *Machiavelli: The Chief Works and Others.* Durham, NC: Duke University Press, 1989.

———. *Discourses.* Preface, trans. Allan Gilbert. In *Machiavelli: The Chief Works and Others.* Durham, NC: Duke University Press, 1989, 1958.

———. *Tutte le opere.* Ed. Mario Martelli. Milan: Sansoni, 1993.

Marcellinus, Ammianus. *Roman History.* Trans. C.D. Yonge. London: Bohn, 1862.

Marescotti, Ercole. *Dell'eccellenza della donna, discorso di Hercole Filogenio.* Fermo: Sertorio de' Monti, 1589.

Marinella, Lucrezia. *Enrico, or, Byzantium Conquered: A Heroic Poem.* Ed. and trans. Maria Galli Stampino. Chicago: University of Chicago Press, 2009.

———. *L'Enrico, ovvero Bisanzio acquistato: Poema eroico.* Ed. Maria Galli Stampino. Modena: Mucchi, 2011.

———. *La nobiltà et l'eccellenza delle donne, co' diffetti et mancamenti de gli huomini.* Venice: Giovan Battista Ciotti, 1601.

———.*Le nobilità et eccellenze delle donne, et i diffetti e mancamenti de gli huomini.* Venice: Giovan Battista Ciotti Senese, 1600.

———. *The Nobility and Excellence of Women and the Defects and Vices of Men.* Ed. and trans. Anne Dunhill. Chicago: University of Chicago Press, 1999.

Martelli, Niccolò. *Il primo libro delle lettere di Nicolo Martelli.* Florence: n.p., 1546.

Matraini, Chiara. *Breve discorso sopra la vita e laude della beatiss. vergine e madre del figliuol di Dio.* Lucca: Busdraghi, 1590.

———. *Dialoghi spirituali.* Venice: Prati, 1602.

———. *Lettere di Madonna Chiara Matraini, gentildonna lucchese con la prima e seconda parte delle sue rime.* Venice: Nicolò Moretti, 1597.

———. *Lettere di Signora Chiara Matraini, gentildonna lucchese con la prima e seconda parte delle sue rime.* Lucca: Busdraghi, 1595.

———. *Meditationi spirituali.* Lucca: Busdraghi, 1581.

———. *Rime e lettere.* Ed. Giovanna Rabiti. Bologna: Commissione per i testi di lingua, 1989.

———. *Rime e prose di Madonna Chiara Matraini, gentildonna lucchese.* Lucca: Busdraghi, 1555.

———. *Selected Poetry and Prose. A Bilingual Edition.* Ed. and trans. Elaine Maclachlan. Intro. Giovanna Rabitti. Chicago: University of Chicago Press: 2007.

Mercurio, Scipione. *La commare o riccoglitrice.* Venice: Giovan Battista Ciotti, 1621.

Monluc, Blaise. *Commentaires de Blaise de Monluc.* Ed. Paul Courteault. Paris: A Picard et Fils, 1911.

Montalvo, Antonio. *Relazione della guerra di Siena.* Turin: Vercellino, 1863.

Morzillo, Sebastian Fox. *Commentatio in decem Platonis libros de Republica.* Basel: Ioannis Oporini, 1556.

Office on Women in the NATO Forces. *Women in the NATO Armed Forces: Year in Review 1999–2000.* Brussels: International Military Staff, 2000. Available at: http://www.nato.int/ims/1999/win/report99.pdf. Retrieved, Friday, 2 May 2014.

Parenti, Piero di Marco. *Storia Fiorentina.* Vol. II (1456–1502). Ed. Andrea Matucci. Florence: Olschki, 2005.

Passi, Giuseppe. *I donneschi diffetti.* Venice: Iacopo Somasco, 1599.

The Paston Women: Selected Letters. Ed. Diane Watt. Woodbridge, Suffolk: D.S. Brewer, 2004.

Petrarca, Francesco. *Canzoniere: Rerum vulgarium fragmenta.* Ed. Piero Cudini. Milan: Garzanti, 1988.

———. *Le familiari.* Ed. Ugo Dotti. Urbino: Argalia Editore, 1974.
———. *Le familiari.* 4 vols. Ed. Vittorio Rossi. Florence: Le lettere, 1997.
———. *Letters from Petrarch.* Ed. and trans. Morris Bishop. Bloomington: Indiana University Press, 1966.
———. *Letters of Familiar Matters.* Trans. Aldo S. Bernardo. Baltimore, MD: Johns Hopkins University Press, 1982.
Plato. *La Republica di Platone, tradotta dalla lingua Greca nella Thoscana.* Trans. Pamphilo Fiorimbene da Fossembrone. Venice: Gabriel Giolito de Ferrari et Fratelli, 1554.
———. *Republic.* Trans. Richard W. Sterling and William C. Scott. New York: Norton, 1985.
———. *The Symposium.* Ed. and trans. Christopher Gill. London: Penguin Books, 1999.
Plutarch. *"Bravery of Women (Mulierum virtutes)." Moralia.* Vol. III: 475–581. Trans. Frank Cole Babbitt. New York: William Heinemann, 1931.
———. *De virtutibus mulierum.* Trans. Alamanus Rinucinus. Brescia: Boninus de Boninis, 1485.
———. "Sayings of Spartan Women." *Moralia.* Vol. III: 451–69. Trans. Frank Cole Babbitt. New York: William Heineman, 1931.
Pontano, Francesco. *"Dello integro e perfetto stato delle donzelle." Raccolta di scritture varie pubblicata nell'occasione delle nozze Riccomanni-Fineschi,* 13–30. Ed. Cesare Riccomanni. Turin: Vercellino, 1863.
Priuli, Giacomo. *I diarii.* Ed. Arturo Segre. *Rerum italicarum scriptores, 24, pt 3. v4.* Città di Castello: Tipi della Casa editrice S. Lapi, 1938.
Quintus of Smyrna. *The Trojan Epic (Posthomerica).* Ed. and trans. Alan James. Baltimore, MD: Johns Hopkins University Press, 2004.
Razzi, Silvano. *Delle vite delle donne illustri per santità raccolte dal p. abate don S. R. camaldolese.* 6 vols. Florence: Cosimo Giunti, 1597–1606.
Ribera, Pierpaolo. *865 donne illustri antiche e moderne.* Venice: E. Dehuchino, 1609.
Ricasoli, Pandolfo. *Orazione in lode della verginità e della fortezza militare fatta nell'occasione della morte del Principe D. Francesco Medici, etc.* Florence: Sermartelli, 1615.
Riccoboni, Sister Bartolomea. *Life and Death in a Venetian Convent: The Chronicle and Necrology of Corpus Domini, 1395 – 1436.* Ed. and trans. Daniel Bornstein. Chicago: University of Chicago Press, 2000.
Sabellico, Marco Antonio. *Dell'historia venitiana.* Venice: Gio. Maria Savioni, 1668.
Sanudo [alternative spelling Sanuto], Marin (il Giovane). *I diarii di Marino Sanuto, 1496-1533: Dall'autografo Marciano ital. cl. VII codd. CDXIX-CDLXXVII.* Ed. Rinaldo Fulin, Federico Stefani, Nicolò Barozzi, et al. Bologna: Forni, 1969–1970.

———.*La vite dei dogi (1474–1494)*. Vol. 1. Ed. Angela Caracciolo Aricò. Padua: Antenore, 1989.

Sarocchi, Margherita. *La Scanderbeide: Poema heroico*. Ed. Giovanni Latini. Rome: Andrea Fei, 1623.

———. *Scanderbeide: The Heroic Deeds of George Scanderbeg, King of Epirus*. Ed. and trans. Rinaldina Russell. Chicago: University of Chicago Press, 2006.

Serdonati, Francesco. *Della perfezione delle donne*. In *Libro di M. Giovanni Boccaccio Delle donne illustri. Tradotto di Latino in volgare per M. Giuseppe Betussi, con una giunta fatta dal medesimo, d'altre donne famose, e un'altra nuova giunta fatta per M. Francesco Serdonati d'altre donne illustri. Antiche e moderne*. Florence: Giunti, 1596.

———. *Lettere inedite*. Ed. Pietro Ferrato. Padua: Penada, 1872.

———. *Libro di M. Giovanni Boccaccio Delle donne illustri. Tradotto di Latino in volgare per M. Giuseppe Betussi, con una giunta fatta dal medesimo, d'altre donne famose, e un'altra nuova giunta fatta per M. Francesco Serdonati d'altre donne illustri. Antiche e moderne*. Florence: Giunti, 1596.

———. *Vita di cinque donne illustri italiane: Cia Ubaldini, Caterina Sforza, Mandella Gaetani, Caterina Cybo, Caterina dei Medici*. Florence: Campolmi, 1869.

Sigonio, Vincenzo. *La difesa per le donne*. Ed. Fabio Marri. Bologna: Commissione per i Testi di Lingua, 1978.

Speroni, Sperone. "Orazione contra le cortigiane". *Opere*. Vol. 3. Venice: 1740.

Stampa, Gaspara. *The Complete Poems: The 1554 Edition of the Rime, a Bilingual Edition*. Trans. Jane Tylus. Ed. Jane Tylus and Troy Tower. Chicago: University of Chicago Press, 2010.

Strozzi, Agostino. *La defensione della donna d'autore anonimo, scrittura inedita del sec. XV*. Ed. Francesco Zambrini. Bologna: Gaetano Romagnoli, 1876.

Tansillo, Luigi. *Capitoli giocosi e satirici*. Ed. Scipione Volpicella. Naples: Libreria di Dura, 1870.

Tasso, Bernardo. *L'Amadigi del S. Bernardo Tasso. A l'invittissimo e catolico Re Philippo*. Venice: Fabio and Agostino Zoppini, 1581.

Tasso, Torquato. *Discorso della virtù feminile e donnesca*. Ed. Maria Luisa Doglio. Palermo: Sellerio, 1997.

———. "Giudizio sovra la Gerusalemme Conquistata." *Prose diverse*.Vol. 1. Ed. Cesare Giusti. Florence: Le Monnier, 1875.

Terracina, Laura. *Il discorso della S. Laura Terracina sopra il principio di tutti i canti di Orlando furioso, di nuovo con ogni diligentia corretto & ristampato*. Venice: Giacomo Gidini, 1577.

Tixier de Ravisy, Jean. *De memorabilibus et claris mulieribus: Aliquot diversorum scriptorum opera*. Paris: Simon de Colines, 1521.

Tornabuoni, Lucrezia. *Sacred Narratives*. Ed. and trans. Jane Tylus. Chicago: University of Chicago Press, 2001.

Ubaldini, Petruccio. *Vite delle donne illustri del regno d'inghilterra, & del regno di Scotia, & di quelle, che d'altri paesi ne i due detti regni sono stato maritate.* London: John Wolfe, 1591.

———. *Le vite delle donne illustri del Regno dell'Inghilterra et del Regno di Scotia.* London: John Wolfe, 1591.

Varanini, Giorgio, and Guido Baldassarri, eds. *Racconti esemplari di predicatori del Due e Trecento.* Vol. II. Rome: Salerno Editrice, 1993.

Vasoli, Scipione. *La gloriosa eccellenza delle donne e d'amore.* Florence: Giorgio Marescotti, 1573.

Vegetius, *Epitome of Military Science.* Trans. N.P. Milner. 2nd ed. Liverpool: Liverpool University Press, 1996.

Virgil. *Aeneid.* Trans. Michael Oakley. New York: Dutton, 1957.

Vives, Juan Luís. *The Education of a Christian Woman: A Sixteenth-Century Manual.* Ed. and trans. Charles Fantazzi. Chicago: University of Chicago Press, 2000.

Xenophon. *Memorabilia and Oeconomicus.* Trans. E.C. Marchant. London and New York: G.P. Putnam's Sons, 1923.

Zambotti, Bernardino. *Diario ferrarese (1476–1504).* Ed. Giuseppe Pardi. Bologna: Zanichelli, 1934–7.

Secondary Sources

Alhaique Pettinelli, Rosanna. "Figure femminili nella tradizione cavalleresca tra Quattro e Cinquecento." *Italianistica* 21.2–3 (May–December 292): 727–38.

Allaire, Gloria. "The Warrior Woman in Late Medieval Prose Epics." *Italian Culture* 12 (1994): 33–43.

Allen, Prudence. *The Concept of Woman: Early Humanist Reformation.* Grand Rapids, MI: Eerdmans, 2002.

Allmand, Christopher. "War and the Non-Combatant in the Middle Ages." In *Medieval Warfare: A History,* ed. Maurice Keen, 253–72. Oxford: Oxford University Press, 1999.

Ammendola, Teresa, and Maria Grazia Galatino. "Nuove sfide per la leadership nell'organizzazione militare." In *Guidare il cambiamento: La leadership nelle forze armate italiane,* ed. Teresa Ammendola, 95–111. Soveria Mannelli: Rubettino, 2004.

Andò, Valeria. *L'ape che tesse: Saperi femminili nella Grecia antica.* Rome: Carocci, 2005.

Andreoli, Ilaria. "*L'Orlando furioso* 'tutto ricorretto et di nuove figure adornato': L'edizione Valgrisi (1556) nel contesto della storia editoriale ed illustrativa del poema fra Italia e Francia nel Cinquecento." In *Autour du livre italien ancien en Normandie*, ed. Silvia Fabrizio-Costa, 41–132. Brussels: Peter Lang, 2011.

Arrigoni, Giampiera. *Camilla, Amazzone e sacerdotessa di Diana*. Milan: Istituto Editoriale Cisalpino – La Goliadica, 1982.

Ascoli, Albert R. "Ariosto's 'Fier Pastor': Structure and Historical Meaning in *Orlando furioso*." In *Ariosto Today: Contemporary Perspectives*, ed. Donald Beecher, Massimo Ciavolella, and Roberto Fedi, 189–224. Toronto: University of Toronto Press, 2003.

———. "Like a Virgin: Male Fantasies of the Body in *Orlando furioso*." In *The Body in Early Modern Italy*, ed. Walter Stephens and Julia L. Hairston, 142–57. Baltimore, MD: Johns Hopkins University Press, 2010.

Balsamo, Jean. "'Ses vertus l'ont assise au rang des immortels': Catherine De Médicis et ses poètes." In *Il mecenatismo di Caterina de' Medici: Poesie, feste, musica, pittura, scultura, architettura*, ed. Sabine Frommel and Gerhard Wolf, 11–38. Venice: Marsilio, 2008.

Barlozzetti, Ugo. "Aspetti e problemi della prassi guerresca di un capitano di ventura." In *Condottieri e uomini d'arme nell'Italia del Rinascimento*, ed. Mario Del Treppo, 29–40. Naples: Liguori, 2001.

Bassanese, Fiora. *Gaspara Stampa*. Boston: Twayne, 1982.

Bateman, Chimène. "Amazonian Knots. Gender, Genre, and Ariosto's Women Warriors." *Modern Language Notes* 122 (2007): 1–23.

Bayley, C.C. *War and Society in Renaissance Florence: The "De militia" of Leonardo Bruni*. Toronto: University of Toronto Press, 1961.

Bearden, Elizabeth B. *The Emblematics of the Self: Ekphrasis and Identity in Renaissance Imitations of Greek Romance*. Toronto: University of Toronto Press, 2012.

Becker, Trudy Harrington. "Ambiguity and the Female Warrior: Vergil's Camilla." *Electronic Antiquity*, 4.1 (1997): 1–13.

Bell, Rudolph. *Holy Anorexia*. Chicago: University of Chicago Press, 1987.

Bell, Susan Groag. *The Lost Tapestries of the* City of Ladies: *Christine de Pizan's Renaissance Legacy*. Berkeley: University of California Press, 2004.

Benedetti, Laura. *La sconfitta di Diana: Un percorso per la "Gerusalemme liberata."* Ravenna: Longo, 1997.

Benson, Pamela Joseph. *The Invention of the Renaissance Woman: The Challenge of Female Independence in the Literature and Thought of Italy and England*. University Park, PA: Pennsylvania State University Press, 1992.

Blok, Josine H. *The Early Amazons: Modern and Ancient Perspectives on a Persistent Myth*. Leiden: Brill, 1995.

Blythe, James M. "Women in the Military: Scholastic Arguments and Medieval Images of Female Warriors." *History of Political Thought* 22.2 (Summer 2001): 242–69.

Boitani, Piero. "Style, Iconography and Narrative: The Lesson of the *Teseida.*" In *Chaucer and the Italian Trecento,* ed. Piero Boitani, 185–99. Cambridge: Cambridge University Press, 1994.

Bonvini Mazzanti, Marinella. *Battista Sforza Montefeltro: Una "principessa" nel Rinascimento.* Urbino: Edizioni Quattroventi, 1993.

Borzelli, Angelo. *Laura Terracina, poetessa napoletana del Cinquecento.* Naples: M. Marzano, 1924.

Boter, Gerard. *The Textual Tradition of Plato's "Republic."* Supplement to *Mnemos* 107. Leiden: Brill, 1989.

Branca, Vittore. *Boccaccio medievale.* Florence: Sansoni, 1956.

———. *Tradizione delle opere di Giovanni Boccaccio. Vol. I: Un primo elenco dei codici e tre studi.* Rome: Edizioni Storia e Letteratura, 1958.

———. *Un secondo elenco di manoscritti e studi sul testo del "Decameron" con due appendici.* Rome: Edizioni Storia e Letteratura, 1991.

Braudy, Leo. *From Chivalry to Terrorism: War and the Changing Nature of Masculinity.* New York: Vintage Books, 2005.

Breisach, Ernst. *Caterina Sforza, a Renaissance Virago.* Chicago: University of Chicago Press, 1967.

Brose, Margaret. "Petrarch's Beloved Body: 'Italia mia.'" In *Feminist Approaches to the Body in Medieval Literature,* ed. Linda Lomperis and Sarah Stanbury, 1-20. Philadelphia: University of Pennsylvania Press, 1993.

Bruscagli, Riccardo. *Stagioni della civiltà estense.* Pisa: Nistri-Lischi, 1983.

Budd, F.E. "A Minor Italian Critic of the Sixteenth Century: Jason Denores." *Modern Language Review* 22.4 (1927): 421–34.

Bullock, Alan, and Gabriella Palange. "Per una edizione critica delle opere di Chiara Matraini." In *Studi in onore di Raffaele Spongano,* ed. Emilio Pasquini, 235-62. Bologna: Boni, 1980.

Burger, Glenn. *A Lytell Cronycle: Richard Pynson's Translation (c. 1520) of "La fleur des histoires de la terre d'Orient" (c. 1307).* Toronto: University of Toronto Press, 1988.

Butler, Judith. *Bodies That Matter.* New York: Routledge, 1993.

Butters, Suzanne B. "Ferdinando de' Medici and the Art of the Possible." In *The Medici, Michelangelo, and the Art of Late Renaissance Florence,* ed. Cristina Acidini Luchinat, 66–75. New Haven, CT: Yale University Press, 2002.

Bynum, Caroline Walker. *Holy Feast, Holy Fast: The Religious Significance of Food to Medieval Women.* Berkeley: University of California Press, 1987.

Caferro, William. *John Hawkwood: An English Mercenary in Fourteenth-Century Italy.* Baltimore, MD: Johns Hopkins University Press, 2006.

Cantagalli, Roberto. *La guerra di Siena, 1552–1559.* Siena: Accademia Senese degli Intronati, 1962.

Carreiras, Helena. *Gender and the Military: Women in the Armed Forces of Western Democracy*. London: Routledge, 2006.

Chiappelli, Fredi. *Il conoscitore del caos: Una "vis abdita" nel linguaggio tassesco.* Roma: Bulzoni, 1981.

Chimenti, Antonia. *Veronica Gambara: Gentildonna del Rinascimento, un intreccio di poesia e storia*. Reggio Emilia: Magis, 1996.

Collina, Beatrice. "L'esemplarità delle donne illustri fra umanesimo e Controriforma." In *Donna, disciplina, creanza cristiana dal XV al XVII secolo*, ed. Gabriella Zarri, 103–19. Rome: Edizioni di Storia e Letteratura, 1996.

———. "Virago e guerriera: La 'Signora di Forlì' nella cultura umanistico-rinascimentale." *Caterina Sforza: Una donna del Cinquecento.* Imola: Mandragora, 2000.

Connell, R.W. *Masculinities*. 2nd ed. Cambridge: Polity Press, 2005.

Connolly, Joy. "Virile Tongues: Rhetoric and Masculinity." In *A Companion to Roman Rhetoric*, ed. William Dominik and Jon Hall, 83–97. Oxford: Wiley Blackwell, 2010.

Cook, Bernard A., ed. *Women and War: A Historical Encyclopedia from Antiquity to the Present*. Santa Barbara, CA: ABC-CLIO, 2006.

Cooper, Helen Margaret, Adrienne Munich, and Susan Merrill Squier, eds. *Arms and the Woman: War, Gender, and Literary Representation*. Chapel Hill, NC: University of North Carolina Press, 1989.

Corsaro, Antonio. "Introduzione." In Ercole Bentivoglio, *Satire*, 5–28. Ferrara: Deputazione Provinciale Ferrarese di Storia Patria, 1987.

Costa-Zalessow, Natalia. "The Personification of Italy from Dante through the Trecento." *Italica* 63.3 (1991): 316–31.

Cox, Virginia. "Gender and Eloquence in Ercole de' Roberti's *Portia and Brutus*." *Renaissance Quarterly* 62.1 (2009): 61–101.

———. *Lyric Poetry by Women of the Italian Renaissance.* Baltimore, MD: Johns Hopkins University Press, 2013.

———. *The Prodigious Muse: Women's Writing in Counter-Reformation Italy.* Baltimore, MD: Johns Hopkins University Press, 2011.

———. *The Renaissance Dialogue: Literary Dialogue in Its Social and Political Contexts, Castiglione to Galileo.* Cambridge: Cambridge University Press, 1992.

———. "Women as Readers and Writers of Chivalric Poetry in Early Modern Italy." In *Sguardi sull'Italia: Miscellanea dedicata a Francesco Villari*, ed. Gino Bedani, Zygmunt Barański, Anna Laura Lepschy, and Brian Richardson, 134–45. Leeds: Society for Italian Studies, 1997.

———. *Women's Writing in Italy, 1400–1650*. Baltimore, MD: Johns Hopkins University Press, 2008.

Crawford, Katherine. "Catherine de Medicis and the Performance of Political Motherhood." *The Sixteenth Century Journal* 31.3 (2000): 643–73.

Crim, Brian. "Women and Warfare in Early Modern Europe." In *A Soldier and a Woman: Sexual Integration in the Military*, ed. Gerard J. DeGroot and Corinna Peniston-Bird, 18-32. Harlow, Essex: Pearson, 2000.

Cristofaro, Carmela. "'Alcuni ammaestramenti per le gran principesse': Donne illustri e ragion di stato in Scipione Ammirato." PhD diss., Università degli Studi di Bari, 2005–6.

Croce, Benedetto. "Ludovico Ariosto." *Ariosto, Shakespeare e Corneille*. Bari: Laterza, 1961.

———. *Storie e leggende napoletane*. 2nd ed. Bari: Laterza, 1923.

Crouzet, Denis. *Le haut coeur de Catherine de Médicis: Une raison politique au temps de la Saint-Barthélemy*. Paris: Albin Michel, 2005.

———. "'A Strong Desire to Be a Mother to All Your Subjects': A Rhetorical Experiment by Catherine de Medici." *Journal of Medieval and Early Modern Studies* 38.1 (2008): 103–18.

D'Ancona, Alessandro, and Orazio Bacci, eds. *Manuale della letteratura italiana: Secoli XVI e XVII*. Vol. III. Florence: Barbèra, 1895.

Dandelet, Thomas James. *Spanish Rome, 1500–1700*. New Haven, CT: Yale University Press, 2001.

de Conihout, Isabelle, and Pascal Ract-Madoux. "À la recherche de la bibliothèque perdue de Catherine de Médicis." In *Il mecenatismo di Caterina de' Medici: Poesie, feste, musica, pittura, scultura, architettura*, ed. Sabine Frommel and Gerhard Wolf, 39–62. Venice: Marsilio, 2008.

De Costa, Mary Michelle. *Hopeless Love: Boiardo, Ariosto, and Narratives of Queer Female Desire*. Toronto: University of Toronto Press, 2009.

De Maio, Romeo. *Donna e Rinascimento: L'inizio di una rivoluzione*. Naples: Edizioni Scientifiche Italiane, 1995.

De Mattei, Rodolfo. *Il pensiero politico di Scipione Ammirato*. Lecce: Centro di Studi Salentini, 1959.

———. "Scipione Ammirato." In *Dizionario Biografico degli Italiani*, Vol III: 1–4. Rome: Istituto dell'Enciclopedia Italiana, 1961.

de Vries, Joyce. *Caterina Sforza and the Art of Appearances: Gender, Art, and Culture in Early Modern Italy*. Burlington, VT: Ashgate, 2010.

———. "Caterina Sforza: The Shifting Representation of a Woman Ruler in Early Modern Italy." *Lo Sguardo*. 13 (2013): 165–81.

del Soldato, Francesco. "Vita di Scipione Ammirato." *Istorie Fiorentine di Scipione Ammirato con l'aggiunte di Scipione Ammirato il giovane*. Vol. II. Florence: L. Marchini and G. Becherini, 1827.

Dialetti, Androniki. "The Publisher Gabriel Giolito de' Ferrari, Female Readers and the Debate about Women in Sixteenth-Century Italy." *Renaissance and Reformation* 28.4 (2004): 5–32.

Di Bonito, Rosario. *Pozzuoli: Uomini e vicende tra Medioevo et età moderna.* Naples: Gallina, 2001.

Doglio, Maria Luisa. "Il Tasso e le donne." In Torquato Tasso, *Discorso della virtù feminile e donnesca*, ed. Maria Luisa Doglio. Palermo: Sellerio, 1997.

Donati, Claudio. "The Profession of Arms and the Nobility in Spanish Italy: Some Considerations." In *Spain in Italy: Politics, Society, and Religion 1500–1700*, ed. Thomas James Dandelet and John A. Marino, 299-324. Leiden: Brill, 2007.

Dufresne, Laura Rinaldi. "Woman Warriors: A Special Case from the Fifteenth Century: *The City of Ladies.*" *Women's Studies* 23 (1994): 111–31.

Eads, Valerie. "The Geography of Power: Matilda of Tuscany and the Strategy of Active Defense." In *Crusaders, Condottieri and Cannon: Medieval Warfare in the Mediterranean Region*, ed. L.J. Andrew Villalon and Donald J. Kagay, 355–88. Boston: Brill, 2003.

———."Sichelgaita of Salerno: Amazon or Trophy Wife?" *Journal of Medieval History* 3 (2005): 72–87.

Edgington, Susan, and Susan Lambert, eds. *Gendering the Crusades.* New York: Columbia University Press, 2002.

Eisenbichler, Konrad. "'Un chant à l'honneur de la France': Women's Voices at the End of the Republic of Siena." *Renaissance and Reformation / Renaissance et Reforme* 27.2 (2003): 87–99.

———. *L'opera poetica di Virginia Martini Salvi (Siena, c. 1510–Roma, post-1571).* Siena: Accademia degli Intronati di Siena, 2012.

———. "Poetesse senesi a metà del Cinquecento: Tra politica e passione." *Studi rinascimentali: Rivista internazionale di letteratura italiana* 1(2003): 95–102.

———. *The Sword and the Pen: Women, Politics, and Poetry in Sixteenth-Century Siena.* Notre Dame, IN: University of Notre Dame Press, 2012.

Elam, Keir, and Fernando Cioni, eds. *Una civile conversazione: Lo scambio letterario e culturale anglo-italiano nel Rinascimento*. Bologna: Cooperativa Libraria Universitaria Editrice Bologna, 2003.

Elshtain, Jean Bethke. "Reflections on War and Political Discourse: Realism, Just War, and Feminism in a Nuclear Age." *Political Theory* 13.1 (February 1985): 39–57.

———. *Women and War*. Chicago: University of Chicago Press, 1987.

———. "Women and War: Ten Years On." *Review of International Studies* 24 (1998): 447–60.

Everson, Jane. "The Epic Tradition of Charlemagne in Italy." *Cahiers de Recherches Médiévales et Humanistes* 12 (2005): 45–81.

———. *The Italian Romance Epic in the Age of Humanism. The Matter of Italy and the World of Rome*. Oxford: Oxford University Press, 2001.

Farina, Fatima. *Forze armate: Femminile plurale.* Milan: Franco Angeli, 2004.

Femenias, Maria Luisa. "Women and Natural Hierarchy in Aristotle." *Hypatia* 9 (1994): 164–9.

Ferguson, Michaele L., and Lori Jo Marso, eds. *W Stands for Women: How the George W. Bush Presidency Shaped a New Politics of Gender.* Durham, NC: Duke University Press, 2007.

Ferrari, Monica. *"Per non manchare in tuto del debito mio": L'educazione dei bambini Sforza nel Quattrocento.* Milan: Franco Angeli, 2000.

Ffolliott, Sheila. "Catherine de' Medici as Artemisia: Figuring the Powerful Widow." In *Rewriting the Renaissance: The Discourses of Sexual Difference in Early Modern Europe,* ed. M. Ferguson, M. Quilligan, and N. Vickers, 227–41. Chicago: University of Chicago Press, 1986.

———. "Exemplarity and Gender: Three Lives of Queen Catherine de' Medici." In *The Rhetorics of Life-Writing in Early Modern Europe,* ed. Thomas F. Mayer and D.R. Woolf, 321–40. Ann Arbor, MI: University of Michigan Press, 1995.

Filosa, Elsa. *Tre studi sul "De mulieribus claris"'* Milan: Edizioni Universitarie di Lettere Economia Diritto, 2012.

Findlen, Paula. "Humanism, Politics and Pornography in Renaissance Italy." In *The Invention of Pornography: Obscenity and the Origins of Modernity,* ed. Lynn Hunt, 49–108. New York: Zone Books, 1996.

Finotti, Fabio. "Women Writers in Renaissance Italy: Courtly Origins of New Literary Canons." In *Strong Voices, Weak History,* ed. Pamela Joseph Benson and Victoria Kirkham, 121–45. Ann Arbor, MI: University of Michigan Press, 2005.

Finucci, Valeria. *The Manly Masquerade: Masculinity, Paternity, and Castration in the Italian Renaissance.* Durham, NC: Duke University Press, 2003.

———. "Maternal Imagination and Monstrous Birth: Tasso's *Gerusalemme liberata.*" In *Generation and Degeneration: Tropes of Reproduction in Literature and History from Antiquity to Early Modern* Europe, ed. Valeria Finucci and Kevin Brownlee, 41–80. Durham, NC: Duke University Press, 2001.

Flemming, Rebecca. *Medicine and the Making of Roman Women: Gender, Nature, and Authority from Celsus to Galen.* Oxford: Oxford University Press, 2000.

Fontana, Alessandro, ed. *La circulation des hommes et des oeuvres entre la France et l'Italie a l'époché de la renaissance.* Paris: Centre Interuniversitaire de Recherche sur la Renaissance Italienne, 1992.

Foucault, Michel. *Discipline and Punish: The Birth of the Prison.* New York: Pantheon, 1977.

Fowler, Kenneth. "Sir John Hawkwood and the English Condottieri in Trecento Italy." *Renaissance Studies* 11 (1998): 131–48.

Franklin, Margaret. *Boccaccio's Heroines: Power and Virtue in Renaissance Society.* Aldershot, Hants: Ashgate, 2006.

Freccero, John. "Medusa and the Madonna of Forlì: Political Sexuality in Machiavelli." In *Machiavelli and the Discourse of Literature*, ed. Albert Russell Ascoli and Victoria Kahn, 161–78. Ithaca, NY: Cornell University Press, 1993.

Friedl, Ernestine. *Women and Men: An Anthropologist's View*. Prospect Heights, IL: Waveland Press, 1975.

Frye, Susan. "The Myth of Elizabeth I at Tilbury." *Sixteenth Century Journal* 23.1 (1992): 95–114.

Gáldy, Andrea M. "Tuscan Concerns and Spanish Heritage in the Decoration of Duchess Eleonora's Apartment in the Palazzo Vecchio." *Renaissance Studies* 20.3 (2006): 292–319.

Gallo, Italo, ed. *L'eredità culturale di Plutarco dall'antichità al Rinascimento*. Naples: D'Auria, 1998.

Gaston, Robert. "Eleonora di Toledo's Chapel: Lineage, Salvation, and the War against the Turks." In *The Cultural World of Eleonora di Toledo Duchess of Florence and Siena*, ed. Konrad Eisenbichler, 157–80. Burlington, VT: Ashgate, 2004.

Gaylard, Susan. "Castiglione vs. Cicero: Political Engagement, or Effeminate Chatter?" *Italian Culture* 27:2 (2009): 81–98.

Gerschick, Thomas J. "Masculinity and Degrees of Bodily Normativity in Western Culture." In *Handbook of Studies on Men and Masculinities*, ed. Michael S. Kimmel, Jeff Hearn, and Robert W. Connell, 367–78. Thousand Oaks, CA: Sage 2005.

Ghazarian, Jacob G. *The Armenian Kingdom in Cilicia during the Crusades. The Integration of Cilician Armenians with the Latins, 1080–1393*. London: Routledge, 2000.

Gilmore, David. *Manhood in the Making: Cultural Concepts of Masculinity*. New Haven, CT: Yale University Press, 1990.

Goldstein, Joshua S. *War and Gender: How Gender Shapes the War System and Vice Versa*. Cambridge: Cambridge University Press, 2001.

Graziani, Natale, and Gabriella Venturelli. *Caterina Sforza*. Milan: Dall'Oglio, 1987.

Green, Janet M. "'I My Self': Queen Elizabeth's Oration at Tilbury Camp." *Sixteenth Century Journal, The Journal of Early Modern Studies* 28.2 (1997): 421–45.

Grendler, Paul F. *Critics of the Italian World (1530–1560): Anton Francesco Doni, Nicolò Franco and Ortensio Lando*. Madison, WI: University of Wisconsin Press, 1969.

———. "Form and Function in Italian Renaissance Popular Books." *Renaissance Quarterly* 46 (1993): 451–85.

Grilli, Alfredo. *Figure muliebri nell'*Orlando furioso. Ferrara: Stabilimento tipografico Estense, 1933.

Günsberg, Maggie. "Donna liberata?: The Portrayal of Women in the Italian Renaissance Epic." *The Italianist* 8 (1988): 33–55.

Hacker, Barton C. "Women and Military Institutions in Early Modern Europe: A Reconnaissance." *Signs* 6 (1981): 643–71.

Hagedorn, Suzanne C. *Abandoned Women: Rewriting the Classics in Dante, Boccaccio and Chaucer.* Ann Arbor, MI: University of Michigan Press, 2004.

Hairston, Julia L. "Bradamante, 'Vergine Saggia': Maternity and the Art of Negotiation." *Exemplaria* 12.2 (2000): 455–86.

———. "Skirting the Issue: Machiavelli's Caterina Sforza." *Renaissance Quarterly* 53.3 (2000): 687–712.

Hale, John Rigby. "Castiglione's Military Career." *Italian Studies* XXXVI (1981): 41–57.

———. "Gunpowder and the Renaissance: An Essay in the History of Ideas." In *From the Renaissance to the Counter-Reformation*, ed. Charles H. Carter, 113–44. New York: Random House, 1965.

———. *Renaissance War Studies.* London: Hambledon Press, 1983.

———. *War and Society in Renaissance Europe: 1450–1620.* Baltimore, MD: Johns Hopkins University Press, 1985.

Hall, Bert S. *Weapons and Warfare in Renaissance Europe: Gunpowder, Technology, and Tactics.* Baltimore, MD: Johns Hopkins University Press, 1997.

Hametz, Maura. *In the Name of Italy: Nation, Family, and Patriotism in a Fascist Court.* New York: Fordham University Press, 2012.

Hankins, James. *Plato in the Italian Renaissance.* New York and Leiden: Brill, 1990.

Hare, Christopher (Marian Andrews). *The Most Illustrious Ladies of the Italian Renaissance.* Williamstown, MA: Corner House Publishers, 1972.

Harness, Kelley. *Echoes of Women's Voices: Music, Art, and Female Patronage in Early Modern Florence.* Chicago: University of Chicago Press, 2006.

Hauvette, Henri. *Un exilé florentin à la cour de France au XVIe siècle: Luigi Alamanni (1495–1556,) sa vie et son oeuvre.* Paris: Hachette, 1903.

Hay, David J. *The Military Leadership of Matilda of Canossa, 1046–1115.* Manchester: Manchester University Press, 2008.

Hewlett, Mary. "Fortune's Fool: The Influence of Humanism on Francesco Burlamacchi, 'Hero' of Lucca." In *The Renaissance in the Streets, Schools, and Studies. Essays in Honour of Paul F. Grendler*, ed. Konrad Eisenbichler and Nicholas Terpstra, 125–56. Toronto: Centre for Renaissance and Reformation Studies, 2008.

Higate, Paul, and John Hopton. "War, Militarism and Masculinities." In *Handbook of Studies on Men and Masculinities*, ed. Michael S. Kimmel, Jeff Hearn, and Robert W. Connell, 432–47. Thousand Oaks, CA: Sage, 2005.

Holman, Beth. "Exemplum and Imitatio: Countess Matilda and Lucrezia Pico della Mirandola at Polirone." *Art Bulletin* 81:4 (Dec. 1999): 637–64.

Horsfall, Nicholas. *Virgil, Aeneid 11: A Commentary*. Leiden: Brill, 2003.

Illston, James Michael. "'An Entirely Masculine Activity?' Women and War in the High and Late Middle Ages Reconsidered." MA thesis, University of Canterbury, 2009.

Innocenti, Clarice, ed. *Women in Power: Caterina and Maria de' Medici.* Florence: Mandragora, 2008.

Jacobs, Jason. "Galiziella's Escape: Interconfessional Erotics and Love between Knights in the Aspremont Tradition." *California Italian Studies Journal* 4:2 (2013): 1–23.

Jaffe, Irma B., with Gernando Colombardo. *Shining Eyes, Cruel Fortune. The Lives and Loves of Italian Renaissance Women Poets.* New York: Fordham University Press, 2002.

Javitch, Daniel. *Proclaiming a Classic: The Canonization of* Orlando furioso. Princeton, NJ: Princeton University Press, 1991.

Jensen, De Lamar. "Catherine de' Medici and her Florentine Friends." *Sixteenth Century Journal* 9.2 (1978): 57–74.

Jones, Ann Rosalind. "Bad Press: Modern Editors versus Early Modern Italian Writers (Tullia d'Aragona, Gaspara Stampa and Veronica Franco)." In *Strong Voices, Weak History? Renaissance Women Writers and the Canon*, ed. Pamela Benson and Victoria Kirkham, 287–313. Ann Arbor, MI: University of Michigan Press, 2007.

Jones, Christopher. *Plutarch and Rome.* Oxford: Clarendon, 1971.

Jordan, Constance. "Boccaccio's In-Famous Women: Gender and Civic Virtue in *De mulieribus claris.*" In *Ambiguous Realities: Women in the Middle Ages and Renaissance,* ed. Carole Levine and Jeanie Watson, 25–57. Detroit: Wayne State University Press, 1987.

Karras, Ruth Mazo. *From Boys to Men: Formations of Masculinity in Late Medieval Europe.* Philadelphia: University of Pennsylvania Press, 2003.

Kennedy, William J. *Authorizing Petrarch.* Ithaca, NY: Cornell University Press, 1994.

King, Helen. "Agnodike and the Profession of Medicine." *Proceedings of the Cambridge Philological Society* 32 (1986): 53–77.

King, Margaret L. *Women of the Renaissance.* Chicago: University of Chicago Press, 1991.

Kingdon, Robert. *Myths about St. Bartholomew's Day Massacres.* Cambridge, MA: Harvard University Press, 1988.

Kirkham, Victoria. *Laura Battiferra and Her Literary Circle.* Chicago: University of Chicago Press, 2006.

Klapische-Zuber, Christiane, ed. *A History of Women in the West. Vol. II. Silences of the Middle Ages.* Cambridge, MA: Belknap Press of Harvard University Press, 1992.

Knecht, Robert J. *Catherine de' Medici.* London: Longman, 1998.

Kohl, Benjamin G., and Ronald G. Witt, ed. and trans, with Elizabeth B. Wells. *The Earthly Republic: Italian Humanists on Government and Society.* Philadelphia: University of Pennsylvania Press, 1978.

Kolsky, Stephen. *The Genealogy of Women: Studies in Boccaccio's De mulieribus claris.* New York: Peter Lang, 2003.

———. *The Ghost of Boccaccio: Writings on Famous Women in Renaissance Italy.* Turnhout: Brepols, 2005.

Kruse, Elaine. "The Blood-Stained Hands of Catherine de Médicis." In *Political Rhetoric, Power, and Renaissance Women*, ed. Carol Levin and Patricia A. Sullivan, 139–56. Albany: State University of New York Press, 1995.

Laqueur, Thomas Walter. *Making Sex: Body and Gender from the Ancient Greeks to Freud.* Cambridge, MA: Harvard University Press, 1990.

La Rocca, Guido. *Storia dell'epistola di Baldassare Castiglione al re Enrico VII d'Inghilterra: Il reperimento del testo ufficiale.* Mantua: Accademia Virgiliana di Mantova, 1972.

Latella, Cecelia. "'Giovane donna in mezzo 'l campo apparse': Figure di donne guerriere nella tradizione letteraria occidentale." PhD diss., Università degli Studi di Napoli "L'Orientale," 2009.

Lazzari, Laura. *Poesia epica e scrittura femminile nel Seicento:* L'Enrico *di Lucrezia Marinella.* Leonforte: Insula, 2010.

Le Goff, Jacques. *St. Francis of Assisi.* Trans. Christine Rhone. London: Routledge, 2004.

Lehtinen, Ullaliina. "How Does One Know What Shame Is? Epistemology, Emotions, and Forms of Life in Juxtaposition." *Hypatia* 13.1 (1998): 56–77.

Lenzi, Maria Ludovica. "Donne e guerra dal XIII al XV secolo: Alle origini del moderno stato militare." *Donna e guerra: Mito e storia*, 79–86. Udine: DARS, 1990.

Lev, Elizabeth. *The Tigress of Forlì.* Boston, MA: Houghton Mifflin Harcourt, 2011.

Levin, Michael Jacob. *Agents of Empire: Spanish Ambassadors in Sixteenth-Century Italy.* Ithaca, NY: Cornell University Press, 2005.

Libby, Lester J. "The Reconquest of Padua in 1509 According to the Diary of Girolamo Priuli." *Renaissance Quarterly* 28.3 (1975): 323–31.

Lipking, Lawrence. *Abandoned Women and Poetic Tradition.* Chicago: University of Chicago Press, 1988.

Long, Kathleen P., ed. *High Anxiety: Masculinity in Crisis in Early Modern France.* Kirksville, MO: Truman State University Press, 2002.

Lo Rey, Salvatore. "'Venite all'ombra de' gran gigli d'oro.' Retroscena politici di una celebre controversia letteraria (1553–1559)." In *Benedetto Varchi*, ed. Vanni Bramanti, 253–94. Rome: Edizioni di Storia e Letteratura, 2007.

Luckyj, Christina. *A Moving Rhetoricke. Gender and Silence in Early Modern England.* Manchester: Manchester University Press, 2002.

Luongo, F. Thomas. *The Saintly Politics of Catherine of Siena*. Ithaca, NY: Cornell University Press, 2006.

Luzio, Alessandro. *La reggenza di Isabella d'Este durante la prigionia del marito*. Milan: L.F. Cogliati, 1910.

Lynn, John A. *Women, Armies, and Warfare in Early Modern Europe*. Cambridge: Cambridge University Press, 2008.

Mallett, Michael E. "Venice and the War of Ferrara, 1482–1484." In *Essays in Honour of John Hale*, ed. David S. Chambers, Cecil H. Clough, and Michael E. Mallett, 57–72. London: Hambledon Press, 1993.

Mallett, Michael E., and Christine Shaw. *The Italian Wars: 1494–1559*. Harlow, Essex: Pearson, 2012.

Mankayi, Nyameka. "Masculinity, Sexuality and the Body of Male Soldiers." *Psychology in Society* 26 (2008): 24–44.

Mansfield, Harvey. *Manliness*. New Haven, CT: Yale University Press, 2006.

Mantovani, Sergio. *Tra acqua e terra. Storia materiale in Transpadana*. Nuovecarte: Comune di Ficarolo, 2001.

Marcheschi, Daniela. *Chiara Matraini. Poetessa lucchese e la letteratura delle donne nei nuovi fermenti letterari del '500*. Pisa: Pacini-Fazzi, 2008.

Maroi, Lina. *Laura Terracina, poetessa napoletana del secolo XVI*. Naples: F. Perrella, 1913.

Masetti Zannini, Gian Lodovico. *La capitale perduta: La devoluzione di Ferrara 1598 nelle carte vaticane*. Ferrara: Corbo Editore, 2000.

Mayhew, Robert. *The Female in Aristotle's Biology: Reason or Rationalization*. Chicago: University of Chicago Press, 2004.

Mazzanti, Marinella Bonvini. *Battista Sforza Montefeltro: Una "principessa" nel Rinascimento italiano*. Urbino: Quattroventi, 1993.

MacCarthy, Ita. *Women and the Making of Poetry in Ariosto's* Orlando furioso. Leicester: Troubador, 2007.

McClure, George W. *Parlour Games and the Public Life of Women in Renaissance Italy*. Toronto: University of Toronto Press, 2013.

———. "Women and the Politics of Play in Sixteenth-Century Italy: Torquato Tasso's Theory of Games." *Renaissance Quarterly* 61.3 (Fall 2008): 750–91.

MacDonald, Dennis Ronald. *The Homeric Epics and the Gospel of Mark*. New Haven, CT: Yale University Press, 2000.

Macdonald, Sharon, Pat Holden, and Shirley Ardener, eds. *Images of Women in Peace and War*. Madison: University of Wisconsin Press, 1988.

McInerney, Jeremy. "Plutarch's Manly Women." In *Andreia: Studies in Manliness and Courage in Classical Antiquity*, ed. Ralph Mark Rosen and Ineke Sluiter, 319–44. Leiden and Boston: Brill, 2003.

Maclachlan, Elaine. "The Poetry of Chiara Matraini. Narrative Strategies in the *Rime*." PhD diss., University of Connecticut, 1992.

McLaughlin, Megan. "The Woman Warrior: Gender, Warfare, and Society in Medieval Europe." *Women's Studies* 17 (1990): 193–209.

MacLean, Ian. *The Renaissance Notion of Woman: A Study in the Fortunes of Scholasticism and Medical Science in European Intellectual Life.* Cambridge: Cambridge University Press, 1980.

McLeod, Glenda. *Virtue and Venom. Catalogs of Women from Antiquity to the Renaissance.* Ann Arbor, MI: University of Michigan Press, 1991.

McLucas, John C. "Amazon, Sorceress and Queen." *The Italianist* 8 (1988): 33–55.

McManus, Caroline. *Spenser's Faerie Queene and the Reading of Women.* Newark, DE: University of Delaware Press, 2002.

Miles, Gary B. *Livy: Reconstructing Early Rome.* Ithaca, NY: Cornell University Press, 1995.

Miller, Laura L. "Feminism and the Exclusion of Army Women from Combat." *Gender Issues* 16:3 (1998): 33–64.

Milligan, Gerry. "Masculinity and Machiavelli: How to Avoid Effeminacy, Perform Manliness and Be Wary of the Author." In *Seeking Real Truths: Multidisciplinary Perspectives on Machiavelli,* ed. Patricia Vilches and Gerald Seaman, 149–72. Leiden: Brill, 2007.

———. "The Politics of Effeminacy in *Il cortegiano.*" *Italica* 83.3–4 (2006): 345–66.

———. "Unlikely Heroines in Lucrezia Tornabuoni's *Storie sacre.*" *Italica* 88.4 (2011): 538–64.

———. "Unmaking the Armed Maiden: The Poetic Debate of the Warrior Woman in Tasso." In *Innovation in the Italian Counter-Reformation,* ed. Shannon McHugh and Anna Wainwright. Newark, DE: University of Delaware Press, Forthcoming.

Milligan, Gerry, and Jane Tylus, eds. *The Poetics of Masculinity in Early Modern Italy and Spain.* Toronto: Centre for Reformation and Renaissance Studies, 2010.

Mitchell, Bonner. *1598: A Year of Pageantry in Late Renaissance Ferrara.* Binghamton, NY: Medieval and Renaissance Texts and Studies, 1990.

Montella, Luigi. *Una poetessa del Rinascimento: Laura Terracina.* Rome: Salerno, 2001.

Morici, Medardo. "Giustina Levi-Perotti e le petrarchiste marchigiane: Contributo alla storia delle falsificazioni letterarie nei sec. XVI e XVII." *La Rassegna Nazionale* 108 (1899): 662–95.

Muessig, Carolyn, George Ferzoco, and Beverly Mayne Kienzle, eds. *A Companion to Catherine of Siena.* Leiden: Brill, 2012.

Murrin, Michael. *History and Warfare in Renaissance Epic.* Chicago: University of Chicago Press, 1994.

Mutini, Claudio. "Betussi, Giuseppe." *Dizionario Biografico degli Italiani*, Vol. 13: 779–81. Rome: Istituto della enciclopedia italiana, 1971.

Nadin Bassani, Lucia. *Il poligrafo veneto Giuseppe Betussi*. Padua: Antenore, 1992.

Najemy, John. "Arms and Letters: The Crisis of Courtly Culture in the Wars of Italy." In *Italy and the European Powers: The Impact of War, 1500–1530*, ed. Christine Shaw, 207–38. Leiden: Brill, 2006.

Nuovo, Isabella. "*Dell'ultilità che si dee cavare dall'andare attorno* di Scipione Ammirato." *Otium e Negotium: Da Petrarca a Scipione Ammirato*, 361–87. Bari: Palomar, 2007.

Orieux, Jean. *Caterina de' Medici: Un'italiana sul trono di Francia*. Milan: Mondadori, 2007.

Ortiz, Alicia Morales. *Plutarco en España: Traducciones de* Moralia *en el Siglo XVI*. Murcia: University of Murcia Press, 2000.

Owen, D.D.R. *Eleanor of Aquitaine: Queen and Legend*. Oxford: Blackwell, 1993.

Padoan, Giorgio. *L'*Orlando furioso *e la crisi del Rinascimento*. Florence: Olschki, 1975.

Pasolini, Pier Desiderio. *Caterina Sforza*. 3 vols. Rome: Loescher, 1893.

———. *Caterina Sforza: Nuovi documenti*. Bologna: Garagnani e Figli, 1897.

Pastor, Ludwig. *The History of the Popes, from the Close of the Middle Ages*. London: J. Hodges, 1908.

Pennington, Reina, and Robin Higham, eds. *Amazons to Fighter Pilots: A Biographical Dictionary of Military Women*. 2 vols. Westport, CT: Greenwood, 2003.

Petrocchi, Giorgio. "Guerriere a cavallo." *Critica letteraria* 16 (1988): 259–62.

Petrucci, Franca. "Isabella Colonna." *Dizionario Biografico degli Italiani*. Vol. 27. Rome: Istituto della enciclopedia italiana, 1982.

Picot, Emile. *Les italiens en France au XVIe siècle*. Manziana: Vecchiarelli, 1995.

Piéjus, Marie-Francoise. *Visages et paroles de femmes dans la littérature italienne de la Renaissance*. Paris: Université Paris III Sorbonne Nouvelle, 2009.

Pieri, Piero. *Il Rinascimento e la crisi militare*. Turin: Einaudi, 1952.

Pioppi, Stefano. "Il ruolo delle donne nelle missioni internazionali." Airpress 31 March 2017: www.airpressonline.it/19162/donne-missioni-internazionali. Accessed 28 April 2017.

Pitkin, Hannah Fenichel. *Fortune Is a Woman: Gender and Politics in the Thought of Niccolò Machiavelli*. Chicago: University of Chicago Press, 1999.

Pizzagalli, Daniela. *La signora della poesia: Vita e passioni di Veronica Gambara, artista del Rinascimento*. Milan: Rizzoli, 2004.

Pomeroy, Sarah B. *Plutarch's Advice to the Bride and Groom and a Consolation to His Wife*. Oxford: Oxford University Press, 1999.

Potter, David. "Chivalry and Professionalism in the French Armies of the Renaissance." In *The Chivalric Ethos and the Development of Military Professionalism*, ed. David J.B. Trimm, 150–82. Leiden: Brill, 2003.

"Provvisione della Milizia e Ordinanza del Popolo Fiorentino, ottenuto nel Consiglio Maggiore *l'anno MDXXVIII, a dì di Novembre." Archivio storico italiano.* Vol. I (1842): 384–409.

Purcell, Maureen. "Women Crusaders: A Temporary Canonical Aberration." In *Principalities, Powers, and Estates: Studies in Medieval and Early Modern Government and Society*, ed. Leighton O. Frappell, 57–67. Adelaide: Adelaide University Press, 1979.

Quilligan, Maureen. "On the Renaissance Epic: Spenser and Slavery." *South Atlantic Quarterly* 100.1 (2001): 15–39.

Quint, David. *Epic and Empire: Politics and Generic Form from Virgil to Milton.* Princeton, NJ: Princeton University Press, 1993.

———. "Francesco Bracciolini as a Reader of Ariosto and Tasso." In *L'arme e gli amori. Ariosto, Tasso and Guarini in Late Renaissance Florence*, ed. Massimiliano Rossi and Fiorella Gioffredi Superbi, 59–77. Florence: Olschki, 2004.

———. *Origin and Originality in Renaissance Literature: Versions of the Source.* New Haven, CT: Yale University Press, 1983.

Rabil, Albert, Jr., ed. *Renaissance Humanism: Foundations, Forms, and Legacy.* Philadelphia: University of Pennsylvania Press, 1988.

Rabitti, Giovanna. "Introduction." In Chiara Matraini, *Selected Poetry and Prose. A Bilingual Edition*, ed. and trans. Elaine Maclachlan, 1–33. Chicago: University of Chicago Press: 2007.

———. "Linee per il ritratto di Chiara Matraini." *Studi e problemi di critica testuale* 22 (1981): 141–65.

Rajna, Pio. *Le fonti dell'Orlando furioso.* 2nd ed. Florence: Sansoni, 1900.

Randolph, Adrian. *Engaging Symbols: Gender, Politics and Public Art in Fifteenth-Century Florence.* New Haven, CT: Yale University Press, 2002.

Ray, Meredith. *Daughters of Alchemy: Women and Scientific Culture in Early Modern Italy.* Cambridge, MA: Harvard University Press, 2015.

———. *Writing Gender in Women's Letter Collections of the Italian Renaissance.* Toronto: University of Toronto Press, 2009.

Rebhorn, Wayne. "Outlandish Fears: Defining Decorum in Renaissance Rhetoric." *Intertexts* 4 (2000): 2–24.

Richards, Jennifer. "'A Wanton Trade of Living?': Rhetoric, Effeminacy, and the Early Modern Courtier." *Criticism: A Quarterly for Literature and the Arts* 42.2 (Spring 2000): 185–206.

Ridolfi, Roberto. "Del carattere italico aldino nel secolo XV." *La bibliofilia* 55 (1953): 118–22.

Rizzi, Andrea. "L'autore dell'Epitome Polinorese e il mito della contessa Matilde di Canossa nella storiografia ferrarese del Trecento e Quattrocento." In *Il principe e la storia. Atti del Convegno Internazionale, Scandiano, 18–20 Settembre 2003*, ed. Tina Matarrese and Cristina Montagnani, 77–90. Novara: Interlinea, 2005.

———. "English News in Translation: The Commentario del successo dell'Armata Spagnola by Petruccio Ubaldini and Its English Version." *Spunti e Ricerche* 22:1 (2007): 89–102.

Robin, Diana. *Filelfo in Milan*. Princeton, NJ: Princeton University Press, 1991.

———. *Publishing Women: Salons, the Presses, and the Counter-Reformation in Sixteenth-Century Italy*. Chicago: University of Chicago Press, 2007.

Robinson, Lillian S. *Monstrous Regiment: The Lady Knight in Sixteenth-Century Epic*. New York: Garland Press, 1985.

Rogers, Katie. "Ban on Women in Combat Lifted: Readers and Veterans Debate on Social Media." *TheGuardian.com*, 24 January 2013. Retrieved 2 May 2014 from: https://www.theguardian.com/world/us-news-blog/2013/jan/24/us-military-ban-lifted-women-combat.

Rosen, David. *The Changing Fictions of Masculinity*. Urbana, IL: University of Illinois Press, 1993.

Rosenberg, Charles. "The Double Portrait of Federico and Guidobaldo da Montefeltro: Power, Wisdom and Dynasty." In *Federico da Montefeltro: Lo stato, le arti, la cultura*, ed. Giorgio Cerboni Baiardi, Giorgio Chittolini, and Piero Floriani, 213–22. Rome: Bulzoni, 1986.

Rossi, Andreola. *Contexts of War: Manipulation of Genre in Virgilian Battle Narrative*. Ann Arbor, MI: University of Michigan Press, 2004.

Rossi, Vittorio. "Di una rimatrice e di un rimatore del secolo 15: Girolama Corsi Ramos e Jacopo Corsi." *Giornale storico della letteratura italiana* 15 (1890): 183–219.

Roulo, Claudette. "Defense Department Expands Women's Combat Role." *American Forces Press Service*, 24 January 2013. Retrieved 6 October 2017: http://archive.defense.gov/news/newsarticle.aspx?id=119098.

Saccone, Eduardo. "Grazia, Sprezzatura, and Affettazione in the *Courtier*." In *Castiglione: The Ideal and the Real in Renaissance Culture*, ed. Robert W. Hanning and David Rosand, 46–54. New Haven, CT: Yale University Press, 1983.

Sandal, Ennio, Petro Gibellini, and Cesare Bozzetti, eds. *Veronica Gambara e la poesia del suo tempo nell'Italia settentrionale*. Florence: Olschki, 1989.

Sandberg, Brian. "Iconography of Religious Violence: Catherine de Médici's Art Patronage during the French Wars of Religion." In *Il mecenatismo di Caterina de' Medici: Poesie, feste, musica, pittura, scultura, architettura*, ed. Sabine Frommel and Gerhard Wolf, 91–112. Venice: Marsilio, 2008.

Schachter, Marc. "'Quanto concede la guerra': Epic Masculinity and the Education of Desire in Tasso's *Gerusalemme liberata*." In *The Poetics of Masculinity in Early Modern Italy and Spain*, ed. Gerry Milligan and Jane Tylus, 215–41. Toronto: Center for Reformation and Renaissance Studies, 2010.

Schettino, Maria Teresa. *Introduzione a Polieno*. Pisa: ETS, 1988.

Schmitt, Charles B., and Quentin Skinner, eds. *The Cambridge History of Renaissance Philosophy*. Cambridge: Cambridge University Press, 1991.

Schulenburg, Jane Tibbetts. *Forgetful of Their Sex: Female Sanctity and Society, ca. 500–1500*. Chicago: University of Chicago Press, 1998.

Schwarz, Kathryn. *Tough Love: Amazon Encounters in the English Renaissance*. Durham, NC: Duke University Press, 2000.

Schweizer, Bernard. "Preface." In *Approaches to the Anglo-American Female Epic, 1621–1982*, ed. Bernard Schweizer, 1–18. Aldershot, Hants: Ashgate, 2006.

Scott, Karen. "'*Io Caterina.*' Ecclesiastical Politics and Oral Culture in the Letters of Caterina of Siena." In *Dear Sister: Medieval Women and the Epistolary Genre*, ed. Karen Cherewatuk and Ulrike Wiethaus, 87–121. Philadelphia: University of Pennsylvania Press, 1993.

Sears, Olivia. "Women Poets and War in the Italian Renaissance: Veronica Gambara, Vittoria Colonna, and the *Petrarchiste* of the 16th Century." PhD diss., Stanford University, 1996.

Segre, Cesare. *Esperienze ariostesche*. Pisa: Nistri-Lischi, 1969.

Shemek, Deanna. "Doing and Undoing: Boccaccio's Feminism in *De mulieribus claris*." In *Boccaccio: A Critical Guide to the Complete Works*, ed. Victoria Kirkham, Michael Sherberg, and Janet Levarie Smarr, 195–206. Chicago: University of Chicago Press, 2013.

———. *Ladies Errant: Wayward Women and Social Order in Early Modern Italy*. Durham, NC: Duke University Press, 1998.

Shepard, Alexandra. "Manhood, Patriarchy, and Gender in Early Modern History." In *Masculinities, Childhood, Violence: Attending to Early Modern Women and Men*, ed. Amy E. Leonard, 77–95. Lanham, MD: University of Delaware Press, 2011.

Shin, John. "Beyond Virtù." *Feminist Interpretations of Niccolò Machiavelli*. University Park, PA: Pennsylvania State University Press, 2004.

Shrader, Charles S. "The Influence of Vegetius' *De re militari*." *Military Affairs* 45 (1981): 167–72.

Sluhovsky, Moshe. *Patroness of Paris: Rituals of Devotion in Early Modern France*. Leiden: Brill, 1998.

Snyder, Jon R. *Dissimulation and the Culture of Secrecy in Early Modern Europe*. Berkeley: University of California Press, 2009.

Spackman, Barbara. *Fascist Virilities: Rhetoric, Ideology, and Social Fantasy in Italy*. Minneapolis: University of Minnesota Press, 1996.

Springer, Carolyn. *Armour and Masculinity in the Italian Renaissance*. Toronto: University of Toronto Press, 2010.

Stadter, Philip A. *Plutarch's Historical Methods: An Analysis of the "Mulierum virtutes."* Cambridge, MA: Harvard University Press, 1965.

Stauffer, Dana Jalbert. "Aristotle's Account of the Subjection of Women." *The Journal of Politics* 70 (2008): 929–41.

Stephens, Walter. "Tasso's Heliodorus and the World of Romance." In *The Search for the Ancient Novel*, ed. James Tatum, 67–87. Baltimore, MD: Johns Hopkins University Press, 1994.

Stoppelli, Pasquale. "Livia Chiavello." *Dizionario Biografico degli Italiani*. Vol. 24. Rome: Istituto della enciclopedia italiana, 1980.

Stoppino, Eleanora. *Genealogies of Fiction: Women Warriors and the Medieval Imagination in the "Orlando furioso."* New York: Fordham University Press, 2011.

Struever, Nancy S. *The Language of History in the Renaissance. Rhetoric and Historical Consciousness in Florentine Humanism*. Princeton, NJ: Princeton University Press, 1970.

Suzuki, Mihoko. "Warning Elizabeth with Catherine de' Medici's Example." In *The Rule of Women in Early Modern Europe*, ed. Anne J. Cruz and Mihoko Suzuki, 174–94. Urbana, IL: University of Illinois, 2009.

Tarnopolsky, Christina. "Prudes, Perverts, and Tyrants: Plato and the Contemporary Politics of Shame." *Political Theory* 32.4 (2004): 468–94.

Tenenti, Alberto. "I corsari in Mediterraneo all'inizio del Cinquecento." *Rivista storica italiana* (1960): 259.

Tessier, Andrea. "Domenichi." *Giornale di erudizione* 11–12 (1888): 166–89.

Tomalin, Margaret. *The Fortunes of the Warrior Heroine in Italian Literature*. Ravenna: Longo, 1982.

Tomas, Natalie R. *The Medici Women: Gender and Power in Renaissance Florence*. Aldershot, Hants: Ashgate, 2003.

Torretta, Laura. "Il 'Liber de claris mulieribus' di Giovanni Boccaccio. Parte III: *I traduttori*." *Giornale Storico della Letteratura Italiana* 11 (1902): 35–50.

Tuana, Nancy. *The Less Noble Sex: Scientific, Religious and Philosophical Conceptions of Women's Nature*. Bloomington: Indiana University Press, 1993.

Tylus, Jane. "Caterina da Siena and the Legacy of Humanism." In *Perspectives on Early Modern and Modern Intellectual History: Essays in Honor of Nancy S. Struever*, ed. Joseph Marino and Melinda W. Schlitt, 116–41. Rochester, NY: University of Rochester Press, 2001.

———. *Reclaiming Catherine of Siena: Literacy, Literature, and the Signs of Others*. Chicago: University of Chicago Press, 2009.

Verbruggen, J.F. "Women in Medieval Armies." Trans. Kelly DeVries. *Journal of Medieval History* 4 (2006): 119–36.

Verci, Giovan Battista. "Vita di Giuseppe Betussi." *Il Raverta*. Milan: Daelli, 1864.

Verrier-Dubard de Gaillarbois, Frédérique. "Les Amazones: Des phobies masculines aux rêves de femmes …" *Laboratoire italien* 2 (2001). Available at: http://laboratoireitalien.revues.org/287.

———. *Les armes de Minerve: L'humanisme militaire dans l'Italie du XVIe siècle*. Paris: Presses de l'Université de Paris-Sorbonne, 1997.

———. *Caterina Sforza et Machiavel ou l'origine du monde*. Rome: Vecchiarelli, 2010.

———. *Le miroir des Amazones: Amazones, viragos et guerrières dans la littérature italienne des XVe et XVe siècles*. Paris: L'Harmattan, 2003.

———. "Pallade e il centauro." In *Donne di palazzo nelle corti europei: Tracce e forme di potere dall'età moderna*, ed. Angela Giallongo, 49–62. Milan: Unicopli, 2005.

Vickers, Nancy. "Diana Described: Scattered Woman and Scattered Rhyme." *Critical Inquiry* 8.2 (Winter 1981): 265–79.

Villoresi, Marco. "Le donne e gli amori nel romanzo cavalleresco del Quattrocento." *Filologia e critica* 23 (1998).

Volpe Cacciatore, Paola, ed. *Plutarco nelle traduzioni latine di età umanistica*. Naples: D'Auria, 2009.

Ward, John O. "Cicero and Quintilian." In *The Cambridge History of Literary Criticism*, ed. Glyn P. Norton, vol. 3: 77–87. Cambridge: Cambridge University Press, 1999.

Westermann, Anton. *Paradoxographoi. Scriptores rerum mirabilium Graeci*. Braunschweig: Anton Westermann, 1839.

White, James Boyd. *When Words Lose Their Meaning: Constitutions and Reconstitutions of Language*. Chicago: University of Chicago Press, 1984.

Williams, R.D. *The Aeneid of Vergil, Books 7–12*. New York: St Martin's Press, 1977.

Wyatt, Michael. *The Italian Encounter with Tudor England*. Cambridge: Cambridge University Press, 2005.

Zaccaria, Vittorio. *Boccaccio narratore, storico, moralista e mitografo*. Florence: Olschki, 2001.

———. "La fortuna del *De mulieribus claris* del Boccaccio nel secolo XV: Giovanni Sabbadino degli Arienti, Iacopo Filippo Foresti e le loro biografie femminili (1490-97)." In *Il Boccaccio nelle culture e letterature nazionali*, ed. Francesco Mazzoni, 519–45. Florence: Olschki, 1978.

———. "I volgarizzamenti del Boccaccio latino a Venezia." *Studi sul Boccaccio* 10 (1977–8): 286–306.

Zanrè, Domenico. *Cultural Non-Conformity in Early Modern Florence*. Aldershot, Hants: Ashgate, 2004.

Zatti, Sergio. "Epic in the Age of Dissimulation." In *The Quest for Epic*, ed. Dennis Looney and trans. Sally Hill and Dennis Looney, 195–216. Toronto: University of Toronto Press, 2006.

Zemon Davis, Natalie. "Women on Top." In *Society and Culture in Early Modern France*, 124–51. Stanford: Stanford UP, 1965.

Zetzel, James. "Plato with Pillows: Cicero on the Uses of Greek Culture." In *Myth, History and Culture in Republican Rome: Studies in Honour of T.P. Wiseman*, ed. David Braund and Christopher Gill, 119–38. Exeter: University of Exeter Press, 2003.

Zimmermann, T.C. Price. *Paolo Giovio: The Historian and the Crisis of Sixteenth-Century Italy.* Princeton, NJ: Princeton University Press, 1995.

Žižek, Slavoj. *The Sublime Object of Ideology*. London: Verso, 2008.

Zonta, Giuseppe. "Note Betussiane." *Giornale Storico di Letteratura Italiana* 52 (1908): 321–66.

Index

www.ingramcontent.com/pod-product-compliance
Lightning Source LLC
LaVergne TN
LVHW090149080826
844660LV00013B/735/J